For Craig –

may you too "see in
golden glory ... "

Alan Culpepper
John 17:3

November 2003

"Eternity as a Sunrise"

Hugo and Ruth Culpepper

"Eternity as a Sunrise"

The Life of Hugo H. Culpepper

R. Alan Culpepper

Mercer University Press
2002

ISBN 0-86554-819-6
MUP/H621

© 2002 Mercer University Press
6316 Peake Road
Macon, Georgia 31210-3960

First Edition.

Culpepper, R. Alan.
  Eternity as a sunrise : the life of Hugo H. Culpepper / R. Alan
Culpepper.
    p. cm.
Includes bibliographical references and index.
  ISBN 0-86554-819-6 (alk. paper)
  1. Culpepper, Hugo H., 1913- 2. Southern Baptist Convention—Biography. 3.
Missionaries—United States—Biography. I. Title.
  BX6495.C795 C85 2002
  266'.61'092—dc21
                                                        2002012203

For Hugo and Ruth Culpepper

Contents

List of Figures

Introduction

At the end of every month Dad would "balance the books." He took the little pocket notebooks that he and Mother carried, totaled up their expenses for the month by category in his ledger, and compared their expenses with their income. So after his death it seemed important to me to take the time to systematically review his life, gather up all his letters, papers, tapes, slides, and pictures, and "balance the books." What I found is that the ledger does not balance—he gave out much more than he took in.

Hugo Culpepper's life story is so rich that it must be told. It is the story of how a boy from a small town lived far beyond the horizons of his early years, both literally and metaphorically. From the beginning, one is struck by his lifelong effort to find and to follow God's leadership in his life. How does one find God's will, and what was it about Hugo Culpepper that allowed his faith to continue to grow and develop throughout his life? Through his years of experience as a missionary and a professor of missions, Dad developed a biblically based theology of missions, and in his later years he explored the challenge of religious pluralism for the Christian faith.

I have sought, therefore, not only to tell his life story and gather up the sermons and lectures that most clearly express his understanding of missions, but also to show how Dad's life experiences helped him to shape his theology. As a result, you can read this book in a variety of ways. You can read the story of his life and skip the sermons and essays, or you can read the essays and lectures and skip the narrative. For those who read both the life story and the essays that reflect his developing thought, exploring the relationship between experience and theology, the book may become a biographical theology.

In some respects this life story also reflects and epitomizes the best of an era of Baptist life in which there was a fervor for missions and a unanimity Baptists have not seen in a quarter of a century. It reflects the spirit and core values of the Baptist heritage before the controversy that has divided Baptists. Hugo's engagement with people from other cultures also points the way for all Christians in our shrinking world and increasingly pluralistic society. Through reflection on Hugo's life and thought, Baptists may come to a fresh appreciation for their heritage as Baptists, a renewed commitment to missions, and an awareness of the importance and potential of learning from the religious experience of people of other faiths.

Such reflection may well lead us to rethink the ways in which we do Christian missions.

Seldom has a life been so fully lived and so richly documented. Hugo kept meticulous records: financial ledgers, lists of Greek vocabulary, typed study notes, records of his weightlifting, and sermon notes. More importantly, the Culpeppers were letter writers. Hugo and Ruth wrote to their parents weekly when they could, and their parents wrote back. They wrote to each other when they were separated. They wrote to the boys when they were college students, and the boys wrote them back. They also carried on an active correspondence with former professors A. J. Armstrong and W. O. Carver, mission board representatives, and friends and colleagues around the world.

The process of finding, organizing, and reading through this treasure trove has been a fulfilling exercise in itself. The technological world of cell phones and e-mail has changed the way we communicate with each other, and one wonders whether these new technologies will be used for the kind of reflective communication that is preserved in Hugo's letters. The challenge has been to select what and how much to include in the book—less, and some of the richness and detail would be lost; more, and some of the focus would be blurred.

In the process, I have sought to let Dad tell his own story in his own words whenever possible. Like Luke the evangelist, I have also sought the help of those who were eyewitnesses, and I have been greatly helped by close friends of Hugo and Ruth at various periods in their lives: Fern Harrington Miles, who was interned with them in the concentration camp, helped me to straighten out geographical and chronological matters in their accounts of this time, supplied me with wonderful stories about the Culpeppers as young missionaries before the war, shared pages from her camp diary, and generously gave me permission to reproduce her sketches of Baguio and the concentration camp. Cecil McConnell, who was a missionary to Chile at the time they were there, read and corrected the chapter on Chile. Jack and Jean Glaze, colleagues in the mission work in Argentina, corrected references and filled gaps in the account of those years, and Glenn Hinson added insights for the chapter on Southern Seminary from 1970 to 1981. Tom Prevost read the first full draft and offered many suggestions that helped me reduce the manuscript to a publishable length. Family members—Larry, Jacque, Rodney, and Erin—read chapters as they were written. They encouraged me to think it was important to finish the book, and we cried, laughed, and remembered together; it is appropriate that the writing of Hugo Culpepper's life story required the collaboration of family, friends, and others who were touched by him.

In the end, Dad would not have wanted the flattery or aggrandizement of a biography, but if the story of his life and thought prompts others who come after him to live more fully, to seek to know God more deeply, to be more actively involved in the life of the church and its mission in the world, and to respond with greater appreciation to persons of faith from other religious traditions, then I think he would be pleased.

Farewell—Foreword

As I have reflected on the uniqueness of Dad's life, I realized that the one thing that makes sense of it all is that he, more than anyone I know, lived out of a deep awareness of the reality of God and an abiding appreciation for God's redemptive love. Seeking to live in response to the knowledge and fellowship of God as he came to understand it accounts for both his commitment to missions and his expectant curiosity about life after death.

In some respects Dad never got far from his humble beginnings—he always loved navy beans, cornbread, and buttermilk. Who could have predicted the life he would lead when he was born at home, at 716 Cedar Street in Pine Bluff, Arkansas, on January 5, 1913? The stories he told us about growing up in Pine Bluff evoke a bygone era. He had pneumonia when he was nine years old, and when his lungs began to fill with fluid, the doctor came to the house and cut a hole in his back between his ribs and put a tube into his lungs to drain the fluid. His parents thought fresh air and exercise would help him regain his strength, so they bought him a horse, which they kept for a while at the cowcatcher's barn and then in a barn in their backyard. At that time he began his lifelong devotion to physical conditioning, bought a set of barbells and built himself up to where when he was twenty-seven he won the Arkansas state weightlifting title for his weight division. How many times did Larry and I hear Dad talk about the importance of growing physically, socially, intellectually, and spiritually? As Luke 2:52 says of Jesus, Dad grew "in wisdom and in stature, and in favor with God and man."

Although his parents were not very religious, they took Dad to church, and it was through the church, the people of God, and the Sunday school teacher and Baptist Training Union leader who took an interest in him that he first experienced the reality of God in his life, came forward after one of the preaching services, and asked to be baptized. After he graduated from high school in 1932, he was nominated for admission to the United States Naval Academy at Annapolis, Maryland, but he failed the math exam. After spending a year at the Marion Military Institute in Marion, Alabama, he made the highest math score of any applicant in the country and went on to Annapolis in the fall of 1933. Just five months later, and to the amazement and disbelief of his fellow plebes, he responded to a growing sense of call, resigned his place at the Naval Academy, and returned to Arkansas, to Ouachita College, to study for the ministry. That summer he had met Mother at the Baptist assembly at Siloam Springs, Arkansas, on the last day of the Assembly, and at the closing service they both committed their lives to full-time Christian service. At the age of fifteen, Mother was already planning to be a missionary to China.

Dad followed her to Baylor, graduating in 1936, and then she followed him to Southern Seminary in Louisville. She received her M.R.E. degree and he his Th.M. in 1939, and they were married that summer. 1940 was an eventful year. Dad was ordained to the gospel ministry, won the Arkansas state weightlifting title in his weight division, he and Mother were appointed as foreign missionaries, and in August they sailed under the Golden Gate Bridge, bound for Chinese language school in Peiping, China.

When conditions there became dangerous, they were moved to the language school at Baguio, in the Philippines. While they were reviewing for their final exam, Pearl Harbor was bombed, and they never took that exam. Immediately, the islands were cut off, and within weeks they were interned in a Japanese concentration camp. When they went into the camp, the Japanese confiscated everything they had, but one of the guards had been educated in the United States, and he recognized Dad's Nestle Greek New Testament, his Souter's pocket lexicon, and Robertson's "Big Grammar" and let him keep them because they were religious materials. In the three years and four months that they were in prison, Dad read through this Greek New Testament twelve times and worked through Robertson's big grammar three times, twice from start to finish and once working through the Scripture index from Matthew to Revelation. For the rest of his life he kept this tattered old Greek New Testament by his chair and read his scheduled section each day.

They were liberated by General Douglas MacArthur's troops on Mother's twenty-seventh birthday, February 5, 1945. I was born the following year. During 1946 and 1947, Dad studied medicine at the medical school in Conway, Arkansas, but he realized that he could not do justice to both theology and medicine. He would leave medicine for my brother Larry to do. When he gave up his medical studies, he gave the microscope his parents had given him to Bill Wallace, who took it with him to the hospital in Wuchow, China, before he was imprisoned and tortured to death there a few years later.

Because China was closed to mission work, the Foreign Mission Board asked Mother and Dad to go to the seminary in Santiago, Chile. They agreed, on one condition—that they not have to go to language school but be allowed to learn Spanish on the field! We sailed through the Panama Canal and down the west coast of South America. Larry was born in

Santiago the following year. After a furlough in Louisville from 1952–53, the Mission Board asked Dad to become professor of theology and church history at the International Baptist Seminary in Buenos Aires, Argentina. There, Dad taught and preached in Spanish and was president of the Argentine mission for three years.

By the time we returned to Louisville in 1958, Dad felt that his work in South America was over, but he did not know what God was leading him to next. It became clear, though, that now it was time for Dad to teach and send others in his place and work to help pastors and churches in the States understand the nature of the mission of the church. Dad finished his Th.D. at The Southern Baptist Theological Seminary on the thought of Miguel de Unamuno, the agnostic Spanish philosopher and humanist who was president of the University of Salamanca. Dad taught missions at Southern from 1959 until 1965, when Dr. Arthur Rutledge invited him to become director of missions for the Home Mission Board, a position he filled here in Atlanta until President Duke McCall invited him to return to Southern as the W. O. Carver Professor of Missions and World Religions, a chair he held until his retirement in 1981. During those years, he and I had the wonderful experience of being colleagues as well as family.

Throughout his life, Dad continued to grow spiritually, to grow in his understanding of the redemptive love of God. Late in life, he reflected on his growth through six stages of faith: first, the role of the church; second, religious experience, in his conversion; third, a sensitivity to the leading of the Holy Spirit; fourth, a deep appreciation for the Bible; fifth, a responsiveness to the leadership of Jesus as Lord; and finally, late in life, after a sabbatical year at the Center for the Study of World Religions at Harvard, the realization that Jesus' mission was to glorify God and that the character of God is our highest authority. The defining purpose for human life is to live for the praise of God's glory, as Paul says in Ephesians 1. As one of Dad's former students reminded me, Dad said, "If God is the ultimate reality, our vocation is to be such as is in harmony with Him."

One afternoon in fall of 1988, I sat in a hospital room with Dad the day before he would undergo heart bypass surgery. He told me that after having studied the New Testament teachings on the end of time and all the theologies of life after death, the only thing that really mattered to him was that "God is," and if "God is,"—that is, the God revealed in the person of Jesus—then nothing else really mattered, and he could face the future in peace and confidence in the goodness and love of God, whatever the future might hold.

But there is much more to the story.

Chapter 1

Boyhood

"My heart leaps up when I behold
A rainbow in the sky.
So it was when my life began;...
The Child is father of the Man;
And I could wish my days to be
Bound each to each by natural piety."[1]

The Culpeppers came to Grant County, Arkansas, by wagon train some-time after 1880. In 1885, John Francis "Frank" Culpepper (1863–1906) married Florence M. Johnson, and Hugo's father, John Hurlston "Hurley" Culpepper, was born in 1891. Frank joined the Pine Bluff, Arkansas, police force and served as a patrolman and then as a city detective before being appointed chief of police. After he retired in 1905, Frank worked as a night watchman for the Bluff City Lumber Company. Shortly after midnight on 5 December 1906, Frank noticed a man "skulking about near the lumber sheds."[2] When Frank approached him, the man shot him twice, in the abdomen and the groin. Frank returned fire, killing the man. Frank was taken to his home, where he died a few hours later.

Hurley, who was fourteen years old at the time, dropped out of school when he was in the eighth grade and became the family breadwinner, selling women's shoes. In 1910, he married Ida Jewel Bradley, and they settled down to raise a family in Pine Bluff, a town of about 25,000 people. No one living in Pine Bluff could have imagined the life that Hugo Hurlston Culpepper would lead when he was born at home on 5 January

---

[1] William Wordsworth, "My Heart Leaps Up when I Behold," Bernard D. Grebanier, et al., *English Literature and Its Background* (New York: Dayden Press, 1950) 749.

[2] *The Weekly Graphic*, Pine Bluff, Arkansas, 8 December 1906.

1913. His sister, Wanda, was born 12 February 1915. Eventually, Hugo's father finished his high school equivalency, and when he retired he was chief of the field division for the Internal Revenue Service of Arkansas.

Early Religious Experience

Hugo's parents were members of the First Baptist Church in Pine Bluff, and as early as Hugo could remember, his parents took him to Sunday school and church. The preaching and teaching were typical of the conservative Baptist tradition. William Matthews, his Sunday school teacher, and Etta Carnahan, a worker in the Baptist Training Union (BTU), took a personal interest in Hugo.

The influence of parents and teachers led Hugo to an early conversion. He joined the church one Sunday evening (not during a revival). Years later, Hugo recalled,

While my parents were never very active as church members—and perhaps this left me more freedom and responsibility to develop my own personal living tradition—earlier than I can remember, they began taking me to church, and the church...became the first step in my experience of religious authority.

One Sunday night during the summer when I was eight years of age, as I saw it then and as I have seen it through the years and still see it, God took the initiative through a rather ordinary sermon— which has always been an encouragement to me personally—and came into my life in a new way. No one else happened to have responded that night to the in-vitation. And I am sure the preacher was somewhat disappointed that only an eight-year-old boy came forward. But I felt that I must respond to the strong sense of God's leadership that I experienced in those moments. I still think it was at the initiative of the Holy Spirit. I accepted Jesus Christ as my Lord and Savior at that time. I did not understand much about the theology of that experience, but I have never for one moment doubted its authenticity or its validity. The Spirit blew where it would that night, and I heard its voice and was born from above.

The personal experience of conversion then came to be the second step in my experience of religious authority, and I moved on into a period of some five years in which I was living in the afterglow, as it were, of this personal experience.[3]

Hugo's first ambition was to be an electrical engineer. His father built a workshop for him in the back yard, and Hugo spent many hours tinkering with electrical gadgets. He built a radio set from blueprints and instructions and a private telephone line from his workshop to a friend's workshop down the street. His workshop and back yard were the meeting places for boys his age.

At the age of nine, Hugo nearly died of pneumonia. The doctors held little hope for his recovery, and looking back years later his parents believed that his life was spared for the work that he would do later in life. The doctors advised rest, fresh air, and sunshine, so his father purchased a saddle horse for him—something else that attracted all the boys to his back yard.

Hugo's Horses

For the rest of his life, Hugo enjoyed telling the stories of his horses and his boyhood in Pine Bluff, first to his sons and then to his grandchildren. A conversation with his grandchildren, Erin and Rodney, who were seven and five, preserves stories that reveal a great deal about him as a boy, a parent, and a grandparent—and about life in a small town in Arkansas in the 1920s:

You may have heard that when your father and your Uncle Larry were little boys, I used to have them sit on my lap after supper at night, and they would ask me to tell them stories about when I was a boy.

When I was about five years old, my mother and daddy moved to a new neighborhood in the town where we lived, in Pine Bluff, Arkansas. We lived about four blocks away from the school, and I walked back and forth to the school by myself.

When I was in about the middle of the fourth grade, I became ill with a bad cold, and it went into influenza, and the infection settled in both of my lungs. It went into pneumonia, and after I had had pneumonia for about two weeks and had been sick for about a month, the doctor said it would be necessary to

---

[3] Hugo Culpepper, "The Bible and Religious Authority," sermon preached at Southern Seminary, 22 October 1980. See below, p. 329.

operate. They did not have penicillin nor any of the antibiotics which they have now to treat pneumonia, and so he said it would be necessary to cut a hole in my back between my ribs in order to put a rubber tube there and drain the fluid off of my lungs to keep me from dying.

They did not take me to the hospital to do this, but our family doctor got a surgeon who was a friend of his to come with him out to our home, and they did the operation there, on the bed in our bedroom. They gave me a shot of medicine to deaden some of the pain, and they cut a hole between my ribs. I remember very well that it hurt very badly, and I screamed so loud that they could hear me for several blocks. But the operation was successful, and they kept the tube in my back, draining the fluid out for about two weeks.

At the end of that time, I had to stay in bed two more weeks after the tube had been removed. By then I had been in bed for two whole months. I had to begin to learn to walk all over again. I was so weak that I literally could not walk, and my mother or daddy had to hold me up and help me to learn to walk.

Now this was from about the middle of January to the middle of March, and by then spring was starting. I did not go back to school that spring semester, but the doctor advised that I get outside as much as possible and get fresh air and sunshine. So my daddy decided that he would buy a horse for me.

Hugo as a boy.

We put a fence up inside of our backyard, which was already fenced in, and had that corner of the yard just to keep my horse in. It had a small barn in a part of it, where the horse had a stable with straw on the floor and a wooden box nailed to the wall on one side. I would have to go out in the morning and again at night and feed my horse out of a sack. I would also have to clean the stall out periodically and put fresh straw down, and then I would groom the horse. At that time, I had no other friends who had a horse. So I had to ride pretty much by myself. My parents thought it would be good for me to get a dog to go along with me as I rode the horse. So we got a white bulldog. I named the dog Mack, and Mack loved to follow the horse. And so I spent many weeks and many months very happy, outside in the warm air and sunshine, riding my horse with my dog following wherever I went.

While we were still living in that neighborhood, some of my friends and I decided it would be fun to have a rodeo one afternoon with my horse. There was a vacant lot nearby that was fenced in. We decided there was plenty of space there that my horse could put on a show for us. Now, in order to make the horse buck, we took a long rope and tied it around the back and stomach of the horse, toward the back part, and had the end of the rope dragging on the ground between the horse's two back legs. There was a slip knot on the rope, we thought, so that thirty or thirty-five feet behind the horse we could pull on the rope, and it would tighten up just enough to make him kick his feet up in the air as he was running.

After we got that rope fixed, I took the bridle off the horse so he would be free to run wherever he wanted to. All of my friends were sitting up on the fence, with their feet on a two-by-four that ran near the top of the fence. So I got down and pulled on the rope and made the horse kick up his feet as he ran, but then something unexpected happened. When that rope would not slip any more, it tightened up and kept tight on the underside of his stomach. The horse kept running and kept bucking, and I had to run and get back up on top of the fence myself because the horse was becoming wild and running all over that fenced-in piece of ground. One time, as he ran around, he ran near where we were sitting. When he kicked his feet up in the air, he kicked the boards on the side of the fence and knocked the boards loose at the top, and all of us who were sitting on them fell over backwards off the top of the fence onto the ground. The horse kept running and kept bucking. Now, I didn't know what to do to stop the horse. I was afraid my horse was going to hurt himself, and I couldn't stop him.

Well, I thought the best thing to do was to go to the telephone and telephone my daddy, who worked in a shoe store downtown at that time. I called him and got him on the phone, and I said, "Daddy, I have a problem." I told him what we had done and how my horse was running and bucking. "Well," he said, "you just stay there and don't get near the horse because he might kick you and hurt you. You just stay there and wait, and I will get our friend the cowcatcher to come out and do something about it."

So we waited, and we waited, and it seemed to us like it was a very long time until finally our friend the cowcatcher rode up on his horse. He saw what had happened, so he took his rope and lassoed the horse. He cut the rope that we had put on the horse. Then he took his own rope off, and the horse quit bucking. He put the bridle back on, gave me the bridle. I had learned my lesson never to do that again.

Well, a little later we moved closer in to downtown. By that time I had become a good rider, and this horse was so gentle and so slow that I wanted a horse that was younger and faster. My daddy thought it was reasonable, and he arranged to trade the horse in and pay some additional money and get a younger horse, one that liked to run some and that was a gaited horse.

Now, this horse I called Black Beauty. He was a beautiful, black-colored horse that had five gaits. He was lively and young and was just an ideal horse—the best I ever had. I still had my bulldog, and so I enjoyed doing a lot of riding on Black Beauty, with Mack following me. In this new neighborhood, I made friends with two other boys about my age, and each of them had their own saddle horse, and the three of us used to go riding together. We would ride out to the edge of town, out country roads and in the woods, and be gone for several hours at a time.

By the time I was thirteen or fourteen, I had gotten a job working downtown after school and on Saturday. My health was much better. I had begun to exercise and to eat the right foods. I was much healthier then and exercising then, and I was busy working and didn't have time for my horse. I hated to let my friend go, but we sold the horse, and a man bought it who wanted to use it to pull a buggy. Now, a buggy has light wheels. It is not nearly as heavy nor as hard to pull as a wagon. So the last time I saw Black Beauty, Black Beauty was going off down Main Street in Pine Bluff, pulling this man in his beautiful black buggy. And I was happy because Black Beauty did not have too hard a work to do and had a good master. He had a good home, and that made me feel good even though I could not keep him any longer.[4]

Hugo's illness, slight stature (never more that 5'8"), and consciousness of health led him to become a physical culturist. Enthralled by pictures of Charles Atlas, he purchased a set of barbells and began a regime of regular

---

[4] Hugo Culpepper, tape recording, 1981.

exercise, lifting weights three days a week from then on until his arthritis made him stop at the age of seventy-two. The barbell workouts and proper diet helped him to develop a strong, healthy body. Participating regularly in worship also laid a foundation for his spiritual development. For about six years as a teenager, Hugo's pastor was Dr. Perry Webb, Sr. The inspiration of his preaching planted seeds for a vocation in Christian ministry that would germinate some years later, as he recalled:

When I was thirteen years of age, I remember very well walking for two miles to church every night with my grandmother to attend one of those old-time Arkansas doctrinal revival meetings. A preacher you probably never heard of, Dr. Allen Hill Autrey, of considerable reputation in Arkansas circles, was the preacher for that occasion. It was a notable week of experience for me.[5]

For several years God as Holy Spirit had been very real to me. I remember so well, as I was at the point of entering into the teenage years, there began to weigh heavily upon my heart and mind the whole question of life, its nature, its responsibilities—the whole question of vocation. "Who am I?" "What am I intended to be?" And, very frankly, I was overwhelmed by it. I turned to the only place I knew to turn. Frequently, at night, after the house had become hushed and the family had slipped off to sleep, I would slip out of bed on my knees, by the side of my bed, in the darkness of my room, and pray pretty much the same prayer time after time. It went something like this: "Lord, life is too much for me. I'm not sure that I'll be able to handle it. But you know who I am, and you know what you intend for me to be. And, Lord, I want to turn my life over to you and trust you to lead me into becoming and into being and doing that which you have for me." During that week of revival the Spirit gave me eyes to see, and I discovered for myself the Bible.[6]

Teenage Years

Hugo also developed intellectually. When he was in ninth grade, Hugo decided he would study hard so he could "take it easy" the last two years of high school. He was surprised to find that he really liked to study, so he continued to do so. In the eleventh grade he was on the debate team. He was

---

[5] Hugo would later say that this doctrinal revival "set" his religious perspective.

[6] Culpepper, "The Bible and Religious Authority."

a member of the National Honor Society and was vice president of the student council.[7] In later years, Hugo recalled that the first great teacher he had was Nannie May Roney, his English teacher during his junior year in high school. He said, "She taught me to learn to love to read. She gave me the gift of enjoying and appreciating reading, one of the most indispensable gifts anyone can receive."[8]

Hugo made As all through high school. When he graduated in 1931 from Junius Jordan High School in Pine Bluff, his father helped him get an appointment to the United States Naval Academy in Annapolis, Maryland. A Baptist deacon from Malvern, Arkansas, Congressman D. D. Glover was instrumental in securing Hugo's appointment, but Hugo failed the math part of the entrance exam. After spending most of the year (August 1931–February 1932) studying math at the Marion Military Institute in Marion, Alabama, he retook the entrance exam. While his classmates crammed the night before, Hugo confidently went to the movies to relax. The next day he made the highest math score of any applicant that year.

Hugo and Ruth at Ruth's graduation from Baylor, 1937.

---

[7] Alvin Hatton, "Meet the Missionary—Hugo Culpepper," *Ambassador Life* (January 1950): 2.

[8] Hugo Culpepper, tape recording of a Sunday school class at St. Matthews Methodist Church, 14 February [1986–1988?].

Chapter 2

Education

"The understanding of the Christian tradition is a lifelong process of growth and development. My ideas about Christianity have changed remarkably in the last decade, and I am sixty-eight years old now.... Early in life I ran into the perspective that the most important thing in life is not success or failure—and that's a milestone when you really come to realize that the most important thing in life is whether you keep on growing or stop growing."[1]

After five months at Annapolis (June–October 1932), and much to the amazement of his fellow midshipmen, Hugo decided that he could not serve the Lord best with a naval career. It was more than the choice of a career; it was a choice of a way of life, one that had been in the back of his mind since the age of fourteen. A career as a naval officer was a sure road to success and security in the midst of the Depression, but Hugo wanted an education that would prepare him for religious work. In a letter to his parents, telling them that he was dropping out of the Naval Academy and asking for their understanding, he wrote:

After long and careful consideration, I have definitely decided that I must resign from the Naval Academy.

For some time I have felt the urge to be a preacher. All summer long the urge has grown stronger. In fact, I rather hesitated upon entering the Academy but drove myself to it because of all the money you have spent on me. I find the course unbearable. Please don't misunderstand and think that I am impulsive in making this decision. I have thought of little else for the last six months, even during my stay at home....

---

[1] Hugo Culpepper, tape recording of lecture for Bishop Stephen Neill's class at Southern Seminary, 22 January 1981.

Because I am convinced that I should preach, and because of my utter distaste for a Naval career, I find the life unbearable for me. I have been unhappy in trying to go on in this way. My appetite has failed, and I have found it difficult to sleep. You may think me silly and unappreciative. I shall never forgive nor fail to censure myself for the expense that I have been to you.

I don't expect to go to school now. What I want is peace with myself. I believe the Lord will provide in due course of time.... I know that jobs are scarce. I am trusting in the Lord for guidance in what I should do next. This one thing I know, it is impossible for me to drive myself into something in which I am miserable. Forgive me if you can. I am tormented for what I have cost you.[2]

His parents received the special delivery letter on Sunday morning. They immediately wired back their consent. After securing his parents' permission, Hugo returned to Arkansas and attended Ouachita Baptist College for a year and a half, working during the summers.

I worked on a college boys' magazine crew trying to sell *Saturday Evening Post*, and I would go up to a house. This was in 1933—sophomore in college—go up to a house—"Yes, they would like to take *Saturday Evening Post*, but they didn't have a dollar for the down payment"—one dollar! I would say, "Well, would you let me catch one of the chickens out there in your yard and let me take it as a down payment?" "Yeah, they guess they could do without one chicken." So I literally would go out and catch a hen, take it, and put it in a chicken coop on the front bumper of that old Studebaker open touring car that five of us were riding around in trying to sell those magazines. We made a dollar, the down payment. That was what we made off of selling a year's subscription. Then they would bill them later for the rest of it. We would take those chickens and take them in to the county seat and sell them at the curb market. What we got out of them was our down payment.

I remember when I went to college. I paid fifteen dollars a month for room and board. It was in an old, wooden two-story house. We had three people to a room, four rooms—twelve people up there using one bath, and it didn't have a shower. It was a bathtub. We had to heat the water in a small washtub on a two-burner gas stove sitting in the bathroom. You would heat a small washtub of water and dump it over in the tub and get in and bathe.[3]

---

[2] Hugo Culpepper, letter to Mr. and Mrs. J. H. Culpepper, Fall 1932 [undated].

[3] Hugo Culpepper, tape recording of lecture on "The Secular: Secularization and Secularism," for Continuing Theological Education Conference "The Mission of Your Church" at Southern Seminary, 20 October 1977.

During the summer of 1933, Hugo attended the Baptist Assembly at Siloam Springs, Arkansas, and met Ruth Cochrane after he had seen her take part in a program.

Ruth Cochrane

Ruth was the daughter of Mr. and Mrs. W. F. Cochrane, who were faithful members of Immanuel Baptist Church in Little Rock. Ruth's mother wrote the following account of Ruth's early years:

Ruth was born February 5th, 1918, in Little Rock, Arkansas, was enrolled in the Cradle Roll of Immanuel Baptist Church almost immediately, and continued through each department of the Sunday School. At the age of nine or ten she joined the church and was baptized. She had been converted some time before she joined the church, but we wanted to be sure she knew what she was doing and she could tell us all about why she wanted to and we were thoroughly convinced that she knew. Almost from the time she was converted, as well as I remember, she said that she wanted to be a missionary, and when she was about 13 years old she dedicated her life in His service as a missionary to China. From that time on she planned her life and education in that direction. It was at one of the Baptist Summer Assemblies that she dedicated her life.

She met Hugo Culpepper the very last night of one of the Assemblies at Siloam Springs, and from then on they were sweethearts. Each one of them had felt the call to service before they met. She was active in G.A.'s, Y.W.A., Sunday School, B.T.U., and a member of a soul winning group. She was also a member of the Rainbow organization for girls. She helped in several revival meetings as a personal worker or with the music and young people during her summer vacations.

Ruth was educated in the Little Rock public schools. At five years old she went to Mary Dodge Kindergarten, and at six years old entered the second grade at Rose School, continuing on until she graduated from Little Rock High School at the age of 16, in the Spring of 1934.[4]

---

[4] A brief, undated account of Ruth's childhood, written by her mother, Agnes Cochrane, sent to Mrs. Ralph Lee Douglas in 1944.

The following note is written in pencil on the back of Ruth's high school diploma: "This was picked up at Baguio in April, 1945, by Capt. William O. Martin, Headquarters, 6th Army, C.A.S.–P C A U #7, Luzon Island, Philippines. Home address: 425 Magnolia, Park Hill, N. Little Rock, Arkansas." Captain Martin brought the diploma home with him and returned it to the Cochranes.

Hugo went to Little Rock several times that summer to see Ruth (he lived then in Pine Bluff, Arkansas). That fall he went back to Ouachita Baptist College, where he was a member of the Ministerial Association. Ruth had one more year in high school, but they saw each other several times during that winter.

Baylor University, 1934–1936

When Ruth entered Baylor University in the fall of 1934, Hugo transferred his credits there. Their romance was a little stormy, and two or three times they broke up, once for several months. Still, they were together quite a bit at Baylor and eventually became engaged, planning their life work together.

Hugo later described how he sensed a call to missions while at Baylor:

I was sitting in the chapel of Baylor University in the fall of my junior year. The chapel speaker was a missionary on furlough from China. He was giving his life to the work of teaching in a Christian university sponsored by the Foreign Mission Board. So far as I know, I had given no thought to being a foreign missionary. In the course of an otherwise rather dull talk, the missionary said, "A young American who has had the opportunity of a Christian education can find no greater opportunity for the investment of his life than in teaching the forward-looking young people of China." Immediately the question framed itself in my mind, "why not you?" At some considerable sacrifice on the part of my parents, I was being given the opportunity of a Christian education. Why should I not respond to the need for teachers in China? This question was no ordinary question. It came home to the deep of my being as though an arrow had been shot into my heart! I could not put it out of my mind. During the weeks and months ahead it was a recurring question. In the spring of the following year, my senior year at Baylor, I attended the annual spring Pastors' Conference at the Southern Baptist Theological Seminary. I heard Dr. Kenneth Scott Latourette speak on "Missions Tomorrow." Also, I had the privilege of hearing Toyohiko Kagawa speak on "The Philosophy of the Christian

Religion." Under the influence of the experiences during that week, a positive response took shape to the question which had been in my mind continuously for eighteen months. That weekend as I stayed overnight at home in Arkansas before returning to Baylor, I shared with my parents the conviction to which I had come by that time, that God was calling me to be a foreign missionary. I also indicated to them that I was willing to answer that call and invest my life in the work of foreign missions. For many reasons that I do not yet understand, my life has not worked out to be that which I expected at that time. However, never have I doubted the genuineness of this call to missions.[5]

At Baylor, Hugo and Ruth were both deeply influenced by Professor A. J. Armstrong and his love of the poetry of Robert and Elizabeth Barrett Browning. They recalled going to Dr. Armstrong's home near the Baylor campus on Saturday nights and sitting and talking on the front porch. Among the memories that Hugo carried of Dr. Armstrong are the following:

My second great teacher was professor of English at Baylor University. He conferred to his students a "megalomania," a "madness for greatness" in terms of life values. He was an eccentric personality but took some students into the inner circle in fellowship with him. During my first semester there, when I was taking Browning as a junior, he asked us to submit a written philosophy of life. Well, I already had a philosophy of life which I had written in the last year or year and a half at my own initiative, simply to try to state at that age what life looked like it was to me, and so without even copying it over—it was written on long sheets of paper, typed, but not with the neat appearance of a theme to be graded—I simply turned in what I had, folded it over twice and put a rubber band around it and turned it in. About a week later, I had stopped by his office for some routine something or other, and he said, "By the way, I was interested in reading your philosophy of life, not so much for what it is but for what it portends."

I remember sitting in his living room and hearing Edwin Markham read "The Man with the Hoe." He opened doors of cultural opportunity and vistas by bringing *The Barrister of Wimple Street* and other great plays to the stage of the auditorium there at the university. I remember on one occasion going over when I had some kind of a little question in my mind—one reason it took us six years to get married was that I was not certain in my own mind that it would be

---

[5] Hugo Culpepper, letter on a single, typewritten sheet, untitled, and undated.

fair to any girl for me to marry, having some of the ideas I had and expecting her to live with me through life—I went over one day in the middle of the morning, called to see if I could come by to his living room and talk with him, and I remember after talking, tears came in his eyes. (He had only one son who lived in Pennsylvania and was no longer at home.) Because of this almost father-son relationship, as we stood up to leave he reached out and embraced me with a fatherly hug.

He taught me a great many things, but it was primarily this sense of values in life. He was thoroughly imbued with the philosophy of Robert Browning. I guess the text for his "megalomania" was Browning's words: "It is better to aim at a million and miss it a unit than to aim at a hundred and gain it", "on the earth a broken arch, in the heavens a perfect round," and other innumerable quotations that express that philosophy.[6]

Ruth majored in English, worked one year in general circulation in the Baylor library, and then was chosen as the student head of Baylor's famous Browning Collection and spent two years as Dr. Armstrong's assistant curator.

Hugo underlined the following statements in his copy of Armstrong's biography: "Never would Dr. Armstrong minimize the teaching of literature; it is a passion with him. Nevertheless, above subject matter he always elevates the human being.... One great teaching objective of Dr. Armstrong is to enable his students to face life with greater equanimity.... He believes that our faith in God should enable us to "take what comes and make the best of it."[7] Hugo's lifelong interest in the life and work of Albert Schweitzer was probably sparked by Dr. Armstrong, who held missionaries in high esteem and called Schweitzer and Livingstone "two of the greatest of the great!"[8]

On 4 December 1934, Hugo bought a copy of *The Complete Poetic and Dramatic Works of Robert Browning* for three dollars. Like all his books, it has the date and cost written inside the front cover. He kept this treasured volume with him the rest of his life, even while he was in the Japanese concentration camp during the war, for it bears the Japanese stamp in the back of it. It is marked with notes, underlined, and has handwritten and

---

[6] Hugo Culpepper, tape recording of a Sunday school class at St. Matthews Methodist Church, 14 February [1986–1988?].

[7] Louis Smith Douglas, *Through Heaven's Back Door: A Biography of A. Joseph Armstrong* (Waco: Baylor University Press, 1951) 254.

[8] Ibid., 256.

typed introductory essays to various poems glued into it. The underlinings are in various colors of ink, no doubt from years scattered across decades of rereadings. The strength Hugo drew from Browning's poetry is evidenced by the fact that one marking in "A Death in the Desert,"[9] Browning's profound meditation on Christianity through the dying Apostle John, is dated 14 October 1942, while he was in the concentration camp. During these years of hunger, illness, and internment, Hugo reflected deeply on the meaning of life itself. Marked in red are the following lines:

If I live yet, it is for good, more love through me to men.

Is it for nothing we grow old and weak,
We whom God loves?

So duly, daily, needs provision be
For keeping the soul's prowess possible,
Building new barriers as the old decay,
Saving us from evasion of life's proof,
Putting the question ever, "Does God love,
And will ye hold that truth against the world?"[10]

Could there be clearer evidence of the value of education in providing a person with the intellectual and spiritual resources from which to live the rest of his or her life? Inside the back cover, Hugo wrote a quotation from Goethe that Dr. Armstrong loved to repeat: "Life is rich as you fill it with the things beautiful to remember."

During Hugo's junior year, he was initiated into the national honorary English fraternity, Sigma Tau Delta, along with several other students. They were required to present an original composition as part of the initiation. He later recalled,

---

[9] See R. Alan Culpepper, "Guessing Points and Knowing Stars: History and Higher Criticism in Robert Browning's 'A Death in the Desert,' " *The Future of Christology: Essays in Honor of Leander E. Keck*, ed. Abraham J. Malherbe and Wayne A. Meeks (Minneapolis: Fortress Press, 1993) 53–65; revised and republished in part in idem, *John, the Son of Zebedee: The Life of a Legend* (Columbia: University of South Carolina Press, 1994) 267–75.

[10] Horace E. Scudder, ed., *The Complete Poetic and Dramatic Works of Robert Browning*, The Cambridge Poets (Boston: Houghton, Mifflin, and Company, 1895) 386–88.

A fellow student, Louise Harper, read an original poem. While she did not reveal it in the poem, she was thinking of A. J. Armstrong when she wrote it. He was our professor of English, the sponsor of the fraternity, and the founder of the Browning Collection. Because of my appreciation of Dr. Armstrong, the poem was meaningful to me in a special sense. But even more than this, the philosophy of life which it expressed "grabbed me" at the moment and has been a lifelong influence.

The poem reads:

> I often wondered as I saw you work,
> If it were life or death
> That held you most in bondage;
> But now I think I know:
> For such as you,
> Life has no day or night,
> No end and no beginning;
> But all is one great dawn
> That sees in golden glory
> Eternity as a sunrise![11]

Ruth's father, who painted in watercolors, drew a sunrise scene that Hugo made into bookplates that he used all his life. Under the scene are the words "Eternity as a sunrise."

One of the assignments Hugo completed for Dr. Armstrong's English 247, on February 21, 1935, was an English translation of the Latin text of the Eulogium pronounced by Mr. J. E. Sandys, Public Orator at the University of Cambridge, on presenting Robert Browning for the honorary degree of Doctor of Laws on June 10, 1879. The fact that a Latin translation could be required in an English course speaks volumes about the classical education provided by the liberal arts program at Baylor in the 1930s.

---

[11] Hugo Culpepper, "Eternity as a Sunrise," sermon preached at Crescent Hill Baptist Church, 27 September 1970. The full sermon is reproduced below, pp. 293-99.

Southern Seminary, 1936–1940

After spending the summer of 1936 working and living with an aunt and uncle in Shreveport, Hugo entered The Southern Baptist Theological Seminary at Louisville, Kentucky. He wrote the following reflections on his experience as a student at Southern:

In the seminary I did all the required reading assigned in the syllabi, studying about five and a half hours a day outside of classes. The most important courses for me were: the first year, Biblical Introduction (Professor J. McKee Adams), and New Testament Survey (Professor Hersey Davis); the second year, Missions (Professor W. O. Carver), and Systematic Theology (memorizing E. Y. Mullins' *The Christian Religion in Its Doctrinal Expression* under Professor H. W. Tribble); the third year, Senior Greek (A. T. Robertson's the "Big" Grammar for 1/2 year, and Textual Criticism for 1/4 year, and exegesis of Romans for 1/4 year with the International Critical Commentary by Sanday and Headlam), all of this with Professor Hersey Davis; Theology of the Old Testament and Theology of the New Testament (Professor Tribble), with term papers each half year as the only introduction to research during the three years, and Christianity and Current Thought (Professor W. O. Carver). A choice between this course and Comparative Religion, each for 1/2 year, was the only elective in the three-year Th.M. curriculum—and I took both courses. I also was permitted to take a graduate seminar on the Philosophy of Religion the third year (Professor W. O. Carver). My grade average for the three-year Th.M. was 96 percent, although I did not know this until years later because we received no report cards.

I continued a fourth year of study, beginning a Th.D. program. My interest would have led me to major in the Philosophy of Religion under W. O. Carver. One day I heard D. H. Daniel say that he had to get back to the Bible because it had come to mean no more to him than any other book. Therefore, I chose to major in Greek New Testament and minor in Philosophy of Religion and in New Testament Archaeology. My most influential professor was W. O. Carver, and the most important insight gained during the three years was a one-month study of the Biblical Basis of Missions that began the course on Missions my second year. I have shared all these details to establish the fact that I had received a solid, traditional theological education.[12]

---

[12] From the typescript essay "How My Mind Has Changed," written during the 80s at Southern Seminary.

W. O. Carver had a profound influence on Hugo's life from that point on. His own theology of missions was shaped by Carver's, and he proudly carried forward Carver's legacy in later years.

Hugo also met fellow students at Southern with whom he would associate in later years. Hugo and Ruth and Frank and Evelyn Stagg took Greek together. Hugo was in the same small group in Dr. Dobbins's "Principles and Methods" class with Arthur Rutledge and went with Rutledge to do a survey for that class of the American Baptist church Rutledge pastored in Indiana.[13]

While a student at Southern, Hugo read a book on the life of Dan Crawford that he often referred to in later years.

A book entitled *Dan Crawford of Central Africa* tells the true story of a seventeen-year-old young man in England who was converted and the next year called of God to go to Africa. With the help of friends he raised the money to go to the heart of Africa (then called the Belgian Congo). [When he referred to Crawford in his lectures, Hugo always added the story of how after Crawford had been in Africa for five years, he decided "it was not good for man to be alone." He remembered a young woman he had met only briefly, wrote her a letter, and asked if she would come to Africa and marry him—and she accepted his proposal!] He learned eighteen tribal languages and then taught himself Hebrew and Greek. This enabled him to translate the Bible into those languages. When he had been in Africa for twenty-two years, he took his first furlough at the age of forty-five. After visiting England, he returned to Africa by way of the United States. In Louisville, Kentucky, he met with Dr. A. T. Robertson, a New Testament Greek scholar with a world-wide reputation. While reviewing the manuscript of Dr. Robertson's "Big Grammar," Dan Crawford pointed out things about the Greek to Dr. Robertson, by comparison with the African Languages, that the great scholar did not know. God called and led a young man as a missionary into Africa; twenty-two years later he returned having grown in knowledge on a par with a world-wide expert. God is able to prepare and use those whom he calls.[14]

---

[13] Hugo Culpepper, tape recording of Missionary Day address at Southern Seminary chapel, 9 March 1968.

[14] Hugo Culpepper, "God and His Love for Us All," Probe, 14 (January 1984): 7-. See George Edwin Tilsley, *Dan Crawford: Missionary and Pioneer in Central Africa* (New York: Fleming H. Revell, 1929).

Hugo was impressed with the story of Crawford's life as a testimony to the missionary's ability to develop exceptional abilities even under difficult circumstances.

Hugo and Ruth in Louisville

During Hugo's first year at Southern, Ruth continued on at Baylor, where she also belonged to Sigma Tau Delta, and further assisted Dr. Armstrong in the Browning Room. She graduated *cum laude* in 1937. The Arkansas Woman's Missionary Union granted her a scholarship to the W.M.U. Training School at Louisville, but the Training School questioned her age. She was only nineteen when she graduated from Baylor, and they did not think she could be ready for the Training School. After investigating her record, however, they accepted her, and she entered the "House Beautiful" as it was called in the fall of 1937.

That fall, they joined the teams of other seminary students who worked in boats day and night to help Louisvillians whose homes and business were inundated by the flood of 1937. The waters of the Ohio River reached the intersection of Grinstead and Lexington Road, near the seminary, and there was so much water in the Brown Hotel that a bluegill was caught in the lobby of the hotel.

Ruth and Hugo dated for the next two years. The rules regarding the conduct of women at the Training School were strict even by the standards of the day. Men were allowed into the parlor only at certain hours. Couples could sit and talk with a chaperone present, and curfews were enforced. Because the Training School was still downtown, Hugo had to go by bus or trolley, and they later recalled the cold wind that blew down Fourth and Broadway in the winter. Ruth chafed under the restrictions of the Training School. Still, she studied Greek with Hugo, and the two enjoyed friendships they would maintain for years.

Ruth's thesis, submitted in partial fulfillment of the requirements for the Master of Religious Education in the Department of Missions of the Training School, was titled "An Outline History of Medical Missions in China." It was sixty-four pages long and drew material from sixty-six different sources. Ruth graduated from the Training School in the spring of 1939.

After graduation, Hugo and Ruth were married on 24 June 1939, the silver wedding anniversary of her parents. Hugo's parents had moved to Little Rock by then and were members of Immanuel Baptist Church also.

They had a beautiful church wedding, and their close friend Wilford M. Lee performed the ceremony. In the fall of 1939 they returned to Louisville, where they made their first home on the campus at Southern Seminary in Rice Hall.

During the 1939–1940 academic year, Hugo began work toward a Th.D., with a major in Greek New Testament and minors in philosophy of religion and in New Testament archaeology. At the end of the year, he submitted a detailed report of five typed pages on his work that year, to which he affixed his signature. He attended all classes, except for two weeks when he went to Richmond. He was certified for the course Greek New Testament Exegesis (E. A. McDowell): (1) "careful reading of all the New Testament (Westcott and Hort text), simultaneously with all six volumes of Robertson's *Word Pictures*, using Thayer's and Souter's lexicons, with the purpose of improving reading knowledge"; (2) "study of Robertson's *Grammar of the Greek New Testament in the Light of Historical Research*, with the following references to the Greek New Testament looked up in the context: Straight through, pp. 1–300; index: Matthew, chapters 1–2; Galatians, all six chapters"; (3) careful study of grammars: Davis, *Beginner's Grammar of the Greek New Testament* (all), Robertson and Davis, *A New Short Grammar of the Greek New Testament*, pp. 1–195; (4) for the Galatians seminar (Hersey Davis) he wrote a paper on "The Date of Galatians"; (5) the reading of ten books on New Testament criticism, which he listed by title. For the course Philosophy of Christianity (W. O. Carver) he read fifteen books (including William Temple's *Nature, Man and God*, which had a profound and continuing influence on him) and wrote a paper on John Baillie's contribution toward building a Christian philosophy, using Baillie's *The Interpretation of Religion* as the basis of his work. For "The Archaeology of the New Testament" (J. McKee Adams), he did research for a paper on "The Language of the New Testament in the Light of Research," reading and collecting notes from eight books. In summary, Hugo certified to his major professor that he averaged, by accurate count, forty hours a week spent in study during the session of thirty-three weeks, that he had read forty books, written three papers and taken notes for another, and that he had done no outside work (i.e., secular employment) during the year.

Hugo also appended a "statement as to plans for remainder of course: I plan to continue my studies during the next five years while in China as a missionary, and take my oral examination and write my thesis during my first furlough, 1945–46." Events that he could not have foreseen would intervene, but to the best of his ability Hugo carried through on this plan.

Hugo later wrote about two conversations he had with W. O. Carver, one in the spring of 1939 and the other a year later:

As both teacher and writer, Carver's thought was too complex to permit, at least for him, ease of expression in a simple style. His sentences were long and involved.[15] He lost most students along the way in the course of an hour's lecture. For those who followed his thinking, it was often brilliant and even scintillating. In the Spring of 1939, the writer [Hugo] was a student speaker for prayer meeting at the Walnut Street Baptist Church, where Dr. Carver was a long-time member. Since he was having some trouble with his eyes at the time, he asked the writer to drive his car for him that night. When we returned to the Seminary campus, we continued our conversation for a time under the maple trees while parked. Since the faculty was having a periodic curriculum restudy, he asked what was the most difficult course I had during the three years about to be completed. The reply was that if by "difficult" was meant sheer mental exertion (rather than time consuming—which would have indicated the second year of Hebrew), then "that missions course" was the most difficult; "by the time one untangles the long sentences, organizes the material, and masters it, he is exhausted." The author of the book, *The Course of Christian Missions*, cleared his throat and said, "I think I know what you mean."[16]

In a note to "Prof. Johnson" [Inman Johnson], on, Hugo related "the rest of the story":

Then I went on to say that I thought probably the most overrated course for difficulty in the Seminary was Senior Greek. I had heard a great deal about its difficulty from upper-class students before I came to it. However, I was taking Senior Greek at that time and was not finding it so difficult. Dr. Carver thanked me for my comments and we went our separate ways.

A few days later in Senior Greek class, Dr. Hersey Davis called on me to recite. At that time we were studying textual criticism of the Greek New Testament, and were using Dr. Robertson's book on this subject as the text. Dr. Davis began by asking me what the real name of Erasmus was. I told him that as far as I knew it was Erasmus. I shall never forget as he wrote on the board two

---

[15] W. O. Carver, *Out of His Treasure: Unfinished Memoirs* (Nashville: Broadman, 1956) 93.

[16] Hugo H. Culpepper, "The Legacy of W. O. Carver," *International Bulletin of Missionary Research*, 5, 3 (July 1981): 120.

Dutch words which he said was the real name of Erasmus: Geert Geerts. Dr. Davis continued to ask me a series of four additional questions. I had to say, "I do not know," to all five of the questions, inasmuch as none of them were in the assigned material for that day's lesson, and all of them were outside of the range of my knowledge. By that time the class was beginning to perk up and to realize that something unusual was going on because the questions were not directly relevant to the lesson. At the end of this dismal showing, Dr. Davis in his unique way made a huge circle with his right arm, clearly demonstrating that he was in the process of writing a zero on my record for recitation that day. Then he looked up under his heavy eyebrows and said, "Brother Culpepper, Senior Greek is not so easy after all, is it?" I was never quite sure whether to be impatient with Dr. Carver for having shared my comment with Dr. Davis.[17]

A conversation with Dr. Carver a year later would come to have even greater meaning for Hugo in his later years:

In the spring of 1940, the writer [Hugo] confronted the question of universalism, as a soteriological and eschatological doctrine, for the first time while reading in the seminary library William Temple's *Nature, Man and God*. On the way to lunch, in the hall he met up with Carver, who was then his professor in a graduate seminar on the philosophy of religion. The student asked the professor what he thought about universalism. As they walked down the hall, stood at length in the professor's office, and continued the conversation on campus at the point their path separated, Carver talked for more than an hour giving his student a private lecture on the pros and cons of the question. He concluded by saying, "I shall have to wait until I am on the other side of the veil to know the answer to your question." The student's reaction was a growth experience: uncertainty as to universalism did not cut the nerve of mission motivation for Carver, whose life had been devoted to missions (he was then seventy-two years old); for him, the glory of God was the motive—the imperative was to make God known as he is![18]

Hugo was as disciplined in his weightlifting as he was in his studies, keeping records of his exercise routines, the sequence of the exercises, the number of repetitions, and the weights lifted. The discipline paid off: In

---

[17] Hugo H. Culpepper, letter to Professor Inman Johnson, 19 September 1960.

[18] Hugo H. Culpepper, "Missions, Evangelism, and World Religions at Southern," *Review & Expositor*, 82 (1985): 72–73; "The Legacy of W. O. Carver," 121.

July 1940 he won the Arkansas state weightlifting title for the middleweight division.

In the spring of 1940 Hugo and Ruth were elected by the Foreign Mission Board as missionaries to China and were presented to the Southern Baptist Convention in session in Baltimore, Maryland. When they were appointed as missionaries, Hugo did not know what a missionary was paid—it never occurred to him to ask. He had been called to be a missionary.

They had a busy summer in Little Rock, helping in various meetings. On Sunday morning, 11 August, Hugo preached at Immanuel Baptist Church on the subject "The Meaning of Missions to a Missionary." In the sermon he quoted the following poem by an unknown author:

His lamps are we,
To shine where he shall say;
And lamps are not for sunny rooms,
Nor for the light of day;
But for the dark places of the earth;
Where shame and wrong and crime have birth;
Or for the murky twilight gray,
Where wandering sheep have gone astray;
Or where the light of faith grows dim
And souls are groping after him.

At 2:30 PM, he was ordained to the Gospel Ministry. Among the ministers who assisted in the ordination were Dr. C. C. Warren, pastor of the church at that time, Dr. Calvin B. Waller, Dr. L. M. Sipes, and Hugo's good friend Reverend (and later Admiral) James Kelly. That week, Hugo and Ruth's last week in Little Rock, was youth week at Immanuel, and Hugo served as youth week pastor. On 17 August, friends and relatives gathered at the station where Hugo and Ruth boarded the train for California.

On Friday, 23 August 1940, they sailed from San Francisco aboard the S.S. *Nitta Maru* (a luxurious new ship making its second voyage), under the Golden Gate Bridge, bound for Peking, China, where they would enter the College of Chinese Language Studies.

After they left, Hugo's parents received a letter from Paul Geren, Hugo's close friend at Baylor, who was completing a doctorate in economics at Harvard.

Hugo and Ruth on Ship, 1940.

Dear Mr. and Mrs. Culpepper,

Though he [Hugo] and I have caught only glimpses of each other for the past four years, and though hundreds of miles separated us then, yet I am conscious of his departure as if it were from my own home.

I shall always be in Hugo's debt. He has been the sunshine and fresh air for my spirit. To hold on to our faith it is necessary to have someone about us who embodies Christianity at its best—so many who embody it at much below its best fill our gaze. So it is that I am able to keep faith because I believe in Hugo's faith. This may have been what the Jews meant when they spoke of the God of Abraham, Isaac, and Jacob. They believed in God because they believed so in Abraham, Isaac, and Jacob who had worshipped Him. Hugo's presence at Baylor was a boon for me. Since then I have been made brave and strong at the thought of his courage and strength of soul. And thanks to the reality of that which is not seen, as I sit in my room in Massachusetts, my heart leaps up with admiration when I think of him and Ruth braving another world for the truth we hold.

God keep us all, here and there, and lead us to nobler lives.

Sincerely,

Paul Geren[19]

---

[19] Paul Geren, letter to Mr. and Mrs. J. H. Culpepper, 16 September 1940.

Chapter 3

Concentration Camp

"And forgive me if I have troubled you more than was needful and inevitable, more than I intended to do when I took up my pen proposing to distract you for a while from your distractions."[1]

On 23 September 1940, one month from the day they departed from San Francisco, Hugo and Ruth arrived in Peking, China. They had spent one day in Honolulu and two weeks in Yokohama, Japan, waiting for a ship to take them across the China Sea to north China. In Yokohama, they met Fern Harrington and Grace Wilson. They stayed with other missionaries at Karuizawa, a beautiful mountain resort. Twenty-six years later, Hugo recalled memories of their brief stay in Japan to Mr. and Mrs. Leroy Seat, former students who had just gone to Japan as missionaries:

We arrived in Yokohama and went to Tokyo, where we spent several days living in a mission home with the H. B. Ramsours.... It was truly exciting for us as we "did" the city for two or three days. I recall I bought the first volume of William Temple's *Readings in the Gospel of St. John* on the Genza. Later I found the second volume of this book in a French bookstore in Peking. We went up to Karuizawa in the mountains and spent nearly a week there resting. It was exciting to rent bicycles and coast down the mountain road and then put the bicycles in a baggage car and go back up to the town on the train. We took a train on back to Tokyo, and from there down to Kobe, where Kagawa lived in the slums.[2]

In Kobe they visited the Shinkawa slums, where 1,000 people lived in one block, then made the four and a half day trip from Kobe to Tientsin,

[1] Miguel de Unamuno, *Tragic Sense of Life*, trans. J. E. Crawford Flitch (New York: Dover Pub., 1954) 330.

[2] Hugo Culpepper, letter to Mr. and Mrs. Leroy Seat [1966?].

China, on board the Tyozyo Maru. Their assignment was to the China
Baptist Theological Seminary in Kaifeng, China, but before they could
begin their work there they had to learn Chinese.

Peking, 1940–1941

Hugo recalled their arrival and the early, ominous developments.

We arrived in Tientsin, the port of north China, on September 23, 1940.
We were met there by Mr. John Abernathy, who was from the same state we
were from, Arkansas, and who had been in China for a number of years, spoke
the Chinese language fluently, and was there to see us through customs and
on [by train] to the city of Peking, in north China, to see us settled there in the
College of Chinese Studies, where we were to begin our study of the Chinese
language. This was a branch of the University of California, located in San
Francisco. We arrived safely there, were set up, and began our language
study.

Only about a week after we had arrived, the tripartite treaty between Italy,
Germany, and Japan was signed, and this was a clear indication to most people
that the Axis nations were preparing for the possibility of a second world war.
Very soon after that, a matter of days, the American State Department sent out
evacuation notices, advising all American citizens in the Orient to return to the
United States. Since we had only just arrived there a matter of days before,
after some consultation we learned that if combat was delayed long enough
for us to complete a year's language study, there would be the possibility of us
going to West China and continuing to serve as missionaries, even if war were
to come. For you see, we were in Japanese-occupied territory in north China.
Since the Mukden Bridge incident of 1937, Japan and China had been at war.
We knew that if America and Japan were to come to be at war, we would
immediately be in enemy territory and would be taken prisoners. We stayed on
in Peking for what turned out to be a period of six months, until we could no
longer study there because of the increasing international tensions.[3]

Hugo and Ruth's first impressions of China are vividly related in a
letter Ruth wrote to a friend, Marguerite Lavender, back in Little Rock.

---

[3] Hugo Culpepper, tape recording of presentation, Mansfield, Ohio, 5 May
1975.

The streets of Peking in 1940 were nothing like this newly appointed, twenty-two-year-old missionary could have imagined.

Dear Marguerite (and Howard),

You can't imagine how thrilled we were this afternoon to receive your letter. We had had one other letter from Mother and then this afternoon we got another one from her and your letter, and that is all the news that we have had from home since leaving there nearly two months ago. Honestly, you would have thought we were wild people when we found those letters under our door when we came in from a sightseeing tour. It was so newsy and nice that we have both had a lot of real enjoyment in reading it. Of course I want you to keep up writing me like you did because it is worth twice its weight in gold when it gets here....

We are most comfortable here in the school. By now I am sure that you have my other letter telling of our trip over and what a grand time we had. We got to Peking the 23rd of September, which was [one] month to the day after we sailed....

Our first impression was that we were entering Mexico—the walls around the cities were of mud, and the houses were also of mud. One of the first things we noticed on our train ride up from the coast was the little mounds that could be seen everywhere. Upon asking Mr. Abernathy, he told us that these were graves and that as long as the little mound stood 5 or 6 inches from the level of the earth the farmers had to plow around them. You might wonder why they don't have graveyards as we have at home, but over here they consult the spirits as to where to bury a person. It might be in the front yard even. So they are just buried at random, wherever the spirit men say the spirits tell them to bury the person....

Hugo riding a bicycle in Peking.

If you were to come to the school, you would be terribly disappointed in our street. It is very hard to get used to things here in Peking. Even though we had been told that everything was behind walls, we have not yet gotten that mode of living in our heads. To get to the school one turns down a hutung (street) but what we would call an alley at home. They are neither so big or nearly so clean as our alleys are. Thus, we have a few main streets in town and the rest are these hutungs. But as I said everything is behind doors and walls, so nothing is seen from the streets but the stores and the people....

You just can't conceive of such when you go down these terrible streets. We are beginning to get used to them along with their terrible smells. You do not know what sanitation and the blessing of bathrooms is at home. Over here there is no privacy, and one uses the public streets for bathrooms. I don't think I have been down our hutung yet that I have not run across people tending to their business out in the middle of the road. Two or three times a day a boy with a wooden basket will go down the hutung and collect the human dung that has been left there. When you get behind him in the stream of traffic you could wish for one of the good old garbage trucks at home to come along. I hope this won't prove too embarrassing for you to read, but I am just trying to give you a picture of the common people here in Peking.

As one rides down the streets here, he can certainly see life in the raw. There are so many people that I hardly believe that the traffic in Washington, D.C. at the evening hour is worse than it is over here at any time of the day. Then, it is so vastly different to what we are used to. Our first purchase was two bicycles, which everybody over here has that can afford them. They are one of the main ways of transportation, though they have streetcars that one does not dare to ride on. They are always packed to running over, so one takes his life in his hands when he gets on one. Especially if he has not had the typhus shots—which we have not yet had. Typhus fever is always fatal and is caused by a fleabite one gets in public places and public rickshaws, so the language school has their own rickshaws that we can use. The school is going to arrange for us to have the shots soon.

Thus, with the mass of people, the bikes, the rickshaws, the streetcars and buses, the few taxis that care not who they run over, and add the wagons on the street, and you can get a pretty good idea of it all. Wagons are not pulled by horses but by three men who are strapped to them like horses. It is really a heartbreaking sight....

I do not know what I would do if I saw a big store like Cohn's. The stores here are very small and dirty places. If they want to attract attention, they play this Oriental music, which is the worst thing yet. It is a terrible, whangy noise with somebody screeching to the top of their voice—hardly a human sound. Thus, when you ride down the streets trying to concentrate on the traffic, one has this horrible sound pounding in his ears making any thought impossible. Now you have a conception of the street scenes in a way, but then you have all kinds of peddlers and beggars going up and down the streets. Meals are cooked and served right on the streets, only adding more to the congestion.

We have successfully passed our first week of school and know about 75 words in Chinese. There has not been a word of English spoken in the class-rooms or outside to the teachers. They are fired if they are caught using any English, though most of the 60 teachers know English. It is the best method of teaching a language that I know of. Our head teacher, called Dearest, comes in the morning from 8:45 to 9:30 and gives us new words, acting out their meaning when necessary or having the object there for us to see. Then he goes out, and every thirty minutes we change teachers, hearing them pronounce and use the words. Thus we are trained to hear the language.

During the day we have nine such teachers. We have a recess from 10:00 to 10:30 and dinner from 12 to 2. We are out at 4 o'clock for tea, and the rest of the day. Interspersed with this come lectures on Chinese history, geography, art, and religion. After this week we will have private tutors for a while each day for us to talk to. Soon we shall start also to learn to write the characters.

On top of all of this I am taking music. There is a man here in Peking who is considered the best musician in all North China, and it is my privilege to take from him. I have an hour's lesson a week. He teaches in two universities here and does concert work, so I feel very fortunate in being able to take from him. We found out that I am going to have charge of all music in our Kaifeng schools because no one out there knows music. The very thought of it scares me to death. I cannot sing and know nothing of conducting choirs etc., but I am going to have to learn. Also, I will have to teach piano—and that is why I am working at it so hard this year.

Take care of yourselves and tell everybody hello for me. Since getting your letter I can almost believe that there is still somebody left on the other side of the world, out of which silence has come words of news, cheer, and love. You will never know how much your letter has meant to us.

Sincerely yours,
Ruth[4]

---

[4] Ruth Culpepper, letter to Marguerite and Howard Lavender, 13 October 1940.

Although their experience in China was much briefer than they anticipated, it had an enduring impact on Hugo:

I shall always be grateful to God for those six months in China proper, there in the area of Peking. It gave me the opportunity to come to know the Chinese people firsthand, to some extent, to know their culture, to learn something of the needs of the people of that part of the world.

I remember, after we had been there just a short time, a Chinese Methodist pastor came to the language school looking for someone who would be interested in teaching English to Chinese college students. We had no Baptist mission work in Peking proper at that time, so I accepted his invitation, since I could not yet speak Chinese, to go every Sunday morning and meet with a group of about twenty Chinese young men who were eighteen or nineteen years of age to begin to teach them the Gospel of John in English. They were interested, of course, in having someone speak English to them. They had had the opportunity to study it for a time in college, and I was interested in the opportunity of sharing with them the knowledge of the Christian faith and of the gospel through Jesus Christ.

Every Sunday morning I would get up and ride for an hour or so on a bicycle across the city of Peking, even during the winter months with snow on the ground. We had Chinese fur caps that covered our ears and a heavy jacket and so forth, and would go there to meet with them in a small, scarcely furnished room, just a table and chairs around, no heat, and mix with them for more than an hour in studying the Gospel of John. I learned something in observing the life of the Chinese, going to and from that meeting each Sunday morning, as I saw the average Chinese at home and on the streets and at work.[5]

It was in the course of these experiences of going out on Sunday morning that I came to realize the cheapness of life there in China in those years. I remember one day passing along, and in a small open space between two buildings...My attention was drawn there to a group of people to the right here, and I stopped to see what had caused them to come together. I was startled to see the body of a Chinese man dangling from the end of a short rope, from the lower limb of a tree, his feet barely clearing the ground. I was amazed, not so much by the fact that they did not remove the body from the tree—I had heard that this would involve them in a responsibility to help defray the funeral expenses. They were waiting for the city authorities to come out, but the thing that impressed me most was the expressions on their faces.

---

[5] Hugo Culpepper, tape.

They were not what I would have expected to have seen. They almost portrayed to me some identification with this one who had taken his own life in the early hours of the morning because of the misery and the hunger and the meaninglessness of existence under those circumstances. It seemed to me that I could almost trace in their expressions there something of a sense of envy of this one who, so far as they knew, had been released from the misery of existence.

I went on and taught my class and an hour later came by, and there they were still standing, for the body still dangled from the end of the rope. I went away feeling surely this was a land in which human personality is cheap. A few weeks later I was again startled when I saw lying in the gutter of the street the body of a boy who had been hit—a rickshaw coolie who had been hit by one of the few passing automobiles in those days—and there he was without anyone bothering even to throw a coat over his head, lying as though he were no more than a dead dog, there waiting for the city authorities to come by and gather up his body. This was the first impact of the reality of how utterly different life was on the other side of the world from all that I had known in my own heritage as an American.[6]

When Christmas came, we were invited by the Abernathys to come to their home in Tsinan, south of Peking in Shantung Province, and spend about a week with them during the Christmas vacation. We went, and in the course of that week I had my first opportunity to see something of the mean-ing of the Christian faith to the Chinese people themselves, for there we had a well-developed Chinese Baptist church that Dr. Abernathy was serving as pastor of at that time. We took a walk one afternoon, out along a new highway that was being built at the command of the Japanese occupying army, through the use of Chinese coolie laborers, for the purpose of military transport.

I saw firsthand something of the standard of living of the Chinese coolie laborers. They were being paid the equivalent of two cents a day of American money, I was told. They were sleeping at night on the ground, even during the cold weather, with just a straw lean-to or a thatched roof over them. They were given two small bowls of rice a day, one in the morning and another in the evening, for their food supply. Little did I realize at that time that in the providence of God it would be only a matter of months until we too would be introduced into a level of life and standard of living comparable to that of these Chinese coolie laborers. At that time, I was too recently gone out from America

---

[6] Hugo Culpepper, tape recording Seminary Family Service, Missions Emphasis Week, 8 October 1968. [Unless otherwise noted, all further references to "Hugo Culpepper, tape" are to the tape of 5 May 1975.]

to be able to identify with them and to imagine what life would be like under those conditions.

By March of 1941, international tensions had become so great that it was deemed advisable for us to leave China. There were seven Southern Baptist missionaries in Peking attending the school at the time, two couples [Rufus and Marian Gray, and Hugo and Ruth] and three single women [Fern Harrington, Cleo Morrison, and Grace Wilson]. It was decided that I should go ahead of the party by train across land to consult with the area secretary for the Orient of our Foreign Mission Board, who had an office in Shanghai, China, and that the group would pack up and go out to the seaport and take a coastal vessel down to the city of Shanghai with our trunks and baggage.

When I arrived there and conferred with Dr. M. T. Rankin, who was at that time the secretary for the Orient, I learned that just recently an order had gone out from the English government in cooperation with the American government that no women or children would be permitted to go through Hong Kong and to take a flight from Hong Kong into West China. They were trying to get women and children, especially, back to America rather than have the responsibility, in case of the outbreak of war, for American citizens in those areas. Therefore, there was no possibility of our going to West China at that time, which was our first choice, either out to Chungking, the capital of the national Chinese government, which had moved west, or to the university center nearby there.

It was deemed advisable for us to join young missionaries of various other churches and denominations and go to the Philippine Islands, which were at that time American territory, to a branch school that had been set up there. We would take along four Chinese teachers from Peking to be our teachers there in the Philippines, and the seventy-five or eighty of us who would go would continue to study the language until we had completed a year of study. Then, we hoped still to go to West China, even if it were necessary to go around and come in over the Burma Road entrance into West China.[7]

The College of Chinese Studies set up a branch school in the Philippine Islands, and the Foreign Mission Board moved them there in March 1941 to continue their language study in Baguio. The U.S. State Department believed that since the Philippines were an American territory, they would be safe there, and should war come they would have time to get out. In reality, the Philippines were a prime target of the Japanese. Although they

---

[7] Hugo Culpepper, tape.

never made it to their assignment in Kaifeng, Hugo and Ruth retained a love for Chinese people and Chinese food.

Baguio, 1941

Baguio provided a striking contrast to Peking, but life in the Philippines still presented challenges for the young American couple. Letters Ruth wrote to their friends Dr. and Mrs. James P. Jernigan that summer provide glimpses of their pre-war experience in Baguio.

Dear Jim and Jenny,

Baguio certainly is a contrast to China because it is about like any American city at home. The strange thing though is that their drugstores are still really drug stores, and if you want a coke or ice cream or such you go to the grocery store or to the theater. In fact, there are just a few places in town that are so brave as to try to sell ice cream. With milk at 35 cents gold a quart you can see why the price of ice cream is prohibitive. Cokes and sandwiches run the same price as they do at home.

But regardless of being a thoroughly American city some of the native customs still exist, and it is quite funny when you see them. A native cannot wear a tie unless he can speak English. Of course, there is no such law, but that is just one of the accepted customs of the people. It is not unusual to see a man coming down the street with a coat, shirt, tie, and collar and no trousers. Honestly, it just got me for a while, but it is getting quite commonplace now. They wear G-strings instead of trousers. Of course, a good many of them wear nothing but G-strings. The native shirt looks like it would be quite a comfortable thing because they are made on the idea of a polo shirt and made out of the thinnest silk [or local fibers—pineapple and banana stalks] imaginable. Most of them though are made out of net. When the women dress up, they wear huge jacket affairs of starched net, and you can't get within three feet of the woman herself because of the huge puff sleeves. They are quite pretty. They wear the prettiest slips here you can imagine. They usually wear a wrap-around skirt and pull it up in the front so the edge of their slip shows. They are all embroidered about a foot deep and have the most delicate cut-out work you can imagine. Even the poorest women have these beautiful slips. They are made out of some kind of white cotton and must be made by the natives since even the poorest of women have them.

Another favorite custom among the women is smoking cigars between 8 and 10 inches long. They nurse their babies and smoke their cigars at the same time. Girls from 8 and 10 years of age on up smoke the same cigars. Men go in for cigarettes much more than the women do. And by the way, if Jim or George ever specialize in obstetrics this is one place he can do business. The birth rate is enormously high here, and I guess one in every three women is pregnant. We live with a doctor here—rent his downstairs apartment—and they have five children already with another one on its way....

Hugo weightlifting,
Baguio, 12 June 1941.

That reminds me of another custom that makes me feel like I am in the midst of Africa. The women carry everything on their heads. I have seen women walk by our front gate with young trees on their heads that they had chopped down and were bringing in to sell. They run about 10 feet long, but they can walk down a steep hill with them on their heads and never put their hands up to balance them. When the maids go out to gather in the clothes, they don't take baskets or anything but just fold each piece up and stack them on top of their heads. I have seen them stack everything from children's clothes to blankets on their heads and bend down and pick up another piece and stack it up there without worrying the least bit about the pieces already up there. It's a marvel to me....

We took examinations last Friday over the part of the Gospel of John that we have done in Chinese. They were a snap and now we have a three weeks' vacation. I am so glad because it will give us time to catch up on some of the things that we have been wanting to do. Hugo is putting a lot of his time in on Greek because he has not been able to do much since we have come to Baguio. We go to school at 7:30 every morning and then we are out every day at 12:30. Since we are in the rainy season, we didn't want to have to get out in the rain twice a day to go to school, so we are having the one long session. It rains here everyday and soon will be raining all day long. We will have several typhoons in the next two months, they say, and then you just have to close all windows and doors and stay inside. We ordered quite a bit of extra canned goods from the store this morning so that we would not be caught, as several people have been, without enough to eat in the house and not be able to get it. We have shellacked everything we could as a precaution against mold: all the books, suitcases, trunks, and every piece of leather that we have. People tell us that we might as well be prepared to lose things because of mold, but I still hate to think of it....

 With love,
 Ruth and Hugo[8]

One of the families who left in December gave the language school a short wave radio. The young missionaries got hooked on a program from San Francisco KGEI, "The Mail Bag," which came on at 10:00 P.M. on Sunday night. Family and friends could send short letters through this program for free, and Hugo and Ruth received an occasional message this way.

A letter to the Jernigans refers to escalating military activity in the Pacific and then describes the daily challenges of living without modern appliances: "I have just about given up cooking on a wood stove. Yesterday afternoon our girl went home sick and so we had to cook supper. That didn't matter so much because Hugo was here to help with it. Today, I left school early and tried to have dinner ready when he got here. When he came home two hours later, I was still trying to get the fire started. I wish I could see a good gas stove again."[9] Later, however, in the camp, Ruth became quite proficient in managing a wood-burning cook stove.

For a period of time, Hugo recalled, the Culpeppers shared an apartment with Mrs. Baker James Cauthen and their two children while Dr. Cauthen made a trip into West China.[10] Dr. Baker James Cauthen,

---

[8] Ruth Culpepper, letter to Jim and Jenny Jernigan, 9 June 1941.

[9] Ruth Culpepper, letter to Jim and Jenny Jernigan, 28 August 1941.

[10] See Jesse C. Fletcher, *Baker James Cauthen: A Man for All Nations* (Nashville: Broadman Press, 1977) 124: "When they arrived in the Philippines, several of the missionaries who had been language school students in Peking and had moved to Baguio, north of Manila, were there to meet them. The Hugo Culpeppers, the Rufus Grays, the Bob Dyers, and Fern Harrington, Grace Wilson, and Cleo Morrison were among those students. The Cauthens traveled with them to the beautiful mountain city, where Eloise and the children moved in with the Hugo Culpeppers."

who later became the executive secretary of the Foreign Mission Board, had
been appointed by the mission board one year before Hugo and Ruth.
Before Pearl Harbor was bombed, Mrs. Cauthen was able to get a transit
visa through Hong Kong, and Dr. Cauthen met them in Hong Kong and
was able to get them into West China with him. Had that not happened,
they would have been trapped in the Philippines along with the
Culpeppers.[11]

A three-week vacation in the fall gave Hugo and Ruth a carefree
respite, their last for several years. Ruth looked forward to the break:

This term of school is over on September 12th and then we have a three-
weeks' vacation before school starts again on October 6th. Believe me, we are
really going to take out and not think of Chinese that whole time. We may have
to make a trip to Manila if Paul Geren, a Baylor friend of ours who is going to
Burma to teach Economics, comes in and doesn't have but a day or so. We
hope, though, that he will be able to come on up here. We are not planning
any long trips, but hope that we can go to the beach and to another place
swimming. Hugo needs to take a lot of sunbaths because the disease on his
neck is getting worse from lack of sunshine. I wish there was equipment here
in Baguio so that he could take treatments like he did in Peking, but they do
not have that sort of an X-Ray machine here. There is one in Manila, but of
course that is too far away.[12]

When medical problems were serious, missionaries had to be sent back
to the States for treatment, and that summer two single women had to
return home for treatment of brain tumors.

Hugo continued his study of Greek, and both Hugo and Ruth read
avidly: "Hugo is reading 'Inside Asia' now for our parallel reading. We get
one school credit on each 1000 pages read, and we are trying to get the
maximum of 6.... I guess it takes about that many pages for one to begin to
get a background of China's thought, life, habits, and customs, regardless of
giving one a background for helping her to meet her problems today. I have
completed around 2500 of my pages. I read a lot in Peking, and what I read
there will count." The letter to the Jernigans ends with accounts of their
recreation, exercise program, and physical condition: "We are taking our
workouts every other day, and Hugo says he is in better condition than he

---

[11] Hugo Culpepper, tape.
[12] Ibid.

has ever been in. He weighs between 160 and 165. I still weigh the same at 120." [13]

Pearl Harbor, 7 December 1941

Radios flashed the news at daybreak on Monday, 8 December, and word spread quickly that Pearl Harbor had been bombed about midnight their time. Hugo described the events as they unfolded:

We continued our language study and had completed a year's work, and were to go to the language school and begin reviewing for the annual examination over the year's work on that eventful Monday morning, which was still Sunday in this part of the world.

We were asleep because the Philippines is beyond the international date-line, and it was already Monday morning there when Pearl Harbor was bombed, somewhere between seven and eight o'clock in the morning. This was about two o'clock in the morning in that part of the world, and we were asleep. We were awakened about six-thirty that morning, just three or four hours after the actual bombing. A neighbor of ours, who was an American retired Navy serviceman, lived just a block down the street on Quezon Hill, at the edge of the city of Baguio. We had invited him in for chicken dinner on one occasion and had given hospitality. He came down to our bedroom window, where we had the draperies drawn for the darkness, and called in through the window, awakening us from our sleep, and told us that America was at war with Japan, that Pearl Harbor had been bombed. He was a rather excitable sort of personality, and we did not know whether to believe him or not because it seemed so inconceivable to us.

We went to the radio and turned it on, and immediately heard the radio station in Manila confirm the news that Pearl Harbor had actually been bombed and that we were at war with Japan. The radio was advising all Americans not to come to Manila with any idea of getting out of the Islands, that there was no way to leave, that actually the Japanese navy was in Philippine waters, and that we had no way to get out at all, to stay where we were. We got up, still hardly realizing the significance of it, had our breakfast, and went on down to language school, as if things were normal.

---

[13] Hugo and Ruth Culpepper, letter to Jenny and Jim Jernigan, 28 August 1941.

At eight o'clock our classes resumed, but at 8:20 we heard the roar of airplanes and very soon the dropping of the first bombs on the northern part of Luzon Island. Japanese planes had flown over and had bombed Camp John Hay, a military reservation located about five miles out to the edge of the town of Baguio. This is the base where the Philippine Constabulary or Philippine National Guards were being trained under the direction at that time of General Douglas MacArthur. We realized then that war had actually come to our front door. Classes were dismissed, and that was the end of our study of Chinese.[14]

Further reports indicated that the Japanese attack had destroyed most of the US planes in the Philippines in a surprise attack on Clark Field Air Base. From then on, any plane they saw was almost certain to be enemy aircraft. Because Baguio is located in a saucer-shaped valley, it was impossible to see or hear airplanes until they were directly overhead. Mayor Halsema proposed that they set up a lookout post on Mt. Santo Tomas, a nearby peak that is 2,200 feet above the city. A direct telephone line was being installed from Santo Tomas to the Baguio power plant. Reports of approaching aircraft could be relayed to the power plant, and a siren sounded to warn people to take cover. The new drainage system, with pipes eight to ten feet in diameter, served as an air raid shelter.

The mayor of the city had secured the most powerful pair of binoculars that were available in town and sent word to the school that he would like to have three young men to volunteer to go out to the highest mountain point in the area, about twelve miles out from the city, and there on the top of the mountain—which was a tourist spot where people climbed the mountain for the scenery, there was a telephone there and so forth—to stand watch around the clock, day and night, and to telephone the city if Japanese planes were approaching to bomb, so that an air raid signal could be sounded. It was a rather hastily improvised security measure, for people were hastily improvising air raid shelters, blacking out their windows, and so forth.

I volunteered along with two other young men, one of whom was a fellow Southern Baptist missionary by the name of Rufus Gray, from Fort Pierce, Florida.[15]

They were taken by car to within two and a half miles of the top. From there they had to carry their bags along the twisting path that led to the top.

---

[14] Hugo Culpepper, tape.
[15] Hugo Culpepper, tape.

Another spotter gave this account of the hike: "Pine trees and tropical trees interspersed and lined the steep declivities above and below us. We made our way along a curving twisting path that dipped and rose with the contour of the mountain. At the bend of a horseshoe turn we could step up a small rise and look far out over the China Sea. As we approached little Zig Zag, the last and steepest and back-breakingest part of our hike, we could turn and looking east see the white buildings of Baguio some seven miles from us and far below."[16]

Those who lived near the business district were advised to spend the night with friends farther out of town. Ruth invited others to stay with her up on Quezon Hill—about a mile from the center of town, where Hugo and Ruth rented an apartment from Mrs. De la Rosa—if they did not mind sleeping on the floor. The Dyers, the Grays, Cleo Morrison, and Fern Harrington stayed with Ruth that night, and Cleo and Fern stayed on until Hugo returned from standing watch.

I happened to be standing watch—we stood watch four hours at a time, and the others would be sleeping—and in the middle of the night watch about 2:00 in the morning, I heard the beginning of the bombing of the coast at Lingayen Gulf where the Japanese made their main invasion of the Philippines. I took the binoculars, which I had in my hand, and could see the tracer shells about 25 miles away coming in from the ships to get the range of the coastline and then to open up with their heavy naval guns, bombarding the coast in preparation for the invasion. I knew then that it was just a matter of time until the Japanese armed forces would reach our town because there were no defenses to speak of in the northern part of Luzon. The few national guardsmen who were there had already gone to the lowlands. You see, we were on a mountain about a mile above sea level, 5,000 some odd feet up the mountain trail, they called it, just one winding gravel road up to where Baguio was located. So I knew it was a matter of time until resistance faded before the invading forces. They would climb the mountain trail and come up and occupy Baguio as well as the other parts of northern Luzon.

At the end of three days we were relieved by three other young men from the language school. We went down to join our families. In the meantime, my wife and the two single women had gone out and bought what food they could secure, had gotten cardboard boxes and other things to shut out the light on the inside of the windows, so that there would be no light at night to

---

[16] M. H. Patton, "Our Concentrated Life: An Account of Life in Japanese Internment Camps" (unpublished typescript, July 1945) 3.

serve as a target for the bombing airplanes, and they had dug in to see what would happen. I joined them there, and we waited there for whatever the eventualities were to be. By this time, it was about the middle of December.

We began to go at night down to the valley, where the center of the town was located, about a mile away, carrying a small suitcase apiece with a change of clothing and a mosquito net and personal articles, tooth brush, and so forth, to have by our side in case of any eventuality. It was our feeling that it would be better for the women to be in a group than to be out at the edge of the town when the Japanese army came in, that they would possibly be safer from attack and so forth, and so by night we would sleep in this small hotel which was located just across the street from the city hall in the very center of the town. In the daytime we would go back up to our apartment of Quezon Hill and live there. We were still preparing our food there and eating our meals in our apartment.[17]

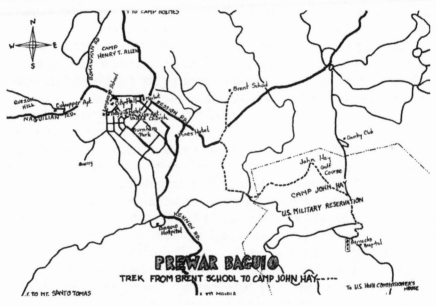

Prewar Baguio. From Miles, *Captive Community*, 28. Used by permission.

When the mission group gathered for prayers at Fern and Cleo's apartment on 21 December, Bob Dyer announced that he had just received a telegram from the Foreign Mission Board: "Advise Baguio group return

---

[17]Hugo Culpepper, tape.

on first available transport." Hugo was the first to speak: "I doubt any ship will be sailing from the Philippines soon. However, it wouldn't hurt to get our names on a list to leave whenever possible." Hugo and Bob agreed to go to Manila the next morning to get ship reservations, but by Monday morning even transportation to Manila was unavailable.[18]

About noon on Christmas Eve, Hugo telephoned Brent School, where many from the mission group were staying, and invited Cleo and Fern to come back and celebrate Christmas with them. About eight o'clock that evening, they got a call saying that the Japanese were expected to arrive at any moment. They were to make their way to the Baguio Hotel, where there would be cars to take everyone to Brent School. The Culpeppers and Fern Harrington spent the night at the hotel. On Christmas Day, they went back to their apartment but continued to spend the nights at the hotel. Hugo remembered the meal they ate that day: "Christmas Day came, of 1941. We had a typical American Christmas dinner...and the ladies baked two cakes for desserts for Christmas dinner. As we were sitting eating that dessert, I commented that very likely before we would have completed eating those two cakes in the next few days, that the Japanese army would have arrived."[19]

During the meal an air raid sounded, but Hugo refused to budge. He said nothing would move him away from such good food.[20]

On the afternoon on the twenty-seventh of December, when we went down to the hotel, we learned that the Japanese army had come up the mountain trail, that they had been met by the mayor and a delegation who had gone out with a white flag of trust to indicate to them that there were no defenses in the city and that no resistance would be made. They could peacefully occupy the town. We learned that they had actually come in and that the city was under the occupancy of the Japanese army. We went on to bed that night as usual, not knowing what to expect.[21]

---

[18] This account is based on Fern Harrington Miles, *Captive Community: Life in a Japanese Internment Camp, 1941–45* (Jefferson City, TN: Mossy Creek Press, 1987) 2–14.

[19] Hugo Culpepper, tape.

[20] Fern Harrington Miles, Camp Journal.

[21] Hugo Culpepper, tape.

Camp John Hay, 28 December 1941–23 April 1942

The night of 27 December marked the beginning of their internment:

About two o'clock in the morning the Filipino in charge of the small hotel came to our door on one of the halls, knocked on the doors, and told us to get up and dress and come to the lobby of the hotel, that the Japanese had come for all citizens of allied nations. We got up and dressed, picked up our suitcases, went to the lobby, and there we were searched, our suitcases were searched, any potential weapons such as knives or scissors or nail files were taken away from us, and we were told to be seated and to wait until others had come down.

During that wait, at 3:00 or 3:30 in the morning, my wife took out the remaining pieces of our Christmas cake, which had been wrapped in wax paper, and we sat there and ate the last bite of American food which we were to have for more than three years' time.

About 5:00 in the morning some empty Japanese trucks arrived and took us, standing up on the back of a truck, out to the edge of the town, to Brent School Building, which was an Episcopal mission school, a two-story boarding school building.

There, we were searched once again and crowded into the building. We were kept there for forty-eight hours, for two days and two nights, while other citizens of allied nations were being rounded up in the area and brought in. Very soon, there were more than 400 of us in that one building. They provided no food of any kind for us to eat for those two days and two nights. We had no water to drink except from out of the faucets in the lavatories of the restrooms. We slept on the floor in the classrooms, between the desks, or in the hallway of the school.[22]

Ruth never forgot the anxiety they felt that day:

After we had been there about forty-eight hours, we were called to go to the tennis court. It was typical of other tennis courts with the high wire fence all the way around it. There we stood while the Japanese soldiers stood every few feet around the tennis court with fixed bayonets in their hands, machine guns fixed, pointing to the tennis court. At this time, we thought, "This is it. This is the end. They are going to mow us down."

---

[22] Ibid.

In a few minutes, the Japanese interpreter got on the little stand they had there for him and said that we were being separated and being moved to another camp.[23]

There were about 500 Americans in the group. The officer informed them that they were now under the control of the Imperial Army of Japan. They would be given food and a place to live. They would not be mistreated as long as they obeyed orders. If they did not obey, they would be shot. The crowd was divided into four groups: (1) children over three, (2) women and children under three, (3) men, and (4) the sick and adults over sixty. At once there was anxiety: Were the Japanese going to take the children somewhere? Would the men be taken off for forced labor? What would happen to the women?

We did not know what all this would mean, and I suppose the darkest hours of our internment experience were the next hour or two as we prepared to leave Brent School. We went then to places where our bags were and said our goodbyes because the men were the first to be led away, then the women, then the children, and then the older people, the sick people, and the babies were to be coming in the fourth group. We did not have any idea that we would ever see members of our families again. It was hard for newly married people to say goodbye, but how much worse it was to walk away and leave a child or a baby laying on the street while you walked on down the street and left that child there.[24]

They later learned that the Japanese officer's name was Mukaibo and that he had studied in the States for the Methodist ministry. Because Mukaibo had studied in the States, he recognized some of Hugo's books and allowed him to keep them because they were religious books. In his suitcase that day Hugo carried his books, among them Nestle's Greek New Testament. In the back of this volume Hugo wrote a reading schedule, which he dated 16 May 1942 and 16 May 1943. Following these schedules and reading eleven pages a day, he could read through the Greek New Testament once every two months. He continued this discipline, reading daily from this Greek New Testament for the rest of his life. He also carried

---

[23] Ruth Culpepper, tape recording of her account of the concentration camp experience, AARP, University of Louisville, 24 September 1981.

[24] Ibid.

Alexander Souter's *Pocket Lexicon of the Greek New Testament*; Robertson's "Big Grammar"; W. Hersey Davis, *Beginner's Grammar of the Greek New Testament*; A. T. Robertson and W. Hersey Davis, *Short Grammar of the Greek Testament*; William Temple, *Readings in St. John's Gospel*; and William Temple, *Nature, Man and God*, which is heavily marked from repeated readings. Temple's concern for experienced faith became a major theme of Hugo's theology. He also carried *The Complete Poetic and Dramatic Works of Robert Browning*,[25] and several other books, each of which has a Japanese stamp in the back of it, showing that it was an authorized item.

Hugo later described his study regimen while in the concentration camp:

> I studied four hours a day and read the Greek New Testament through twelve times. Robertson's "Big Grammar" has about 21,000 references to the Greek New Testament. I read the Grammar three times: twice straight through, and a third time following the index from Mt. 1:1 to the end of Revelation. Each reference was looked up and studied in the light of Robertson's explanation.[26]

After retrieving their belongings, those who could, walked. The others were put on trucks. After half an hour or so, they were relieved to find that they were all being taken to Camp John Hay. The barracks consisted of an empty rectangular-shaped wooden building about 35 feet wide and about 130 feet long with a barbed-wire fence around it.[27] The trucks made two trips before they were ordered to stop. A large quantity of foodstuffs, bedding, and personal belongings was therefore left behind at the very outset. The barracks that had been built to accommodate 60 soldiers now housed the group of about 500. Everyone slept on the floor, with aisles a foot wide between sleeping areas. Hugo described the experience:

> We were told that the women and children were to go to one end and the men to another end, the assumption being that there would be some space for privacy in between with no one there. But by then there were 500 or slightly more of us.
>
> My friend Bob Dyer and I were together. We helped our wives and some of the single missionaries and some of the other elderly people into the far end

---

[25] See above, p, 14.

[26] From "How My Mind Has Changed."

[27] Hugo Culpepper, tape.

of the building. I had carried on my back, in addition to my suitcase and my wife's suitcase, a heavy two-inch pad—a small mattress for a single bed. I had rolled it up, it was in Brent School, and had put it on my shoulder and carried it those five miles with the idea of having a pad for my wife to sleep on if she had to sleep on the floor. I spread that out on the floor for Ruth and helped others get settled in....

When it got time to go to bed, we were all slightly embarrassed. We had never gone to bed with 500 other people in the room before, and it was a new experience for all of us. We put up our mosquito nets, tied them to the window or to the wall or to a post or to whatever we could because mosquitoes were there and we had to sleep under mosquito nets, and we spread a sheet, out of the suitcase, onto the floor and another sheet very modestly to cover ourselves with. Then we got under the top sheet to try to undress and to put on pajamas—500 people all at once doing this—and then we went to bed and turned the lights down low and tried to get some sleep.

The guards would come in, as if we were real great threats to them, and march up and down the aisles between the feet of one row of people and the heads of the people of the next row. It was difficult to sleep that first night. I remember the next morning when we tried to reverse the process and dress under the top sheet. You can imagine that by the time three years were over the 500 of us were all members of one family, just like we were all of the same household, but this was the initiation into the experience in getting to know each other. Bob was having some difficulty—it seemed that his trousers just wouldn't come up as he reached under his top sheet to try to pull his trousers up. He would raise his hips up from the floor and try to pull up on those trousers, and they just wouldn't come. So he lifted up the sheet and put his head under and peeped down. Then, he turned to this very attractive mother and said, "Pardon me, lady, but would you mind unpinning your baby from my trousers."[28]

Ruth shared quarters with a group of friends. After a few days, the men were taken out of the building and put in another building just like it, and the women were allowed to spread out some. The bathroom was one big open room with commodes and urinals, no stalls. The Americans solved the bathroom problem by designating alternate half-hour periods for men (on the hour) and women (on the half hour). Because there were no lights, everyone went to bed at dark.[29] About four o'clock in the morning they

---

[28] Ibid.
[29] Miles, *Captive Community*, 23–31.

found that the water was turned off. Upon investigation, they found that the water tanks were empty and the electric pump was broken. They were without water for two full days. Drinking water was brought in from outside in small cans by a number of the men. "At this time, the greatest struggle we had was starvation, and for the first forty-eight hours, lack of water. We had no water whatsoever, except for a half a glass, given to us in the morning, with which we could drink, wash our teeth, take a bath, wash our face—whatever you can do with a half a glass of water. That was all you would have until the next morning."[30]

Some of the internees became dehydrated and began to lose weight rapidly: "It was a hard struggle, and many of us were losing maybe two pounds a day. I myself fell to the low weight so fast that it did things to my insides that resulted, about eighteen months later, in an operation, but at this time it was just the pain and the nausea that I could not stand, and could not stand up."[31]

The first months were extremely difficult, as Hugo later recalled:

As I look back upon this time, I think this was the darkest period in the whole experience because we were undergoing the period of transition—psychologically, physically, spiritually, and in most any way one could think of. We were being bombarded with propaganda, radio broadcasts through loudspeakers mounted at the guardhouse in front of our barracks. We were being told of the continuing successes of the Japanese armies, of how Singapore had fallen, how they were almost down to Australia by then, and how it was just a matter of time before America herself would be taken.[32]

With the permission of the Japanese, the internees elected a committee for the regulation of their internal affairs and communication with the Japanese. A dining room detail was formed for serving meals and a kitchen group for preparing them. Carl Eschbach wrote the following description of the daily regimen during these early days of internment:

The Japanese ordered the segregation of the sexes and established strict regulations concerning the contacts between men and women. All food was to be prepared in the men's kitchen, and only the cooks were allowed to carry food to the women's barracks.... The men had roll call

---

[30] Ruth Culpepper, tape.
[31] Ibid.
[32] Hugo Culpepper, tape, 8 October 1968.

every morning at seven o'clock, followed by setting-up exercises, and later in the morning the women and children were required to assemble for roll call. We were required to be in the building at seven o'clock for the evening, and lights were turned out at 9:30 by the Japanese.[33]

The next few months were especially difficult because of the forced separation. Beginning on 15 February, families were allowed to meet with each other for an hour each Sunday, from six to seven in the evening.

We were not able to see our wives, except for one hour each week. On Sunday afternoons, they would let us go inside a double-wired, enclosed tennis court that had been there in the pre-war days for the recreation of the officers who were training the national guards. The Japanese soldiers would patrol the outside of the fenced-in, double tennis court, and the internees would go in. The men could be on one side and the women the other, but they kept about a ten-foot gap in between us for part of the period. We would stand on each side, lined up facing our wife, to have a conversation. There would be somebody on your right and somebody on your left. They would be trying to talk to their wives, so it wasn't a very satisfactory arrangement, and the children would have to be put down by the mother to crawl those ten feet over to the father to get to visit with the father even for the period of that one hour a week. After a period of [two] weeks, they began to relax this a bit and to let us walk, if we kept moving in a circle, round and round, and thus we could be closer together to talk.

Life at this point went on this way for the first four months. We began to settle in for whatever the future might bring. They had mounted a radio, for propaganda purposes, at the guardhouse just outside of the barbed-wire fence between these two buildings. We heard of the fall of Corregidor [in May 1942]. We heard of the fall of Singapore. We heard of the pushing of the American forces to the far south in the Pacific, and we realized that if this were true we would have a long period of time there.

For the first three weeks we lived off of American food that various people had brought in, canned goods and such things as this. Our American men who had had experience as cooks were permitted to use the kitchen of the barracks building to prepare the food, and we would have two small servings a day, one in the morning and the other in the afternoon. By the end of three

---

[33] Carl B. Eschbach, "The History of the Japanese Army Concentration Camp #3," unpublished typescript.

weeks the American food had run out completely, and then they began to bring in rice to feed us on.... We were fed two servings of rice a day, one in the morning and the other late in the afternoon.[34]

Procuring food for the camp of 500 was a constant problem. During this time the internees had to feed themselves. Dues were collected, and rations were purchased and prepared. The authorities allowed some of the men to go to the city market and buy food for the camp. The internees had two meals a day, one at nine o'clock in the morning and the second meal at four in the afternoon. Mothers and fathers would save a banana from the morning for a midday snack for their hungry children. Most of the internees began to spend several hours a day resting in order to save their strength, and Hugo studied during these hours of forced rest.

The authorities made no effort to supply them with food, so they had to establish their own financial organization within the camp. Each person was assessed two pesos (one U.S. dollar) for this purpose and another two pesos for a hospitalization fund. On 10 January they were visited by a Japanese civilian, accompanied by a number of Japanese who said they were acting under orders of the Japanese army. The internees were ordered to turn over to them all personal money in excess of 50 pesos per person, or 100 pesos per family. In addition to this, they ordered the internees to turn over to them all stocks, bonds, insurance papers, bankbooks, checkbooks, traveler's checks, and all other securities and legal papers. No receipt was given for the securities or the money that was taken. The internees were asked to turn in the articles demanded, and their baggage, bedding, and other belongings were searched by the Japanese.[35] Rings and jewelry were also collected, but Ruth was able to keep her wedding ring by hiding it under a rock close to the barracks.

On 18 January, they began to allow a few men to go out every day under guard with a cart and loot stuff left by the American army. The "looting gangs" collected items and supplies, medical supplies, firewood, mattresses, blankets, and tools. Eschbach recalled how the internees were able to gather much needed items:

One of the first needs of the camp was firewood for cooking. A detail was organized which was permitted to go outside the fenced area and bring in firewood in a small two-wheeled cart, collecting it from

---

[34] Hugo Culpepper, tape.
[35] Eschbach, 7.

the homes of the ex-personnel of Camp John Hay. Fortunately, the guards who accompanied this detail were very lenient in the supervision of the items which were brought into the Camp. In this way, we were able to supply practically all internees with mattresses, with a supply of towels, sheets, clothing, toilet paper, soap, cleansing powders, brooms, mops, light bulbs, books for the library, equipment to start the shoe-shop, a sewing machine to start the first clothing repair department, a number of tools, such as hammers, saws, chisels, etc., to enable the men to do repair work and make the living quarters presentable; a number of chairs; cooking utensils, dishes, tableware, and two drums of gasoline for the Japanese authorities to use in sending our truck to the market.[36]

A water pump and electric plant were put in order, and a hospital was established in the former homes of officers near the camp. The hospital in Baguio was used for the more seriously ill patients, and those who returned from the hospital brought vital news from the outside world.

The population of the camp consisted of three groups: miners and mining officials, business and retired people, and missionaries. Quite a few gold mines were located in the vicinity of Baguio, and the attitudes, language, and lifestyles of the miners often clashed with the missionaries, whom they held in low regard. M. H. Patton described the situation:

Missionaries did a lot of studying and were generally soft spoken. The hearty, flavor-some cussing of the miner was alien to that. To some miners we were simply "the damn missionaries." Some missionaries helped along this feeling by being too vocally evangelistic. Nothing suggestive of a "holier-than-thou" attitude would go. We were under constant watch, and any slip-up in ethics or accepted miner etiquette was seized upon as reason for further damning. We were either too human or not human enough—hence the bitterness. This feeling gradually wore away as we came to know each other, but it certainly persisted for some time. With some it never dissolved.[37]

---

[36] Ibid., 5.

[37] Patton, "Our Concentrated Life," 8. For other accounts of the experience written by fellow internees, see R. Renton Hind, *Spirits Unbroken* (San Francisco, 1946), and Evelyn Whitfield, *Three Year Picnic* (Corvallis, Oregon: Premiere Editions International, Inc., 1999).

The Japanese were suspicious that the language school was training spies to go into Japanese-occupied China as undercover agents for the U.S. government under the guise of being missionaries, so they started interrogating the missionaries, taking a few of them into Baguio each day for questioning. The inquisition began on Saturday, 24 January.

They came in and for a period of a week took five missionary men out each morning to cross-examine and question. They began to take us in alphabetical order, and therefore I was among the early group to go out, on the second or third day, because my name was in the Cs.

We were taken down to military police headquarters, put in a room, and then one by one were taken out of the room, into another empty room. There, in the presence of a Japanese officer who spoke only Japanese and a Japanese civilian interpreter, we were cross-examined. After more than an hour of cross-examination, I simply took the position, for whatever they asked me, that I was there only because of my love for mankind. My only desire was to tell them of the gospel, and I made a consistent reply to all their questions from this viewpoint. My friend Bob Dyer followed me. We were taken to a separate room and did not see the others until all had been examined. Then we were taken back to the camp, and another group was taken out.

When they arrived at the Fs [24 January], a Church of the Brethren missionary by the name of Flory was taken out. He had gone out to be an agricultural missionary. He, with his group of five, was taken out, but he was not brought back that afternoon. No explanation was given. He had a wife and baby in camp with us. Of course, great anxiety began to arise, particularly since another group of five would go out the next morning.

The next day, another of our Southern Baptist missionaries, Rufus Gray, whom I mentioned earlier, from Fort Pierce, Florida, was taken out. He had slept the night before leaving that morning just a few feet from me on the floor. He left a wife and baby in camp, and he was not returned that afternoon. A day or two later, a Norwegian Evangelical Lutheran missionary by the name of Loddigs was taken out with his group of five, and he was not brought back. He left only a wife, no children in that case.

You can imagine the anxiety of these wives, not knowing where their husbands were nor what their condition was. At the end of about ten days of this procedure, they came out—no report had been given on the condition of these three men—and got all of the missionaries on trucks and took us down to this little hotel [the Baguio Hotel], which we had been sleeping in before the bombing of Pearl Harbor, just across the street from the city hall and the city jail. The Japanese had taken this hotel over as an office headquarters. There, they processed us and told us that we were being released to live inside the city, to go back to our homes. We could stay there and be free to go out and buy food and be on the streets of the town, but we could not leave the city limits. They said that orders had come for the missionaries to be released.

We were greatly encouraged and hoped this meant we would be out for the duration of the war. So my wife and I and the two single women missionaries of our mission went back up to the apartment on Quezon Hill. So far—this was about five weeks after it began—everything was still there.[38]

Cleo Morrison and Fern Harrington stayed with them that night because their apartment building had been taken by the Japanese Intelligence Headquarters. That night they prepared a feast from the pantry: Tomato juice, cornbread, beets, corn, lima beans, corned beef, scrambled eggs, peaches, and pineapple—enough food for a week in camp. They started eating with gusto, but soon were so full they could not eat another bite.

About 10:30 we went on to bed and had planned to get up the next morning and take our shopping bags and go down to the curb markets and buy vegetables and begin to live as normally as we could. About midnight, as we were just dozing off to sleep, there was a knock on the door of the apartment. I went to the door, and here two or three Japanese officers in uniform and a Filipino, who was associate pastor of the Union Evangelical Church there in the town of Baguio and was serving as a guide at their command, asked if they might come in. They came in, and we were seated. The officer asked how many other people were there in the apartment. I told them my wife and two other women, and he said, "Would you have them get up and come in?" And I said, "Is it really necessary to disturb them? Couldn't I give them any message?" He said, "No. They must come in," so I went to awaken them and they got up and put on their housecoats and came in the living room, and there at midnight we had a brief visit with them.

They told us that we were to come back and report at that small hotel the next morning. I immediately became suspicious that we were to be taken back into camp, and I asked him directly if that is what it meant. He said, "Oh, no, no, nothing like that. We just want to give you more information." We were still naïve enough to believe them. The next morning we got up and had breakfast, got our shopping bags, went back to the hotel, and expected to be

---

[38] Hugo Culpepper, tape.

free to go on and do our vegetable shopping and return to the apartment. We got there, and they kept us waiting indefinitely.[39]

When Marian Gray returned home, she found her house in shambles. Rufus was an avid photographer, and his photographs were strewn everywhere. When they later learned that Rufus had been killed by the Japanese, the missionaries surmised that they had seized his pictures as evidence of his undercover activity.

The Japanese told us that a mistake had been made, that only the missionaries who were assigned to do work in Baguio were to be permitted to stay out, and the other missionaries would have to go back into the camp. They were going to take us directly then on trucks back to the camp. But we began to object and to impress upon them that we must be able to go back to our apartments and get our suitcases with a change of clothing and some things like this.

There was a great deal of uproar and confusion for a moment, and finally I asked the Japanese who was near me if I might go. In his desperation, possibly not knowing what he was doing, he said yes. With that I turned and immediately left the crowd and started walking off across the valley to go up to the apartment. They missed me soon and asked where I was. This led finally to permission being given for one person from each household to go and get together things for whoever stayed at any given house. Then they sent a truck around to make a circuit and pick us up, and then took us back into camp. That is the only time we were outside of the camp for the more than three years.[40]

By 8 March 1942, the internees' funds were almost exhausted, and the Japanese began receiving funds regularly for the prisoners' upkeep. The experience was taking its toll, however. Hugo came down with dysentery and had to be isolated from the camp. For a week he took only rice water, since there were no drugs to treat the dysentery. Even in this desperate state, he continued to read his Greek New Testament. Improbable as it seems, it was one of the turning points of his life.

It was Tuesday afternoon, March 10, 1942, about 7:00 P.M. The place was Camp Holmes, a civilian concentration camp in the Philippines, located about five miles north of Baguio on Luzon Island. The scene was a beautiful sunset

---

[39] Ibid.
[40] Ibid.

over the China Sea. The situation was existential: it was a matter of life or death, both physically and spiritually. Physically I had lost 20 pounds of muscle in ten weeks' time and had been suffering from bacillary dysentery for ten days. For four days I had been isolated from the community, living outside the barbed-wire fence in a cottage with six other patients fasting on rice-water. Spiritually I was sinking in a state of lethargy, not caring much, whether I lived or died. As I was leafing through this copy of the Greek New Testament, looking for some word of hope from God, I came upon I John 3:23: "And this is his commandment..."—a word from God for me in that hour of crisis. I looked more closely; it said two things: (1) "that we should *believe* in the name of his Son Jesus Christ"; and (2) that "we should *love* one another...." My heart leapt up! I had found a reason for being–a rationale, an underlying reason, for life: first, the basis of *trust* in life is the *character* of God revealed in the nature of Jesus Christ; second, what one does in life is to spring from "*loving* one another," from respecting the inherent worth of one's fellow human being.[41]

Another experience, shortly thereafter, imprinted itself on Hugo's memory. The internees received their first money from Tokyo and took some of it to buy a water buffalo.

After a period of a week to ten days, I had recovered from the bacillary dysentery. We went for a whole week without a bite of food to eat in order to let our digestive systems heal. I had lost eighteen pounds by then and was just beginning to learn what it is to be hungry, not just in the pit of your stomach but in the cells of your arms and your legs and all over your body. I had returned to the barracks building, and still had just the two servings of rice [gruel] a day to eat.

They let us buy a water buffalo, a carabao. We brought that animal behind the barbed-wire fence, behind the barracks building, and some of the American men prisoners who had had experience as butchers slaughtered the animal, drained the blood out, prepared the animal for eating, and for about three or four days the 500 of us had a small serving of carabao meat once a day with our rice. When we had eaten all of the meat, they took the bones and boiled them in water to make soup stock and put some of the rice with it, and we had soup for another three or four days.

---

[41] Hugo Culpepper, "The Rationale for Missions," *Education for Christian Missions: Supporting Christian Missions through Education*, ed. Arthur L. Walker (Nashville: Broadman Press, 1981) 37.

I happened to be standing with eight or ten other men on the back porch of the barracks in which I was living when the American men prisoners, cooks, brought several black kitchen pans from the kitchen filled with bones of the carabao. They were bleached out white and bare except for shreds of meat in the joints, in the cracks and crevices of the bones. I remember how at the sight of this, even in our hunger, we pounced down over those pans, surrounding them on our knees, and began to pick with our bare fingers for just a shred of meat here and there to put into our mouths or into an empty tin can to share a bite with our wives or families.

There came over me the feeling that slowly but surely I was sinking to the level of an animal. I was becoming a scavenger for food anywhere I could find it. Then, I looked up at the contrasting expressions of two men on the other side of the pan from where I was working. One was a young man; one was an elderly man. They were both as hungry as I was. They were both picking for bites of food. But they had contrasting expressions on their faces. I had learned that the young man was a millionaire. He was a typical young American adventurer who had come out to the Philippines a few years before in search of wealth, had staked out a claim, and struck a vein of gold and had acquired over a million dollars within a matter of a few years. He had investments back in the United States that would have made him independently wealthy for life, but the conditions shut him off from the source of his meaning in life, and his spirit had been possessed by hatred, by fear, by apprehension, and the expression on his face radiated nothing but the negative aspects of the human personality.

I looked into the contrasting expression of the other man, who was sixty-five years of age [Bill Mather].[42] He had spent forty years in China, literally walking from village to village in the interior to preach the Christian gospel to people who had never heard of God's love before. He was on his way back to America to retire and happened to come up to Baguio for a few days, waiting for the next ship out, was trapped there along with us, and spent the three years in the concentration camp after forty years in China. But he radiated nothing but the fruits of the Spirit, of love and joy and longsuffering and peace, and I saw in that moment, in the contrast of those two facial expressions, the two ways of life in our world today—one that is lived in harmony and fellowship with God through faith in Jesus Christ and the other the state of the person who does not have the peace of God in his heart and who is left alone in crisis without adequate resources to carry on or to bear up

---

[42] See William Arnot Mather, *Grace Burroughs Mather: A Sower of Living Seed in China* (Passaic, NJ: The George Dixon Press, 1946).

under the pressures of life. I have never forgotten those two contrasting expressions. They have been a source of strength to me day after day through life, reaffirming the all-importance of faith in Jesus Christ and the love and joy and peace and tranquility that comes from it, regardless of what happens in one's environment or in the world round about.[43]

On 5 April, Nakamura allowed the internees to have an Easter sunrise service, but only Scripture and music—no original thoughts were to be expressed. It was the first public gathering that had been allowed. By 6:45 A.M., the whole camp had crowded into the tennis courts. As the sun rose over the distant mountains, the Japanese guards assembled nearby for their worship of the rising sun, and the internees sang two Easter hymns. One of the men read the biblical account of Jesus' resurrection, and Mary Dyer sang "I Know That My Redeemer Liveth," accompanied by a violin. At breakfast the children found an Easter egg by each plate, which the women had decorated with crayons. Carl Eschbach was the Easter Bunny. That evening, the single women joined the married couples walking around the tennis courts and had an Easter parade. The Japanese guards were annoyed by the internees' gaiety as they laughed at the outrageous hats the women had fashioned. One had a roll of toilet paper perched over one eye at an angle and secured with a ribbon tied under her chin. Had the internees known the American troops were being defeated in Bataan that very day, they would not have been so giddy.[44]

Rolland Flory and Herbert Loddigs returned to camp on Tuesday, 14 April, having spent ten weeks in the city jail. They had not seen Rufus Gray, but reported that the Filipinos believed he had died from torture the day he was taken for questioning:

They were afraid to talk at first. They had not seen Gray at any time, and after about a year the men told us of the experiences they had had. They had been cross-examined, as we had, trying to force them to admit to being spies. They were beaten with shaved-down baseball bats and leather straps, and after that they were strapped flat on their backs on a table and had water forced down their throats. After they had been forced to drink all they could hold, they were beaten or stomped on their abdomen until they fainted and passed out. Cold water was thrown in their face, and this was repeated three times. At

---

[43] Hugo Culpepper, tape.
[44] Miles, *Captive Community*, 59–61.

the end of the third time, when they came to, they had been placed in solitary confinement in a city jail cell.

We assumed that that is what happened to Rufus Gray and that either he got a blow on the head from the baseball bat or suffered an internal hemorrhage of some sort under the treatment and probably died under torture that day that he was cross-examined. They said, after a year, that he had gotten ill, and they had put him in the hospital, and he had died and been buried, but there was no record in the hospital of his ever having been there. There was no indication anywhere of his burial. Even his wife never knew what became of him.[45]

Camp Holmes, 23 April 1942–27 December 1944

With the approach of the rainy season, the Japanese realized that the internees could not remain at Camp John Hay. Since Bataan had fallen, they felt secure in moving the prisoners to a camp without tall fences because it would be difficult for the prisoners to escape. Ruth explained:

> Really, it was a state of anarchy the first few months that we were in camp. We kept thinking each day the Americans would rally, push back up the mountain, and we would be free. We kept thinking each day there would be landings of American soldiers, that the navy would have had time to get out there, and hope never died that the Americans would be pushing back into Baguio soon. However, with the coming of the rainy season [after the fall of Bataan] we realized that it would be impossible for them to come in until after the end of the rainy season.
>
> Our roof in this first camp was nothing but a sieve, where they had strafed the building. We could look out at night through the roof and see the stars. The Japanese realized that they could not keep us here during the typhoon season, so we were taken to Camp Holmes, outside the town of Baguio, and put there in this camp, which turned out to be our salvation because there we had more than just a tennis court when we could be outside.[46]

On Monday, 20 April, the internees were notified that they were to be transferred to Camp Holmes at Trinidad, about five miles from Baguio.

---

[45] Hugo Culpepper, tape.

[46] Ruth Culpepper, tape.

Thirty-five men were sent ahead to make arrangements. On Thursday, 23 April, the transfer to Camp Holmes was made by truck. Camp Holmes overlooked a long sweep of mountainous country to the north and had a fine view of the China Sea to the northwest. Across a spacious parade ground were three barracks. The Chinese were assigned to the two-story building on the right. The women and children were given the upper floor of the middle building; the lower floor was the dining hall, and the men and boys took up residence in the barracks on the left, a one-story green building with a porch across the front. There was less floor space here than at Camp John Hay. The women's bunks were barely eighteen inches apart, and the men had no more than a seven by three foot space on the floor. One's belongings had to be stored in the space allotted. After much negotiation, Mukaibo allowed the internees to use a cottage down the hill for the sixteen mothers with babies under a year old: "The Baby House." At first the Japanese attempted to maintain restrictions on conversations between husbands and wives by putting up parallel fences six feet apart in front of the green barracks, but within a few weeks they quit attempting to enforce the separation, and eventually families were allowed to eat together outside.[47]

The internees organized a kitchen, cafeteria, school, blacksmith shop, electric shop, and wood-cutting gang. A mathematician did a survey of hours the internees spent in camp work and then apportioned camp work according to one's personal responsibilities. A woman without children worked three hours a day, women with children less.

After five months or so we were permitted to begin to have church services, and except for a few groups, such as the Roman Catholics and the Seventh-day Adventists and one or two others, we all met together outside and took turns preaching. There were twenty-one different denominations in the camp. I learned more about the beliefs of various denominations in that camp than I ever learned in a seminary classroom because we lived and worked together and came to be on a first-name basis and were able to share our religious understandings and experiences with each other.

Everybody worked for a half a day. My work was on the wood crew along with other able-bodied younger men. We went out under armed guards into the woods, up on the mountain, and would fell trees and saw them up into logs. We had three wheelbarrows with a short rope at the front of each wheelbarrow. Three men were assigned to a wheelbarrow, one to take the handle-

---

[47] Miles, *Captive Community*, 63–68.

bars, one to pull on a stick run through the end of a rope at the front of the wheelbarrow, and the third man would rest. We rotated from handlebars to rope to rest. Finally, we would bring that wood from as far away as a mile from the camp, over a dirt path, rolling it down the edge of the mountain for perhaps three or four hundred feet through a gully. Another crew of men would take these logs and with wedges and sledge hammers break them up into firewood and stack them crosswise under a hut to dry, and we used them to cook our rice with during the first two years.

We had a choice in our menu as we went by to be served, cafeteria-line style. We could take hard rice or soft rice. That depended on the condition of our digestive system. If we were suffering from dysentery at the time, we would take soft rice. If we were normal, we would take hard rice. It became quite commonplace; I said we all became one family. The standard greeting each morning was "What kind of a night did you have?" meaning whether or not you had become ill with dysentery in the course of the night or were in good condition, digestively speaking.[48]

Ruth worked at The Baby House from the time they arrived at Camp Holmes. Her qualifications, as she said, were that she had never had dysentery, and being a missionary she could be expected to be honest.

My particular job was making baby formulas. It was uncanny how the Chinese had planned for such events. They had cached food in all of the mountains there, and when word got out about the babies being born in camp and no milk, the Chinese sent in food or smuggled in food and milk for these babies. Since I had no baby and since I was not prone to have dysentery, I was a logical selection to make the baby formulas. We used what we could for bottles and nipples that the doctor brought in from the hospital, and each morning I would make some fifty to sixty bottles for the babies, never giving more than two ounces of milk per bottle, then filling it with sterile water the rest of the way. It was necessary that I keep a very definite record of everything I did, every can I opened. I even opened it up full so that I could pour boiling water in it and rinse the can out, because when your baby is starving and you have no way to feed it, you want to be sure it is getting everything it can. Thus, I made the formulas and set them there in full view of everybody.

---

[48] Hugo Culpepper, tape.

Then on Saturday morning of every week I went before the medical committee—we had some six, eight doctors in camp, and they formed the medical committee. I went before them with my records and showed them how many cans I had used, how many cans were left, and made it a public record so that there could be no feeling that some were getting milk and others weren't, for in what was called The Baby House, in four very small rooms, with one very small bathroom, there were twenty-seven mothers, with thirty some-odd babies and small children. Therefore, we had quite a bit of bedlam, as four or five mothers to a room were housed there with their other children. In fact, you could not walk at night without walking on somebody so that you really had to walk with care if you had to be up in the night because there was no room on the floor even for a passageway.[49]

Together with Fern and Cleo, Ruth made the formulas, pureed vegetables and fruit, sterilized baby utensils, and measured out milk with an eyedropper to ensure that each baby got the same quantity. When the supply of canned milk ran low in June, chemists in camp worked out a formula for "bean milk," which required mixed mongo bean puree, coconut milk extracted from freshly grated coconut, sugar, pineapple juice, and vegetable liquid to produce a formula similar to milk.[50] It tasted terrible, but it was nourishing and not as hard on the children's digestion as beans. Pigs, a dozen hens, and milch goats were added to the menagerie.

At the end of some two years, The Baby House was closed officially, and I was given the job of teaching American history in junior high school. We had this very small school building that the men had erected with some planks and things, with a board that we could write on as a blackboard. Each morning when we went into the classroom—I had about five children there—we put words on that board so that if the Japanese came through the building, as they could do at any time, they would see that we were studying spelling and not American history because that was taboo.

The school was a topflight school. Limited though their books were, the children did well. Some graduated from high school at this point. The schoolteacher had to have at least a master's degree before they could be considered as teachers in the school. Many of the professors

---

[49] Ruth Culpepper, tape.
[50] Miles, *Captive Community*, 74.

there had Ph.D.s, so the children, while they lacked in books, had a great store of knowledge that could be drawn on from the teachers that they had. Sometimes only one student was tutored in some particular course—by an engineer or by somebody who had done special work in that field.[51]

In May and June, the last two months under Nakamura, the quality of life in the camp improved in many ways. The Chinese were released the first of May, so the men moved into the Chinese barracks, and women without children moved into the men's barracks. The additional space seemed like a luxury. One of the men fashioned an outdoor stove for private cooking. Those who used the stove had to scrounge for firewood, but there was always a group of women at the stove heating a can of food procured from the outside. Beginning in June, entertainment on Saturday nights brought out songs, yarns, mimes, whistling, short plays, quips, and readings. To pass the hours during the rainy season (most of the summer), some of the missionaries broke down their aversion to playing cards and learned to enjoy bridge. The missionary choir broadened its membership and its repertoire and became a community chorus. Classes were offered in a wide range of subjects, drawing out the expertise of various internees. Some gardened; others worked in the shop.

Ruth remembered events that broke the monotony of camp life.

During this year they let us begin to have meals together in the dining room, meals consisting of boiled rice. In the evenings, they let us come together, play cards, sit and talk, do whatever we wanted to there in the dining room, and then on Saturday nights we would have programs. It was amazing the talent we had in camp with us. Different people would do different things on Saturday nights to entertain us. Sometimes plays were put on, sometimes scholarly lectures were given—always something that we could look forward to on Saturday nights.

We formed a small group, some six or eight of us, and on Wednesday nights we would have games together in a room because one of the men [Bob Dyer] lived at the hospital as an orderly, and we could go down there to the room, the eight of us, and have an evening together. We looked forward all week to this because it was the one night we would pool our resources and maybe make some kind of an

---

[51] Ruth Culpepper, tape.

ersatz pie or cake or something like that, that we might have just a little bit of something sweet once a week there on Wednesday night to close out our fellowship and fun hour.

All that time we had not received any packages, we had not received any mail, and we had no idea what was going on outside those barbed-wire fences except what came in as authentic rumors. We learned a little later that actually there was a radio in camp. Dr. Dana Nance, who was the head doctor in the camp, would go out to the hospital, where he used to be the head doctor, and he would tell the Japanese that he was bringing in supplies. Indeed, he did bring in supplies in a pull case, but underneath the supplies would be part of a radio. They assembled this radio, had it in the hospital down there, and because we were friends with one of the orderlies—a Baptist missionary—we were privileged to hear authentic rumors. We did not know just where this was, but we always knew that Bob knew things and would slyly pass them on as something he had heard. We came to find out that actually Bob stood guard for Dr. Nance when he went in under the stairway of this house and turned on the radio, beamed toward San Francisco at news time, to hear the news. He could not do this every day because of the great danger. It was a capital offense to have a radio, so extreme care had to be taken when they would go in to listen to the news.

This went on for about a year. We would hear these authentic rumors, nothing good, but finally we did begin to hear of the Americans coming back toward the Philippines, and we would begin to wonder where on the maps this or that was.[52]

At the end of July, Hayakawa, the new commandant, confirmed Rufus Gray's death. The next Sunday, 2 August 1942, the internees held a brief memorial service for him, which Hugo led, reading Bible verses on the future life and comforting Marian as best they could.

A short article in the *Arkansas Gazette* reported that after having received no word from the couple for a year, relatives in Little Rock were notified that week that Hugo and Ruth were interned at Baguio.[53] A message from the International Red Cross said they were in good health; relatives were advised not to worry.

---

[52] Ibid.

[53] *Arkansas Gazette*, 12 December 1942.

Activity around the camp picked up as Christmas neared. No Yankee ingenuity was spared in making Christmas gifts with the limited tools and materials available. M. H. Patton and Fern Harrington both recalled the beehive of activity in the shop:

> For weeks ahead there was much scraping and carving of coconut shells and fitting together of pieces of the same in the making of bracelets, brooches and rings, belts, or necklaces. Children's toys were made of scrap lumber, cardboard, bamboo, and tin cans. "Have you some small nails I could borrow?" "What about your homemade drill when Jack's through with it?" "Can I see how you wired together that belt you're making for your wife?" "What will you take for two squares of that heavy cardboard?" "Who has a file they will lend me?"[54]

> One man made a set of drinking glasses for his family from bottles he had collected. By setting fire to a kerosene-dipped string tied around the bottle and plunging it into a bucket of cold water, he neck snapped off easily. After smoothing sharp edges he had some beautiful drinking glasses.[55]

Ruth, too, recalled the presents she and Hugo made for each other.

> We had no way to buy presents. Therefore, we had to make our presents. I still have today rings and pins that Hugo made me out of the bones cut from animals' legs that would form the ring that would slip on your finger, and then with a very small knife and great patience he would whittle a coconut shell down to the part just between the dark and the light part of the shell, and when he reached that part, then he could form a scene or something like that using the two tones of brown that would be at that part.
> My only way of giving a gift to him was to knit something. I knitted belts; I knitted socks. Knitting was quite a task. The men would go out to the fence, the barbed-wire fence, and cut pieces of wire, and then they would take a rock and take the wire and, by rubbing and rubbing, rub a point on the wire. These were our knitting needles. Actually, there is no article of clothing that I have not knitted. The Catholic sisters—in their rehabilitation of Filipino women—sent in

---

[54] Patton, "Our Concentrated Life," 14.
[55] Miles, *Captive Community,* 90.

from their supplies a room full of twine, just plain grocer's twine like they used to tie packages in the grocery shops. This we took and knitted into every kind of an article of clothing. This, then, I would use to knit Hugo various things to wear. Since I had no children in camp, I knitted for the children because as they grew larger, naturally, they had nothing to wear.... The women had long since taken their skirts and made shorts and a halter, just enough to cover themselves as best we could. Being in Baguio, it was rainy and cold several months of the year. All of us had coats that we used and sweaters. We always had to have our mosquito nets; these things were essential to us in that cool, damp climate, especially during the rainy seasons.[56]

The wood crew brought down a huge pine tree for the community Christmas tree, which they put up and decorated on Christmas Eve. The Japanese guards even supplied strings of Christmas light (no doubt looted from American homes). A Christmas pageant at a nativity scene retold the Christmas story. A huge three-dimensional star lantern made of thin paper over a bamboo frame supplied light over the stable. A baby goat from the camp flock added to the realism of the pageant.

Christmas Day began with the a cappella choir singing Christmas carols at five-thirty down at the guardhouse. After a worship service at ten o'clock, everyone gathered to wait for Santa's arrival at the Christmas tree. A few minutes later Santa appeared from behind the shop, carrying a rice sack full of toys for the children, who squealed with delight. In addition to the toys, each child received two oranges, candy, and peanuts, purchased with money donated by the internees. That afternoon, the Japanese permitted Filipinos to bring gifts for relatives and friends, and the mothers at The Baby House had a party for Ruth, Fern, and Cleo and gave each of them a bag of fruit, homemade cookies, and candy.

Our Christmas dinner was a fitting climax to the day: roast pork, rice, green beans, squash, candied tropical yams (a whiter, mealy type of sweet potato), with steamed pudding and coffee for dessert. The dining hall, festooned with red paper streamers between pine boughs and silver paper bells, helped create a festive atmosphere.[57]

---

[56] Ruth Culpepper, tape.
[57] Miles, *Captive Community*, 92.

Green Barracks. From Miles, *Captive Community*, 119. Used with permission.

Many remembered Christmas 1942 as the happiest time of their internment. Their Red Cross relief kits were the only things missing that year. Two days later, they quietly marked the first anniversary of their captivity. Optimists were convinced the Americans would come before the rainy season; pessimists believed they might not come before 1944.

Since their cameras had been confiscated, Fern Harrington made sketches of camp scenes. Ruth's cubicle was on the backside of the green barracks, just across from the door. Two sketches show Ruth's cubicle, which she shared with three other women, one dated 18 December 1942 and one June 1943. The later sketch shows their living area after the two beds had been hung from the ceiling to make more room.

Ruth's cubicle, 1942. From Miles, *Captive Community*, 93. Used with permission.

The spring of 1943 brought more outbreaks of dysentery and debates within the camp about voting rights for women and representation on the General Committee. Eventually women were allowed to vote, and a camp judicial system was established.

Ruth's cubicle, 1943. From Miles, *Captive Community*, 93. Used with permission.

At Easter, they staged an elaborate, outdoor Passion play that culminated with the crucifixion. The Japanese brought in four spotlights, one for each of the scenes: the Last Supper, betrayal in the garden, trial before Pilate, and the crucifixion. Ruth helped with the costumes and the staging. The pageant was staged on the hillside just west of The Baby House. Terraces for flowers on the east hillside made a perfect place for the audience to view the pageant enacted on the west hillside, where the four scenes were set up. Ruth remembered the event vividly:

> When the night came, we wondered whether the Japanese would come. We wondered how it would be received. That evening, as dark came, all of the Japanese left the guardhouse, came down in single file, filed in, and sat down on the ground on what would be the front row of the audience. All of our guards left the guardhouse and came [and a carload of Japanese came out from town for the pageant].... It was a very impressive thing. It was beautifully done and well handled by people who were just ordinary people who had tried to memorize and work out the part in the spirit of Easter.

After the play was over, and Jesus was left hanging on the cross, everybody filed away from the mountainside with absolutely no talking, in utter quiet, and went back to the barracks. The Japanese soldiers went back to the guardhouse, and when our leader went to report to the Japanese that all were accounted for in camp that night—because we had a roll call check at 11:00—the Japanese were just sitting there. Finally, one of the men said, "What happened to that man on the tree? Why did he have to die? He didn't do anything wrong." Then the man who was head of the camp committee [Carl Eschbach], being himself a missionary, was able to explain to these Japanese guards what the whole story meant and how this man came to save them as well as Americans. He said, "But this is not the end of the story because on Sunday something else happened." And he said, "At sunrise on Sunday morning you will see the rest of the play."

So Easter morning, at sunrise, we met on top of the hill that day, all of us who were there, and the Japanese all came back, and it was [a] glorious morning of song and reading of the resurrection of Jesus and of what happened later. It was a glorious day when we could sing, "Up, Up from the Grave He Arose." Thus we were able in some ways to witness, to be true to a calling that had led us out to the Orient and indeed had led us into the concentration camp.[58]

The camp doctors dealt with medical emergencies as best they could, with little equipment or medication, and surgeries were performed in very primitive conditions. "There was very little ether in camp, and the doctors who had brought in their own equipment and what supplies they had when they were taken prisoners used spinal anesthetics as far as possible and saved the ether for children and for head surgery. The pastor of the First Baptist Church in Manila suffered a tumor, a malignancy of the brain, and they did head surgery there under those rustic conditions in camp, drilled holes through the skull, released the pressure and so forth, but were not able to save him."[59]

On 22 June 1943, Ruth had to have emergency surgery. Dr. Dana Nance performed the operation.

[Ruth] underwent an acute abdominal surgery with an attack one night. I was awakened after midnight by the doctor and left my building, went to the

---

[58] Ruth Culpepper, tape.
[59] Hugo Culpepper, tape.

hospital, and another doctor examined her, and they decided exploratory surgery was the best thing, to try to see what the difficulty was. I asked if I might watch the operation, and they gave me permission. The doctor had been working on the wood crew, the same as I had that day. He had on just shorts up above his knees, worn-out trousers that he was still using. A gold miner friend of his was standing by his side with a carbide miner's lantern. In case the one electric globe that was fed from a Delco—that was hanging down over the kitchen table which served as the surgical table—failed, he would be able to shine the carbide light down so that the doctor could complete the surgery.

And I stood there and watched the exploratory abdominal operation. Removing all the internal organs and feeling them to see what the difficulty was and finally the removing of the appendix and sewing her back up took over an hour. The incision was jagged and crooked because the doctor's scalpel was too dull to cut a straight line. It was under those primitive conditions that we had medical attention.[60]

In August, a repatriation ship, the *S.S. Gripsholm*, came to the Philippines to pick up internees to exchange with Japanese internees from the United States. Hopes soared, but only those who had been caught on ships in the Manila harbor were able to go. Only one internee from Camp Holmes was repatriated. He memorized the names and mission boards of as many of the internees as he could. The Japanese let them send one letter, typed on a single sheet of paper. It was the only letter they were able to send home during the war. Their letters give a sense of their condition and daily activities, while putting the best light possible on the experience for loved ones at home and avoiding taboo subjects.

Dearest Mother and Dad:

Everyday, as we have remembered you in our prayers, our greatest desire has been to let you know how well we are. Now that the opportunity has come, we are hoping that you will have this letter by Christmas. We were interned on December 28, 1941, at Camp John Hay, Baguio. On April 23, 1942, we were moved to Camp Holmes, five miles north of Baguio, where we have remained since then.

Beautiful mountain scenery, colorful sunsets, cool weather, and a good water supply combine to make this an ideal campsite. We have about five hundred people interned here, of whom about 190 are missionaries representing 21 denominations. (In some respects this has been better than a

---

[60] Ibid.

post-graduate seminary course.) The women with children in one, the women without in another, and the men in a third barrack. Much of our time is spent in camp work, doing everything from the bathroom detail to log-rolling. We are fortunate in having a small camp library as well as a considerable number of our own books. The 35 ministers alternate in church services on Sunday mornings. One of the best features of camp life is adult education classes in most everything from calculus to seminars on Christian thought.

Perhaps you would enjoy a description of a typical weekday routine for Ruth and me; I get up at 6:45 when the rising whistle blows and [Note: no reference to the daily roll call] study my Greek New Testament until 8:00. Ruth gets up about 7:30, and we meet under her barracks, around our own little table with two stools, for breakfast at 8:00. In the dry season, from October until June, we move the table out into the open. Both of us get to our camp work detail at 8:30. I roll logs for camp firewood from 8:30 until 11:30. We transport logs in wheelbarrows for about a half-mile on top of a mountain near the camp. Ruth works from 8:30 until 10:30 and again from 5:00 until 6:00 preparing the milk formulae for baby bottles. I enjoy a cold shower at 11:30 and then relax until I meet Ruth for lunch at 12:30. We have all three of our meals in the same place. From 1:30 until 4:30 I study hard in continuation of our regular language study; and also in preparation for my degree examination in Greek. We have dinner at 4:30. Ruth reads and sleeps in the afternoons and does her language study in the mornings, after 10:30. After dinner, from five until seven I read Theology, Church History, novels and so on, for recreation. We spend the evenings together 7–9 in the dining hall, playing various games with other couples, reading, or studying our language course together. Every Saturday evening there is a camp entertainment program. Lights are out at 9:30. There is little variation in this routine for us.

Our health is good, but we have an excellent hospital and surgeon if needed. Beds are comfortable, and food is adequate. Dining hall menus are: Breakfast—hard or soft rice, syrup and a banana; Lunch—soup, two vegetables, and a banana, and a slice of bread three times a week; Dinner—meat and vegetables stew, steamed rice, two vegetables and a fruit. We are also fortunate in receiving two market bags of food a week from town including banana, coconuts, papaya, mangos, sugar, onions, lemons, eggs, and even meat occasionally. There is also a camp store at which we buy things. Ruth prepares these extra foods at lunch and for desserts in the evening. I weigh 145 and have a good healthy tan from working barefooted with nothing but a loin cloth on. Ruth weighs 114 and feels fine.

This experience has been educational in many ways and has been helpful spiritually. We have no regrets, but are completely happy in our vocation of teaching.

Please send a copy of this letter to the Board in care of Dr. Maddry, and also to Dr. Davis at the Seminary. All of our group here are well. We are all here except Rufus Gray, who passed away in January 1942. We send our love to you and all our friends. May the peace of God keep your hearts in Christ Jesus.

Lovingly,

(Ruth and) Hugo H. Culpepper[61]

Dearest Mother and Daddy,

It seems too strange after 20 months to be writing again. We were told a few days ago that through the kindness of the Japanese authorities we could write to you. We are both in good health—Hugo weighs 145, and I weigh 114. We have had no sickness except in March of 1942 Hugo had bacillary dysentery for a week. On June 22, 1943, I had an exploratory operation which turned out to be an appendectomy. Dr. Nance thought it was gall bladder trouble and made the incision about 6 inches long just above the gall bladder down. He examined the gall bladder, took out my stomach and examined it and the intestines for ulcers, but found nothing but an inflamed appendix, which was out of place, being under the gall bladder and causing it to give me trouble. I am fine now, having gained back most of what I lost. Outside of this we have had no sickness.

We were interned Sunday, December 28, 1941. We had Christmas turkey that year. Mother's package with the grey wool dress, and socks, ties, make-up kit got here. That was the only Christmas presents we had. No other packages got here. I have practically worn the grey dress out in here. Until April 1942, we were interned in the Igorot [mountain tribesmen] barracks at Camp John Hay. Since then we have been interned at Camp Holmes, which is about 5 miles from Baguio. It is rumored that we are going to be moved to Los Baños, which is south of Manila soon, but as yet we have had no official announcement. There are just about 500 in camp now.

The sameness of our daily routine in here makes the days go about twice as fast. Hugo works on the wood detail—bringing wood down from the hills around for camp use. The rest of the day he spends

---

[61] The letter makes no reference to the circumstances of Rufus Gray's death. Hugo Culpepper, letter to Mr. and Mrs. J. H. Culpepper, 21 August 1943.

studying Greek and continuing regular language study. I have charge of making all the formulae for the babies, so I work both morning and afternoon. In the evenings we play bridge or rook or read. We eat all three meals together: breakfast—8:00, lunch—12:30, supper—4:30. We are fortunate enough to receive a bag on Tuesday and Friday from the market in Baguio with fruit, eggs, flour, coconuts, and meats in it. This helps a lot to give us extra nourishment, though the camp diet is quite adequate. One of the nice things about our situation is the great variety of fruits available. Hugo gets up at 6:15 and I at 7:15. Lights are out at 9:30. We live in separate barracks.

Our whole mission group is just fine except that Rufus Gray died in January 1942. Most of us are continuing our studies and looking forward to the time when we can get back to our work. As our group stands, it includes Fern Harrington, Cleo Morrison, Bob and Mary Dyer, Marian and Billy Gray.

The camp has a good library, and with the private books in camp we are getting a lot of reading done. From the studying he has done, Hugo will be ready to take his degree, and the experiences we have make us feel that we are far better suited to be missionaries; we hope this is just the final touch to our preparation for a life of usefulness in His service. We are fast learning "in whatever state I am to be content," and "my God shall supply your every need according to his riches in glory." Truly this has been a glorious experience in making us face and live on the fundamental realities of life.

We hope you are well and happy when this reaches you. I do hope it won't be too long until we can hear from you.

Lovingly yours,

Ruth (and Hugo) Culpepper[62]

The *Arkansas Baptist*, the Arkansas Baptist state paper, carried a banner headline on 22 December 1943, which read "Letter from the Culpeppers." Below, it printed a picture of Hugo and Ruth from before they left for China, a brief report of their situation, and the text of Hugo's letter. Ruth's mother asked for prayer: "Pray that the Lord will keep and preserve them and that they may come out of all this turmoil in good health and be better prepared to serve and honor Him."[63]

---

[62] Ruth Culpepper, letter to Mr. and Mrs. William F. Cochrane, 22 August 1943.
[63] Undated letter from Agnes Cochrane, to Mrs. Ralph Lee Douglas in 1944.

The year 1943 had been perhaps the best year of their captivity. In the spring of 1943 a new commandant, Rokuro Tomibe, took charge of the camp. He was a Japanese army reserve officer, from a prominent Japanese family, well educated, and—the internees agreed—a gentleman. He reprimanded Peeping-Tom guards who spied on women in the bathroom and flogged guards who stole their chickens. He sought to improve living conditions, gave the Americans permission to go up on "the hill," the southern boundary of the camp, for picnics, secured extra food on special days, and allowed the wood crew to go further from camp to maintain the supply of wood.

Tomibe also allowed Carl Eschbach to visit the American leaders at two other camps, Los Baos and Santo Tomas. There he learned that their Red Cross packages the previous year had been distributed in Manila because of lack of transportation to Baguio. Tomibe sent two committee members to Manila to see that the Red Cross packages were put on a train and guarded en route. Because the Japanese army had commandeered every truck in Baguio, he promised American cigarettes from the care packages to the manager of the copper mines that lay to the north if his drivers would carry the packages to the camp. On 22 December, seven trucks rolled into camp with all 502 Red Cross food kits. After the war Ruth described the arrival of the trucks:

> One of the most vivid recollections of my camp experience was that night in December, 1943, when trucks began to roll in loaded with American food, clothing, and medicine. From the headlights one could see the mingled emotions upon the faces of those who looked with all their hearts at those heaven-sent supplies. Tense were those moments as we stood by watching the unloading begin. A dream fulfilled. Relief tangible before our eyes. With hope and cheerfulness in our faces we thanked God that someone, somewhere had given and relief from hunger and pain was ours.[64]

On Christmas Day, they doled out a box of food to each internee.

> At the end of the second year—one time only—we did get a large package, of about forty-eight pounds, I believe, of food from the American Red Cross. Since the Japanese government does not recognize the Red Cross, this came through the international YMCA

---

[64] "I Perish with Hunger," *The Commission*, 8, 9 (October 1945): 9.

organization, but it was food for us: canned milk, jelly, Spam, beans, sugar—the sort of things that made all the difference in the world to us during that third year of imprisonment, when the rice had all been shipped back to Japan, and now we were down to eating a half a cup of cornmeal mush in the morning and another half a cup of cornmeal mush in the evening.

This menu was given a variation at Thanksgiving and Christmas. During that year at Thanksgiving, the cooks put up a sign that said, "Genuine pancakes Thanksgiving morning." I remember the children standing there, and one child asked his mother, "Mother, does 'genuine' mean big or small?" That was the only thing [that] mattered when it came to food, how much, not how good, or what, or other things, just so if we could possibly have enough to eat.[65]

Every internee unpacked his or her box and examined each item. Then came the question of how to handle this incredible surplus. Some ate it in the next few weeks, expecting the Americans would come soon, but most hoarded it and rationed it out through all of 1944.

On New Year's Day the rest of the Red Cross shipment was distributed. For the first time in two years, each of them received a roll of toilet tissue, a bottle of vitamins, a box of tampons, a toothbrush, soap, shoe polish, a comb, a pencil, a sheet, and clothing. The internees then began the process of swapping with each other in order to gain the items they prized the most.

Tons of mail came on the same ship with the Red Cross supplies, but censorship slowed its delivery. On Friday morning, 21 January 1944, Hugo and Ruth received a letter from his mother that she had written the year before. Hugo's father had been made chief of the field division in the Arkansas internal revenue office, and "there have been so many changes in Pine Bluff it does not seem like the same place any more."[66]

By this time, their food supplies were dwindling, meat was scarce, bananas appeared less and less frequently, and prices were rising. Beginning 1 February 1944, the Japanese put the internees on army rations. Theoretically, each person was allowed a daily quota of fourteen ounces of rice, seven ounces of vegetables, three and a half ounces of meat or fish, and small amounts of salt, oil, sugar, and tea. In actuality, they never received the stipulated amount. The Japanese bought the cheapest vegetable available, so during February they had cabbage every day. So

---

[65] Ruth Culpepper, tape.

[66] Mrs. J. H. Culpepper, letter to Hugo and Ruth Culpepper, 11 January 1943.

much of the fish was rotten that it could not be eaten. Their diet quickly deteriorated to rice and cabbage, supplemented with a little fish or meat every other day.[67]

On 9 March 1944, Hugo and Ruth received fourteen letters, dated from 17 December 1942 to 9 May 1943. The families had been so relieved to hear that they were alive and to know where they were. Ruth's family had received several letters from Dr. Armstrong and Mrs. Russell at Baylor in 1942, asking about Ruth and Hugo. Wanda wrote a newsy family letter: "I seem to find so little time these days to do what I want to"; "Daddy is just grand. He has strictly been O.K. for over two years now [Note: a reference to his alcoholism]. He has gotten the promotion and two nice raises. I am so glad, cause I think it has made him realize what he can do if he tries."[68] Ruth's mother wrote her on her twenty-fifth birthday: "My what I would give to have you all here with us today. Twenty-five years ago tonight the Lord sent you to us, and what a blessing you have been ever since. I am so unworthy of you, but I do love you so much and I just had to tell you that again today. Let us hope we can all be together on your next birthday."[69] Hugo's mother wrote that Wanda was three months pregnant after nearly eight years of marriage, thrilled, but having to be very careful with the pregnancy; Grandma Bradley had lost her eyesight; Grandma Culpepper "had a terrible sick spell last fall, but she is up and feeling lots better"; Monroe F. Swilley, Jr., from Eldorado, had just gone as pastor to the First Baptist Church of Pine Bluff.[70]

As conditions became more difficult, the worship services became more vital. M. H. Patton described the change: "You would notice this in the preaching. Men were no longer so anxious to present their point of view. They seemed (most of them) more concerned to make of their everyday convictions a source of help to others. Less theology and more inner experience began to appear on the Sunday menus. The sermons were helpful and the services well attended. All of us had been mellowed a bit by finding beneath differences of creedal beliefs a common human striving, failure and aspiration."[71]

---

[67] Miles, *Captive Community*, 123.

[68] Wanda Bedell, Hugo's sister, letter to Hugo and Ruth Culpepper, 10 January 1943.

[69] Mrs. William F. Cochrane, letter to Ruth Culpepper, 5 February 1943.

[70] Mrs. J. H. Culpepper, letter to Hugo Culpepper, 26 February 1943.

[71] Patton, "Our Concentrated Life," 17.

In April the routine was shattered by the escape of two of the miners to join the guerillas in the hills. When the escape was discovered, roll calls became longer, trips "up the hill" for picnics were canceled, private gardens were curtailed, as were store privileges, and the daily rations grew slimmer. Some of the miners were taken away for interrogation and beaten and tortured before they were returned. Commandant Tomibe told the camp that they had betrayed his trust after he had done everything in his power to make life easier for them.

In a lecture in 1977, Hugo gave the following account of these events, referring to a journal he kept while in camp:[72]

I say this in the context of my own personal, existential struggle with the issue of the disciple of Christ's role in a time of war.

When the war began and we were taken prisoners by the Japanese on December 28, 1941, in the Philippines, on the island of Luzon, in the city of Baguio, I at that time considered myself to be a conscientious objector—not in the official sense of being registered as a conscientious objector, but in the sense of having the conviction that the ethic of Jesus was an ethic of absolute love, that he lived and died by it, that I was called to be his disciple, a pupil of his in the school of life. It was just that simple for me. I quote here from my personal journal, which I composed in camp, a thing that I rarely have ever done. Quote:

"April 8, 1944, Saturday 9:00 A.M. On Wednesday morning April 5 Richey Green and Herbie Swick escaped from camp." (Richie Green was [a] coal miner, a single man. Herbie Swick was a captain in the American army who had donned civilian clothing and put himself off as a civilian and succeeded in being put in civilian camp instead of having to go to the military prisoner of war camp. These two men escaped from camp on Wednesday morning April the fifth.) "They were missing that night at roll call at 9:30 P.M. Thursday morning all the men, and then all the women, were called to the dining hall. Mr. Tomibe, the Japanese commandant of the camp—he was a lieutenant in the Japanese army—spoke regarding the escape and laid down four new rules: 1. No more hill picnics. (He had been the most lenient of our commandants and had given us extra privileges.) 2. Cannot get outside the fence. 3. Commandant takes charge of roll calls, and 4. Camp must share the responsibility of preventing further escapes. Therefore everyone must take turn standing watch at night to report any attempted escapes. This last provision (I am still quoting from my

---

[72] To my knowledge, this is the only recorded reference to Hugo's camp journal. I have never seen it, nor did I ever hear him speak of it. RAC

journal) has caused some concern to many people in camp. The Executive Committee of the camp, composed of fellow internees by camp vote, refused to take this responsibility, but were told that we must accept it. Yesterday, a notice was posted giving two reasons for our standing watch. Quote: Explanation of duties of night watchmen of internment camp: 1. Prevention of fire and protection of internees; 2. To establish connection with the commandant's office in case of emergency. This statement from the commandant does not make clear any withdrawal of the responsibility indicated in his original statement. At the best it is ambiguous. Therefore, I have felt compelled to write a letter to be forwarded to Mr. Tomibe unless a formal removal of 'responsibility' is announced. I turned the letter over to Carl Eschach, chairman of the internees camp committee the morning I wrote it, last Saturday.

April 8, 1944

Saturday, 8:30 A.M.

Mr. Tomibe,

Commandant of Japanese Army Internment Camp Number Three,

Baguio, Philippine Islands

Dear Sir:

I have conscientious objections as a disciple of Jesus Christ to participating in the war activities of any country, including the Unites States of America. To stand watch with the responsibility of reporting any possible escape of internees is in my opinion the function of a soldier. Since I would not accept this responsibility nor this activity for my own country, I cannot comply with your request to stand watch with this responsibility. I have no duty "to prevent liberty of action" even so far as standing watch to report attempted escapes. I have no objections to standing watch for prevention of fires or other purposes not related to military activities. This explanation is courteously presented in an effort to make clear the convictions by which I am led in this matter.

Sincerely yours,

Hugo Culpepper

April 16, 1944, Sunday 11:30 A.M.: "In regard to guard duty the general committee had a meeting Saturday afternoon, April 8 (incidentally it was that day that I had written and given my letter to Carl) and framed a protest which was given to Mr. Tomibe. Several days later the Executive Committee had a conference with him. He indicated that while he might be willing to make it mere fire watchman and to remove the responsibility as to reporting internees escaping and so forth he did not feel that the military police would agree to this. Today I learned that the committee is not forwarding the refusal of some of us. (I have a question mark here about "some," though that is in my journal. I don't know that anybody else wrote any communication. I know there were some members of peace churches, the Church of the Brethren, some Mennonites, and so forth, who were opposed to it and probably would have taken a stand when the showdown came, but I don't know of any other letter written, and that is why I am not clear in my memory as to what "some" referred to except in that general way.)

Today I learned that the committee is not forwarding the refusal of some of us to Mr. Tomibe but is exempting us and assigning us to other work upon their own responsibility.

May 3, 1944, Wednesday, 9:10 A.M. (This is some two weeks later, you see): I spoke to Carl again about night watching. In the Committee meeting minutes of last week there was a paragraph stating that the commandant has signified his intention of standing with his approval of the committee's letter of protest. (And later he did that and removed the required responsibility, which of course removed the element of conscientious objection because to serve as night watchman would merely be a civic duty and contribution to the community, but no military dimension to it.)[73]

On 1 July 1944, Tomibe was replaced as commandant by Oura, a Japanese military officer, who was as vindictive as Tomibe had been conciliatory. Food rations were cut further, and the quality was poorer. Everyone was required to work in the garden to grow vegetables for camp use, in addition to their regular work assignment. He also began weighing every internee every two weeks, which revealed that the average weight of the internees was declining steadily.

On 24 July 1944, Hugo and Ruth received another bundle of letters, some written as early as 13 December 1942. Paul Geren was teaching at a college in northern India; James Tull was in China and Jim Jernigan at Pearl Harbor. On 25 November 1942, the Culpeppers had received a cablegram indicating that ten missionaries and their families were interned at Baguio, among them Hugo and Ruth. The American Red Cross also advised them, by letter, of Hugo and Ruth's location, that they were well, and not to worry. Fourteen letters they had sent to Hugo and Ruth were all returned. A letter from Monroe F. Swilley, Jr., dated 13 March 1943, recalled their friendship at Ouachita and at Southern Seminary. As pastor in Pine Bluff, Swilley had visited Hugo's grandmother and aunt.

---

[73] Hugo Culpepper, tape recording of lecture on "Civil Religion: Discipleship and Patriotism," for "CTEC—The Mission of Your Church," Southern Seminary, 17–20 October 1977.

The Culpeppers and the Cochranes kept writing every month, not knowing whether their letters were getting through. In Little Rock, the summer of 1943 was the hottest summer in sixty-five years. Hugo's father wrote: "You should be here on our back porch. I am in my BVD's, Mother in her slip, and boy is it hot, have two fans going, am sure that it has been a long time since either of you have [had] hot weather. You would enjoy it."[74]

On 22 September 1944, their thousandth day of internment, they heard airplanes flying north along the coast and loud booms, followed by anti-aircraft fire. The Japanese later confirmed that American planes had hit a military base on the coast and destroyed many of their planes on the ground. Hopes were raised that they would soon be liberated, but weeks dragged by and conditions only grew worse. Ruth sat with other women, separating kernels of rice or corn from the dirt and bugs.

At the end of two years the rice supply was exhausted. They began to bring in hard-kernel, yellow-shelled corn that had been eaten by the weevils and was molded. I always felt that it was the remains of the rice that had been stored in the warehouses for the Japanese army. There was chaff and small rocks and dirt mixed in with it, and the older people who were too old to do any other kind of work would sit for hours each day and pick the rice grain by grain off the edge of a table into their hands. We had to pick the weevils out and wash the mold off and spread it out on the ground to dry. We had one hand-turned coffee mill, and we took turns, day and night if necessary, to keep that handle on the one coffee mill turning to grind the hard kernels of the shelled corn into cornmeal flour. We boiled that in big iron vats that were in the kitchen of the national guard's barracks where we were staying, with the firewood that we brought in. And for the last one year and two months we had molded cornmeal mush to eat, one bowl in the morning and another bowl late in the afternoon. We got down to as low as 700 calories a day during the last year.[75]

The camp newssheet posted the menu each day and the number of calories.

On 30 October, Hugo and Ruth received brief letters from each family indicating that their letters had been received by Christmas 1943. On 25 November, an American plane buzzed the camp, setting off wild excitement. In the days ahead, other planes would fly over, but still they waited.

Commandant Oura ordered the internees to vacate the houses on the lower level next to the highway, including the Baby House and the hospital.

---

[74] Mr. Culpepper, letter to Hugo Culpepper, 4 July 1943.
[75] Hugo Culpepper, tape.

Much to their surprise, he brought them a steer on the hoof for their Christmas celebration, saying they could have it if they would butcher it and give the guards a front quarter. Pressing the limits of survival, the internees prepared for their third Christmas in captivity. This year there was no hope of Red Cross packages because even Japanese ships could no longer bring supplies to their own army. Still, Christmas worked its magic, as M. H. Patton remembered:

> Christmas looked pretty bleak to us, but as it drew near we threw ourselves into preparation and once again the perennial miracle came to pass. Again Christ visited Camp Holmes, and the angels sang and the rest of us re-echoed the angel's song. "Glory to God in the highest and on earth"—What? Well, it would come some day and the more we really sang "Glory to God" the sooner it would come. Christmas dinner was rather slim, but we added bits from our thin stores and made the occasion as festive as possible. Santa Claus was present, and toys for the younger ones and Christmas music. The old lifting of the spirit returned.[76]

Bilibid Prison, Manila,
28 December 1944–5 February 1945

About nine o'clock Tuesday evening, 26 December, they were informed that the camp would be moved. They were not sure but surmised they would be taken to Manila. Sixty percent of the camp would be moved on Thursday, the rest on Friday. The first group was to have their baggage ready for inspection at eleven o'clock the next morning. Time for lights out was being extended to midnight to give them time to pack. Each person was limited to a half cubic meter of luggage, a bedroll, and lunch.[77]

Excitement rolled through the camp as they packed and speculated about where they were going and what the move meant. The kitchen crew slaughtered their small farm of livestock: fifty to one hundred chickens, two cows, several pigs, and a dozen goats. The next day they had meat at every meal.[78]

---

[76] Patton, "Our Concentrated Life," 19.
[77] Miles, Captive Community, 149.
[78] Patton, "Our Concentrated Life," 19.

At nine o'clock Thursday morning three trucks left camp with as many people as they could pack onto each truck, sitting on top of baggage piled to the top of the cabs. Hugo and Ruth went out the next day. The trip from Baguio to Manila took twenty-four hours. The highway was a mass of Japanese troops, tanks, and equipment moving north from Manila toward the mountains. "You can imagine something of the problems and sanitary conditions, with men, women, and children riding for hours on hours, all mixed together there, jammed in like cattle on the back end of a truck."[79]

Ruth, too, recalled the ordeal:

Our truck put us out, and we were told that we would have to walk the rest of the way. We felt sure by then we were being taken to Manila. We knew that we had many miles yet to go, and the sun was broiling hot—temperature above 100. We were sick, without water, and without food. We struggled along as best we could, carrying the one suitcase that we had, leaning on each other for strength, trying to help each other down the road, as we tried to make our way on to what we were feeling sure was Manila. By mid-afternoon it was obvious that we could not go on. We were sick; we were just prostrate. Many people were not able to even stand or sit up, so they herded us over into a grove of trees off of the road and told us just to stay there until they decided what to do with us.

It was at the end of one military command and the beginning of another military command, as the Japanese army was divided. But sometime along after dark they did come with trucks and took us into the trucks again.... We rode on down the road, slowly making our way as best we could in the dark with practically no lights on anywhere. We got down to Clark Field and were held up a long time there at Clark Field, taken on down the road, and then just before dawn we were taken on into the city of Manila, through the streets, and then through some big, tall, concrete walls.[80]

Finally, they arrived at Bilibid Prison, in the center of Manila:

About four o'clock in the morning we pulled into the city of Manila and were taken to Bilibid Penitentiary. We went in through the main gates of the prison and were taken to the hospital area, which was a vacant building that

---

[79] Hugo Culpepper, tape.
[80] Ruth Culpepper, tape.

had been condemned before the war. The third floor had been dismantled, windows and doors taken out. It was just a shell of a reinforced concrete building with the first and second floors remaining. The 500 of us were put in that one building. We had to improvise the best living conditions we could.[81]

Bilibid was an old Spanish prison that had been condemned before the war as unfit for human habitation. The internees were moved into the so-called Hospital Building, built in 1908. The first arrivals had begun the process of cleaning it up as best they could, with nothing but their hands with which to clean. They had been told that mattresses would be provided, but the mattresses they found were not only alive with bedbugs but also contaminated with blood, urine, and diarrhea stains. Most of them had to be discarded. The filth was indescribable. Rats scurried in and out of piles of trash, dirt, and garbage in the building. Before long, however, the beds, toilets, rooms, and yard were cleaned as well as possible, and a camp routine was established.[82]

They were inside a compound about 200 by 600 feet, surrounded by thick walls. Only the shell of the building remained. A tin sink outside, ten to fifteen feet long with faucets, was the only water supply for bathing and cooking for the 500 prisoners. A homemade masonry stove stood nearby. Roofless outdoor toilets left by the previous inhabitants provided a latrine. The prisoners had to straddle a sloping trough with their feet on rough wooden beams on either side. Ten to twelve feet long, it could accommodate several people at a time.[83] The oppressive heat in Manila made the living conditions even more miserable.

Guards were kept at the gate. No news from the outside reached the internees. For three weeks the internees at Santo Tomas did not know they were there. The food situation grew even worse. From 300 grams a day the ration was dropped to 200 grams a day per person.[84] Their meat allotment for January was the snout and ears of a pig butchered by the guards. They were reduced to eating mush made from moldy cornmeal with black specks of weevils and the leaves of *talinum*, an edible plant that grew in the courtyard.[85] Slowly, they were starving to death, and many had symptoms

---

[81] Hugo Culpepper, tape.

[82] *Santo Tomas Internment Camp, 1942–45*, with a foreword by Gen. Douglas MacArthur (Limited Private Edition, Frederic H. Stevens, 1946) 322.

[83] Miles, *Captive Community*, 153–56.

[84] Ibid.

[85] Ibid., 159.

of beriberi due to vitamin B-1 deficiency. Another epidemic of dysentery broke out.

Rows of crosses lined the cemetery in the northeast corner of the compound, and soldiers' dog tags hung on crude crosses. Ruth and Hugo brought back the dog tags of two Arkansas soldiers and returned them to their families. Hugo fashioned a bed for Fern, nailing legs to the corners of a frame of chicken wire Fern had found and claimed. In return, she gave Hugo her mattress, since he had been sleeping on the bare concrete floor.[86]

They learned that they were not the only residents at Bilibid:

> We found out through our camp commander that across these twenty-foot walls were the American military men who had made the march of death [the Bataan death march], who were the remains of the military. These were the men so badly crippled, so badly sick, that they could not get out of their beds, or if they did they had to hobble on a piece of stick or something for a crutch. They were the men unfit for work, and therefore they had not been shipped out to Japan for work and labor camps in other parts of the Japanese empire. We heard that these men were there. We weren't sure of it, so we wanted to communicate with them, but we were not allowed to communicate in an ordinary way.
>
> Therefore, having had this wonderful choir to sing with us through our experience, we decided that we would give a concert on Saturday afternoon.[87]

The choir stood on an outdoor balcony on the second floor that extended over the front steps of the building.

> So that Saturday afternoon, everybody lined up out there. The choir began singing and sang only the songs that an American sings, like "Way Down Upon the Suwanee River," "Carry Me Back to Old Virginny," "My Old Kentucky Home," and all of these old, old favorites, even one or two football songs—things like this that would identify us indisputably as Americans, and not only that, there were women singing. You should have heard the catcalls that came across those walls, the shrill whistles, the claps, the noise. After we were liberated, some of these men told us it was the first woman's voice they

---

[86] Ibid., 156.
[87] Ruth Culpepper, tape.

had heard in over three years, and then to hear an American woman singing just did something to them, so we got our point across that day. They knew that we were next door, and we felt sure that they were next door to us, though no communications were allowed....

Through talking to our guards, Carl Eschbach found out that these men next door had yellow-kernel corn to eat. They had a little wood given to them to cook that hard-kernel corn, about the hardness of popcorn. No wonder they were dying in such numbers, so we asked the Japanese if they would give us the privilege to use our little coffee grinder that we had salvaged from the camp up there to grind their corn to make cornmeal mush like we were doing for ourselves. They said all right, and so we kept the grinder going twenty-four hours a day. My husband and I ground corn from midnight till two o'clock in the morning. That was the time that we were assigned to grind corn so that the boys next door, some 800 of them, could have food that would be much better for their intestines than it had been.[88]

After they started grinding the corn for the American soldiers, they noticed that the death rate, which had been about fifteen a day, was cut in half.[89]

Under these most desperate circumstances, Hugo still made time for his daily study of his Greek New Testament:

By then we were so weak—I had lost forty pounds, my wife thirty pounds. We had to lie down on the concrete floor to sleep. There was no bedding of any kind. By then we were all one big family. Everybody was just sleeping side by side, wherever you wanted, and we had to lie down about seventeen hours out of every twenty-four. We only had enough physical energy to be up about seven hours out of every twenty-four, and I remember early in the morning, when I would get up, I would go outside by myself and sit down at the back of a row of three outdoor cells on the curbing there, within about fifty feet of the wooden crosses that marked the grave sites of the military prisoners who had been there for three years.

---

[88] Ibid.

[89] Brian W. Burton, "Hugo Culpepper: Still a Seeker after Truth," *Western Recorder* (30 May 1989): 7.

Inside Bilibid. From Miles, *Captive Community*, 157. Used with permission.

During that month of January 1945, I studied through the Gospel of John once again for thirty to forty-five minutes every morning. I read along with it, as a commentary on John, the book by William Temple entitled *Readings in the Gospel of St. John*. I think I had the most profoundly probing spiritual experiences during that month of Bible study, under those conditions, that I have ever had. I think I have never felt God to be nearer, nor more real to me, than I did under those conditions. I had come to the point that physically it didn't matter too much. As long as I still lived by this profound trust in God and love for others, bitterness could not obsess my soul. It mattered not to me what men could do so long as I was in close fellowship with God.[90]

Against that somber background of the issues of time and eternity, Hugo said,

"I discovered once again in the Gospel of John what I came to see as the true nature of life, of real life. In John 17:3, I had read, 'This is eternal life, that

---

[90] Hugo Culpepper, tape.

they should know thee, the only true God.' I came to see that an experiential knowledge of God is life, absolutely and eternally."[91]

In the copy of Temple's *Readings in St. John's Gospel* that he was reading that day, Hugo underlined the following comments on John 17:3: "Eternity cannot be too long for our finite spirits to advance in knowledge of the infinite God.... If a man once knows the Spirit within him, the source of all his aspiration after holiness, as indeed the Spirit of Jesus Christ within himself, as none other than the Spirit of the Eternal and Almighty God, what more can he want? *This is the eternal life.*"[92]

During January the internees regularly saw formations of American bombers fly over them on their way to Grace Park Field and other targets. One morning they watched in horror as one of the planes was hit by anti-aircraft fire and crashed.[93] A few days later one of the guards informed the internees that American forces had landed at Lingayen Gulf, about 125 miles north of Manila. Then, Ruth recalled, they received an unusual message:

> We had no other contact with them [the military prisoners], except one Saturday afternoon a strange thing happened. Actually, it was Friday afternoon of this week, a strange thing happened, because over the wall came a rock, and on the rock was a piece of paper, and this had never happened before, but we heard—it went through our camp—that a note had come, to be ready for liberation at any time. That was all the note said, "liberation at any time." Well, naturally this buzzed through our camp and raised our hopes greatly, though we had nothing to base it on.
>
> We later found out that they also had made a homemade radio in their camp. One of our friends that we later found out was in that camp had lost a leg there on Bataan, and in his wound, where the leg had been taken off at the hip, they put a piece of a radio and bandaged it over so that this young man knew that there was a radio, because in his wound he brought part of the radio. They took it when they all got into camp, assembled it, and over it made something like a baseball

---

[91] Hugo Culpepper, "The Bible and Religious Authority," tape recording of sermon in Southern Seminary chapel, 22 October 1980. Full text below, pp.329-34.

[92] William Temple, *Readings in St. John's Gospel* (London: Macmillan, 1940) 2:310.

[93] Patton, "Our Concentrated Life," 22.

game, one of the games that they play now where they make a lot of racket and all, so that each night they would gather around, make a lot of noise while one man climbed underneath and found San Francisco radio and got the news. Sometimes the Japanese guards played the game while an American was underneath, listening to the radio. The Americans told them that a man had to be underneath to make the game work. They found out through that radio that the Japanese were fighting the Americans at the river just outside Manila.[94]

The *Immanuel Record*, the church newspaper published by Immanuel Baptist Church, reported that the families had received brief messages on postcards from Hugo and Ruth (written in April 1944):

> Ruth weighs 119 lbs.; Hugo 152. Just permitted to live together. Have a shanty of our own. Ruth teaching kindergarten. Hugo teaching New Testament class. Ruth C. Culpepper.
>
> . . . .
>
> Received first letter of December 1942. Also letter from Warren, Swilley, Edmonds, Mathis. Preaching series sermons four Sundays September. Weight 144. Hugo Culpepper.
>
> . . . .
>
> Hugo and I are living together in one room having moved July 13. Much more comfortably situated. Taking Vitamin B2 for sore mouth. Weight 110. Ruth Culpepper.[95]

Almost simultaneously, a letter came from a lady who had recently been repatriated from their camp. She recalled that Hugo and Ruth

> took their full share of the load of the camp.... He and others of the younger missionaries did volunteer for the less popular jobs.... Mr. Culpepper also kept up his studying—I cannot imagine either of them happy without that—and I remember well seeing the two of them sitting out in the open working at Greek together, and plainly finding satisfaction in getting ahead with it.... I do have a very clear memory, however, of seeing her going quietly about the camp, always cheerful and with a kind word for everyone, and of seeing them together at

---

[94] Ruth Culpepper, tape.
[95] *The Immanuel Record*, 18 January 1945.

every chance, and obviously happy in each other and their common study.[96]

Liberation, 5 February 1945

Finally, the moment they had been praying for came. On the evening of 3 February, they heard the rumble of tanks. It was the First Cavalry, 37th Division, and 4th Tank Battalion, less than 1,000 strong.[97] Their first objective was the liberation of the 3,000 internees at the Santo Tomas Camp. The Americans were unaware that the civilians had been transferred from Baguio, so they did not know there were Americans in the Bilibid Prison. Ruth recalled the following memories of that day:

> A very curious formation of planes came in. We had never seen a V-shaped formation of planes come at that time of day before. They came, and within fifteen to twenty minutes in came tanks, and they rumbled all around the streets. We could see, we could hear these tanks. One man chanced and went up above, on the open roof of our building. When he got up there, he heard one GI say to another, "We've been down this street before," and he realized that this was not only an American out there, but he was a Southerner, because of his accent. Therefore, we knew the Americans were there. We knew the pitched battle was going on outside the camp. Immediately the Japanese came in and rushed up to the top of our building to begin firing off of our building.[98]

---

[96] Letter from Mrs. Barbara M. Hayes, January 1945, quoted in *The Immanuel Record*, 18 January 1945, 1, 3; and *Arkansas Baptist*, 44,3 (18 January 1945): 1,9.

[97] *Santo Tomas Internment Camp*, 323.

[98] Ruth Culpepper, tape.

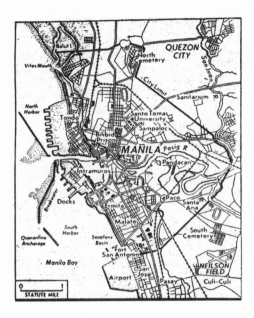

Manila. The *Courier-Journal,*
February 1945.

Fires flared. The whole block east of the prison was aflame. The guards ordered everyone on the second floor to move their bedding to the lower floor, while they fought from the roof of the building. All night the battle for Manila raged over the internees. Hugo described the liberation in the following words:

And then that eventful, dramatic, February the third, Saturday afternoon, 1945, came. About the beginning of dark we heard the rumbling of tanks. We went up, a few of us, and looked from the top floor of the building, through a window, across to the north, and saw the tanks, a force of 700 American military, entering the city of Manila. They had come from the invading force at Lingayen Gulf and were on a forced march, about thirty-six hours ahead of the main body of American troops.

Immediately, a group of them surrounded our prison, not knowing that there were civilian prisoners there, but only that there were military prisoners. The rest of the 700 went to surround Santo Tomas University, where the Manila people, totaling some 3,000, were interned. They made a break through the door and had a dramatic seizure of the building, with the people rushing upstairs and the guards on the second floor, and it was a dramatic showdown there.

A pitched battle began at our camp for the next seventeen hours. From eight o'clock that night we were all on the bottom floor, lying flat on the floor. The seventy guards were on the top of our building, sniping out over the wall at the American troops. There were machine gun nests surrounding the prison. They began to send up flares to try to get a line on the snipers, not knowing that we were in the building on the bottom floor. We were lying there, waiting for all eventualities.

They saved back some soybeans for an emergency, and the camp committee, who were like aldermen or mayor and aldermen in the camp, our fellow prisoners, decided that probably an emergency had come under those conditions and that we would eat those soybeans. So they took the autoclave that was used to sterilize sheets from one of the doctor's hospitals, used it as a pressure cooker, and cooked soybeans, and...in the morning they passed out, crawling around from one to the other, a serving of soybeans, as we were under the siege with the pitched battle going on outside.[99]

Just before noon, Carl Eschbach returned from the commandant's office and called everyone to meet in the foyer. Before he could speak, the Japanese soldiers who had been fighting on the roof marched past them and out the front gate to join the other Japanese troops in street-fighting against the Americans. When the gate closed behind the soldiers, Eschbach said, "I have our official release from the Japanese." After he read the statement, the internees burst out singing "God Bless America." Then someone produced an American flag the women had made back in their first camp—Camp John Hay. Ruth had sewn the Arkansas star on the flag. A Britisher, ironically, grabbed a bamboo pole and hoisted the flag on a balcony above them. The internees tried to sing the National Anthem, but were so choked up with emotion that they could not finish the first verse. There was a huge explosion nearby and shrapnel fell around them. The gate opened again, and a Japanese soldier advised them to take down the flag as it would only draw fire from the Japanese guns.[100]

The internees were in limbo. The Japanese had left, but the Americans did not know they were there, and the battle for Manila raged around them. All that day the battle raged over them as they watched the city burn. Fern Harrington Miles described their first meeting with American GIs:

---

[99] Hugo Culpepper, tape.
[100] Miles, *Captive Community*, 161–63.

Before the day was over, U.S. soldiers accidentally stumbled upon us. That evening when infantrymen of the 37th division were looking for a place to spend the night, they heard POWs inside Bilibid talking. Thinking they were GIs, a soldier yelled, "How'd you guys get in there?"

"Never mind how we got in here. We want to know how in the hell do you get out of here! We've been trying for three years."

The American soldiers knocked out a boarded-up hole in the wall and came in.

The first two or three GIs who came into our compound looked petrified as women and girls swarmed around, hugging and kissing them. These shy country boys, who had not seen white women in thirty months of fighting in the Pacific, were totally unprepared for such a passionate welcome.[101]

Hugo was struck by the GIs' response to the prisoners, especially the children.

The next morning, the American soldiers began to come into the camp. The first soldiers who came into our prison area were Ohio national guardsmen. They were big six-foot-three, six-foot-five men who had come up, island hopping across the Pacific. They had not seen any prisoners, and as they stood there and saw the emaciated bodies of 500 of us—down to three-fourths of what we weighed when we went in—big tears began to roll down their cheeks. Some of them had not seen an American woman or child for more than three years. Some of them had candy in their pockets, and some of the children had been born in the first months in the camp and had never seen candy. These Ohio national guardsmen had them reach their hands into their pocket and take out a piece of candy and put it into their mouth and watched the expression on the child's face as they tasted a sweet for the first time. Then they told them to reach in and take a handful.

That night, the fifth of February 1945—was my wife's birthday. We were rejoicing because the American army had finally arrived. It was about 5:30; we were sitting with some friends there. We heard the first sound of demolition bombs. Then we learned the Japanese were setting off demolition bombs as

---

[101] Ibid., 164.

they retreated, and the fire began to loom up. We were in the path of the fire [that came] through the streets of the city of Manila.[102]

To celebrate their release and Ruth's birthday, Cleo and Fern baked a cake, but they had none of the normal ingredients. They used panocha syrup for sugar and milk, rice flour and a little flour ground from the roots of the elephant's ear plant, a cup of rice gruel, cinnamon, for shortening three tablespoons of Red Cross unscented face cream, and some powdered "Japanese Stomach Pills" (for sodium bicarbonate). The cake turned out surprisingly well. Enjoying the celebration on their bunks, they scarcely noticed the din of explosions as the Japanese were setting fires and blowing up buildings around them. Word passed that there were explosives in a tunnel under their building and that they were to evacuate immediately, taking only a bedroll and change of clothing. Leaving the cake half-eaten, they hastily grabbed things to take.[103] Hugo grabbed his big suitcase that had his books.

Hugo later recalled the events of that day and the following days many times as he recounted their experience for churches back home:

The next morning they came in in greater numbers. This was on Monday, the fifth of February, which was my wife's birthday. We knew that her name would be on the prayer calendar of people in our churches back home and that they would be praying for us and our safety during that particular day. About five o'clock in the afternoon of that day we heard demolition bombs, which were set off by the retreating Japanese in street-to-street fighting. They began fires, and the flames began to sweep down upon our prison camp.

Immediately, word came from the American command, for we were then behind the American lines, that we were to leave and go out the back gate of the prison. As many as could walk, walked toward the north, down the one highway. Those who were too weak to walk, they would come in and get. And so they came in the jeeps and trucks and ambulances and took out the 800 military and the 500 Americans.[104]

The military POWs were taken first, then the civilians. They walked for two or three blocks, marveling at the new army vehicles and the clean-cut, robust American GIs who lined the streets.

---

[102] Hugo Culpepper, tape.
[103] Miles, *Captive Community*, 164–65.
[104] Hugo Culpepper, tape.

I was still able to walk and began walking with others, and when they got the rest out, they came back part way and carried us on out to field headquarters, which was at the Ang Tibay shoe factory, an empty shoe factory where they had set up field headquarters temporarily.

That night we mixed and milled among the troops who were off duty. We had some k-rations to eat—the first food we had had. It tasted wonderful to us. We could not understand why the soldiers were griping about the k-rations. We were with them there all night. We heard the communication sound truck, which was picking up the short wave broadcast from San Francisco of the broadcast to the American people of the release of the prisoners and of the city of Manila being on fire and all that was going on. We were standing there watching the flame on the horizon and being a part of all the excitement as we heard the sound truck.

The next morning—we had not slept all night under the excitement—we heard that they had cooked too much oatmeal and that if we would go down to the field kitchen we could get a bowl of hot oatmeal. So we went down and had the first hot, prepared American food that we had had. Then they said that there was no place to put us, so they took us back into Manila, back to Bilibid Prison, under sniper fire that day, and we went back into the same prison area. The Filipinos who were behind the American lines thought that we were being shipped back to America, and they had come in and looted our suitcases and what we had left behind, so we had nothing left that we had not carried with us for that overnight leaving of our site.[105]

Had Hugo not taken his big suitcase full of books, they too would have been lost.

The experience of mixing with the American soldiers that night led Hugo to reexamine his views about war. In a 1969 article titled "War and the Christian Conscience—One Man's Struggle," he described the intense soul-searching he experienced for the next three months:

The life and work of Jesus Christ impressed on me an ethic of absolute love. All that he was and did was determined by his love, it seemed to me. As his disciple, I believed that my life should be shaped by this love also. I rejected the term pacifist, because it smacked of political pressure. But I did feel a deep conviction that I must be a conscientious objector to war as a follower of Jesus Christ....

---

[105] Ibid.

Throughout the three years and two months of our imprisonment, I found my conviction as a conscientious objector to be a great source of strength. It helped save me from self-pity, bitterness, and hate. The love of God, which led me to love all men, both captors and captives, kept life sweet and meaningful, even though we lived on a starvation diet and I lost forty pounds. It also gave me courage when my conviction was put to the test....

My convictions were unchanged until the end of imprisonment. On February 3, 1945, the American Army returned to Manila. Two days later we were liberated in the midst of the battle for the city. We were taken to the American field headquarters at an empty shoe factory five miles north of the city. Here I stayed up all night mixing with off-duty American troops and watching the army pour into the battle as it moved from the north down the highway toward Manila.

In the midst of this experience, I gained a new viewpoint. I recognized war as the result of the sins of men. But I saw that it was the result of my sin also. Because of the fact of social solidarity, I was inextricably involved. I had lived a way of life, along with all others, that resulted in war. What right did I have to stand aside now?

If I could transcend society and live on an island in complete isolation, perhaps I could. But this was impossible. I also felt a close identification with these young Americans who were no more possessed by demonic spirits than I. They belonged to me and I to them....

This was the beginning of an intense struggle which went on within me for the next three months. I came to feel that the Christian faith, based on an ethic of absolute love was impractical, but that nominal Christianity as popularly held was irrelevant. This left me on the horns of a dilemma. I came near to rejecting Christianity. While the storm raged in the top of my mind, somehow the grace of God in the bottom of my heart carried me through.

I have never resolved the conflict. I live on under the ethical tension of what is and what ought to be. I have not been a conscientious objector since that struggle. But I understand and respect those who are. I still believe that Jesus lived by an ethic of absolute love. I hope I shall always feel the pull of his spirit. I have no longer any basis to be a conscientious objector. I am involved whether I want to be or not.[106]

The next day General Douglas MacArthur came to see them and promised to send them all home soon. The army medics checked each

---

[106] Published in *The Southern Baptist Chaplain*, 1, 3 (July–September 1969): 1, 4, 5, 8.

internee. Hugo weighed 128 pounds and Ruth 98 pounds. American Red Cross workers brought mail from home and allowed them to write one letter each. Ruth wrote:

Dearest Folks:
We have another opportunity to write to you. The Red Cross has just come in with magazines for us. I have just finished reading a Jan. 15th *Time*, which is the first magazine we have had in over three years. We feel like Rip Van Winkle just waking up and finding out things. We did not know who the Vice President was until Sunday night when we talked to our first American soldiers. We assumed that Roosevelt was still president because in almost every conference the committee had with the Japanese they referred to Roosevelt by using all kinds of dirty names. It is a wonderful feeling to be able to talk news without setting a person to keep watch while you whispered what few rumors you could pool together. As I said in the letter yesterday, freedom and security are the two greatest joys we are enjoying. Freedom to talk without fear of being overheard, freedom to move about (only in the compound now) without being heavily guarded with soldiers and fixed bayonets; security from bombing—knowing it is our own planes, security of knowing the right army is protecting us, security of three meals a day and no long period of actual starvation facing you—all these things create such a sense of relief it is hard to describe to you.
I'm terribly sorry we have caused you so much worry, but I truthfully say that the experiences which we have had have so deepened and strengthened our outlook on life, and taught us what things are worthwhile and of lasting value, that it has been worth all the suffering we have had to undergo. Our faith in the Lord has been greatly strengthened. I think both of us feel that it was God who led us here to this place, and we feel that He has taken care of us through it. This was our third choice, and it seemed that circumstances over which we had no control sent us here. As we look back over it, and even as we were in the worst of it, we had the sense of security in feeling we were where God would have us be. I think no matter whatever we do in life, life will always be richer because we have gone through this. Our appreciations have changed considerably, and we have learned to appreciate just the simple things of life in a way we'll never forget.
We mentioned yesterday that all our possessions could be put into two suitcases, and this is true so far as we know. Our landlady had our sterling, and silver service, pictures, strongbox, and a few other things

in her care and when we last saw her (December 1943), these things were still safe even after other things had been looted. However, in October 1944 we heard that all residences on Luzon Hill were emptied and the whole hill made into Japanese hospitals. We do not know whether she was able to get our stuff out or not. Even if she did, we understood that when the Americans found out we were no longer there they just cut loose and leveled the city; and also that the Japanese burned it about as badly as the one we are in now. Consequently, we do not expect to find anything there. Then too, we will no doubt be shipped out long before we would have the opportunity to go back up there.

As far as our health, we are in comparatively good shape. My last blood count showed a hemoglobin of 65 percent in the mountains, which at sea level is about 55 percent. My B-1 deficiency has showed up in my sinus, but we are being given tremendous dosages of B-1 each day now. My feet—due to improper shoeing—have given me trouble. Both arches are broken. As for teeth—in October 1944 I had to have a jaw tooth pulled, and at that time I had one very bad cavity. I have not had the opportunity to have that fixed. Due to vitamin A deficiency our eyes are weaker, but nothing noticeable. Hugo finds reading at night impossible, but his glasses need changing. His B-1 deficiency seems to have caused digestive disturbances. He was actually laid out the week the Americans came, but with good food now for four days his digestion has returned to normal. The difference the mood makes is amazing. Since coming here we had been spending from 14 to 16 hours a day in bed because we were so weak we didn't have the energy to sit up. Now we are absolutely bubbling over with energy—going to bed about eleven and can hardly wait until daylight to get up. We have had no light since coming here, so daylight hours are precious—and especially now with new magazines to read.

To be home again with you is going to be our greatest joy. We have got to have rest and quiet for a while, and there is no prospect of having it before we get there because things are quite hot and noisy now which makes things keep at a keen pitch of excitement. I can hardly realize that David is a college graduate now and Mary is working. I do hope we can see Billy before leaving—if he's near here or in these islands. Love to all of you. The Major said today that two weeks would see us out of here. We are counting the days.

Ruth[107]

---

[107] Ruth Culpepper, letter to Mr. and Mrs. William F. Cochrane, 8 February 1945.

Their sense of security was shattered shortly before dawn on 15 February, when a Japanese plane dropped a bomb just outside their wall. As Ruth later wrote, "This bomb hit about a hundred feet from where we were sleeping. Two of the boys had been up and eaten some fudge that we had made in a tin can, using chocolate k-rations. They gave us the sugar and chocolate. They were killed after they went to sleep that night, and never woke up again. We were really touched by this. One boy had said that his favorite hymn was 'Peace, Perfect Peace.' " [108]

One day in February, Hugo and Ruth, the Dyers, Cleo Morrison, and Fern Harrington hitched a ride on a military vehicle to visit the wounded at the 71st Evacuation Hospital. As they went from tent to tent, Cleo introduced herself by saying, "I'm Cleo Morrison from Telephone, Texas. Do you know what Texas is famous for?" After a pause she answered, "Oil wells, white-faced Herefords, and beautiful women." A GI from Arkansas looked her over from head to toe and then drawled, "Well, she ain't no oil well." Hugo and Ruth enjoyed telling this story for years.

On 20 February, Mrs. Cochrane, Ruth's mother, hardly felt well enough to get up. After tending to her, Ruth's father went to work as usual. At 9:00 A.M. he received the following telegram from the Lerch Provost Marshal General in Washington, D.C.: "Am pleased to inform you that information received indicates the rescue by our forces of Hugo H. and Ruth C. Culpepper physical condition good formerly interned at Santo Tomas stop you may send free through American Prisoner of War Information Bureau this office one only twenty-five word message stop."

Word of their release spread quickly. Mr. Cochrane shared the story with family members in a letter:

You can rest assured that we lost no time sending the twenty-five word message. Immediately, I called Agnes and gave her the information, and a miracle was performed—she got well right now. In fact, the poor girl had worried practically all night about Ruth and Hugo.... It is my understanding from talking to those who have been in these Japanese camps, that on account of the rotten condition of their food and etc. the internees get just as wormy as little puppies, and that they have to go to the hospital and be dewormed, after which they will make the return trip home....

---

[108] Ruth Culpepper, handwritten annotation in Miles, *Captive Community*, 171.

I don't think I have ever seen anything travel over the city, county, state, and even adjoining states like the news of the rescue of Ruth and Hugo. We have had calls even from out of state. It was in both of the Little Rock papers and broadcast over the radio.

We went to prayer meeting last Wednesday night and there were nearly three hundred people there. Dr. Wade called Agnes and me up and made the announcement, and before he finished he was half crying. He called on Agnes to say something, she spoke a few words and quit half crying. He then called on me, and between him and Agnes and approximately three out of four people crying, I had to quit and handed Dr. Wade the telegram, and he read it. The thing that got me most was an old judge out in the audience who was crying and just shaking all over almost. The same thing happened in a meeting at Pine Bluff, Arkansas, last night.[109]

Mr. Culpepper received an identical telegram at the same time. An hour later, he wired back: "Prayers answered with word of rescue you and Ruth and health good both families well anxiously waiting more news from each and return home love." The same day he wrote Professor Armstrong at Baylor and relayed the good news to him, saying in closing, "I think this is one of the happiest letters I have ever written."

Back in Manila, Hugo and Ruth remained in Bilibid Prison.

We were kept there the next six weeks. During the battle for the city of Manila all the artillery went over our prison into the walled city where the Japanese made their last stand. We were fed American food, however. They began to bring in steaks, fruit cocktail, powdered eggs, and all the good food that we had dreamed of. Some of us gained a pound a day for the first three weeks. This Flory, mentioned earlier, was still in good organic physical condition, and he literally gained a pound a day for twenty-one days. He looked like a bicycle tire being pumped up. Every morning his face would be filled out just a little bit more.

At the end of six weeks, they flew us out on DC-3s, I believe they were, with the bucket seats, down to the island of Leyte, where the Americans had occupied the island of Leyte before they had gotten to Luzon. The men were put in an army replacement center near Tacloban on the island of Leyte, and

---

[109] Mr. William F. Cochrane, letter to family, 23 February 1945.

the women were put in convalescent hospitals on the beaches twenty-five miles down the island.[110]

The army began moving the internees out of Bilibid by lottery. Hugo and Ruth were flown out on 15 March. Hugo remembered the events.

By the middle of March the city had been secured, and we were flown out by planes to the island of Leyte, there to spend the next month in convalescent hospitals at the army replacement center near the town of Tacloban, waiting for empty troop ships to take us back to America. This was the time when troops were being sent out for the Okinawa invasion, and we were to return on one of the empty ships. I remember very well an experience during that period of a month there when I was standing in line one day waiting to go into an army dining hall, realizing that my aluminum tray would be loaded down with more good American food than I would possibly be able to eat. I noticed to my left at the other end of the dining hall a line of hungry Filipinos forming, waiting for us Americans to eat all we wanted and then to go out and scrape into these garbage cans a great deal of what we had been served. Our stomachs had shrunken to the size of a clinched fist, and we could eat only a very little and were not able to eat more, though we continued to be hungry in every cell of our body—arms and legs—and not just in the pit of our stomach.

As I thought about this, it seemed to me that the two worlds of our time had come to a meeting point within my own self. My body was still identified, as was my spirit, with the hungry, suffering people of the Orient. A few weeks before we would have been better fed to have had that garbage than the food which we were eating in the prison, but my stomach had already returned home to America and was being fed the finest food available.[111]

On 16 April they sailed for home on board the Dutch ship *Japara*.

We were placed on the empty troop ships after one month, my wife and me, and started back across the Pacific to America. There was a Japanese submarine on our tail, and we had to take a zig-zag course, trying to shake the submarine, lest we be torpedoed.

I did not know much about what it was like in the navy—though I had been a midshipman in the naval academy, preparing for a naval career when I was called to the ministry—but in the course of that voyage there were gallon cans

---

[110] Hugo Culpepper, tape.
[111] Ibid.

of fruit juice, tomato juice, orange juice, and so on put out on the deck as we neared San Francisco, and we asked what they were going to do with them, and they said, "We had too much. We dare not take supplies back in because they will not give us a full quota the next time we go out, so we are going to throw them overboard." Well, we just could not stand to think of food being thrown away, and we asked them if they would mind if we drank it, and they said no. So the repatriates who were on the ship—a large number of us—had a fruit juice party that night, and we drank most of those gallons of fruit juice that were there on the deck, just simply to keep them from being thrown away.

We pulled in to San Francisco [on 9 May] dressed in GI clothing. My shoes were a size ten. I normally wear a size seven, but these were size ten high-top shoes, and the top of the shoe is what kept my foot in the shoe, as it was laced tight. We had baggy GI trousers and coats and so forth as we went a-shore there, and had to wait for about three days to get a train back across the continent. We arrived in our hometown of Little Rock, Arkansas, on Mother's Day, May 13, 1945, for a glorious homecoming.[112]

They sat up the whole way to Little Rock. The services at Immanuel Baptist Church let out early that day so that everyone could go down to the train station to meet them. The next Sunday evening, 20 May, Hugo preached at Immanuel, sharing for the first time their experiences in the concentration camp. For the *Commission* magazine the next fall, Hugo summed up his response as follows:

After thirty-seven months of hunger and insecurity in a Japanese intern-ment camp, one returns to America with a deepened sense of stewardship and responsibility. We had never understood, as we do now, what it means to be "hungry—thirsty—a stranger—naked—sick—in prison"! Human misery is no longer oceans away from us; it is constantly pressing at the door of our heart for relief. If we can always feel the flood tide of human need over-whelming us, and share with others this sense of urgency, we shall have no regrets. As American Christians, repatriation does not bring renewed oppor-tunity for self-indulgence; it means liberation for another chance at life—a life which must give itself to a needy world.[113]

As he retold the story often in the ensuing years, he ended with the following reflections.

---

[112] Ibid.

[113] "I Perish with Hunger," *The Commission*, 8, 9 (October 1945): 9.

And then we came home again, and yet one can never completely come home from such an experience as that. My first reaction was one of gratitude: gratitude to God for the sparing of our lives and for the privilege of returning to America, which I saw now as being an island of luxury in a sea of desperate need. We arrived home on Mother's Day, which was Sunday May the thirteenth, and it was a great privilege to be home again with our loved ones and members of our family.

I had a second reaction, though, after a time, which was one of an almost overwhelming sense of responsibility for the stewardship of life and talent and energy and opportunity, and I came to see that we could never again take life for granted, but that God's goodness to us gave us the responsibility of using that which He gave us, both materially and spiritually, as a means for bringing blessing and the knowledge of God into the light of others. And so since then it has seemed to me that in many respects we have been living beyond the death line, for other friends were left behind who did not have a second opportunity at life and ministry and service....

My colleague, Rufus Gray, lies still buried under the soil of the Philippines. I will never know why in the providence of God my life was spared and his was taken, but it has always given me the responsibility that somehow I must do twice as much in life for the glory of God.[114]... I had some fellow internees whose souls shriveled within them because they did not know the love of God in Christ. They were left to themselves, and they were seized by bitterness and hatred and ill will. As I would pass their bunks on the floor, I could hear one particular man cursing under his breath his enemies, the Japanese. He was literally eating out his soul, and he was not qualified to live after he was released. And so I have felt, coming back to an island of luxury in a world of tremendous need, gratitude to God and a sense of stewardship and responsibility for the gift of life that is overwhelming. We Americans, who have spiritual freedom, the opportunity to know and to react to the love of God in Christ, and the gospel, have a greater responsibility probably than any other people on earth, to use that which God gives us for his glory.... By the grace of God we have tried to take advantage of every opportunity since those days because of

---

[114] It is probably more than coincidence that this sentiment echoes a story Prof. A. J. Armstrong used to tell his students when he introduced Richard Conwell's book *Acres of Diamonds* in his classes. Dr. Conwell was "the only son of a widowed mother, whose friend volunteered to substitute for him in army service. The friend lost his life, and Richard Conwell said, 'Now I must do two men's work.' " Lois Smith Douglas, *Through Heaven's Back Door: A Biography of A. Joseph Armstrong* (Waco: Baylor University Press, 1951) 74.

His goodness to us and because He had kept His promise, "and lo I will be with you every day until the end of the ages."[115]

---

[115] Hugo Culpepper, tape, and a second, undated, tape recording.

Chapter 4

Medical School

"Ah, but a man's reach should exceed his grasp,
Or what's a heaven for?"[1]

Returning to the United States brought welcomed rest, nourishment, and time with family. Hugo and Ruth were still citizens of two worlds, however, America and the Orient, and that tension within them continued to shape their thoughts and plans for the future. The correspondence with close friends that they saved from these years vividly reflects their friendships and their commitment to finding God's leadership for the next chapter of their lives. Part of their time was spent in hearing news from close friends who had been caught in the war elsewhere.

Their friend Paul Geren wrote to them on and shared some of his experiences during the war, while he waited to hear from them:

> I began teaching in Judson College, Rangoon, in November 1941. I was very happy and hopeful. On my birthday, December 5, came the news of the death of my brother John of an obstruction in his intestinal tract. You must remember him, the youngest. It was a shattering blow. I have never had such an experience before or since, though some since have partaken of its quality. When the war came a couple of days later, I was insensible to it. And partly insensible to the bombings of Rangoon which began two days before Christmas, 1941.
>
> The College was closed and the students dispersed. Many of the missionaries began to come to India. Dr. Seagrave, a medical missionary in the Baptist Mission in Burma, organized a mobile hospital to help in an emergency. I joined along with others of the

---

[1] Robert Browning, "Andrea del Sarto," *The Complete Poetic and Dramatic Works of Robert Browning*, ed. Horace E. Scudder (Boston: Houghton Mifflin Co., 1895) 346.

College, as an ambulance driver. In time we were assigned to the Chinese troops who had come into Burma to fight. I was in a couple of months of action. It was full of despair. We were being hopelessly beaten, the planes in the air were those of the enemy, the Chinese were not equipped and were suffering terrible slaughter. At the end we found a Japanese encirclement about to close about us, and we began to retreat—in vehicles as long as the roads held out, and after that on foot. We walked across the mountains between Burma and India in a party led by General Stillwell who was the American Commander in this theater.

For the first four months in India, June–September, 1942, the hospital unit I had joined in Burma worked with Indians and Chinese coming from Burma. This time the suffering and death were repeated, but the cause was disease rather than enemy action. All the people who had walked over from Burma were ravaged by starvation, exhaustion, and disease.

In September 1942 I was offered a commission by the army and at the same time the American Presbyterian Mission invited me to teach economics in Forman Christian College, Lahore, Punjab, India. I debated this and decided to stay in missionary work, especially since there was no immediate prospect of active war in this theater. I had a very profitable year of teaching Indian boys. I learned a great deal about this sad, inexhaustibly complex country. But as the war began to speed up, I began to be haunted by the feeling of being left out and enjoying a comfort to which I was not entitled by our times. (I don't know whether this is a valuable sentiment or not—certainly both of us have been more or less chronically affected by it.) At any rate, I joined the army in India, went back in medical work as a private and served for ten months with Chinese infantry in North Burma. It was a sad experience and I was afraid or in some way miserable most of the time. There were some mean little personality conflicts to rob the tragedy of war of some of its dignity and make it considerably harder to bear. I can elaborate this some day, though it is not worth it....

I don't know what I shall do in the future. It is problematical whether Judson College will ever be reopened. I have been asked to come back to Forman Christian College. I have thought of working among the hill peoples in Burma. I have thought of going into politics. I should like to talk these things through with you.

In my spirit, I have had ups and downs and am more or less reconciled to this as the path the life of my particular spirit is going to play over. I have had some great insights of faith and some supreme moments. I have had others when I could believe or trust nothing. But I think I have only rarely doubted that the insights were truer than the doubts.[2]

Hendrix and Central, 1945–1946

Almost immediately, Hugo decided to pursue a medical degree. In this decision he was influenced both by his firsthand experience of the pressing need for doctors in the Orient and by the example of Albert Schweitzer, whom he held in high regard. Perhaps not altogether coincidentally, Dr. A. J. Armstrong was also enamored with Schweitzer.

A letter from M. T. (Theron) Rankin certified Hugo and Ruth's losses in the Philippines for a full payment of $1,000, and he added:

It was a joy to have you and Ruth in Richmond with us. You helped us greatly by your message as well as by the fine spirit of you and Ruth both. Since I have had more time to think about your plan to take medicine, I must admit that I feel a keen sense of loss in our plan for theological training in the Orient. You have superb qualities for that type of work. Even so, I could not try to persuade you against your definite feeling of leadership in making your plans to study medicine.

After you had spoken on Sunday night at Barton Heights Church, one of the men in the church in speaking to me said, "That man has got something; something which all of us tremendously need." I agreed with him fully that you do have "something." I could hope that there still may be a place for you to render what you have through our foreign mission program, but we shall leave that with you and our Lord. The whole world is in His program and wherever and however you serve, I know you will be serving in His plan.[3]

---

[2] Paul Geren, letter to Hugo and Ruth Culpepper, 3 April 1945. Paul Geren later became president of Stetson University, serving from 1967 until his death in an automobile accident in 1969. For more on Geren's experiences in Burma and India, see: Paul Geren, *Burma Diary* (New York: Harper, 1943); and, *The Pilgrimage of Peter Strong* (New York: Harper and Brothers, 1948).

[3] M. T. Rankin, letter to Hugo and Ruth Culpepper, 22 June 1945. See J. B. Weatherspoon, *M. Theron Rankin: Apostle of Advance* (Nashville: Broadman Press, 1958).

Hugo had planned to take his examinations in Greek New Testament at Southern Seminary in September but decided against doing so. W. O. Carver wrote:

> I am very sorry to have missed that interrupted visit of yours before your leaving Louisville. I appreciate your writing me of your decisions which I accept in all good faith, without any loss of my confidence and my love and in general of my hopes for you and Ruth. My prayer for you is in terms which I appropriate from Paul in 2 Thessalonians 1:11-12. And my prayer is a prayer of assured faith. I shall always be glad of my associations with you.
>
> I am particularly interested in your hopes toward February, which I trust will come to most satisfying fulfillment. You made an abiding impression upon Mrs. Carver and me in your Walnut Street talk and I know that the good of it will long influence most of the people who were there.[4]

While Hugo was making plans to study medicine at Hendrix College in Conway, Arkansas, he received an invitation to teach classes in missions and theology at Central College, the Baptist junior college for women in Conway. While teaching at Central during 1945–1946, Hugo took basic sciences—chemistry, physics, and zoology—at Hendrix and preached wherever he was invited on Sundays.

That fall, Hugo and Ruth received a letter from Robert Chang, a young Chinese man they had met at the Bible class in Peking. Although the English is a little rough in places, the sense of the letter is clear.

> My first dear Foreign Friends,
>
> As soon as the surrender of Japan was announced by the radio this noon, with extreme excitement over the fact that the world peace has been restored after all through strenuous dead-lock and the hope that sooner or later I can meet my friends again, especially Mr. and Mrs. Culpepper, who left me before the outbreak of this war, I intended to write a letter to you.... But I am not sure whether it could be received by you or not as I do not know which corner under the sky you are staying at, Arkansas, Manila or Chungking. I do hope that it will be able to forward to you and that you would give me an early response.

---

[4] W. O. Carver, letter to Hugo Culpepper, 9 August 1945.

God saved us from eternal disasters and helped us to subdue the treacherous and atrocious chauvinists. Suppose, if the atomic bomb were invented by our truculent enemy, would this world become a hell? We should try to build an everlasting fraternal and prosperous world under the law of mutual love decreed by our gracious Lord and to prevent any hostility in the future with all our might.

Be grateful to Americans who have offered very much to the enforcement of world peace that narrowly escaped from deterioration in the hands of aggressors. We appreciate your help to the Chinese for our emancipation from suffocating yoke. Let us pray for the intensifying of the friendship between America and China in the future.

I am still able to recall vividly the words you told me and the conditions in your room while I paid you the last visit before you left Peiping for Manila in the evening of March 9, 1941....

Though under frequent and censorial and scrupulous examinations, I still keep the "souvenir note" on which you both had kindly written some words full of friendly love. The "five-year diary" you gave me is kept well too. After coming back from your lodge in Tung Tan Pai Lou at the midnight of March 9, 1941, on the first page in that diary I wrote the following sentences: "This diary was given by Mr. and Mrs. Culpepper, two kind, gentle and friendly young American pastors, who with an enthusiastic heart came from the other hemisphere to spread the gospel message in this land, when we parted. It is a marvel that we made a good friendship through so short a time of acquaintance, as if our friendship is based on intuition. I very regret that we met so late and parted so hurriedly. I shall keep this diary through all my life as a token of possible human fraternity. God bless them wherever they go."...

Hoping this letter will be received by you, trusting you will please reply by return mail, thanking you in advance for your help and wishing we can meet again.

I remain,

yours very faithfully,

Robert Chang

P.S.: Today I met several American Marine Officers. When I told them I intend to send you a letter, they all would transfer it for me. Really, every American is talkative, frank and generous. If all people in the world would be so kind to each other, how could war happen, and the word "war" would be cancelled from the dictionary. This letter will be trusted to a certain officer.[5]

Subsequent letters from Chang reported deteriorating conditions in China.

On 2 March 1946, Alan, Hugo and Ruth's first child, was born in Little Rock, Arkansas. Theron Rankin wrote: "We are so glad that Richard Alan has come to your home to live and grow up. In the choice of his parents he has shown wise judgment at an early age. I hope he will make up for you some of the delayed happiness that you experienced in the years of internment."[6]

In a revealing letter, Hugo reflected on their year in Arkansas, their continuing commitment to missions, and their hopes to return to the Orient.

Dear Dr. Rankin:

We have been back in the United States a year, having arrived in May, 1945, which brings us to the end of our one-year furlough and to the time for our becoming inactive, suspended, or for resigning—according to whatever status or term you prefer.

This has been a good year in our lives; perhaps, it has been the happiest year we have ever known personally. Of course, the contrast with the three years in camp would make this likely, but it is true for deeper reasons than this. The deepest of these reasons is the satisfaction we have of following God's will for our lives as we see it. I have been engaged in the type of activity I would like to have all my life. Through the week most of my time has been given to scientific work, taking Chemistry, Physics, and Zoology at Hendrix College. Two hours a week I have been teaching a class of nineteen girls at Central College, which is our Baptist junior college for girls in Arkansas; the first semester I taught missions, and the second semester, theology. On Sundays I have been busy preaching in the Baptist churches all over the state, having been in forty-one different churches and spoken sixty-two times. This is the combination of activities I have always dreamed of following on the mission field. It has been encouraging to find it practicable, without one detracting too much from the efficiency of the other. (Of course, I realize that medical school for the next four years will be more demanding and temporarily make this combination impossible.) Somehow I feel that the breadth of ministry and the combination of services in the Kingdom's work more than compensates for

---

[5] Robert Chang, letter to Hugo and Ruth Culpepper, 15 August 1945.

[6] M. T. Rankin, letter to Hugo and Ruth Culpepper, 22 March 1946.

the limitations in each separate type of work. However, this year none of these activities has suffered from the demands of the others.

You will recall that I have always tried to express myself candidly and fully to you, without reservations, as for example in our conference in Shanghai in 1941, and in Richmond in 1945. In these two instances it was easier to do because we were speaking face to face. For the last few days I have been pondering the matter, seeking the best way to share our present state of mind with you. This is my conclusion: In February I was invited to be one of the thirteen speakers who were selected to make recordings at the radio station in Little Rock for the Arkansas Baptist Hour which was begun a few weeks ago on a statewide network. This invitation was accepted as an opportunity to bear witness to the worth and needs of the missionary enterprise as we now feel them. With that in mind, I sought to express myself just as I would like to do if I could sit down with Baptist people in small groups in their living rooms all over the state. (My hour is scheduled for the week of June 23rd.) At the time of writing this talk, I had no idea of sending it to you. However, it occurred to me recently that I had expressed the attitude of Ruth and myself toward missions better in this talk than I could in a few words in a letter to you. Because of that I am enclosing it now. After reading it, if you have the time, please return it at your convenience, as I would like to put it with some other papers to serve as a journal entry at this time of our lives.

Since the health of both of us is robust, I believe we shall have thirty years of service ahead of us, by the grace of God, in foreign missions, even after completing the medical training five years from now when I shall be 38 years old and Ruth 33 (and I prefer thirty years there with medicine, to thirty-five years there without it.) However, I realize that will put us above the age limit of the Board and it may be contrary to their policy to even consider us then. If we could, we would much prefer to continue on in the work under Southern Baptists to whom we feel obligation in many ways, and to whom we are grateful for their investment in us thus far. In any event, if God continues to lead us as He seems to be doing now, we believe there will be a place for us somewhere in foreign missions....

We have re-outfitted only to a minimum extent of personal clothing. The back salary and war losses fund are being budgeted to last as long as possible. We try to live on $125 a month, but with rising prices we are finding our monthly expenses nearer $150 a month, especially since the baby came. Even at this we have enough for the first three years, and we can borrow the money for the last two when the time comes if we cannot provide it ourselves....

We shall be praying for you as you plan for the years to come in China. I am gravely concerned about the future opportunity for work there, because of the question of Russia and her growing influence. By the time we are ready again, the trends will be more apparent perhaps. There are only two questions in our minds which might be a barrier for us in foreign mission work. One is the incurring of too large a debt, three to four thousand dollars, to be repaid from a missionary's salary. The other is the situation in the world which exerts tremendous pressure to shut us up into national units in a practical way. Against this the missionary enterprise is unalterably opposed. But it is a factor in any realistic thinking and planning. Or perhaps my idealism has not yet fully recovered from the strong dose of realism I experienced during those dark years. As Paul says (2 Timothy 4:2) we must "press forward, having good opportunity or having no opportunity." If in pressing forward we are ever completely shut out from China, I am glad to see our work is also growing throughout the world in other fields and in new directions in which we are also vitally interested.

In closing, I hope I have not been too presumptuous in taking so much of your valuable time with a long letter and the even longer enclosed talk which is a fuller expression of our minds now. Please remember that we deeply appreciate your patience, and gracious and generous attitude toward us. May all of these things turn out to be further investments in the work of the Kingdom.

Cordially yours,
Hugo Culpepper[7]

With this letter Hugo enclosed a copy of a sermon he preached for broadcast:

"The Missionary Motive"

Is there any good reason for being [a] missionary in such a world as ours? Are people who devote themselves to missions in one way or another, at home or abroad, engaged in a work of primary significance, or is their work of small consequence in a secular world which is preoccupied with other things to the exclusion of spiritual values? It is not enough for us who are disciples of the Christ to answer such questions as these with an energetic affirmative. We must be able to give a reason for the faith that is in us today! First of all, to others, who might be unsympathetic or even antagonistic to the Christian way of life expressed in the missionary enterprise. But most of all to ourselves, who

---

[7] Hugo Culpepper, letter to M. T. Rankin, 21 May 1946.

otherwise are likely to lose heart and go away discouraged by the overwhelming demands of a world in need.

We went out to the Orient in 1940 as missionaries, with certain motives which led us to prefer that way of life above any other. For five years (three of them in a concentration camp), these motives were adequate to sustain us in our hours of deepest need. I share them with you today, before going on to mention newly acquired convictions which are leading us through additional years of preparation with the purpose of returning to the Orient, hoping to have a larger usefulness there.

The center of the missionary motive is a personal experience of redemption through faith in Jesus Christ. Until one has experienced what God can do for a man in lifting him out of a self-centered and rebellious life, in giving him an inner peace and harmony, with a purpose and a power that makes living for Christ a joyous privilege, he has no message for others and no missionary motive. But when he has come into fellowship with God through Christ, his eyes are opened to see the ways of God among men. We read our newspaper to see what men are doing in the world; and sometimes they are motivated by the Evil One. The Christian reads his Bible to understand what God is doing in the world. There is an over-all strategy by which God is working out His purposes. The Apostle Paul calls it "the plan of the ages which God made in Christ Jesus our Lord." This plan is unfolded in the Bible, beginning with the call of Abraham, continuing through the history of the nation of the Israelites, the ministry of Jesus and his disciples, the history of the Christian churches, and on through our own day until the end of time. When one has this viewpoint of life and history, he is motivated to give himself to be used of God in achieving his ends in the world.

But there is yet another motivation which is usually even more decisive. It is the compelling urgency of the spirit of Jesus within, which leads a person to relate himself in some way to missions. In his prayer to the Father on the night before the Crucifixion, Christ said, "Righteous Father, the world did not know you, but I knew you, and these (disciples of mine) know that you sent me." A few days later, on the night after his resurrection, Christ said to the disciples, "Just as the Father sent me, I also am sending you." This commission has been an impelling force in the lives of his disciples through the ages. We have come to see that Christ is continuing to work out the purposes of God in the world through his disciples who give themselves to meeting the needs of their fellowmen. And the greatest of these needs is the knowledge of God! "This is eternal life, that they should know thee, the only true God, and him whom thou didst send, Jesus Christ."

This then was the motive with which we went to China five years ago: A personal experience of redemption through Christ, a belief in God's plan of the ages as being the clue to history and the meaning of life, and a compelling desire to help continue the work of Christ in bringing a knowledge of God to those in need.

Our experiences in the Orient deepened these motives which we already had, and brought additional ones to bear upon our hearts. First of all, we saw the difference that Christ makes in lives which are lived out in an environment of deepest sin, ignorance, and disease. While in Peking, China, I led a group of young Chinese college men in a Bible Class. We met early on Sunday mornings in a cold, bare room near their Normal College located in the Chinese city, outside the main gates of Peking. In our conversations together, as we talked about the life in Christ while studying the Gospel of John, I gained an insight into the inner life of the young Chinese of our day. They were desperately hungry for the Gospel. Some of them had never heard of Jesus before coming to this Bible Class. Those who responded to the message of the New Testament manifested an enthusiasm seldom seen among Christians here at home. During the Christmas holidays that year, two of them wrote us letters of gratitude for their new found life in Christ; they told of witnessing for him in their homes among members of their families who were Confucianist, and who insisted on observing the rites of ancestor worship at the family altars before the ancestral tablets. I could not fail to see that these boys had found "the pearl of great price." In their homes there was spiritual darkness. In the neighborhood where they went to school in Peking, there was filth, and disease, and moral corruption, and abject poverty. Life was cheap, and the future was bleak and barren. It was not a startling thing to see the body of a dead Chinese lying for hours in the streets, as a dead dog sometimes does here at home; on one occasion, as we rode our bicycles through the narrow street approaching the Bible classroom, we saw the body of a man hanging by his neck from the lower limb of a small tree just a few feet to the side of the street. The battle of life had been too much for him and during the cold night he had ended the nightmare of wretchedness and hunger, because he had apparently lacked the spiritual resources within his life for coping with his situation. But with these boys it was different; their life had taken on new meaning in Christ Jesus!

Perhaps you are saying, "Yes, but missions are a failure because they have reached so few people during all these years of work." I too, have felt the discouragement of this pessimistic viewpoint. But I have come to believe that our basic failure lies in our failure to make Christianity sufficiently real, comprehensive, and actual, anywhere at what we call the home bases. No more than about half of our people in our own land have been successfully evangelized in the sense of even professing to accept Christ as Savior. With little concern, less anxiety, no heartbreak, we allow them to remain unevangelized. Satisfied, if only our faith assures us of heaven when our inevitable quitting of earth comes, we do not press energetically into the kingdom of heaven. Most of us even resist all serious suggestion that we shall come wholly under the reign of God here and now. We need seriously to face the question, "How much Christianity do we have anywhere that satisfies the heart of Christ?" (W. O. Carver).

But we must also remember that the ideals and demands of Jesus are so high that they are never fully followed. They create a tension and produce modifications in social practice and institutions. They revolutionize some individual lives. Others they alter, although not so profoundly. Now and again, as in the fields of education, though, and political theory, they bring about startling innovations. Yet never has a society and probably never has an individual fully embodied them. It may be that this side of the grave they never can and never will. However, that does not mean that Christianity has failed. The measure of the influence of Jesus is not the gulf between his teachings and the practices of individuals and societies, but the changes which have been produced" (K. S. Latourette). To see the difference that Christ makes, in a land where the contrast is greater than here at home, is to gain another motive for being missionary!

The other half of the world is in tremendous need of help from us who have so much. The need would be overwhelming, if we did not know the difference that Christ makes. A realization of the stark need of China is the only thing that could ever take us back. The romance of a foreign land with new sights, new sounds, new customs, new people—and the romance of missions is almost always an unconscious influence in the going of young missionaries—this romance is gone for us now. We know that. China is in many respects an unattractive place for making one's home. But still, one cannot get away from the great need of these open sores, these dark spots in the world. (I am speaking of China because I am most familiar with it; but you also know of other places such as India, Africa, and the Near East.)

From almost any point of approach China impresses one with her appalling need! Physical suffering is beyond description. There are two main reasons for this. The first is economic in nature. The Chinese are an emaciated people because of over-population and the lack of food for proper nourishment. While about 85 percent of them are farmers, most of them barely subsist, living off rice in the south and kaoliang in the north, with an occasional vegetable such as cabbage. Because of this condition they are the ready victims of disease. And unfortunately their health program is altogether inadequate to meet their need. Since coming home I have heard people complain of the shortage of doctors here. Ordinarily, we have one doctor for each eight or nine hundred people in this country. But in China, there is only one doctor for each 70,000 people. For example, at this rate Greater Little Rock would have about two doctors. And there is no relief in sight for China in the near future. If she continues training doctors at the same rate as of 1939, it will take her 450 years to have one doctor for each 2,000 people. The need of the people cries out for a healing ministry, but there is small answer to their cry. During Christmas week of 1940, we visited in Tsinan, a city of north China, in Shantung province. While there, a biologist of Cheeloo University told us that the intestinal parasites inhabiting the people of Shantung province would equal the body weight of 25,000 men. Can you feel something of the physical suffering of China?

Illiteracy and lack of education is another cause of suffering in China; and intellectual poverty can be the cause of much evil. [Eighty-five] percent of the Chinese are illiterate. Less than one-third of the men and less than two percent of the women can read or write. Of the 42 million children between the ages of six and twelve in China today, only one-fourth are in school. It was the challenge of educational missions which first turned my attention to China; I repeat the words of a missionary which were so challenging to me: "There is no greater opportunity to be of service in the world today, than in helping to educate the forward looking young people of China!" (J. B. Hipps).

What can one say for the religious need of China? The revolutionary events of the last few decades there have torn the younger generation from the traditional sources of comfort and strength, such as they were, which their parents had. The older Chinese look to Buddhism for eternal security, to Confucianism for a way of life in this world, and to Taoism for a means of warding off evil spirits, the fear of which constantly haunts them. They seem not to be disturbed by the inconsistency of professing three different religions at the same time. But this situation does not give them peace and harmony. The impact of science from the Occident has broken the hold of these inadequate religions on the younger Chinese, and the spiritual hunger is there, waiting for the satisfaction which only Christ can give! The Christians of China cannot meet this need alone. Less than one-half of one percent of the Chinese are Christians. They need our help, if the need is to be met!

With such a sense of the need of the rest of the world, human misery is no longer oceans away; it is only hours away today! Indeed, it is all about us, for the missionary motive must lead us to begin where we are in meeting human needs, and keep on meeting them in Christ unto the ends of the earth. There is no difference in the nature of ignorance, disease, and sin here at home; it is only that the human forces for combating them are numerically smaller on the other side of the world.

Can you, as an individual, catch the vision of a great Christian of the Orient who wrote,

"Today
A wonderful thought
In the dawn was given.
And the thought was this:
That a secret plan
Is hid in my hand,
That my hand is big,
Big,
Because of this plan.
That God,
Who dwells in my hand,
Knows this secret plan
Of the things He will do for the world,
Using my hand!" (T. Kagawa).

One cannot do anything much alone; but many of us, as workers together with God can do much! And that is the Missionary Motive![8]

A letter from Rankin, acknowledges Hugo's plans to enter medical school and proposes placing the Culpeppers on inactive status. W. O. Carver, ever the teacher, recommended more reading for the first-year medical student:

My Dear Hugo:
How good of you to write me of your present status and plans, of your feelings and aspirations in all of which I am deeply interested. My love and greetings to all the three of you. How glad I am over Number Three. It is no surprise to be able to discern in your letter the tremendous amount of effective missionary advocacy both you and Ruth have been able to do while at the same time carrying on so effectively in your new responsibility. I shall be following you now in your medical work with the same expanding interest which I have had through the years. If it shall be the will of God I shall have joy in seeing

---

[8] Hugo Culpepper, "The Missionary Motive," sermon preached on the Arkansas Baptist Hour, 23 June 1946.

you back in China some day. But I shall have joy in your work wherever the providence of God may direct it.

I am glad you are still thinking, as of course you would be, in terms of basic philosophy. Have you found time to read Brunner, *The Divine Human Encounter*, or (and) Miller's *Christian Truth in History*? Do you see the *Review & Expositor*; and have you had occasion to read the first of my Norton Lectures? The second will appear in the forthcoming number. Whether the other two will be published I do not now know.

You will be interested in knowing that I am still trying to carry through my Ephesians project [*The Glory of God in the Christian Calling*]. It is my present hope and purpose to finish the manuscript by the end of this year.

If you find time in the midst of your strenuous activities, I could stand a biennial report without waiting another full year.

Heartily yours,

W. O. Carver[9]

The Decision to Give Up Medical Studies

In the fall of 1946, Hugo plunged into medical studies at Hendrix College. His parents bought him a microscope, but within a month Hugo realized that he had made a mistake. He saw that he could not give himself to both medicine and theology and maintain his missionary work and his interest in theology. The following paragraphs come from a letter he wrote to Theron Rankin and then reproduced in a letter to Baker James Cauthen a week later:

While you will probably be surprised to have the news which this letter brings to you, perhaps it will not be so much of a shock to you as one might expect. After one month of study at the medical school, I discover that I have made a mistake in taking up the study of medicine. Although I was maintaining an academic average in the upper half of the class, it was being done at such a serious cost to my spiritual and physical health that I have withdrawn from the school.

The pressure of the work was no greater than I had at the seminary; apparently the difference is that one was my vocation and the other is not. I seemed to be out of my element here and the work I did was under a strain

---

[9] W. O. Carver, letter to Hugo Culpepper, 6 October 1946.

which resulted in chronic nervous indigestion and sleeplessness. Along with this physical maladjustment, which seemed to be due to a temperament that is incompatible to the demands of this type of work exclusively, I was losing a sense of the presence of God in my life and work. The realization that four years of work under these conditions would disqualify me from any future usefulness in mission work brought me to the point of accepting my limitations and being willing to live and work within them. My mistake has been made because I aspired to do too much.

During the past year we have been happy in our work, but half of the time was spent in teaching and preaching. I made A's in getting the premedical sciences off, but that work was in the nature of a discipline which consumed only a part of our time and energies; I discover that while disciplined work is good to an extent, all of life cannot be discipline without undue strain. My heart has to be in the work too. The most satisfying work I have done was in teaching the Bible class I had in Peking, and in teaching the classes in missions and theology at Central College for a couple of hours a week last year.

I am grateful that this past year has been almost as full of deputation work for Ruth and me as it would have been had I not been taking the premedical sciences. Because of this I feel that the time lost from mission work has been reduced to a minimum, and that in the long run the experience is a wholesome one and will result in more effectiveness in our mission work because of the attitude engendered.

The letter to Cauthen continues:

The above paragraphs are excerpts from the letter I wrote last week to Dr. Rankin. Since they explain my recent experience and decision as clearly as I can put it, I have repeated them here. Yesterday afternoon I talked with Dr. Rankin for a few minutes over long distance.... Characteristically, his attitude is one of sympathetic understanding. He regards this experience as "just one step in becoming reoriented" after the long concentration experience.

As of the first of this month, we have been returned to the active list of missionaries and are doing deputation work here until a decision is reached as to what is best for us to do in the immediate future. Dr. Rankin mentioned that he was writing to you with reference to this matter; he indicated that there were several urgent needs out there now which you might feel that I should help in, or that you might think it best to resume language study—either at Peking when they reopen in the spring, or at Yale here.

We are grateful that you two have recently traveled extensively in China and that you are on the scene there and in immediate contact with the present needs. This will be of inestimable help in our finding the Lord's will as to the place for us to work. In our deliberation as to the best place to fit us into the picture as a whole, we thought it might be helpful if we wrote expressing our interests, attitudes, and general spirit regarding the matter. Then you can bring this into harmony with the places of need and come to some conclusion. It is in this spirit that we are writing.

When we were appointed in 1940 it was with the idea of my teaching in the new seminary which had been founded recently in Kaifeng. In the hour just before we were presented to the Board, Dr. Rankin approached us with reference to our working in the Pooi Ching Boys' School at Canton, setting up a Bible department and teaching. However, at that time we leaned rather strongly toward seminary work. Since then our interests have broadened greatly. Just now we are eager to get into the work somewhere, "to get our roots down," which is perhaps only natural after these years of delay. We discovered a new joy in our work on the campus at Central College this past year with the students there. This has created an interest in some such place on the mission field. We have read of the reopening of the University of Shanghai and also of the establishment of a Middle School on the Baptist compound in Shanghai, and have wondered if there is possibly a place for us in either of these places. My studies thus far have been rather broad: at Baylor I majored in English and minored in History; at the seminary I took the Th.M. and did the year's residence work in Greek N.T.; this past year I have studied general chemistry, general physics, general zoology, quantitative analysis, and organic chemistry. This breadth of studies might qualify me for general school work of some kind more than an advanced specialty. I have specialized in Greek N.T. more than anything else (having read it through twelve times in camp, etc.), although by aptitude I am not given to languages as much as to sciences and math, nor as much as to theology and philosophy by interest.

Just now I am tired of studying "in the abstract" and because of that am indifferent to pushing through to a doctorate in some field just for the sake of taking a degree. Perhaps, at my age of 33 it is natural to have become more practical minded and to desire to get into a job that needs to be done, and then if necessary take any additional studies later on, the need for which arises naturally out of the job.

I hope that the above information will be helpful to you in placing us. Please be assured that we are not willful in any respect in the matter. We would welcome work in a middle school, college, Bible school, seminary, etc., or general teaching work in a mission station somewhere if you feel that we are most needed there. I have mentioned the school work in Shanghai merely because it seems that Ruth has something to contribute in student work and seems to have a strong leaning in that direction, and because I feel that the work would also be congenial to me. We want above all else to be in God's place for us and I am sure that is also your first desire in leading in such problems as these.[10]

Dr. Rankin replied:

Dear Hugo:

I have read your letter of October 29 with much interest. The information that you have decided that you cannot go on with your plans for taking the medical course and that you are ready to make yourself available for missionary work in China is no great shock to me. In fact, although I was not in any sense expecting this news, it does not come even as a great surprise. Your decision to begin at this time on a medical course was to me a rather staggering undertaking—and I could not help but wonder if you would find it possible to carry the plan through. In a sense, your present condition brings something like relief in my thinking about you....

I do not think that you need to consider that the decision to try the medical course was a mistake. I would look upon it as a step in readjusting your thinking after the experiences which you had while you were in the Orient. As the matter now stands, you will be able to pursue your pathway from here on with a sense of confidence and permanency.

I am not certain as to just where or in what line of work it will be best to assign you in China. I had rather Dr. Cauthen would take this under consideration and correspond with you about it. Meantime, unless he recommends differently, we will look toward your continuing language study in Yale at the next semester, which I think begins in February. On the other hand, should Dr. Cauthen think that in view of the language study you have already had it would be advisable for you to go to Peking to continue the study, he will write you to this effect....

As soon as I can hear from Dr. Cauthen, we will take up the question of your language study next spring. Meantime, I suggest that you go ahead with your schedule for such speaking and deputation work as you are called on to do.

---

[10] Hugo Culpepper, letter to M. T. Rankin and Baker James Cauthen, 29 October 29 and 5 November 1946.

With best wishes to you and Ruth, I am
Cordially yours,
M. T. Rankin[11]

Hugo's friend James E. Tull, who was at the time studying philosophy at Columbia University and Union Theological Seminary, affirmed Hugo's decision to leave medical school and shared his own experience in struggling to find God's direction in his life.

Dear Hugo and Ruth,
We of course were surprised to hear that you have decided to quit medical school. However, in view of how you came to react to your studies, I don't blame you a bit for quitting, and I think that your decision was wise. In my own case I have wondered many times lately just where the fine line is drawn between wisdom on one hand and a commendable tenacity on the other. If you have found that line (and I believe from what you say that you have), you cannot help being the gainer for it. Besides this, you have the faculty for absorbing what happens to you, of making experience out of it, so that your studies in science will not be so much lost effort. No doubt it has altered your perspective, and will in the long run more soundly ground your faith.

I am aware from the background of my own experience too, that your decision probably was not one just of a cool-headed choice between two alternatives, but must have involved something of a mental and spiritual crisis itself. This long continued series (on my part, anyway) of starts and stops, of aspirations and frustrations, of tangents and detours, has left an undeniable residuum of disappointment with me, though I comfort myself by thinking (perhaps some would say that I am rationalizing) that a unity of purpose has run through them all. Since for years I have had a very wholesome respect and appreciation for your life-purpose, I think I can well understand that any change of plan on your part is not a breaking-off to something new, but is an accommodation to a unified purpose. In short, Virginia and I both feel that we quite understand your motive, and continue to wish you well in your new plans. We will follow you with our interest and our prayers, as we have done.[12]

---

[11] M. T. Rankin, letter to Hugo Culpepper, 5 November 1946.
[12] James Tull, letter to Hugo Culpepper, 13 November 1946.

Tull later became a professor of theology at Southeastern Seminary,[13] but in 1946 he could hardly have known how prophetic the next paragraph of his letter was.

Virginia and I hope eventually to return to the South to spend our ministry. Whether we can get back, or whether they will let us stay, I don't know. My experiences of the last five years have given me very intense convictions, that some of us are going to have to begin fighting some of the things with which Southern Baptists are cursed—a pernicious spiritual isolationism, an authoritarian system which makes a mockery of our tenet of freedom, a Biblicism from which the very heart of the Christian message has escaped, a retreat from the task of bringing Christianity to grips with fundamental issues, while fanatically exalting secondary ethical considerations into the chief place, a killing of the spirit by adherence to the letter of the law. I recognize that I may have veered too far to the other side (in ethics, not in theology). This is not to say, though, that I condemn Southern Baptists wholesale. I am proud to be one, and I think that one of our greatest sins has been in our failure, through a self-righteous isolationism, to share some of our principal values with other groups, such as our evangelistic emphasis, for example. In short, I may be all wet, and there are many people who think so, but Virginia and I want to spend our ministry in whatever capacity the Lord wants us in, in the South, attempting to deal, however ineffectively, with some of the problems which I have mentioned. It would be a hard road, and I am not at all sure that I would have the courage, the resourcefulness, or the tenacity to follow through, but at any rate, that is how my conviction lies.

This letter grows too long already, so I must quit and get to Aristotle. Anne had her second birthday two days ago. She is a great joy to us, and a constant source of surprises. I am sure that you are finding Alan to be so too. Write to us again when you have time, and be assured of our continued interest, prayers, and friendship.

---

[13] James Tull authored the following books: *The Atoning Gospel* (Macon: Mercer University Press, 1982); *High-Church Baptists in the South: The Origin, Nature, and Influence of Landmarkism* (Macon: Mercer University Press, 2000); *A History of Southern Baptist Landmarkism in the Light of Historical Baptist Ecclesiology* (New York: Arno Press, 1980); *Shapers of Baptist Thought* (Macon: Mercer University Press, 1984).

Sincerely,
James[14]

Personal and Spiritual Crisis

The "deputation work" of speaking in churches, revivals, and mission emphases, led Hugo around the state and to several other states, traveling by bus and train to speaking engagements. The separation from Ruth and the uncertainty of their future soon led them into one of the most difficult periods of their married life. Several undated, handwritten letters to Ruth chronicle Hugo's experiences and provide a glimpse of their intensifying struggle as they made plans to return to China.

Dearest Ruth,

When I am in situations like this, where the people seem backward and untrained, it makes me realize how far our opportunities have removed us from the viewpoint of the "common man" of the world. Our problem is to learn to bridge the gap and get next to them. It is not easy. This morning the service was quite cold, the "crowd" a scattering; I hope the Lord can use me to help some during the week.

Monday

I suppose you could tell from the tone of my letter that I was not very enthusiastic yesterday over the prospects here. My morning message was a flop—it seemed to bounce right back in my face, to me. Both meals yesterday were in migrant-workers' houses, depressing surroundings and food that was not relishing. And yet in one of the houses, the older son is a senior in high school and plans to go to Ouachita next year. He is very interested in piano. Practically all of his time outside of school is spent practicing. The piano is in the corner of the kitchen (a four-room frame house they built themselves, bit by bit). He has taken [piano lessons] for two years. Now he plays all classical stuff. Recently he managed to buy an inexpensive record player (single) and a few albums of Beethoven, Brahms, etc. Now he practices the sheet music, then listens to the records, and improves his own playing.

I don't expect any tangible results from the meeting. The pastor has planned no organized visitation nor efforts at enlistment. If we have done nothing in this respect soon, I think I'll suggest it. There were 132 in Sunday School yesterday. The empty seats yesterday morning were more noticeable

---

[14] James Tull, letter to Hugo Culpepper, 13 November 1946.

than the filled ones. All of this together with my loneliness for you all, and the feeling of strangeness in a new place, made for a depressing day yesterday. Even then, I felt something like a spoiled kid; I realized we have been reared in luxury and came from wealthy homes compared to these people.

Beginning at B.T.U. things have taken a sharp turn upwards. I was invited for an informal talk to the adult union. I turned it into a question and answer period. That broke the ice. They were very responsive. When we went to the auditorium, it was nearly full—many more than the morning service. This surprised the pastor, because it is usually just the opposite. It was a definite encouragement to me. I did well in preaching the new sermon on Romans 1:18—"The Wrath of God Is Being Revealed." Everyone paid close attention, and I have hopes that we got off to a good start then, and will have good night services all week. At least they will hear some things that should be helpful....

This is really a mission field here, discouraging as it is. I have a certain satisfaction in knowing that I am directing their attention toward enduring realities and eternal truth. That is my compensation.

We were right in not bringing Alan, but had it been possible for you to be here you would have found many opportunities to be helpful with the women—and how much more there would be in life for me these days with you here. I don't feel "wholly" myself; while we are living and working together, all is well.

Lovingly,
Hugo[15]

The letters from Hugo written during the week before Thanksgiving reveal the turmoil they were experiencing, Ruth's misgivings, and the pressure they were experiencing from their families not to return to China.

Dearest Ruth,
If you were here also it would all be quite enjoyable. I have an excellent, large room on the seventh floor of a hotel that is similar to the Ben McGehee, located in the heart of the city (70,000 pop.) and three blocks from first church. Have breakfast in the cafeteria of the hotel. The week's program is pleasantly full. I enjoyed speaking to about 1,000 people (844 in Sunday School) this A.M. in a large auditorium with a public address system. My message will be the same all week: The outline from the radio sermon I preached on the theme, "the Missionary Motive," with about 7 or 9 minutes of description of concentration camp life worked in at the pastor's request. It was well received. I

---

[15] Hugo Culpepper, letters to Ruth Culpepper, no date.

speak each night in a different church, through Friday night, all in the Port Arthur area....

On Thanksgiving, we all go to Beaumont for a morning meeting of all three groups of speakers, have Thanksgiving dinner, and a sightseeing trip in the afternoon on buses. I'll leave here on the train at 9:15 A.M. Saturday and get to Shreveport at 4:00 P.M., leave there by bus at 11:00 A.M. Sunday arriving in Little Rock about 6:30 P.M. on the Mo. Pac. (not Greyhound station) from Texarkana....

I wish we had arranged for your Mother to keep Alan and you had come, not only for us to be together, but also because I believe you would find it stimulating and helpful psychologically to get away from home there for a while and see things more objectively. This, along with Dr. Carver's "Christian Missions in the World Today," which I got into on the train yesterday, are reassuring and strengthening to me in the step we are taking, bringing me to a deeper appreciation of the nature of the missionary enterprise through the ages as the framework for life's meaning. I hope you will read it when I get back.

While I tremble when I think of many of the little practical problems of living facing us out there, just as you do, I have been lifted to an assurance that this work gives one an opportunity in life to be engaged with the central, strategic matters of life, history, and destiny. I don't really believe that you in our better moments prefer an "easy life" at the sacrifice of this opportunity. If only our parents had the opportunity to get this perspective, and we could leave without so much heartache! I wish your folks would read this book I mentioned above, and "Missions in the Plan of the Ages." I am praying constantly for all of us on this problem....

With my love,
Hugo
Monday, 3:45 P.M.
Ruth, dear,
Because of my message being so different and based on our experiences, I seem to be receiving an enthusiastic hearing, as evidenced again last night. And even this morning when I spoke very informally for the fellowship meeting of the workers, after sharing "Random Thoughts on Foreign Missions" (personal viewpoints and observations) they questioned me freely, and then got me off on concentration [camp experiences] and kept me going an hour and twenty minutes altogether....

I appreciate the plan which you described and see the merits, but I also see the other side. I expect the policy to be (as it should be) to get the missionaries to China as soon as practical and not keep them at Yale any longer than necessary now that Peking is reopening. Then too, in spite of the problems, perhaps they are not as great as they would be at Yale for us, because we do have rooms in Peking. Then too, I expect the American dollar to procure most foods, even canned milk, where American business can possibly get the stuff in. We know from experience that language study is better *in China*.

As to our family problem, I surely do realize its seriousness .... All in all, I cannot but feel that we have "set our hand to the plough" and should not look back any more. We must learn to adjust constantly to the demands of the work, and not fashion the work to our situation. Perhaps, we shall never be settled in our external situation, but I believe we can learn to accept peace and quiet within ourselves, and in the end to have permitted God to work through us in his mission for us—and that is what counts. Departure would be just as hard a year later, even more complicated with two children. I believe the sooner we lose our lives in the work, the sooner we shall have peace within. I am experiencing that this week to some extent, and only wish that you could be sharing it.... I hope you can enter into the planning and preparations by the time I return, so we can get on with it.

I almost fear that we shall not really be happy again together, now that we are going on in mission work, until we get away again from the home ties and dominations there. I'm trusting that then you can find "joy in the work" again which I believe you once had out there. If you can't, it will be tragic, regardless of how the situation ultimately resolves itself. Meanwhile, I almost dread to pass through the agonizing period of those last weeks at home with everybody depressed, when they should be weeks of joy and happiness, redeeming the time to the full for all of us.

So few people here at home in the States seem to find joy in their work. I was impressed in Shreveport with the burden of irksome, unsatisfying work which both Dale and Uncle Oscar bear and openly protest against; they are miserable, though living an "easy life." How grateful we should be for our opportunity at significant work, which can be a joy if we attune our spirits to it and keep them in harmony. If only again our love for each other can bloom full, and fill our home! I long for understanding and love and peace together; then the world about us can't touch us or affect us.

Sincerely,
Hugo[16]

Life on the road brought Hugo into contact with all kinds of situations. In one letter he wrote: "It will be necessary for me to flag the train tonight to

---

[16] Hugo Culpepper, letters to Ruth Culpepper, no date.

get him to stop. There will be no one else at the station, but they say a lantern is available.... I'll take the first train out of Kansas City tomorrow after speaking."[17] From another town Hugo wrote:

The crowds have been increasing a little at each service. However, my contribution is limited largely to the better element in the church membership. I've never known of a situation in church and town quite like it is here. It is too long a story to go into before I see you. In short, it is heart-sickening. For the last couple of nights I haven't slept well because of concern over it, but I've come to realize that my efforts are limited. The people who are entering into the meeting seem to be getting a blessing and inspiration. All in all, this week is proving to be quite educational to me in the way of practical experience in the knotty life-situations some have always, and we will perhaps have some of.

Last night the Colemans kept me up till 11:00 telling me the history of the situation here: e.g., one preacher was choked in the pulpit, one had his house burned down by a church member and lost everything, etc.

With all that on my mind, when I woke up about 3:15 this morning I couldn't get back to sleep for a while.... I'm looking forward to the hours we'll have together before next week's separation (I don't think about that). Kiss Alan for me too.

From another town Hugo registered again the pain of separation and traveling by himself:

When I got off the bus I went first and got a sandwich and milk shake, then for a haircut, and then to the church to try and find someone and see what arrangement had been made for me. I finally got the church secretary on the phone, and she called someone and then called me back to tell me that a room was reserved for me at the second-class hotel here. The preacher was away in a meeting. I went to the hotel, took a bath in the general public bathroom, tried to relax, but my headache was bothering me too much. Then I dressed and went for some aspirin and took two. It was 4:00 P.M. by then. I walked slowly around the main section of town, bought some razor blades and half a dozen oranges. Finally, I wound up in the park downtown and sat on a bench eating two oranges and watching the stream flow by. I felt miserable, but didn't want to go back in the room. Never would I make a traveling salesman![18]

---

[17] Hugo Culpepper, letter to Ruth Culpepper, no date.
[18] Hugo Culpepper, Letter to Ruth Culpepper, no date.

Plans to Go to Chile

Events happened quickly in January of 1947. Fortunately, Hugo reflected on the recent events and detailed the changes in their plans in a round robin of letters they sent around among several couples.

Dear Fellows:

Things have been moving fast with us since I last wrote a page for the robin.... On November 1st we resumed an active status with the Mission Board, with the request that we have the opportunity to get to a field of work as soon as possible. We had grown weary of being missionaries on furlough. By the first of December, word came that the language school in Peking would reopen on March 1st and that we could go there; we were to prepare for departure late in January. That threw us into feverish activity to re-outfit as completely as possible for the three of us to live where whatever "we expected to have we must take with us," as our people out there wrote back. By January 4th, we had accumulated and had crated a total of about 3,800 lbs. net, or 5,200 lbs. gross of freight which occupied 399 cubic feet. On authorization from the Board, we shipped this on to San Francisco on January 4th in time for it to go with us.

You might be interested in what we included in our outfit. We had two crates of household goods which contained the things we already had bought: two platform rockers, a study table, two steel folding chairs, a chest of drawers, a radio table, a Frigidaire (in a separate crate), a bicycle; we also bought a floor lamp, a Beauty Rest mattress and box springs, a Simmons bed, a hot plate, a Whizzer one cylinder motor bike, a C-3 Argus 35 mm. camera and an Argus projector, a tripod, a Weston light meter, a National NC-46 high frequency radio communication receiver with four bands and a band spread tuner (such as was built and used by the Navy during the war), a quantity of books to begin a library again; of course, we had such incidentals as our dishes, china and crystal, wear-ever utensils, etc. I have just completed building a table model phonograph cabinet finished in dark walnut. In it I mounted the motor, turn table, and playing arm. Then a technician placed a jack in the back of my radio so that I can plug it in and get the tone value of the 11 tubes in playing the phonograph. We selected about 25 records to begin with. I managed to get an auto-transformer for converting 220 volts to 110 volts where necessary, such as in Peking.

For Alan's food problem we had two crates containing 10 cases of Carnation Milk, 38 cases of chopped fruits and vegetables, 5 cases of soup, 48 pounds of powdered milk; for ourselves, 4 cases of meat, 3 of cheese products, and 73 pounds of Klim. A large box of drugs and vitamins was included. Incidentally, we had to secure an export license from the Department of Commerce to take this food out as freight; it was too heavy to take as baggage which would have been permitted without a license. My barbells were in two boxes. I have quite a supply of tools, but they will have to be included among the personal things in our five trunks. I realize this sounds like a lot when it is all gotten together, but when spread out in a house it would be pretty thin and some essentials even would not be on hand. I have written the foreign freight agent of the American Express Company to hold the stuff for us in Frisco, and I suppose he has it by now.

On January 6th, two days after shipping the stuff, we received a letter from our Secretary for the Orient in Shanghai, Dr. Cauthen, suggesting that it would probably be better for us to attend Yale in view of the trend of events in the Communist situation in North China. For the first time we became somewhat concerned as to the wisdom of our going to Peking just now. I suppose we had cast caution to the wind in our desire to get back. The next day, Tuesday the 7th, I left for the little town of Hawesville, Ky., via Louisville. A small church there had "adopted" me as their missionary and wanted us to get acquainted. On the way up I read the letter in the *Christianity* from Perry Hanson, a Methodist missionary in Peking, telling of the situation around there. This added to my concern, but I felt that we had come to an impasse. We definitely did not want to continue living under uncertainty of waiting here, even at Yale. Yet it began to seem unwise to go into Peking just now.[19]

Two letters that Hugo wrote to Ruth, one from Memphis and the other the next morning from Louisville, give a fuller account of his experience:

Ruth, dearest,
I am terribly homesick for you. The trip thus far has been miserable. Unless we can regain our love and live in a spirit of harmony, nothing else in life seems to matter. The most important decision of our lives is facing us: I cannot make it alone.

An hour before arriving in Memphis I had decided to take the next train back home and not go on. The responsibility is too great for me to take you and Alan back to China now against your will. It is a "dangerous opportunity" that faces us, I realize, and I cannot go on, knowing that you feel as you do.

I believe our vocation is mission work. If we cannot go on in that, I would prefer to turn away from the ministry and make the best living possible for you

---

[19] Hugo Culpepper, letter to several couples, 29 January 1947.

and Alan. Perhaps, with a year or two of training I could make an average living for us at something else. Perhaps your Dad could get me a job with the company somewhere. Maybe we would be happier at that.

I'm sure we would, if we cannot regain a spirit of religious devotion and consecration together that will give us courage to make any necessary sacrifice for the Lord's work. We will be miserable without such a spirit.

It is not too late to turn away. Public opinion should not phase us. I would be happier here as a layman living an average life than we could be there in China without our love and harmony and courage and devotion to the work.

Please think and pray seriously about this. I don't want to be hasty this time, and so I'm going on and shall decide when I return. Then I won't seem "bull-headed" as formerly.

If we can go on in missions in the right spirit and relation, I don't want to take something here as a minister just for a living. I'd rather keep our self-respect and do something else—which I'm willing to do. Love Alan for me. All my love, Hugo[20]

The next morning Hugo wrote the following letter.

Ruth, dearest,
I have just stepped off the train here. My letter last night gave me a relief from the burden I have been carrying lately. I had a sense of sharing it; I think the fact that I acted—did something (i.e., wrote the letter)—broke the tension.

On boarding the train I got into a brief conversation with some Orientals (I think Japanese), and then went to bed. I had a song in my heart for the first time in a long while. It was the solace of religion, at a time when there is no other refuge. I prayed as I have not been able to lately. The words of two songs were in my mind as I fell asleep: "I'll Go Where You Want Me to Go," and "Are Ye Able?" and yet, my mind is truly open to go, or stay and work at something else. Our peace and harmony together is a prerequisite for life anywhere. If you prefer, and have the self-reliance and independence of spirit, we can start over here at something else. I have found peace for myself with God and I hope with you, in not being self-willed, but in honestly being ready to do anything. I hope you can have found this peace by the time I return and have some suggestion to make.

With this hope and faith I expect my trip to be more light-hearted now. I love you dearly.
Hugo

---

[20] Hugo Culpepper, letter to Ruth Culpepper, 7 January 1947.

P.S. I cannot believe that we can compromise wisely now. It seems to be either stay here at something else, or go on to China. But I'm willing to do either.[21]

The letter to the "round robin" continued:

That night on the train I prayed as only a desperate man can pray for guidance.... The next morning I read of Marshall's appointment as Secretary of State and his report on China. After this I had to face the probability of a drawn out struggle there, even though I had been hopeful of some early settlement heretofore. After a 24-hour visit with the church, I started back on Thursday, the 9th. On reaching Louisville, I read in the evening paper of fighting within 5 miles and within 13 miles of Peking, and of the transportation difficulties up there. Then while walking to a cafeteria for supper, the thought occurred to me for the first time in recent months of our possibly transferring to another country for work.

Back in 1940 after our appointment but before our departure, a seminary friend from Chile—a native from there—had tried to get us to go back with him to work there. He had told us much of the situation there. We had not taken him seriously because our faces were set toward China. In 1941, while we were in Baguio, we had a letter from him. He was writing as the President of the Chilean Convention of Baptists and again urged us to come there since we had to leave China then. Again we shelved the invitation, but with the thought of perhaps turning to it if we should continue in mission work and for any reason left China. With this background it was not surprising for my thoughts to turn to Chile. As I rode from Louisville home, I took the position in my plans of not bringing up the possible change unless the initiative for not going to China came from outside ourselves; otherwise we would sail on January 27th as scheduled. I had been writing Ruth these few days while gone. When I arrived home I learned that Ruth had received a long-distance phone call from Richmond, Va., the day before. It was the secretary telling her that our passage had been cancelled because the army was taking over the space on the boat and that they could not secure passage for us until March. Meanwhile, they had come to feel that it would be unwise for us to go to North China now; they did not want to assume that responsibility. Would we go to Yale instead, and stay as long as we desired? Was there any reason why we could not? They had housing for us there, etc. Ruth replied that I was away but that we would talk it over went I got back the next day and then write them.

---

[21] Hugo Culpepper, letter to Ruth Culpepper, 8 January 1947.

When I heard of this, I felt that the impasse was broken and that the whole matter was up for decision again. Then Ruth and I went into a huddle and for the day discussed the pro and con of transferring to Chile. As all of you have probably felt yourselves, we were wearing pretty thin at waiting around. Our Baguio experience with the language gave us no interest in study at Yale. Even after a year and a half there we had no assurance of material improvement in the China situation. On the other hand, we could probably learn Spanish to the point of proficiency as soon as we could Chinese since we would have only about a 6 months start over a younger couple who might begin now on Chinese. Would it not be wiser for the Board and us, considering my age of 34, for us to settle into a work in Chile and let some younger couple take our places for China? We think so!

Shortly after our minds were made up, we had another call from Richmond, one day after I had returned and two days after the first call; I took the call. It was the secretary again saying that they had just gotten word that we could be taken on the boat for the 27th; did we insist on going, or would we follow their preference and go to Yale? I explained briefly our idea about transferring, provided there was a need for us there, and said I would write a letter that day. The Executive Secretary in Richmond cabled the Latin-America secretary. The reply was that we are needed for a term of fieldwork and for educational missions after that period of orientation.[22]

The cable received from Dr. Gill, who was in Paraguay at the time, read, "Chile needs new workers but seminary sufficiently staffed after one term field work educational opportunities probably open Culpepper." M. T. Rankin relayed the content of the cable and indicated that he was prepared to ask for their transfer to Chile. He added, "I do not think there is any question but that a place will open up for you to do educational work in Chile and in all probability that place in time will be in seminary work. Your qualifications and your natural ability in that line will almost inevitably call you into that kind of work."[23]

Hugo's letter to the robin continued:

Last week I wrote back accepting the proposition and officially requesting the transfer. About 20 minutes ago we had a letter saying that the necessary steps for the transfer are being pushed: it must be approved by the Board in session early in February (I rather expect any such recommendation by the

---

[22] Hugo Culpepper, letter to several couples, 29 January 1947.
[23] M. T. Rankin, letter to Hugo Culpepper, 17 January 1947.

Executive Secretary will be routine); the Latin-American secretary is being written for a suggestion as to our location there and to make sure housing will be available. The letter today said transportation to Chile is very difficult to secure but that it will be pushed. All in all, it will probably take several weeks to arrange for our departure.

Meanwhile, I am writing today to see if there isn't someone to whom I could send the freight on by water from Frisco to avoid unnecessary storage there. I realize we are "carrying coal to New Castle," in regard to the food—fancy taking meat and milk, etc., to a country bordering on Argentina....

P. S. We gave the new microscope to the Stout Memorial Hospital in Wuchow, China. Dr. Wallace, on furlough and studying at Tulane, came by and got it to take back.[24]

Hugo with microscope. Family photograph, printed in the Sunday Magazine, *Arkansas Democrat*, 28 April 1946.

Dr. Bill Wallace traveled from Memphis to Little Rock to pick up Hugo's microscope. Dr. Wallace sailed to China in the summer of 1947, where he was later arrested by the Communists and murdered by them in February 1951.[25] Hugo indicated their eagerness to get to the mission field and their willingness to do field work wherever they were needed before moving into educational missions in a school or the seminary there. He

---

[24] Hugo Culpepper, letter to several couples, 29 January 1947.

[25] See Jesse C. Fletcher, *Bill Wallace of China* (Nashville: Broadman Press, 1963).

added, "Ruth first became interested in foreign missions while hearing Miss Anne Lasseter of Temuco while she was here on furlough about sixteen years ago."[26]

Espinoza sent an encouraging response by return mail:

> Your letter has given us a very agreeable surprise. We shall be very happy to have you working here with us. As I should like for this letter to reach you soon, I shall not enter great details in assuring you that whatever might be your vocation for mission work, here you will find a place to use that vocation. The best thing would be for you to come on and study the language here in Santiago and during that time you will hear what the missionaries advise you and you will see for yourselves the situation of the work and its most urgent needs, and after that you can decide the work that you will do during the first period of your stay in Chile. Any decision that you make beforehand might prove to be a mistake.
>
> We want to help you in all that we can in the broad sense of that term. I will get professors for your study, we will look together for a house that will be most convenient for you, we will discuss frankly together the work with the sincerity of friendship and the knowledge that comes through confidence in men that have had a common task.[27]

Hugo, Ruth, and Alan, 1947.

---

[26] Hugo Culpepper, letter to Honorio Espinoza, 3 February 1947.

[27] Honorio Espinoza, letter to Hugo Culpepper, 12 February 1947.

In May the Culpeppers traveled by train to New York, where they visited with James and Virginia Tull and with Marian Gray, Fern Harrington, Cleo Morrison, and other friends from the concentration camp. They stayed at the King Edward Hotel for six dollars a night, but Ruth thought it was no better than a four-dollar room at an Arkansas hotel! While in New York, they visited the Empire State Building and Radio City Music Hall and took in two plays. Then, on 16 May, they set sail on the *S.S. Santa Maria*, of the appropriately named "Grace Line," bound for Valparaiso, Chile.

Chapter 5

Chile,
1947-1951

"I profess no other share
In the selection of my lot, than this,
A ready answer to the will of God. "[1]

Fern Harrington and Cleo Morrison saw the Culpeppers off. The ship departed on schedule at 5:00 P.M. on 16 May 1947, and they sailed past the Statue of Liberty as they left the harbor. The *S.S. Santa Maria* was a luxury liner that carried only fifty-four passengers, and their stateroom was as large as a bedroom at home The itinerary scheduled seven stops and passage through the Panama Canal on the eighteen-day trip to Valparaiso, Chile.

When they arrived in Valparaiso, they were met by Howard Bryant, a fellow missionary. The crates that had been sent ahead to San Francisco had arrived some days earlier, and an agent was engaged to take care of getting the crates through customs. After lunch, Howard Bryant took the Culpeppers on to Santiago in the mission station wagon.

Getting Settled, First Impressions

At first, it was unclear where the Culpeppers would settle. The language committee of the Chilean mission was made up of five members, two from Temuco and three from Santiago. Each contingent wanted the Culpeppers to come to their city for language study, with the hopes that they would

---

[1] Robert Browning, "Paracelsus," *The Complete Poetic and Dramatic Works of Robert Browning*, ed. Horace E. Scudder (Boston: Houghton Mifflin Co., 1895) 15.

settle there. Hugo and Ruth also realized immediately that they would probably need a car. Gasoline cost about the same as it did in the States, and most missionaries had cars (purchased with money from the annual Lottie Moon offering for foreign missions). There was a coal strike, and gas was being rationed. For several days it was cut off at one o'clock and turned back on at seven in the evening. Ruth assured her parents that they were in no danger, though as a precaution they were staying off the buses and avoiding crowds.

Within a week it was decided that they would stay in Santiago for their language study. Ruth had a woman from Ecuador to come each evening during the week for an hour, and she gave Ruth forty to fifty words or phrases a day. By 20 June, they had located a bungalow with a backyard. To get to the seminary, they had to walk seven blocks to a main thoroughfare to catch a bus or streetcar. The Andes Mountains appeared to be only a few blocks from their front door.

Their letters to the Culpeppers and the Cochranes back in Little Rock are filled with accounts of Alan's health and growth, their language study, getting the house set up, and arranging for a maid. By the first week in August they had unpacked all their crates and trunks, down to the last shoebox. Staple items were cheaper in bulk, so on one occasion they reported buying a 100-pound sack of flour from a bakery at black market prices. On another, Hugo went to the seminary to divide out some lard and sugar that the missionaries had bought; they expected their share would be forty-five pounds of lard and twenty pounds of sugar. Imported items were expensive; when they found Heinz catsup, it was $1.75 a bottle.

A new language teacher came to the house two days a week, and a seventeen year-old boy came three mornings a week for conversation. Hugo wrote:

I asked him if he were a Catholic and he said no, that he knew nothing about religion—that he had no faith—but that he would be very grateful if I taught him a faith. That is representative of the paganism here—sheer ignorance of what Christianity really is!

There has recently been a turn of public opinion against Communism here. They have been turned out of the Cabinet and a new one formed. But the masses of the people are in great material need, and unless capitalism can successfully meet their needs the present set-up can't go on forever.[2]

---

[2] Hugo Culpepper, letter to his parents, 11 August 1947.

In the middle of August, Howard Bryant sent his family on ahead by airplane to their new field of service in Antofagasta and then left Santiago the next day to make the 900-mile, five-day trip in his 1931 model A Ford sedan.

On 7 September, Hugo preached his first sermon in Chile, through an interpreter, at the Third Baptist Church in Santiago. He hoped to be preaching in Spanish by Christmas. Again, he added a comment on the political situation:

In September a burglar broke into the house while they were away for a picnic in the mountains. Petty, their maid, and a neighbor chased him, and he dropped the bag he was carrying, so he only got away with things he must have had in his pockets: a pencil and pen, nylon stockings, money, jewelry, and a gold pocket watch Hugo's parents had given him in 1930. He also damaged some of the furniture by trying to get into locked drawers. From then on, Hugo and Ruth were very cautious about security.

Just now the evangelicals here are much concerned about a bill pending in the legislature. It has passed the Senate and will probably pass the house. The bill makes it compulsory for a Catholic priest to teach religion in all the schools of the country which are recognized by the government and give degrees. Our recognized school in Temuco would be affected. This is where we shall probably work. All the Catholic children, and all others except where the parents write a request for exemption, would be in the class. The school has to pay the salary of the priest for teaching the class. This gives you an idea of the scheming of the Catholics here to keep their hold on things. While it will be a deplorable situation, and some of the missionaries here think we should close the school rather than do this, some of the others of us (including Honorio [Espinoza]) think we should go on with the school open (even if the bill passes) and compete with the priest for influence on the children. After all, we have five missionaries teaching there, as over against the one priest who might be there![3]

In October there was another coal strike. The gas was turned off except from 10:00 A.M. till 1:00 P.M. and from 7:00 till 10:00 P.M., and the electricity was turned off two days a week from 8:00 A.M. till 9:00 P.M., so they burned candles those evenings until the electricity came on. Hugo's running commentary on the political situation continued:

---

[3] Hugo Culpepper, letter to his parents, 15 October 1947.

In an unusual way the three-cornered struggle for world power comes to a focus quite clearly here in Chile: Communism, Roman Catholicism, and Evangelical freedom along with democracy. While the forces of Communism are stronger here than anywhere else in the Western Hemisphere, probably, fortunately we have a strong man as President here who stands up against them....

Across the street this morning a hearse completely white in color, drawn by two black horses covered with white veils, came for the body of a 17 months old baby who died of pneumonia. The family is the caretaker of the big orchard you can see behind the wall in the pictures from the front of our house showing the mountains. Probably faulty diet and exposure to the chilling night caused this example of infant mortality—about the highest percentage in the world. No funeral was held. The casket was very tiny, and while no funeral was held it was an expensive affair for the family to hire the hearse and two cars to take the body to the cemetery. The mother did not go, but the father went alone as is the custom here. It was a poor girl from this family that gave the alarm of our burglar. Even the poorest of families here are put to exorbitant expense for weddings and funerals. I suppose this custom is in keeping with their religious background, which makes much of these times and scarcely touches them at other times.[4]

At the mission meeting in Temuco, Cecil Moore approached Hugo about being pastor of the Baptist church there, which had about 500 active members. Moore wanted to move to Santiago the next summer to develop a Baptist bookstore there. Hugo thought the church would be the greatest opportunity they would have in Chile, but he had doubts about the wisdom of taking on such a large church so soon after coming to Chile.

Gradually, Hugo began to take on more responsibilities at the seminary in Santiago, as Ruth related in a letter.

Friday night we had a station meeting [of the missionaries] over at the Woods. Hugo has been asked to teach English in the seminary this year. Classes begin in about three weeks. Then he is taking over Ivey Miller's Bible class for English-speaking people, and they will meet each Wednesday night at the seminary. The Millers are moving to Valpo [Valparaiso] soon. Then Hugo was appointed chairman of a committee to plan Bible studies for the missionary group here. It looks as though he will be getting into the work more and more from now on. Next

[4] Ibid.

Sunday morning he is to preach at the closing exercises [the seminary's graduation ceremony] at the Second Church here. He will have to prepare a 15-minute sermon this week. We voted to have a missionary Bible study once a week at the seminary—each Wednesday afternoon.[5]

The invitations to preach meant that Hugo began to spend more time in sermon preparation: "I will also be preparing sermons as regularly as I can because there are plenty of opportunities to preach. I had to turn one down tonight because I didn't have a different sermon prepared for that church yet."[6] One of the sermons he preached early in their time in Chile was titled "Living with Jesus." The sermon was based on John 1:35-39, the same text he had preached on his first sermon in China some years earlier. After affirming the value of historical-critical study of Scripture, he emphasized the importance of reading Scripture devotionally. In these verses from the Gospel of John, Jesus asked his first two disciples what they were seeking. Hugo commented:

As the Lord of life puts the question to you, "What are you seeking in life today? What does life mean to you?" How are you going to answer it? If we are all honest with him and with ourselves, these would be some of our answers....

But others would say, "I am seeking the good things of life." I once asked a young doctor friend of mine why most doctors crowd into the cities to compete with each other and leave the rural areas neglected. He said, "Primarily because most of the good things of life are to be found in the cities." He was speaking in terms of material values in life—money and the things money can buy and the recreations and pleasures that make up life for most people. But how characteristic that is of most people! They are seeking "the good things of life" in terms of material values, and all too often to the exclusion of spiritual value. This is the definition of secularism, which, to my mind, is the basic difficulty in the life of the world today: We are preoccupied with the pursuit of material things to the utter exclusion of spiritual values. This explains much of the impotence of even those of us who call ourselves Christians. In contrast with these and other possible answers which people would give to the question "What are you seeking?" Jesus said, "Seek ye first the kingdom of God and His righteousness, and all these things will be added to you."

---

[5] Ruth Culpepper, letter to her parents, 29 February 1948.
[6] Hugo Culpepper, letter to his parents, 14 March 1948.

The first disciples also asked Jesus, "Where Do You Live?" Hugo continued the exposition:

Christianity is experiential. We must come to know Jesus for ourselves in our own experience. This is the authority of reality—we might call it ontological authority. The only way to come under this highest form of authority is to enter into the arena of life and come to experience the reality of living. The only way really to know Jesus is to enter into fellowship with Him, by repentance and faith, and live with Him day by day in spiritual communion, making Him the supreme authority in our lives.

This is a continuous experience. In some respects, it is a progressive development that makes life become sweeter and better with each passing year. The poet [Robert Browning] has shown rare insight when he wrote, "Grow old along with me, the best is yet to be, the end of life for which the first was made." Living with Jesus lends vitality to life even now as we grow older. One of the most remarkable people I know is a man who is old in years but remarkably young and alert in body and spirit. For forty years he was an itinerating missionary in China, spending most of his time walking from village to village to tell the story of Jesus to those who had never even heard His name before. Guillermo [Bill] Mather loved his work; indeed, for him it was not work—it was a glorious privilege. No doubt, the constant exercise of walking helped build a rugged constitution, physically speaking. However, his spiritual poise and devotion also contributed much to his energy, endurance, and alertness, I believe. I came to know him as an inmate of a Japanese concentration camp when he was seventy years old. His attitude and way of living under such conditions was an inspiration to me. Before the three years were up, he was thin and weak, as were all the rest of us. He was not expected to last through the closing months. But he walked out of the prison, without assistance, when we were liberated, and returned to the States. After an operation to remove cataracts from his eyes, and after a few months of rest and good food, he grew young again. He resumed his hobby of mountain-climbing in California, although he was past seventy now, and later returned to his home in the East where he bought a bicycle to ride in, going about visiting his friends, some of whom lived fifteen miles apart. Later, he resumed his research in Chinese, studying in Columbia University. Perhaps you can account for such vigor on a purely naturalistic basis, but for me his daily fellowship with Jesus is a large part of the explanation. He had learned to live with Jesus.[7]

---

[7] Hugo was referring to Bill Mather. See above, p. 54, n. 42.

Some years ago one of the most noted psychiatrists in the United States, Dr. Sadler, was lecturing to a group of seminary students on pastoral counseling. In the course of his comments on the nature of life as involving change, he emphasized that we were made for continuous growth throughout our lives. Then he said, "None of us knows exactly what eternity will be like, but for my part I believe it will be a long, long climb upwards, and I am looking forward to it with the keenest anticipation!" Perhaps he is right. At least we know from Christian experience here that the follower of Jesus is supposed to "keep on coming," to continue growing in the knowledge of his Lord.

You Shall See. This was the promise of Jesus to Andrew and John: "If you want to see where I live, keep on coming and you 'shall see.' " For the Christian there is a goal in life, there is an end to be achieved: it is the growth of a Christlike personality. If we have this as the deepest conviction of our lives, then we believe that the spiritual values of life are primary in the nature of reality and that all the physical world is instrumental to these spiritual values. To begin with the individual, one's body is the instrument of his spiritual personality; in the same way all the physical world is instrumental to spiritual personalities. That is why God created the universe—in order that it may be used as the arena for growing souls that could become qualified to appreciate eternal fellowship with Him. History, thus, is seen to be a soul-making process. It has an objective, a purpose....

What are you seeking in life? Where do you really live? Keep on following Jesus, and you shall see Him for whom you were made. Then you shall have eternal fellowship with him forever![8]

A Sacrificial Gift

In March 1948 Hugo and Ruth received a letter from Mrs. Francis Rowe, president of the WMU at Immanuel Baptist Church, explaining that they wanted to give the Culpeppers something special for their work in Chile, and the gift of a car had been suggested. She was writing to ask if they needed a car, what kind of car they preferred, and what the duty and tax would be. She added, "You may rest assured that we will not embarrass you or your family by a 'drive' to raise money. We plan only to give those who wish to do so an opportunity to do what they have expressed a desire to do."

Hugo and Ruth replied:

---

[8] Hugo Culpepper, "Living with Jesus," sermon preached in Chile.

It is impossible for you there to realize fully what such a demonstration of continuing interest on the part of the folks back home can and does mean to young missionaries who are struggling to make the adjustment on a foreign field to language, climate, people, and pressing needs that are hard to meet. It gives one the feeling that we really are your extended hand reaching out here to try to love and lift and bring a blessing to those in need of God here: we are not alone, even in the sense of human companionship in the work. This experience and feeling of your presence with us is worth far more than whatever gift you might send. In fact, without it the gift would have little meaning. And so be assured that the tidings your letter brings are already proving to be a blessing to us.

We do not know, and, after some consideration, cannot think of anything that would be of greater value to us and be of more service in the work than an automobile, as you suggested.... As time passes, very likely our ministry will be reaching farther afield and a car will facilitate this. In our work here in Santiago, a city of a million people, we have mission points scattered from one edge of the city to the other. Perhaps, the greatest "drain" on one's energy and time is in riding the overcrowded, and usually old, buses from place to place....

Again let me express our appreciation of the spirit of your letter as it reveals the spirit of the people there. We would be exceedingly reluctant to even consider accepting such a wonderful gift, if we did not feel that it has come to be considered as the result of a spontaneous movement; if it should come to take on anything of the nature of a "drive," please quietly drop the matter because that would mar that which we value most about it all.

With our love and appreciation,
Ruth and Hugo Culpepper[9]

Confidentially, Hugo and Ruth left open the question of whether they would return to Chile for a second term. Ruth had not adjusted to life there, as Hugo explained in a letter to his parents.

As to our personal feelings about continuing on with the work here after this first term, that is a long time off and we really cannot be sure as to what we will want to do until then. Meanwhile I am continuing to study and work just as if we knew we would be here all our lives until retirement; as the newness wears off in respect to the language and the people, I expect we will increasingly feel

---

[9] Hugo and Ruth Culpepper, letter to Francis Rowe, 14 March 1948.

more at home—I already am experiencing this, and I hope Ruth will by the time the children get a little older and she can do more in the work and get around easier and more often...[10]

In a letter shortly later, Hugo explained their feelings about Chile further:

I have a definite sense of being on a mission here, feel a challenge for the possibilities, and would be happy to be permanently settled in the work here. I have been trying to study the language with this attitude, and have until now. However, I realize that if Ruth continues to feel as she does, we probably would not come back after the first term regardless of how I feel, although I have no idea of what we would really want to do in the States.[11]

Fathers with the car, 1948.

By November 1948 the wonderful people of Immanuel had bought the car, a new Chevrolet. Following a brief dedication ceremony, photographed for the *Arkansas Democrat*, the Culpeppers' parents drove the car to New Orleans, where it was loaded on a ship for transportation to Santiago—the best Christmas present they ever received.

---

[10] Hugo Culpepper, letter to Mr. and Mrs. J. H. Culpepper, 14 March 1948.
[11] Hugo Culpepper, letter to families in Little Rock, no date.

In the midst of the language study and increasing responsibilities in Chile, Hugo continued to study, as his correspondence with James Tull indicates. In response to a request from Hugo for a reading list, Tull sent a bibliography of works on medieval and modern philosophy. He encouraged Hugo to write to Dale Moody, whom he felt would be much more qualified to guide Hugo's reading, and added that Moody had just come through New York on his way to Europe to spend the summer studying under Barth and Brunner. Tull's letter confirms that Hugo's thinking was already turning in a direction that would ultimately lead him to the topic of his doctoral dissertation:

> I think you have envisaged a very worthy and necessary project when you are thinking of doing in future years some work in Christian apologetics and in setting out the Christian message in a way which will commend itself to the intelligence of educated people down there. I know you are very well qualified to do this from the standpoint of natural ability, and by reason of having naturally a logical and systematic mind. Though I can't see how you are going to have the time to do all the many things you have to do, this is certainly a field which apparently has been neglected. I hope you will persevere in it. I think we Southern Baptists have taken too much comfort from the fact that 'not many wise, not many mighty' are called, and have therefore conceived that our mission was to reach the uneducated and illiterate. While such people are not to have their importance minimized in the least, I think we have not realized that, from a long-term point of view, the attitudes of the educated people are determinative beyond what we usually think. In other words, a general cynicism among the intellectuals today will almost inevitably filter into the attitudes of the common people tomorrow, as is happening right now in this country.[12]

Tull added that he had arranged for Hugo subscriptions to *Christianity and Crisis*, *Christianity and Society*, and *Theology Today*, and he commended the last as one of the most valuable theological journals. He begged Hugo not to send him any money for these subscriptions, saying they did not amount to much and that he and Jenny thought that "if we can do any little amount to help in your work in Chile, we are making an investment of our own lives to that extent."[13]

---

[12] James Tull, letter to Hugo, 9 May 1948.
[13] Ibid.

On 14 May 1948, Paul Lawrence "Larry" Culpepper was born in Santiago. The family was complete, and Hugo's desire to give part of his life to medicine would eventually be realized.

Family in Chile.

The Invitation to Move to Buenos Aires

That winter (summer in the northern hemisphere), it was decided that Hugo should stay in Santiago and teach in the seminary rather than go to Temuco to pastor the church there. Almost immediately, an invitation to come to Buenos Aires, Argentina, to teach was extended by Jack Kilgore, who was a missionary in Argentina at the time. Kilgore informed Hugo that at their last mission meeting they had appointed a committee to study the idea of establishing an international seminary for all the work in South America. He recognized that personal and sectional interests would oppose the proposal and lamented that the mission effort did not have "an A-1 seminary at the moment, and at the rate we are going I do not see such an institution at any time within the near future." He ventured that the institution should be independent of existing organizations so that the faculty would be free to devote itself to teaching. The "Junta de Education" should be representative of all the groups represented in the institution, and the faculty itself should be the real policy-making body of the institution. He knew there would be an effort to locate the seminary in Buenos Aires, but he questioned whether pastors trained there would be willing to go back to the small towns, and he noted that they would not benefit from the "denominational politics" they would see there. More immediately, they faced a crisis in the next year with a shortage of teaching staff. Kilgore therefore confidentially raised the possibility of their making an emergency request for the Culpeppers to transfer to Buenos Aires for one year. He commented pointedly on the character of the mission in Argentina: "Your mission is probably somewhat like ours—it varies from conservatism to reactionary-ism in its theological make-up. We even have some rather strong and outspoken 'pre's' [pre-millennialists] here and some brethren who know so much theology that they have not found it necessary to read any serious theological work in 15 years."[14]

The invitation to teach at the new international seminary appealed to Hugo, and he began to explore it actively. Hugo received another welcomed letter from W. O. Carver with reflections on Hugo's plans and mission strategy, and news from Southern Seminary:

I am not a mind reader nor in any sense a modern "psychologist." Certainly I am not an absentee psychoanalyst. Yet I think I understand rather fully the processes through which you have been seeking, missing, and finding your way through these last six years. Indeed, I think that perhaps you had even prior to that an element of tentativeness in your decisions, with a door left open for revisions. I sincerely hope that now you have come to stand on definitely solid ground. At the same time, I would not wish you ever to come to feel that new leadings of the Spirit of God could not reach the citadel of your personality....

I definitely approve the idea of winning an element of what we may call the "cultural leadership" of Chile. Such an ideal is necessary to the highest achievement in missionary work. You may recall the comparisons which I used to make in my missions course among Anderson, Wilson, and Duff in their strategy in India. All of them were needed, and all of them together were only providing for the Christian cultural leadership in a land where "the common people" must, as in the ministry of Jesus, be the main objective of the gospel enterprise. It is good to remember that while "He had compassion on

---

[14] Jack Kilgore, letter to Hugo, 29 August 1949.

Hugo baptizing, Christmas day, 1949.

the multitudes" and always took care that "the common people heard Him gladly," He also definitely undertook the training of a leadership. Again, I used to say that in the light of His example, in the long run, "it is more important to indoctrinate a dozen than superficially to evangelize a million."

In China Timothy Richard pursued a policy that looked toward the whole of China, its masses and its culture, its entire civilization. There were many missionaries who won more converts. There were very few who did as much for the influence of Christ Jesus on China. You will have noticed, I am sure, that Luke is always careful to record the fact whenever people of position, influence, and leadership ability were won by the gospel. It is not a question of this or that, but of both. I notice with much satisfaction that you are "enjoying working with a group of about seventy in a mission point." Always find time for doing much in that line. Give my love to your colleagues and as far as it may be of any possible value share these sentiments with them.

We must not indulge in vain regrets. Yet I have always wondered whether you had not been making a mistake in not majoring on the philosophy of religion. I hope that you will do that on your furlough, as you suggest...

In the midst of last session I broached with the different men whose departments were involved and then with our President the idea of a new approach to the theological curriculum. I was surprised at the readiness with which approval of the idea was met. The idea is that the story of our Christianity and its interpretation should be studied historically by its great periods; that the various aspects of it, expansion, institutional development, worship, philosophical contexts, and consequent theological formulation, should be studied together. To some extent that method is being put into operation. Thus, while Price is technically in the Department of Church History, he is not to be limited to history in the ordinary technical sense. Similarly, the other men in history are to take a more comprehensive view. There is to be inter-departmental co-ordination and co-operation in a measure not heretofore practiced. At least, such is my hope and my understanding.

May I venture to add that I think that Dale [Moody] will outgrow his Brunner-Barth complex....[15]

As he wrestled with the invitation to move to Buenos Aires, Hugo corresponded with Dr. Everett Gill at the Foreign Mission Board, with his close friends, with H. B. Ramsour, who had been in Argentina and transferred to Honolulu but was being invited to return to teach at the seminary, and with Jack Kilgore, who was on furlough during 1949 (at Baylor, where he would remain for the rest of his career). The majority of the missionaries in Chile strongly opposed the proposal to establish an international seminary in Buenos Aires. Hugo and Ruth, however, communicated to Everett Gill late in August that they felt inclined to move to Buenos Aires and help start the international seminary there. Indeed, Hugo was apparently the first person officially named to the faculty of the new seminary, according to Bill Cooper, who would be named as the first president of the school: "Perhaps it would be better to say that, so far as I know, you are the first member of the faculty of the new institution that has been named. Several of us hope and feel that we will form part of that faculty, but we have not been formally named yet."[16]

A letter from Kilgore provides an inside view of the dynamics at work in the founding of the seminary in Buenos Aires.

Dear Hugo:
Your recent letter was forwarded to me here. Your questions and problems are of such moment that I hesitate to tackle them....

While in Louisville last Spring I had an opportunity to speak with Rankin for about an hour. I tried to present a case for the building of a good seminary somewhere in southern South America. My approach

---

[15] W. O. Carver, letter to Hugo, 14 September 1948.
[16] Bill Cooper, letter to Hugo Culpepper, 3 September 1949.

was not that of eliminating any of the others (however this might have logically and administratively followed). My point was simply that the work was in need of such an institution with a sufficiently trained faculty and the necessary equipment.

I think the prime movers for the combination institution were Cooper and the various visitors to our fields (and you?).... The news that I received of your probable transfer to the seminary in Buenos Aires was the "most encouraging" I have had in regard to the work there—with the exception of the move to attempt to build a decent seminary somewhere down there.

Any institution that we may have there will be greatly dependent upon the faculty which it has. I certainly hope that it will not be filled up with reactionaries with one or two of us having to bear the brunt of carrying the ball against it. I certainly hope to see you there when we return!

From an Argentina standpoint, it would be difficult to move the seminary out of the country. Uruguay would be more favorable than Chile from that angle and even then you might have another "Bible Institute" on your hands.... [17]

In spite of his attraction to the proposed seminary in Argentina, Hugo could not feel released from his commitment to the mission in Chile. Hugo expressed his change of heart about the move in a letter to Everett Gill with copies to Bill Cooper and Jack Kilgore. After detailing a number of considerations, he wrote:

I suppose the above considerations are really just contributing factors. Probably, a more basic consideration is that I have come to the conclusion that we would possibly be entering a "blind alley." I have indicated in letters to you in the past that the violent reaction here against the whole plan has considerably dampened my first enthusiasm and taken the "heart out of me." I am still as fully convinced as ever as to the need for such an institution. But I believe the wholehearted cooperation of *all* the missions involved, and of the large majority of all the missionaries in each of the missions, is absolutely necessary for any promise of success, especially with reference to the securing of more and better students for the institutions. I see no hope of this being possible now. Furthermore, perhaps in recognition of this also, I get the impression that the leaders on the Board and there in Richmond are "making

---

[17] Jack Kilgore, letter to Hugo Culpepper, 5 October 1949.

haste slowly," are going to *not* push the matter too much just now but will let it work itself out slowly as seems expedient; probably that is the only thing to do in the nature of the case. Furthermore, I am convinced that, very likely, the con-tinuation of the school here in Santiago will result in practically no stu-dents going from here to Buenos Aires. I am sure, as you say, that this proposal has caused all of us to think more seriously then ever before (though not always constructively) about the problem of theological education in these countries, but this will not suffice. All of the petty national pride on the part of the nationals and even missionaries (I fear), all of the bickering and conflicting opinion, makes it difficult to get positive, constructive action.

All of what I have said can be summed up in this mixed figure of speech: I can not see my way clear to change horses in the middle of the stream and ride off up a blind alley (possibly) with an ailing wife (possibly [Ruth had trouble with asthma, but it did not persist]).

Although we are not going to Buenos Aires now, we shall continue to favor the development of an international seminary as being a much needed institution and will use whatever influence we might have to support it.[18]

In response, Cooper wrote:

> Dear Hugo:
> Sometimes one receives more blows than he can well withstand. Thus they have been coming these last few days. Your letter was one of those blows. However, being a miserable diehard, I am slowly recovering. We regret that you will not be with us for next year. We do not want to accept your letter as a final note, but will let it be so far as next year and maybe even the next are concerned.[19]

By February of 1950, Hugo had made a trip to Buenos Aires to meet with the mission leaders there. In August 1950 Cooper wrote again, asking for Hugo's help in shaping the curriculum of the new seminary and again expressing hope that he might come to teach history and theology. Hugo responded with a six-page letter after a month of careful consideration, expressing his frustration in feeling that he was not able to give himself more fully to theological education in Santiago, his sense that there was some duplication of expertise among those in the seminary in Santiago at

---

[18] Hugo Culpepper, letter to Everett Gill, Bill Cooper, and Jack Kilgore, 2 November 1949.

[19] Bill Cooper, letter to Hugo Culpepper, 13 November 1949.

that time, his hopes for the new seminary in Buenos Aires, and his openness to continue to explore the matter with Cooper.

Early in the letter he provided the following summary of his activities in Chile. When he corresponded with Dr. Rankin about going to Chile, he expressed a strong preference for seminary work. Rankin said that although there was no opening in the seminary at that time, he felt sure that Hugo would move into teaching later on. At the end of just one year of language study, he was pressed into teaching in spite of his language deficiencies, and he thoroughly enjoyed it. At the same time, he became increasingly conscious that the situation in Chile left much to be desired. Because of this, he was enthusiastic when he learned of plans for an international seminary that would make possible a more adequate program of theological education. He also found that he was taking on more and more responsibilities. He began teaching Old Testament and English. The next year he taught Philosophy of Religion, Church History, Old Testament Criticism and Interpretation, and Apologetics. In 1950 he was teaching New Testament Criticism and Interpretation, Biblical Introduction, Greek, and Homiletics. He was also Treasurer for the Junta de Cooperación and spent a lot of time handling funds and wrestling with problems pertaining to the relationship between the Mission and Chilean pastors. While they were basically quite happy in Chile, he did not find the satisfaction that comes from participation in a creative work. On the contrary, he felt that he was merely helping feed grist to the mill to keep the wheels turning.[20]

A month later, Hugo wrote to Dr. Gill at the Foreign Mission Board and to Bill Cooper, indicating that while he was not seeking the position in Buenos Aires, if the board supported Cooper's plans for the seminary there and supported the request for Hugo to join the faculty there, then he and Ruth were ready to respond positively:

We have come to feel that all of this has come to us from without, that we have not sought it, and that the Lord is in it. Because of that, we are in dead earnestness now in trying to be very careful to feel our way along and not to rush into something. I am deeply impressed by how you and I seem to see eye to eye with reference to what the Seminary should and can be. The only hesitance I feel now is as to whether Richmond is in a position to fully back us in the matter; I believe they are or they would not have gone this far along, although problems will have to be worked out along the way as they come up. If Dr. Gill

---

[20] Hugo Culpepper, letter to Bill Cooper, 26 September 1950.

so recommends, we are definitely ready to make the change this summer and be there for next year.[21]

Dr. Gill replied that he was ready to recommend the Culpeppers' transfer to Argentina wholeheartedly, and added: "I am ready to back up the program of making the Seminary in Buenos Aires a first-class institution, in which the professors will be giving the major portion of their time to teaching and study."[22] Dr. Gill's recommendations were adopted by the Foreign Mission Board on 7 December 1950.

In February of 1951 Hugo returned to Buenos Aires on his way to Montevideo, Uruguay, to spend a week teaching at a pastor's retreat. On the way back he attended the Pan-American Games in Buenos Aires and met with the seminary faculty.

In a letter written from Montevideo a couple of days later, on Sunday, 19 February 1951, Hugo reported to Ruth that while he had been in Buenos Aires he had looked at apartments, trying to locate suitable housing for the family. Some on the faculty wanted the Culpeppers to get a temporary visa and move to Buenos Aires before classes began on 3 April 1951. Hugo wrestled with the decision: the need in Buenos Aires, the difficulty of finding housing and renting out the house in Santiago, the effects on the family, and the question of the visa. Bill Cooper and the rest of the faculty planned to arrive in September. At the end of the letter Hugo added a handwritten note, saying that he had reread the letter and that getting away from Buenos Aires, resting, and writing the letter had helped him to clarify his thinking about the matter and that he thought it best to wait for the regular visa and make a more orderly move, rather than rushing things and having problems in the move.

In his next letter, at the end of the week in Montevideo, Hugo related his experience with Uruguayan pastors:

There was a full program all morning and every evening, and after the afternoon nap we played volleyball. I had an hour's class each morning and one each night; they were really the principal part of the program as it turned out.

In Uruguay there are 14 Baptist Churches and 10 pastors besides the three missionaries. All three missionaries and all the pastors except one were there with their families. All of the pastors have been to the seminary. There

---

[21] Hugo Culpepper, letter to Bill Cooper, with copy to Everett Gill, 16 October 1950.

[22] Everett Gill, letter to Hugo Culpepper, 30 October 1950.

were about 23 to 25 of us present all the time. The men are better educated and more cultured than our pastors in Chile. I was well impressed by them. They are living sacrificial lives and are trying to serve the Lord with all they have. We thoroughly enjoyed the fellowship together during the week. Apparently they were quite appreciative of my teaching, judging by the interest shown during the classes and the way they entered into the discussions. Ricardo Alverez (the one who had dinner with us our first year in Chile out on Santa Julia), who is a graduate of Louisville Seminary and has his M.A. from Yale, was quite profuse in his words of appreciation for my efforts at the closing session this morning. He has invited me over to his home for dinner this evening at 8 P.M. Numbers of the fellows said that they wanted to invite me back again next year. All in all, it was a week well spent I think.[23]

He still thought it best to take their time with the move to Buenos Aires. Hugo wrote again, three days later, now inclining definitely toward remaining in Santiago until they could get a permanent visa and make an orderly move. Ruth had written that she was willing to make the move then and "make the best of any situation." Hugo was thinking of delaying the move for some months but moving before their furlough and being in Buenos Aires for the opening of the seminary early in 1952. They could continue their work in Santiago, and a new missionary to Chile was expected in September, who could pick up some of their work there. The rest of the week, Hugo visited with personnel in Buenos Aires and attended the weightlifting and track and field events at the Pan-American Games. He was especially excited about getting to meet and talk wih Bob Richards, a preacher working on a Ph.D. in philosophy and the second man ever to pole vault fifteen feet. A friend, Bob Hoffman, invited them to a steak dinner: "With our Spanish we managed to get back to town on a street car and bus (he wanted a taxi but none was available). By 9:00 we were seated to the best steak dinner I've ever eaten (it was really a baby beef roast, nearly three inches thick) with melon, tomatoes, and canned peaches for dessert."[24]

---

[23] Hugo Culpepper, letter to Ruth Culpepper and Mr. and Mrs. J. H. Culpepper, 23 February 1951.

[24] Hugo Culpepper, letter to Ruth, 28 February 1951.

Home to Little Rock

Leaving friends in Chile was painful, and fellow missionaries greatly regretted the decision to move to Argentina. After Hugo's return to Santiago, plans changed again. In view of the needs of the mission in Santiago, the requirement of a two-year lease on housing in Buenos Aires, and the timing of their furlough, it was decided that they should move up their furlough, sell most of their belongings in Chile, return to the States before the end of 1951, spend a year in study at the seminary in Louisville, and then go to Buenos Aires in time for the beginning of the school year, early in 1953. Hugo would serve as professor of theology and church history. H. C. Goerner advised Hugo: "Since more than ten years have elapsed since you were actually in residence, and since there would be a change of major in which there would be little carry-over from the previous year's study [1939–1940], it will be necessary for you to begin your work in the field of Theology *de novo*."[25]

In September 1951, Dr. Gill approved their request to return home on furlough six months early in order to begin studies at Southern on 15 January, and the Culpeppers arrived in Little Rock on the eve of Thanksgiving. The *Immanuel Record*, 13 December 1951, announced that Hugo and Ruth had moved their membership to Immanuel Baptist Church and that they would be speaking there for a "missionary rally" on Monday evening, 17 December.

Culpeppers arriving in Little
Rock, Arkansas, 21 November
1951.

---

[25] H. C. Goerner, letter to Hugo Culpepper, 17 February 1951.

In an article in the *Arkansas Gazette*, Hugo articulated a principle for missions and government programs:

> Rev. Hugo Culpepper believes that the same problem of wise assistance faces missionary work as well as international government relations in South America. How to help the Chileans wisely without hurting their initiative and leadership and without offending their pride is the major difficulty for missionaries as well as government workers, he declared.
>
> "We have to learn quickly the discreet use of American influence and power. The common people appreciate the economic contributions the United States is making, but they strongly resent any hint of external domination or dictation," he explained.[26]

In January 1952, Hugo left the family the family in Little Rock, while he went on to Southern Seminary to continue his doctoral work there.

---

[26] "U.S. Must Be Humble Partner in Aiding World, Pastor Says," *Arkansas Gazette* (the clipping is undated).

Chapter 6

Furlough in Louisville

"Let us insist that every Christian shall feel that missions is his one business.... It needs to be made the test of orthodoxy [Hugo: and what Southern Baptist wants to be unorthodox!], if not of saving faith itself."[1]

In January Hugo left the family in Little Rock while he went on to Louisville to begin work on a Th.D. in theology. The separation was painful, but he immersed himself in his studies in preparation for his role on the faculty in Buenos Aires. If possible, he hoped to complete the comprehensive exams before returning to Argentina.

Dear Ruth, Alan, and Butchie,
I am becoming much better adjusted here. In fact, I am becoming somewhat concerned now about finding enough time for real studying. This morning I got up at 7 (en punto ["on the dot"]) as usual (by the alarm, although the noise here wakes me around 6:30 usually and I doze), had breakfast (typically one scrambled egg, oatmeal, orange juice, a glass of milk for 33 cents), shaved, and went to the library at 8:00. That gave me an hour to study before N.T. Theology at 9:00. Chapel was at 10:00. Dr. Pettigrew, pastor of Walnut Street gave a helpful talk on "Our Biggest Problem is the Big I," that is, thinking too much of ourselves. I realized that I have done the despicable thing of succumbing too much to self-pity these last few days, when really we have so much to be thankful for. At 10:40, immediately after chapel, I went to Systematic Theology class until 11:40 and then to Theology Seminar (on the Atonement) until 1:00. I had to rush to get to lunch before the deadline at

---

[1] W. O. Carver, *Missions and the Kingdom of Heaven* (Louisville: John P. Morton and Company, 1898) 3. "Prefatory Remarks," quoted by Hugo Culpepper in his faculty address, "Mission in the Twentieth Century: A Perspective in the Theology of Mission," *Review & Expositor*, 70, 1 (Winter 1973): 98.

1:15. Had Mexican macaroni and chipped, ground meat, okra, fruit jello, and buttermilk (55 cents). I lay down to rest for 30 minutes. At 2:15, just as I was walking out to go to the library to study until supper time, a telephone call came from the main office saying that the barbells had arrived.... I hope to get in 5 or 6 solid hours of reading besides the classes and seminars each day. I like the studies. However, there is so very, very much that I do not know whether it will be possible to take the written exams or not. In any case, it will have been well worthwhile, as a planned reading course. When we get back together, I'll enjoy the studies even more, and I think we shall have a delightful year up here all together next year if we get an apartment. Otherwise, we will not come unless we can find something entirely desirable for the whole family.

Tomorrow will be another full day, with classes and chapel from 9:00 till 11:40 as every morning from Tuesday thorough Friday, and the Philosophy of Religion seminar for the first meeting from 3:30 till 5:30 in the afternoon. I think this will usually meet on Wednesday afternoon. I have been pleased to find that I have a very good orientation for the studies, from the slow, general, interested reading through the years. The fellows have the details on their fingertips, and have the advantage on me in this way, but some of them lack a certain maturity that I feel I have. That is to be expected, of course. What I need is to sharpen my wits now, grateful that I seem to have a quite adequate general orientation. I am by no means lost—and that is what the intensive study of the next year should do for me. If I can successfully complete this course of studies, exams or no exams, my work in B.A. will be a pleasure. I'll have lots to share with them, and will feel more sure of my bearings in doing it.

That is about all I have for today. I am so happy that you are resting with Alan and taking the time to read him good literature. I realize more than ever that they are our dearest possession (you and I as one) and that nothing is so important as to invest our best in them. It is wonderful for me to know that they have a Mother like you to do this so well. I feast on every little detail you write about all of you....

Lots of Love,
Daddy[2]

Dearest Ruth and Boys,
Your two letters were like a tonic for me today. I got up this morning feeling quite low. Last night I returned from studying in the library and went to bed by 10:00 P.M. to get some extra rest, planning to sleep as long as I could and then get something to eat in the student center before the 10:00 A.M. class. I

---

[2] Hugo Culpepper, letter to family, 24 January 1952.

was hoping that getting caught up some on my rest would help my general feelings. I woke up about three this morning with those burning acute pains in my stomach and could not doze off for a couple of hours. I really became suspicious of an ulcer then, and realized that it could cause us some inconveniences and change of plans. I determined to see a doctor today, if I could. However, it was a spiritual blessing to me because it made me realize in an experiential way (. . .) that we are really only creatures of God and utterly dependent in our nature as man.... I came on to the room and read your letters. All along I have figured that my emotional condition was probably the cause of my indigestion, etc. Your letters were a real lift to me, and I soon found myself humming and singing for the first time since arriving here.... I'll be there with you all two weeks from right now!...

I leave at 8:00 and get back late. I think I'll speak only once in the morning, to save some nervous energy. I'm going to have to alter my speech [on their experience in the concentration camp] so as not to have such an emotional reaction myself every time I speak. I think that is a factor in my condition too. Of course, it always costs one to really put himself in his talks, but I must make some adjustment about this....

My paper on [William] Temple is my main project, but I hope to get in other reading also. The time should pass better for me now that I have something to look forward to....

Lovingly,
Hugo[3]

Ruth and the children spent part of the summer of 1952 with the Culpeppers and the Cochranes in Little Rock. A happy event marked that summer—Alan's childhood conversion—which Hugo faithfully recorded so that Alan could remember the details of it when he grew older.

Alan was converted during the first two weeks of August, while we were living at Ridgecrest in Mrs. Marian Cowherd's apartment. One night his father read the story of the crucifixion for his and Larry's bedtime Bible story from Egermeier's Bible Stories. Alan's eyes filled with tears as he was visibly moved; he said, "Daddy, I just can't understand it—I try to, but I just can't." I explained to him that I did not understand all about it either, but that it made plain to us the love of God and the reality of sin. Each night after that, Alan prayed about his sins and confessed them one by one. For example, one time he said,

---

[3] Hugo Culpepper, letter to family, 26 January 1952.

"Forgive me for telling Cris a story today." A few days later he told me that he wanted to come into the room where I studied and talk to me about something.

The next morning he came in and climbed up in my lap. He said, "Daddy, you know all those Bible Stories that we have been reading—well, I want you to tell me the meaning of them." I began and told him the story of creation and the fall and redemption on through the meaning of church membership and the ordinances. At points he would say, "I understand that, go on." At other points he would say, "I don't understand that, explain it." The following night or so, on Thursday, August 14, Alan said, when we had our prayers at bedtime (he had been wanting to say them with me alone, and his mother with Larry because he said Larry would not understand our praying about his sins) he said he wanted to get up after Larry went to sleep and come in the living room and tell his mother about "what we had been doing." He did, and asked me to tell his mother. Then he said to us, "I want to do something—guess what—it ought not to be hard for you to guess, because it is about the church." I asked him if he wanted to join the church and be baptized and he said, "yes, do you think I am too young? Mr. Vaught said in Bible School that children my age were not, but that he wanted to talk to their parents first." I explained again that joining the church did not save him and he understood.

A few days later he wanted to "tell the people" (make a profession of faith) in Blacksburg, Va., at the Tull's, but I explained that we would be back in Immanuel at Little Rock the following Sunday. On Sunday, August 24, I told Frank Shamburger (W. O. Vaught was on vacation) of Alan's experience and then he talked with Alan. Alan joined the church in the morning service after John McClanahan had preached from Hebrews on "Let us go outside the camp, bearing His reproach...." At the opening of the night service I baptized Alan (he was the only candidate), opening my remarks with the verse, "By grace are ye saved through faith, and that not of yourselves, it is the gift of God." I related his experience and then baptized him saying, "In obedience to the command of our Lord and Savior, Jesus Christ, and upon your own profession of faith in Him, I baptize you, my son, Alan Culpepper, in the name of the Father, and of the Son, and of the Holy Spirit. Amen"

After church, on the way home, Alan said to me, "Dad, do you remember what the Bible says about coming up out of the water to a "new life" —well, that is just how I felt when I came up; I didn't even want to play with paper in church. I said to myself, 'No, I'm going to listen to the sermon'." He was especially interested in the illustration of the little boy who made a boat and lost it on the waters of a flash flood, and later saw it repainted, for sale in a show window. He bought it after recognizing it as his own, and said, "Now you are twice mine—I made you and I have bought you." I explained to Alan what this meant as we rode home from church.[4]

At the end of the summer, the whole family moved to Louisville, to the missionary apartments, adjacent to the tennis courts on the campus of Southern Seminary. Hugo continued his graduate studies throughout the fall and winter. W. O. Carver retired in 1952, so Hugo treasured this final opportunity to study and spend time with his mentor. Near the end of the Culpeppers' furlough, the Carvers took Hugo and Ruth out for lunch at the Canary Cottage in St. Matthews. Hugo always remembered that on that occasion Dr. Carver told him, "My father taught me to think for myself," which Hugo understood as Carver's giving his father credit for his originality of thought. After lunch, they returned to the Carvers' home where Ruth took a picture of Hugo with the Carvers.

Hugo with the Carvers, in their home, 1953.

Hugo did not attempt the comprehensive exams that year, feeling that he was still unprepared to do so. Foreshadowing things to come, however,

---

[4] Hugo Culpepper, record of Alan Culpepper's conversion, 26 August 1952.

Hugo's interest in the writings of Miguel de Unamuno was already taking form, as evidenced by a note written in the back of one of his Nestle's Greek New Testament and dated 17 March 1953:

"The thought of Unamuno centers round two main ideas which he clothes with religious significance: the idea of vocation or mission, and the idea of agonizing struggle, especially of struggle to live forever. Truth breaks and life is fulfilled only upon the road when one is pressing onwards, loyal to the heavenly vision."[5]

On 14 May 1953, the Culpeppers moved to Little Rock for some time with their families before returning to South America. The Baptist church in Stuttgart, Arkansas, wanted to call Hugo as their pastor, and in later years Hugo often speculated how his life, and the lives of others in the family, might have been different had he decided not to go back to South America at that time. Hugo had been having trouble with gum disease (pyorrhea) since their experience in the concentration camp. Following his dentist's recommendation, he had all his teeth extracted and wore dentures for the rest of his life. Because of this dental work, their departure for Buenos Aires was delayed, and they had to fly rather than go by ship in order to arrive in time for the beginning of the second half of the school year in July. They flew from Little Rock to Houston on 28 June 1953, then on to Mexico City, where they spent a day sight-seeing. From there they flew to Panama and on to Santiago. After a day of visiting friends in Santiago, they flew on to Buenos Aires, arriving on 2 July.

---

[5] John MacKay, *The Other Spanish Christ: A Study in the Spiritual History of Spain and South America* (New York: MacMillan, 1932) 149.

Chapter 7

Argentina
1953-1958

"Verbalization of the gospel is not enough. We must make the gospel
incarnate. Even God could not find a better way."[1]

The Culpeppers arrived in Argentina in July 1953, almost exactly fifty
years after Dr. Sidney M. Sowell, the first Southern Baptist missionary to
Argentina, disembarked in Buenos Aires (23 September 1903). Dr. Sowell
was still in Argentina, living at the seminary with his daughter, Anne
Sowell Margrett, when the Culpeppers arrived. His death some months later
marked the end of an era for the Argentine mission. By 1953, however,
there were 160 Baptist churches in Argentina. The Baptist seminary in
Buenos Aires was founded in 1912. Dr. Sowell had become the president of
the seminary in 1918 and served in this capacity for twenty-three years. In
1922, with fourteen students, it moved to its present location. By 1927 it
had reached an all-time high of seventeen students, and the following year
it began requiring a sixth-grade certificate for admission. The year the
Culpeppers arrived, the W.M.U. Training School of Rosario and the
seminary united to form the International Seminary for the five
southernmost countries of South America and began the year with fifty-six
students.

One of those students was Franz Boretsky, who made an immediate
impression on Hugo. Boretsky wrote the following account of his life
experience:

I was born in the Soviet Union the 13th of March, 1924, into a
family of atheists. From no one did I ever hear talk about God, and

---

[1] Hugo Culpepper, Charge to Missionary Appointees, Ridgecrest, 22 August
1970. See below, p. 288.

when I was older I took advantage of every occasion I could to show to those who did believe in God that He did not exist.

At the beginning of the war I was deported to Nurenberg, Germany, where almost as soon as I arrived, I was put in prison. After a short time, I was sent along with a group of 250 people, to a concentration camp in Mathausen, Austria. There almost any form of life was impossible; we were made to work far beyond our strength, we were beaten with whips until unconscious, we suffered from acute hunger, and were tortured in all forms. Every day before my eyes hundreds of persons died, and as is only logical, for the first time, I began to think of God. Up to this point I had led the life of an atheist. I trembled at the very idea of death because I felt that something very terrible waited for me in the life beyond. I began to think all I was suffering was nothing but punishment from God for all my sins. When my companions of misfortune died during the torturing, cursing God instead of pleading for His Mercy, I took the side of God, even though I did not know Him. I imagined God as One of vengeance, all-powerful to punish, and I could not imagine how it would be possible for Him to let me live. With all my heart I desired some information about this unknown God; but, shame though it is, none of the deported people knew or loved God. Many times my life hung by a thread, but I noted that in every case a superior force saved me, and foolish as it is, I called this force "good fortune."

Time passed. The year 1945 arrived. In May the North American troops liberated me from this terrible camp of death; by this time I was almost a skeleton. When we were liberated our group, that was 250 people, was now reduced to three. I lived for a time with the American soldiers, and then I decided to go back to my native country. But I could not realize my intention to go to the place of my birth because in the Soviet zone in Austria I was captured and put into the Russian army. The great desire I felt in my heart was to desert, but it was without any purpose or reason that I felt this way. I felt a mysterious force in me that gave me the impulse to flee, and I could not understand what had happened inside of me. After I had battled this temptation for a good while, I finally decided to flee.

For several months then I was a vagabond in the different zones in Austria. I fell into the hands of the frontier guards, but in all dangers and hopeless situations, I always found a force unknown to me who always returned me to liberty. Finally, I resolved to become something, and I became it—a thief. It was a work that according to an old

Russian saying "was pleasing to my heart." From small jobs I climbed up the ladder in a short time to doing big-time stuff, and it always made me as happy as a child to read in the newspapers of my latest exploits.

In November 1946 I left Austria and slipped into Italy, where I continued to live my risky life, being a slave to all the passions. Here I lost my soul day after day. One afternoon in Rome, as luck would have it, I fell into a meeting of Russian Baptists—this was in February of 1947. All were singing with great devotion, and I felt ashamed to be in their midst. When I rose to leave, the preacher started to talk of God, of sin, of repentance, and he awoke again my interest in such things. He talked about an eternal life that was completely unknown to me, of a new birth that was completely incomprehensible to me. I listened to the sermon as if it was a beautiful fable. Finally, he painted a particularly clear picture of a life without God, and I felt that he was talking of me. I put my naked soul before me, and I discovered something that I did not want to face—my past condition, and my present one. I felt like I was on thorns, like a rat caught and stuck. At the end, the preacher gave me a New Testament and a little book entitled "The Salvation of God." All the believers greeted me warmly and invited me to come again. I left that church alarmed at the sermon I had heard, but at the same time comforted by knowing of such a great love.

I tried to erase from my mind all the things I had heard about God, but it was useless. I decided then to get thoroughly drunk, during which I gained my purpose of forgetting what was bothering me, and I threw into the corner the books that had been given to me. Then came the day of the next meeting and I returned to the place of the meeting, where such a sympathetic and cordial reception was given me that it left me giddy. I informed them of my financial status, and my necessities. The meeting began. They spoke again of the Kingdom of God, of the impossibility of a person entering who had not been born again, and of the second coming of Christ to take the ones who belonged to Him and to leave the unrighteous. Again, it appeared to me a second time that the preacher was talking of me, and wanted my repentance. Even though I was accustomed to living a life full of risks, I felt a profound terror of God; my past life ran before me, and I felt horror to see in what condition I was before God. At the end of the service, they took me to an adjoining room where they gave me a pair of shoes. Satan took hold of my heart again, and I stole several jars of jelly, when I should have been grateful for the shoes that had been given me.

But I had hardly reached the street when, for the first time in my life, I felt remorse, such a great remorse that I felt constrained to enter again and put back in their place the things that I had stolen. From this moment there was born in me an inner struggle which I could not overcome, and I saw clearly that I was lost. On my way home, I saw neither people nor streets. The picture of my condition was continually before my eyes. What should I do? How could I live? These and other questions came to my mind, and I could hardly wait to get home to find the book, "The Salvation of God." I began to read it eagerly. When I arrived at the point where it says that our sins have been washed in the blood of Christ, that all that is necessary for our salvation has already been done by Him and that He will refuse no one, I understood with surprising clarity that the Lord would not refuse even me. I fell on my knees, and crying furiously I said to the Lord, "Lord God, I am not worthy to raise my face to heaven, let alone to be on my knees before you, but in your great mercy, take me just as I am, dirty, ruined, and lost."

I not only felt saved, but I put all my past life, my present, and my future at His feet, and in that instant I felt a new force penetrate my being. My heart was happy. All the weight of my sin left me, and there is no one in the world who could convince me that I was not pardoned. Words of gratitude filled my soul, while at the same time I was crying for joy because of my glorious salvation. Oh what consolation! Words cannot describe it, but one can only live it and feel it in the heart. There is nothing so precious in all the world as to know that Christ has forgiven sin and saved one. Looking back over my past life, I now see clearly the way by which the Savior has chosen to bring me to himself.

Now I can testify to the many things that Christ has done for me: He has given me victory over sin, and has brought me to see the purpose of my life. I am happy, and I am afraid of nothing because I know God is with me and I feel His presence. I am continually praising God and testifying as to how He has been able to transform a dangerous delinquent into a child of His. For this reason, I am dedicating my life to His service; my heart rejoices in living only for Christ.[2]

Hugo added the following note.

---

[2] Franz Boretsky, "I Was Lost and I Was Found," from typescript in Hugo's files.

Mr. Boretsky has continued to live a Christian life. His first step after his conversion was to win a fellow-countryman to his Christ. Within the first month, this friend, an ex-lieutenant in the Russian artillery, was led to Jesus. This army officer found his way first to Argentina. Just last year he was graduated from the International Seminary in Buenos Aires. At present he is a home missionary under the Argentina Home Mission Board working down in Patagonia, which is a very southern, cold province.

Mr. Boretsky himself soon fell in love with a beautiful Italian girl, a daughter of one of our Baptist families in Rome.... With his wife, Mr. Boretsky too migrated to Argentina and settled in the southern part. After working for several years, he entered the International Seminary here this fall, along with his wife and five children. Being a very industrious person, he has taken an old shack on the seminary campus and has made it into a livable home for his family. Four years of school are ahead of him, but he is undaunted in his spirit and energy as he faces them with his wife and children.[3]

Growing Responsibilities

Because there was no other suitable housing available when they arrived, the Culpeppers moved into an apartment in the men's dormitory. In January, Hugo went with the other missionaries to the camp at Bialet Masse in Cordoba, a resort area in a low mountain range in Central Argentina, about 800 miles northwest of Buenos Aires. His letters to Ruth describe the rigors of the trip, his activities, the strain of his heavy schedule on the family, and the dynamics of the Argentine mission at that time.

Dear Ruth and Boys,
We had a more pleasant trip on the bus than I expected. It was cool and the air was clean. I found it restful just to sit down all day again for a change. The bus was like a Greyhound.... We made stops at 11, 3, 5:30, and at 9:45 arrived at Cordoba. There we had hot dogs for supper and orange crush. Then, at 11 P.M., we took a rattling old bus out to Bialet Masse. About midnight we got off, and it was hard carrying my 57 pounds of luggage [mainly books, no doubt!] besides the brief case of books and canteen down a dark road for 6 or 8 blocks. A daughter of the caretaker got up when we arrived.... We slept from 1:00 till 8:30 and got up for a cup of coffee with milk and bread.... My first impression is that it is not bad for a "missionary Shangri-la," but that we will

---

[3] Hugo Culpepper, ibid.

never develop a camp here. It is not attractive enough and is too remote from Baptist Centers, it seems to me. The boys would like it here, but it would be hard on you. Julia Askew washes in the river!... We are about half a mile high, and nearby a big, long mountain is another half mile up.... I read fifty pages in a commentary on Galatians yesterday, and plan to spend as much time reading and resting as possible.... Tonight I'm going a 10-minute bus trip down the highway to preach to a Baptist Church at 9:30 P.M....

Lots of love to you and the boys,

Hugo

P.S.: In general we are about like being out at the edge of Conway [Arkansas] (at Mrs. Gunn's where we lived) on the thinly settled edge of a small town with dirt streets. Within a block or two is a river and open country.[4]

Dearest Ruth and Boys,

I have just gotten up from a siesta and have come down to the dining hall to have a table to write on. This is the hottest day we have had. The weather here reminds me of Santiago in the summer time—hot in the day and cool at nights. The camp program here is going along very nicely. There were 43 in Sunday School this morning. They have as closely scheduled and as full a day as Siloam [Springs Baptist Assembly in Arkansas] or even more so. It would be hard to work the boys into the schedule, or to fish, etc. with them without disrupting the schedule. I am trying to put as much as I can into my teaching. This takes time for preparation. Consequently, I don't sit through all the classes. The first class is mine from 8:20 to 9:10. Then I prepare for the following day till morning preaching at 11:20–12:10. After lunch is siesta and more study for me. They have a hike 2:30 to 4:30. Tea at 4:30. From 5 to 6 I am one of the lifeguards at the river. We soap up and bathe there along with our swim. After supper is preaching, camp fire service, dormitory devotionals, and bed at 11 P.M....

Dear, I'm sorry you have been so unhappy lately. Whatever part of it has been my fault in any way, I hope to be able to change. It is distressing to see you depressed. After all, we mean more to each other than anything else, and I'm sure neither of us wants to cause the other to suffer. When the light is gone out of your eyes and face, it casts a shadow over our home. If there is anything I can do to help you in relieving your depression, I hope you will let me help. Anyway, I hope I can be more sympathetically understanding and manifest the affection which I really feel but have found it hard to let express

---

[4] Hugo Culpepper, letter to family, 7 January 1954.

itself. Has that been part of the trouble, or has it been concern and sharing of your father's retiring, etc.?

I hope we can organize our work better in the future, both school and house, and leave time for leisurely being together some each day as a family and doing things together. Try and get rested up, and love the boys for me. Alan, you, and Larry, you, help your mother all you can and be careful while you enjoy your playing.

Love to each,

Hugo[5]

Dearest Ruth, Alan, and Larry,

I have just finished the last class of the first week on Galatians. We completed the epistle, and it has been a personal blessing for me to study it two or three hours a day as I have done. I really started my preparation last Wednesday morning on the bus and have carefully gone through the 250 pages of G. S. Duncan's commentary in the Moffatt series with the Greek text and dictionary and the Spanish text and dictionary. I have learned quite a number of new words in Spanish. This is really the way to study the Bible. It just shows that the best way to learn is to teach. I hope to eventually have studied the whole Bible this way, and especially the New Testament. Now I start 1 John, but I've done this before and have C. H. Dodd's commentary in the Moffatt series underlined and the Spanish Bible marked, so it will take less time. I'm reading a little book on the thought of Unamuno, in Spanish.

The following paragraph from the same letter reveals Hugo's skill in reading groups and analyzing disputes—a skill he often used in later years in mediating differences and working out solutions for harmonious relationships in divided groups.

We have had good discussions the last two afternoons between all the missionaries about the "seminary-mission" problem, and will continue next week. There seem to be four factors in our analysis: (1) Professors "running things" of the mission as members of the Executive Committee in Buenos Aires; (2) the budget of the seminary hogging [the] allowance for Argentina and leaving field needs neglected; (3) Almost half of the votes in the mission are seminary, but mission has little control over the seminary on the other side; and (4) "Professional ethics" in working relations between professors and

---

[5] Hugo Culpepper, letter to family, 10 January 1954.

district missionaries in contacts with churches—professors [should] consult district missionaries first. We have no solution yet.[6]

On 24 May 1954, W. O. Carver died at the age of eighty-six. His prayer at the last chapel service he conducted, a few weeks earlier, repeated themes and emphases that had made a profound impression on Hugo:

> We thank you O Lord our God for this day. We pray Thee that Thou wilt help us to learn more and more how so to relate ourselves to Thee, and to Thy purposes for us in Christ Jesus, and to Thy living presence in the Holy Spirit, as to enable us to thank Thee for every day. There are some days that we call good days; there are some days that seem to us bad days. But in Thy providence and purpose and in Thy grace they may all be for us, and for Thy interest and concern with us, good days.
>
> Help us to learn how to walk with Thee and talk with Thee, and help us to learn how to listen and hear that which Thou dost say and which Thou art ever ready to say to Thy servants and to all men who will listen.
>
> We thank Thee for the years and the days of Thy providence and of Thy grace, and we pray Thee that these young servants of Thine may early learn how to live, and move, and act, and plan, as living in God, consciously; with all the constraints that go with that glorious privilege, and with all the restraints which our own wills and our own limitations impose upon our living.
>
> Help us, we pray Thee, to effect harmony and unity in our progress. Give, God, an inner experience; and in life, as we work with God according to Thy purpose, help us that it more and more become true of us as Jesus said of himself: that the Son can do nothing on his independent initiative, but that he does lay hold on everything which he sees the Father doing in relation to him, and that he undertakes to do it and to do it in the same manner in which the Father is doing it.
>
> And so grant, O God, that in our experiences we may constantly be growing in grace and in knowledge and in service of our Lord Jesus Christ, for His name's sake. Amen.[7]

---

[6] Hugo Culpepper, letter to family, 13 January 1954.

[7] W. O. Carver, *The Tie*, 22,6 (July 1954): 4.

Hugo enjoyed a close relationship with his own father also. A paragraph in a letter written by Hugo's father reflects the loving relationship between father and son: "Your letter received yesterday, and your remarks for Father's Day was all any father could wish for. No father can or could have a son to be as proud of as I have. In fact, Mother and I have much to be thankful for in having a son, daughter, son-in-law and daughter-in-law, and grandchildren. We are happy with them all, only wish that we could do more for all of you and show our appreciation and love."[8]

The Culpeppers' annual report to the Foreign Mission Board in 1954 gives a synopsis of their first year in Argentina.

We arrived in Buenos Aires on July 12, 1953, to begin our third term of missionary service, after a first term in the Orient and a second term in Chile. The challenging opportunities for work in the seminary and churches were all that we had hoped for and expected. With the beginning of the second half of the school year a few weeks after our arrival, we took up our regular duties. Ruth began giving private lessons in piano and playing for the choir in the seminary. Hugo began teaching Theology, Philosophy, and Church History, and directing physical education. Because of the gradual transition to the new curriculum, the only course he offered for the second semester of 1953 was the History of the Reformation. We moved into the bottom floor of the boys' dormitory temporarily and have been counselor for the boys.

Invitations from the churches to preach have taken up about 3/4 of the Sundays during the year. Near the end of the year we became members of the Velez Sarfield Baptist Church, and at the beginning of the year Ruth began playing for the Sunday School and Hugo became teacher of the adult Bible class, a deacon, and a member of the finance committee. During the month of December, Hugo was supply pastor for the Baptist Church in Eva Peron, and in February for the Velez Sarfield Church. In January he spent two weeks at the summer camp near Cordoba, teaching Galatians the first week and 1 John the second week. February and March were spent in preparation for a heavy teaching schedule the first semester of this year: courses in general Church History, Biblical Theology of the Old Testament, and History of Philosophy.

In the course of the year we have been working on plans for building a mission house on the property near the seminary and have just let the contract for construction to begin in a few days; the contract calls for completion of the house in eight months. It is gratifying to be able to give our full time to seminary

---

[8] Mr. J. H. Culpepper, letter to Hugo Culpepper, 20 June 1954.

work on the mission field for which we have been preparing for so many years. We are thankful for all those who are making this possible.[9]

After the annual mission meeting in Buenos Aires in mid-July, the Culpeppers and Baker James Cauthen flew to Asuncion, Paraguay, for a mission meeting there. They stayed with medical missionaries assigned to the new hospital in Asuncion. On the return trip, they sailed down the Parana River from Asuncion to Buenos Aires.

In August work began on the brick home that was being built for the Culpeppers. Hugo supervised each step in the construction and was amazed at the process and the amount of brick, cement, and metal reinforcement that went into the construction. Every day at noon, the workmen would stop, build a fire, grill their steaks, eat their lunch of salad, bread, steak, and wine, take a siesta, and then resume construction. The projected eight months of building drug on for fourteen months before the house was finished. Hugo often joked that it could withstand a nuclear blast. It had concrete reinforcement between the floors and bars on the windows. A small yard surrounded it, and between the front yard and the street there was a twelve-foot brick wall with barbed wire on the top—a necessary and typical precaution in Argentina.

Sturdy construction ran in the family. Hugo and his father had perfected the craft of building crates for shipping goods overseas. Hugo's father shared the family secrets with Jack Glaze when the Glazes were packing to go to Argentina:

We know what a big job you folk have in packing these items with Jack's freight. I wish I could be there to help do the building of crates which will be needed. Hugo and I have had so much of this type of packing to do and each time we improved the building of crates and system of packing.

We found that in building the large boxes that it was best to cut 2 X 4's [for] frames for each end, having the 2 X 4's outside at each end. This gives the inside a smoother inside, lining the box with heavy paper, use 1 X 12's for sides, top and bottom. After it is nailed (plenty of nails), we covered the nails with a metal strip around each end. This

---

[9] Hugo and Ruth Culpepper, annual report to Foreign Mission Board, 12 July 1954.

will be a big protection and will keep thieves from breaking in on the boat and [in the] warehouses. Just thought I should mention this.[10]

When Bill and Kitty Cooper had to return to the United States for several months for medical reasons late in 1954, Hugo was made acting president of the seminary. Their annual mission report for 1954–1955 (written by Ruth) provides a succinct glimpse of the daily demands on a missionary's time.

Since we are here as Seminary professors, probably the first thing in our report should be the work done in that field. Hugo has carried three courses each semester. These classes entail preparation and the grading of papers which are often overlooked when one thinks of three hours a day in class. During the months from September [1954] until February [1955] Hugo was acting president of the school as the Coopers were on emergency leave in the States. Ruth has taught piano classes and played for the school choir during the school months.

In our church, Velez Sarsfield, Hugo teaches the adult class each Sunday morning, while Ruth plays the [pump] organ for the services in the morning. Also during the months of December through February Hugo served as interim pastor of the church. He is also serving as a deacon in the church, and through this means he is being able to help in making some plans that we hope are for the betterment of the church—this includes the budget, plans for a new building, and reorganization of the Sunday School.

Hugo in his office in Argentina.

---

[10] J. H. Culpepper, letter to family, 12 December 1954.

Hugo has averaged preaching more than once a week throughout the year. He has had special series of sermons in Caballito, Velez Sarsfield, and Nueva Chicago. For the past several months he has been teaching a class in the north district on Monday nights. In February, he had the privilege of being Bible teacher at one of the young people's camps held out on the Tigre River.

During the summer Ruth spent much time working on a textbook for one of Hugo's classes, typing nearly four hundred single-spaced official length stencils and supervising the running of them. Ruth has served as president of the Women's Organization for the missionary women, and has also served as chairman on the mixed committee for planning the G.A. and R.A. camps.

Mission meeting, 1955.

As president of the mission during the past year, Hugo has presided at each of the bi-monthly meetings of the executive committee. During February, there was the general mission meeting held in connection with Dr. Means' visit. Ruth has served as chairman of the hospitality committee which has had a lot to do this past year.

We want to take this opportunity to thank the mission again for the trip that we made to Paraguay as their representatives to the mission meeting there. We made this trip last July-August, and we feel we gained a great deal of insight into the work there which we hope will make us better teachers of those students who come from there to the seminary. Hugo was given several opportunities to speak while he was there, and we felt that the week spent in Paraguay was well worth the time and trip. So we want to thank the mission again for the privilege of making the trip.[11]

Hugo's mother's letter reveals her characteristic gentle humility and the pain of separation from her missionary son:

First let me thank you son for the sweet words you sent me for Mother's Day. You just don't know what they mean to me for I look back over the years and see where I have made so many mistakes. Don't feel that anything I ever done was a sacrifice. It was because I loved you so much. It seems now that it was so little that we ever done for you children, but at the time it was all we could do. I am so grateful to God that we have been blessed with two fine children and that you both added the pleasure that you have by falling in love with Ruth and Buddy [Wanda's husband], and have given us the wonderful sweet grandchildren that you have. We could not ask for more.... Some times I want to be with you all so much. It would be so wonderful if you was where we could have you run in or we could go see you. We will always miss that, but again that is life.[12]

La Facultad, the ecumenical seminary in Buenos Aires, sponsored the annual Carnahan Lectures and invited scholars whom Hugo held in highest esteem. John Baillie gave the lectures 19–21 July 1955, and Kenneth Scott Latourette gave the lectures the following year, 3–6 July 1956. Hugo encouraged his colleagues to support the Carnahan Lectures, and the Culpeppers entertained these guests in their home—as they did so many others over the years—while they were in Buenos Aires.

Ruth taught Alan the second-grade curriculum by "Calvert Course," and in the spring of 1954 the Culpeppers enrolled Alan and Larry in an Argentine school. The following year they entered the American Community School, which was quite a distance from the seminary. The Argentine government required that every child in the country have at least six years of education in the public school system in order to raise the literacy level in Argentina. Because there were a large number of American and British industrialists, military personnel, businessmen, and missionaries in Buenos Aires who wanted an English education for their children, they worked out a compromise with the government. At the American Community School, the children had classes each morning with Argentine

[11] Ruth Culpepper, annual report to Foreign Mission Board, 1955.

[12] Mrs. J. H. Culpepper, letter to Hugo Culpepper, 18 May 1955.

teachers and curriculum and then classes in the afternoons with American or British teachers. Homework was in Spanish one night and in English the next.

Political unrest in Argentina erupted into revolution in 1955. Relations between Juan Perón, the Argentine dictator, and the Roman Catholic Church had steadily deteriorated. In November 1954, Perón accused a group of clergymen of "agitation" against the government. The same year, in the face of Catholic opposition, divorce and prostitution were legalized, and benefits and legitimacy were given to children born out of wedlock. As a result, Perón lost the support of the church, and then part of the armed forces turned against him. On 16 June 1955, elements of the Argentine navy and its air arm rebelled, but the army remained loyal, and the rebellion was crushed in forty-eight hours. Then, on 16 September 1955, concerted efforts by insurgents from all three branches of the military, spearheaded by the air force and navy, resulted in a three-day rebellion in which an estimated 4,000 people were killed. Naval ships sailed down the Rio de la Plata and began shelling the executive building, the Casa Rosada, from the bay. Hugo and Jack Glaze had to pick up the boys from school, which was normally a forty-five minute trip across town. This time, they had to wind their way for two hours through side roads to get back to the seminary because city buses and tanks blocked all the main arteries through town. The army units in Buenos Aires who remained loyal to Perón dug in, while the navy and air force shelled their positions. For the duration of the revolution, the missionaries stayed at home and followed the news on the radio. Classes were suspended both in the schools and at the seminary, and an armed guard was stationed in the foyer of the seminary administration building. When they ventured out for groceries, they passed tanks and soldiers with machine guns stationed at the major intersections. Hugo and Ruth telephoned their parents to tell them that they were in no danger, however. Perón took refuge on a Paraguayan gunboat in the harbor and then fled the country. On 20 September General Eduardo Lonardi took office as provisional president.

Although they were not put into effect, there were plans for the evacuation of the North Americans should that become necessary. Jack Glaze reported:

> Prior to the successful revolution, I was summoned secretly to meet with the Consul General. Buenos Aires had been divided into sectors where North Americans lived. I was given an assignment of contacting and coordinating the evacuation of those living in our area of the city,

if indeed it became necessary. The Baptist Seminary would be the gathering point. A North American aircraft carrier with helicopters and marines was in the South Atlantic and would evacuate us. I was given the code word, etc. that would signify the beginning of the operation. Fortunately, the order was never given![13]

Finally, in October of 1955 the house was finished and the Culpeppers moved out of the men's dormitory and into the new two-story brick house. Money had run out before the walkways could be finished. The yard needed to be seeded, and Hugo planned to fence in the back yard and build a one-room detached building that could be used for a workshop and tool shed, and for his barbells and inclined board (for sit ups).

Later that month the son of another missionary was thrown off the train on the way home from school. He fell under the train and lost his leg. A railroad track worker was inspecting a switch and saw him fall. Although the leg had been amputated below the knee, he applied a crude tourniquet, carried him to the station platform close by, and saved his life. Apparently the attack was politically motivated, and he was thrown off the train by some young "Peronistas." After this tragic incident the Culpeppers and the Blairs took turns taking the missionary children to and from school, which involved riding public transportation (train, bus, or street car) since the Culpeppers did not have a car.

The Conference in Rio de Janeiro

In January 1956 all the missionaries went to Bialet Masse for their semi-annual mission meeting. The next month Hugo flew to Rio de Janeiro for several days of meetings with missionaries from various parts of South American and representatives from the Foreign Mission Board in Richmond. They met to discuss the future of Baptist theological education in Latin America. Before leaving, Hugo wrote and the following prayer for the twenty-fifth anniversary reunion of the class of 1931 of Pine Bluff High School:

---

[13] Jack Glaze, e-mail to Alan Culpepper, 6 July 2001.

Our Heavenly Father, as we pause in the midst of our busy lives to renew our fellowship of other years, we feel ourselves drawn closer to Thee from whom all love and true friendship comes. We thank Thee for those years that we shared together in study and in play, and for every teacher and classmate who made us want to achieve the best in life. As we parted twenty-five years ago, we went out into the world with our heads held high and our hearts warmed with dreams of things to come. Life has been a song for some, and a disappointing failure for others; but for most of us, it has been filled with much joy and some suffering—and through it all we have lived in constant need of Thee. We invoke Thy presence with us during these hours of reunion; may they be hours beautiful to remember in the years to come. But even more, we invoke Thy continuing presence in our lives, to the end that we may become full-grown Children of God, prepared to fellowship together with Thee and with all Thy children forevermore. Come and be with us now, drawing us to a closer walk with Thee, for we pray in the name of Jesus Christ our Lord and Savior. Amen.[14]

From Rio, Hugo wrote to Ruth about the trip up and their activities there.

Dearest,
We had a fairly rough trip, running into rain in Sao Paulo and Rio de Janeiro. Lightning played all around the plane a lot. Our stomachs were well churned from the bouncing up and down, but I did not get sick. The two Orricks and Sanderfords got on in Montevideo. Also Moore and Parker. Then there were ten of us. They met us in cars, and we drove through rain to the Training School. We are very comfortably housed (I like a hard straw mattress, but poor Dan [Carroll]! He says he aches.) It is semi-dormitory style with six beds to a large room. Moore, Parker, Swenson, Sanderson of Brazil, and I share a room.... Lunch is a big, heavy meal—the other two are light.

---

[14] Hugo Culpepper, tape recording of prayer, 13 February 1956.

Missionaries en Route to Rio Conference, 19 February
1956. (l-r): John Parker (Chile), Dan Carroll
(Argentina), Matthew Sanderford (Uruguay), Ben H.
Welmaker (Columbia), Hugo Culpepper (Argentina),
Cecil Moore (Chile), E. Swenson (Argentina), Alex
Garner (Argentina), and B. W. Orrick (Uruguay).

My devotional Monday morning was prepared Sunday 5:00 P.M. in flight. It
was on 1 John 1:5-9, with emphasis on

1. God is light—We need that light for these days.

2. Koinonia (Fellowship)—We need to improve the quality of our
fellowship.

3. Humility (Blood of Christ, i.e., His "life principle" living in us)—We need
to be humble as we approach our problems.

And all this under a sovereign God who is "faithful" (trustworthy) and
righteous. It was well received.

Monday morning I moved to change the horaria [schedule] of Committee
meetings for the first four days and it passed—later I learned that Dr. Means
had prepared it! But it didn't matter—we still improved it. Monday afternoon
was given to the Theological Education Committee. (Before the change in the
horaria the Total Program Committee was meeting at the same time as the
other Committees, and everyone on Total Program was also on some other
committee. The issue of international seminaries as related to national theological institutions has the Committee hopelessly deadlocked. Nobody wants

to give an inch! The 1949 policy will no doubt be a dead duck when we leave here! We resume the Theological Education Committee today for three hours in the morning and three hours in the afternoon. Last night Total Program discussed self-support. Chile and Argentina are advanced on this. Only one or two others are doing anything! I had to keep asking questions till I learned this (Dr. Means affirmed my "probing" as he said in the meeting). A sub-committee was named to draft a recommendation on self-support and report back tonight: Chairman, Culpepper; Secretary, Sanderson (Brazil); and Parker (Chile).

We drew this up between 10:00 and 11:15 P.M. last night. I got to bed at 12:00 and up at 6:10 A.M. A cold shower sends me into a new day fresh. Ben Oliver is having Welmaker and me for lunch in his home today. It is not hot yet, and I'm too tired at night to notice mosquitoes. It's 8:30 A.M. and time to start. Must run.

Lots of love,
Hugo[15]

Another letter to Ruth includes candid observations about the meetings.

In general, the Conference has value. In the Theological Education Committee, the shadow of Mrs._____is with us too much, resulting in pussyfooting expediency! About the only value here is the possibility of getting some good texts into Spanish. Theological Co-Education is the issue in Brazil; _____ is another [Mrs.] _____ on this question. It is spoiling our work. I've come to the conclusion that our Seminary must achieve distinction—these "acuendos" don't mean much. _____ lacks backbone! _____ of Mexico is too conservative. Tell Jack he wants Young's book in O.T. instead of _____'s. I admire David Means, also McConnell's objective fairness.[16]

The day before leaving for the Rio conference one of the students at the seminary had reported to Hugo a matter of sexual misconduct involving one of the missionaries. Hugo's response to the situation over the next several months demonstrated his concern for the mission as well as for the missionary and his skill in handling difficult situations—which would be called upon in the future both at Southern Seminary and at the Home Mission Board. At the meeting in Rio, Hugo outlined the situation in very general terms to Frank K. Means. Together, they decided that Hugo should present the matter, in the same indefinite terms, to the executive committee of the Argentine mission. The executive committee decided that he should take one other missionary into his confidence and investigate the matter further. Every effort was made to deal with the situation discretely and protect the identities and reputations of those involved. After further investigation, the two reported back to the executive committee in June 1956, and it was decided that Hugo should write a report to Frank Means, revealing all the details. The report was signed by all seven members of the committee. In response, they received a telegram stating that the report had been received and that the next steps would be taken in Richmond. Further letters reported that Frank Means and Baker James Cauthen, then head of the Foreign Mission Board, had met with the individual, and without attempting to pass judgment it was mutually agreed that it would not be wise for the missionary to return to Argentina.

Years later, several close national friends and pastors shared with Jack Glaze, confidentially, their concern at the time and their gratitude for Hugo's handling of the matter. Glaze wrote: "Had it not been handled effectively, mission credibility would have been completely destroyed. The lesson in ethical responsibility and Christian discipline was critical in the light of the Mission/Convention tensions—the standards were not double (one for the pastor and another for the missionary)!"[17]

In March of 1956 a polio epidemic broke out in Buenos Aires. Hugo and Ruth began to try to get the recently developed Salk vaccine for the boys and kept them in as much as possible to minimize the risk of exposure. Their school was closed for three weeks as parents tried as best they could to protect their children from the dreaded disease. Before any Salk vaccine could be secured, a shipment of Gamma-Globulin arrived, and everyone went to the school to take the serum in a sugar cube.

That winter the Culpeppers were assigned one of the mission cars, a 1947 Ford that had a tendency to get a vapor lock on hot days. Consequently, they always carried a coffee can and a rag in the trunk so that when it developed a vapor lock, they could wet the rag and wrap it around the fuel line to cool it off so that they could get under way again.

For Father's Day 1956, Hugo wrote the following:

Dear Dad,

---

[17] Jack Glaze, e-mail to Alan Culpepper, 6 July 2001.

We hope this letter will reach you on Saturday before Father's Day next Sunday. Remember that we shall be wishing we could be with you and will be grateful for you and all that you have meant and done for us through the years. I have been most fortunate to always have the assurance of a Dad who stood behind me, always ready with a helping hand in life when it was needed. I wish that you could have had the same blessing and not have had to be on your own since you were about 13. One of the things we are proud of is the splendid manner in which you have made an uphill pull in life to come out on top in so many ways in spite of obstacles. May you have a full life in the years to come as you enjoy some of the fruits of your efforts.[18]

In response to Hugo's letter, his father wrote:

Hugo, your Father's Day letter was well timed. It arrived Saturday about 10:00 A.M. I appreciate your letter beyond words, with which to express how I feel on this Father's Day, other than to re-state here if possible how proud I am of having such a fine son and daughter, with families such as each of you have, knowing that each of you has had an uphill pull also, and each has come out on top, in spite of the obstacles. My only wish is that I could have done more to help each of you. Not having been able to do more in the past, I still have a chance to help. Being a father as I see it requires this, and I am happy to keep on doing all that I can for the fine families (Ruth, Alan, Larry, Buddy, and Sherryl) the remaining years of my life. I can and do enjoy it, knowing that I will not leave an estate of much value in world goods. My greatest investments are in all of you, and I am receiving my dividends all along. Few fathers can equal the fruits I now have.[19]

In their annual report in June 1956, Hugo reflected on the events of the year past. The report gives another snapshot of the life of a busy missionary:

As we look back over the past months, we think of the oft-repeated phrase, "Thank God for strength He gave today"; for the tasks of the last year have been many and varied, and [were] often confronted without [the] wisdom and insight necessary to solve them. But God has supplied the many necessities, and we can truthfully say it has been a good year.

---

[18] Hugo Culpepper, letter to Mr. J. H. Culpepper, 11 June 1956.
[19] Mr. J. H. Culpepper, letter to Hugo Culpepper, 17 June 1956.

Naturally, the large part of my time has been taken up with seminary duties. I have taught Systematic Theology, Philosophy, Church History, and this half-year have supplied for Dr. Cockburn in the Greek interpretation course. Serving as interim president of the seminary during Mr. Cooper's absence has taken much time....

In the mission, I have served as chairman during the past year. One needs only to mention this because all know the duties that are required by this office. As for work with the mission and convention committees, I have served on the Executive Committee of the Convention and the Publication Committee. This year at the convention I was asked to serve on the newly formed committee to set up and administer the Cooperative Program funds.

Since last December I have served as District Missionary while Mr. Watson was at home on furlough. I cannot give details about the churches here, but would only mention that I have tried to visit nearly every church in the district for a service—not to speak, many times, but just to visit and listen. These have been real blessings to me, as I would drop in and see the work going on in a fine manner....

In my own church I am chairman of the building committee. We feel we have won a true victory there in remaining firm about the educational space, when the church did not want it. A reworking of the plans left the church and the committee much happier than either of the two opposing original plans. Also in my own church I serve as a deacon, member of the finance committee, and teach the men's Sunday School class.

I have spoken an average of a little more than once a week in a church service. Also it has been my privilege to continue to teach a class in the San Isidro church—last year going once a month, and this year twice a month.

One of the highlights of the year was the Rio trip and the opportunity to participate in this conference. I feel deeply humble for the experience there, and for the responsibility of being selected as chairman of the Continuation Committee on Theological Education. Our main project is the translation and securing of adequate textbooks for our seminaries. The task requires much correspondence, but we feel all effort is worth it to secure the best for our students.

Ruth's work is confined to her home and the seminary. She has greatly enjoyed getting moved into the beautiful new home that the Board has supplied us with. It has been one work that has been completed in the past year, and one project to write a happy "fin" to. We are grateful both to the mission and to Richmond for such a lovely place to live, and trust that it will be a blessing to all those who come to visit us there.

Ruth is teaching twelve hours a week in the seminary, and is chairman of the Course committee. In the mission she has served on the personnel committee.

For Thy leadership and strength in days past, Lord we thank Thee, and for Thy leading footsteps in the future, Lord we beseech Thee.[20]

At the mission meeting in July 1956 Hugo was elected president of the Argentine mission, adding further to his multiple responsibilities and activities. At the same meeting plans were put in place to secure ten new cars, over time, for the missionaries. The need for transportation is reflected in the following paragraph of a letter from Hugo's father:

The new house in Buenos Aires, 1955.

Glad that you now have some pressure off the work, it looks like Ruth should also get out from some of her pressure (a new car would be a big help in that direction) for this would help much in getting the boys to and from school. Ruth, we are sure you was not serious about moving to a house near the school, but we do know how disgusting it is to have so much trouble about transportation, and no one can be happy about the disadvantages, but think of the many others who do not have a home like all of you now have. None of us can have everything just as we would wish. Glad a carport is being built. This

---

[20] Hugo and Ruth Culpepper, annual report to Foreign Mission Board, June 1956.

shows that all of you plan on having a car soon, and I wish I could do something to speed it up.[21]

When the Culpeppers went to Argentina, the term of service was six years between furloughs—meaning that their next furlough would come in 1959–1960. Paul Geren, who was then vice president at Baylor, wrote, inviting Hugo to

> make Baylor your headquarters during your furlough in 1959 and teach in the expanded program of Studies in Foreign Service. I have cleared the matter in principle with the Foreign Mission Board. They furnish the housing and pay the regular missionary salary. They have no objection if Baylor pays an honorarium. Even if you feel you cannot spend three quarters, maybe you can spend one or two at a minimum. Please think about this. Devout scholarship is a rare quality. I have always thought you have it. Some have devotion and many have scholarship, but the combination is the need here at Baylor.[22]

Hugo's father thought the invitation sounded good and hoped Hugo would accept, but added that he knew it was important for Hugo to write his thesis and get his Ph.D. while on furlough. Still, the invitation from Baylor might give him the time and opportunity for research and study, to say nothing of the honor of being selected. In October of 1956 the board changed the term of service from six to five years, so the Culpeppers would be back in the States in 1958–1959 instead of 1959–1960. By November the mission was working smoothly. The Coopers were expected to return to Argentina, and their return would mean that Hugo could pass the presidency back to Cooper and devote his time to teaching and preaching, which he enjoyed more than administration and for which he felt better suited. A new 1957 Opel station wagon, purchased by the mission, arrived just in time for a long-planned vacation—the first real vacation the Culpeppers had had since arriving in Argentina. After the meeting at Bialet Masse in 1957, the Culpeppers spent a restful week at a small resort, Hosteria San Jorge (a 1950s-style motel with a swimming pool), not far from Bialet Masse.

---

[21] J. H. Culpepper, letter to Hugo Culpepper, 19 August 1956.

[22] Paul Geren, letter to Hugo Culpepper, 23 September 1956.

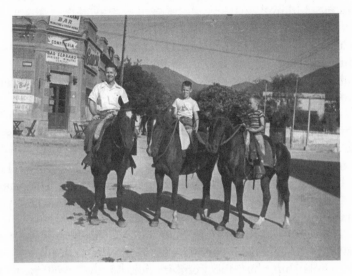

Hugo, Alan, and Larry, Bialet Masse, 9 January 1956.

The Decision to Finish His Th.D.

By February 1957, Hugo had indicated to Paul Geren that he felt he had to give priority to finishing his graduate work when they returned to the States the following year, but he also told him that he was beginning to feel that his work in Argentina was coming to a close and he did not know what lay ahead for him. Geren responded, affirming his decision to give his time to finishing his Ph.D. but expressing hope that the Culpeppers could spend a quarter at Baylor, and confidentially he left open the possibility of conversation about a long-term relationship with Baylor.

The decision about whether to return to Argentina or not following their coming furlough plunged Hugo into emotional, spiritual, and physical turmoil. In a letter to his parents, Hugo laid out the dilemma he faced as he made plans for the coming furlough:

Dear Mother and Dad,
We were so happy this morning to receive your letter and to know that your plans have taken shape and that you have a definite job to look forward to

that will be just "what the doctor ordered," so to speak. It all sounds wonderful.... As you say, it is worth a lot to have peace of mind now and to be able to go to bed at night without your subconscious pushing up questions to your attention while you are sleeping or trying to sleep. You should be able to get along well financially on this set up also. . . Sometimes definitely making up one's mind is the most difficult part, especially if one makes the right decision as things work out.

I wish I could come to know what is the best decision for me to make, with reference to the future. I have not mentioned before to you that I was thinking anything about this, because I did not want to burden you with even knowing that I was thinking, so long as you had your own plans to be worked out. But I think the time has come to share my thinking with you, even though it is too undeveloped to be very significant.

The realization that I faced a definite decision in the near future was suddenly pushed on me with the news that our terms of service have been shortened by one year to a total of five years. Until then, furlough was far enough out in the future for me to live in hope of being freed from other duties enough to be able to give adequate time to serious study, looking toward finishing up my doctorate this furlough. When a year was suddenly cut off and I now have only 15 months till furlough—well, I felt almost overnight as if "my execution" were awaiting me tomorrow and I might not be ready. You see, I had expected to be able to give all my time here to teaching and studying, and to be free from extra mission responsibilities. That was the agreement I had with Dr. Gill. Things have not worked out that way, and I am not griping about it because we cannot but feel that in the providence of God we have been here in Argentina at a strategic time in the life of the work and that unique and unusually significant opportunities have been placed in our hands for making a lasting contribution in working out and setting up long-range policies in both the seminary and the mission. In some respects the work was not far enough advanced here to make the Mission feel that freeing of professors was justified. Then too, the administration changed completely in Richmond, and they are not in agreement with the view we had reached with Dr. Gill. Then, the tragic illness and accident in the Cooper family necessitated my taking the seminary administration for a year and a half. (I've had the presidency of the mission for 3 years now, and will be relieved this July.) Then shortage of personnel made it necessary for me to take a district for 6 months. Much time was taken up with building the new home. All of this adds up to an entirely different picture from what I expected this term of service to be. I am grateful to God for the sense of satisfaction we have in feeling that through us a worthwhile contribution has been made; but, I am sorry and disappointed that I have not been able to apply myself to basic research more and be ready to take the written examinations immediately upon arriving home and then have the year to finish a 20,000-word thesis that I had also hoped to get started on. In order to get the degree this furlough, I would have to pass five written examinations of 4 hours each (they take five days straight, all morning each day), a total of 20 hours of examinations written, in September, 1958, after arriving home the end of July. Then I would have to do the studying and write a 20,000-word thesis and hand it in by March 1, 1959, which would be a little less than 6 months later. If this were possible, I would get the degree May 1st and be ready to return here in July. An extension of furlough would be out of the question; they are tightening up on that. For the written exams I need to study carefully about 100 to 150 books, some of which I have read but many of which I have not, and none of which I feel that I have mastered. If I do not finish this furlough, my time will run out and I will no longer be a candidate for the degree. There you have the making of our dilemma.

Of course, there are two sides or two ways to react to it; if there were not, it would not be a dilemma. Let me analyze the two sides as I see them: (1) it would seem to be the part of wisdom to accept my limitations, forget about taking the degree, come home, and enjoy our furlough doing deputation work in speaking and traveling, or spend some time at Baylor on Paul's [Geren] invitation, and then return here to continue on with our work and forget all about ever taking another degree. This has many sensible points about it. I will be 45 next year. That is only 20 years until retirement. Spending another 15 or 16 years in Argentina, along with furlough time, would bring me to age 65. We would retire with the $150 plus a small cost of living allowance (which may be discontinued since social security came in), plus our social security which would bring us up to about $285 to $300 per month retirement income, plus enough to buy a small home to live in and thus avoid rent (this from our present savings in bonds and from insurance, after paying for the boys' education). I already know more than enough for the actual needs of the teaching work here. A doctorate is not a requirement to teach here. We are very well set up in a lovely modern home, well furnished (at an investment of about $3,500 dollars in addition to what we brought down here—that is that much spent here), and we could probably continue living there after we return from furlough. There is a possibility that we would continue to have some kind of a car after furlough also, but not certain. This would be safe and secure and be taking no chances. While we do not seem to have much of an income, actually when everything is added in with all the allowances and benefits, we enjoy a standard of living that would take an income of at least $6,000 or slightly more in the States to equal (we are able to save about $75 dollars a month, for example). I am basically happy and get a real satisfaction out of teaching, and Ruth has made a better adjustment here than in Chile, seemingly. She possibly has an easier time here by having a maid, than she would have in the States. While the number of students is not very large, with whom we work here, we have a deep satisfaction in feeling that our being here makes a lot of difference in their lives by the grace of God. They seem to have opened their hearts to us and enabled us to have a strong influence in their lives. Cooper has intimated to me that he probably will not continue on as president after another 4 or 5 years. Possibly Richmond would turn to me for this placement then (not that I want or would want it) on the basis of this term's experience. The boys seem to be fairly well adjusted for missionary children and are getting along well in general and no doubt are freed from many temptations they would have in the States. That is one side of the picture.

2. On the other hand, there are some things that lead me to think of not returning after this furlough. (I have no thought of not finishing this term, since it is only 15 months away, and my duties have been so lightened already as to offer the prospect of as good progress in studying here, while serving, as I could have anywhere. Then we will have one year of furlough coming to us with salary even if we announce that we do not plan to return because it comes as due [to] one after the term of service. In the first place, I hate to think of dropping the doctorate without finishing it (there is a certain sense of satisfaction that I would never have, and would possibly always have a sense of regret over it); but, I also hate to think of attempting it until I feel that I am prepared, and running the risk of failing it and being rejected. (Although this would not rule me out here.) Right now the doctorate is not so important here. Only one professor (Cockburn) has it. But Glaze and Carroll stayed at the seminaries two or three years after graduation until they had gotten their written exams off. (That is the only way for a missionary to do from now on; there just isn't time here to work at it.) They will be able to write their theses between now and the end of their furloughs and return with their degrees. The new professor coming next year already has his degree. As Ruth points out, in another 8 to 10 years the degree will be important. Then too, one never knows what the future holds and a doctorate is an absolute prerequisite to teaching in the States; not to get it would shut me up to staying on here regardless of any circumstances that might develop. I honestly do not want to have the administration of the seminary when Cooper leaves, if he should step out in another term. However, I know of no one else immediately in view that would be the indicated man for it, either. A difficult situation could develop in a few years.... _____ wants to be president, but he repels people and would be an intolerable dictator. (Does this sound strangely like conditions up at your

office? I have often chuckled to myself that problems are pretty much the same the world over in all kinds of work.) I wish we had a strong, capable administration in whom we could have confidence that the future of the institution would be properly developed and be left to our teaching duties. I do not want to study just to take a degree. I love the work and the studies, but I want to do it without too much pressure so as to really get it assimilated. Therefore, I have thought of selling out here, returning to the seminary for furlough (doing the necessary speaking from time to time) and being able to take the written exams by the end of furlough probably. Then I could take another year, living from our savings for one or even two years if necessary, to finish up the thesis, possibly doing the research at Louisville or possibly at some other strong theological center (Yale, possibly). Then I could hope for a teaching job there in the States somewhere.

In replying to Paul and explaining why I felt I must decline his invitation I mentioned this whole matter to him confidentially (he is the only other person who will ever know anything about it, unless we should decide to stay in the States). He replied that he would prefer to wait and discuss the pros and cons of it with me when he sees me in the States—he has taught there and also been abroad so that our experiences are similar enough to enable him to be sympathetic and at least understand the factors involved—but he did say that if we should decide to stay there that he hoped we would "keep Baylor in mind." This was possibly just "being nice," or he might have really meant that he hoped it might work out for us to teach at Baylor permanently if we finished up the doctorate. This would be nice in many ways, but I think I would like to be open until the studies were actually finished. If a strong smaller school opened up, it might have some advantages, for example. I am sure that Ruth and the boys, as a matter of preference, would like to stay in the States. The heavy financial loss we would take on selling out here would be of comparatively small importance in view of the availability of things there. It would be wonderful, from the viewpoint of personal comfort, once the studies were finished to settled down at last somewhere and not be disrupted again (not that this is a worthwhile end in life!). It would mean so much to all of us to be able to see all of you more often, and then later on not to be separated from the boys when they grow up (but of course, one cannot plan on this. What if they should be missionaries?—or war!) I am convinced and have demonstrated to myself, at least, that I love teaching and would prefer it to pastoring, although it is not as well paid. I am not too confident that I would succeed as a pastor. In some respects, this seems like a lot of sacrificing of money, time, and security to exchange situations that in effect would be just the difference of living in the States instead of here. Once we resigned, we would forfeit all retirement benefits from the Board, and until we resumed with an income, our social security would not be advancing either. We would probably have a lower standard of living there, teaching (college or seminary professors there are lower salaried; than we are here. The average salary of Baylor teachers is: Instructor—$3,550; Assistant Professor—$4,400; Associate Professor—$5,200; Full Professor—$5,700. Seminaries range from about $4,000 to a top of $7,000 after years of service. That is why they all must accept every opportunity for supplying in churches, etc.

The bright side of doing this is: something of a feeling that possibly our work and contribution here has been accomplished; the attraction of pushing on to complete the degree once started and having the zest of accomplishment; the opportunity of giving myself more exclusively to teaching; the feeling that our experiences give us an unusual preparation to be able to be helpful to young people in teaching there for the next 25 years that would be left us, possibly. There would also be certain attractions and advantages for the family there. I feel that there would be a place of rewarding service where we could well invest our lives without breaking faith with our vocation and dedication to the Lord's work.

The discouraging possibilities: To what extent would the immediate economic insecurity of cutting off all retirement benefits (once I was settled they would start building up again, of course), the possible using up of from a half to all of our savings (We would have about $14,000 to $15,000 dollars as a backlog) and then settling down without a home on a lower standard of living just when the boys would be ready for college, the possibility of not having enough peace of mind economically to really apply myself to the studies, the possibility of sickness, etc. Perhaps, "nothing risked—nothing gained" and maybe these are lots of bridges we would never need to cross!

3. There is a third possibility: not making any decision now, but giving myself to my studies as I am increasingly trying to do with a view to being ready for the written exams as soon as possible; saying nothing before leaving here but packing up things here as if we were sure of returning and then see how well we got along on furlough. This would be burning no bridges behind us, and would leave the decision open until the end of furlough. I think Ruth would possibly incline to this position. There are disadvantages to it, as well as advantages. If we should decide not to return, it is not fair or satisfactory to ask someone here to liquidate our situation. Then too one cannot take anything out of the country after being away 6 months—not even a trunk. Someone else would have to bring out anything as their own. I could return at my own expense to liquidate, but this would waste about $1,000 dollars in travel. It is just putting off a decision to try and be sure. One cannot "have his cake and

eat it"; we cannot maintain the present security and still gain any benefits from staying on there. Sometimes I feel that maybe we should try and reach a decision soon and maybe even announce it so as to make it definite and thus be able to throw our whole heart into one plan or the other; at other times, I feel that maybe we should put it aside from our thinking for another year, give myself to seeing how much progress I can make in my studies and then decide about March or April of next year something definite. That is what I have been doing in recent weeks, and been sleeping well and studying well (in contrast with a rather acute agitation I felt last summer here, about the time we went on vacation); your letter today brought me around to writing all this out to share with you, since it still pushes up to my consciousness from time to time—depending on my mood.

I am afraid I have made you weary after so much wandering around in this maze of indecision, so I will not write more now. It may be some time before I shall have any more thoughts to speak of on the subject, but I did want to share these with you now. I shall be interested in your reactions. Please remember that I (the real "I") haven't really changed any. I still want to make the best use of my life by the grace of God in his service, and am still ready to do His will. But it isn't always easy to know what that is. Sometimes I wonder if I could not be used more fully by Him there than here. Some of my teachers have suggested to me that when it comes right down to the test I have more ability in the "pinch" than I have confidence in myself beforehand; however, I know I do not have the "push" (of oneself) that opens so many doors of opportunity back there. The most effortless way would be to sit tight, take no chances, and enjoy the security I have achieved. Would this be doing God's will by serving at my best here, or would it be failing to follow on into larger fields of usefulness there? I could launch out and uproot us here with a view to fuller preparation and larger use of our lives there. Would this be abandoning an established place of service and taking foolhardy chances with my—and my family's—future? That is what makes the question hard. (I do know that this is probably the top teaching opportunity in all of our foreign missionary fields, and there are many who would jump at the chance of stepping into my place here. Switzerland and Japan compare favorably and in some respects surpass it, but they have other unattractive features too.) So much for this now....

I have written for 2-and-a-half hours. I hope it does not take that long for you to read. I can imagine that it will give you all something to think and talk about for a few days though, and I did want to share these thoughts with you, even if nothing should ever come of them in the way of any change.

I'm leaving now to meet Ruth and the boys for supper and bowling.
Lots of love,
Hugo[23]

Hugo's mother's response to this letter reveals her uncommon love, faith, and insight. Its glimpses of Hugo's future look providential, and we can only assume that it played a significant role in Hugo's eventual decision not to return to Argentina but to give himself to teaching others who were preparing themselves for mission service.

Dear Children,

I have just finished my work this morning, and while I was working I was thinking.

Son we was glad to get your letter Friday morning, and I have been thinking of it ever since it came. Of course it would be the easiest thing in the world for me to say right away without hesitation "come home to stay," but I know also that would be strictly a personal, selfish feeling, and as I have done so many times when I get so lonesome to see all of you and think how wonderful it would be if you could be closer to us, I start asking forgiveness for putting my feelings before the Lord's work, and begin thanking him for having a son like you that has a wife like Ruth, and I pray that the boys will follow in your all's footsteps. I know you all have done a lot of thinking about your situation, and there are as you say, several different ways to look at it, and in the end no one can tell you what to decide to do. All we can do is express our views on it, but that does not mean that you should do that way. This is just how I feel about you all coming home to stay in the States.

When you stop and think how long and how hard you have tried to serve the Lord on the foreign field, and in the beginning the different ways you was blocked, and after finally getting settled in Argentina things not having turned out as was first planned, it makes one wonder if it is not the Lord having his will in a way that we do not understand. I also feel that there are many young people that are going to prepare themselves for mission work, and since you all have given fifteen years of your life, it would be, if you could be satisfied in doing it, a great thing to have a part in preparing younger folk to take up where you left

---

[23] Hugo Culpepper, letter to Mr. and Mrs. J. H. Culpepper, 12 April 1957.

off, and perhaps that is the reason you have not been able to do the work that you went to Buenos Aires to do.

You are so right in many ways of thinking, as far as the living being different here than there. Of course there is a big difference I am sure, but on the other hand you realize you all do have the boys to think of. You spoke of having to be separated from all of us, as you are, and that is one of the bad things of being so far away that we cannot get together even once a year, but I have often thought of the time when the boys will have to stay here and you all there. That is when it will be hard for you and the boys, for wherever they are and regardless of the school and environment—it could be the very best—I think they would need you and Ruth as much as they do now, and it would be awfully hard for you to be separated, *I know*. Of course you could, and I am sure you both would, feel whatever would be the Lord's will you would want to do, but that does not keep you from having that longing feeling that one has when their own are so far away.

You know it is a coincidence: it has not been more than two weeks ago that we were talking about how the time was flying and that it would be time for you all to come home before we knew it. I was out at Wanda's, and she said then that she wondered if you all had given it any thought about staying in the States when you come home this time. I told her then that as far as our feelings was concerned I wished you could feel that you could serve the Lord here in a great way, but that as always, when I think about it, I know the Lord will guide you and whatever is His will is the way we want it. We do know that He works in a mysterious way sometimes, and He alone knows what the future holds for us. We will pray that you will be shown what is best for you to do and that you will not worry too much. I do think it would give you a feeling of satisfaction to get your Ph.D., and as Daddy said you know we want to help in any way we can if you decide to stay here and finish it....

Son, try and not get too disturbed in trying to think things out, for we know prayer can do so much to give one a peace of mind, and we will pray that everything will work out all right. Must go and give Jesse his lunch. He is here working the flowerbed. All our love for all of you!

Lovingly,
Mother[24]

---

[24] Mrs. J. H. Culpepper, letter to Hugo and Ruth Culpepper, 22 April 1957.

The response from Hugo's father was more direct:

Now about your decision pending, I will try to turn on the light for you, and by so doing help you make the correct decision so here goes: no need to take 10 months to decide, do it now and have more time to liquidate all your assets there. You can do a better job and receive better prices for all items you want to dispose of by not being rushed and not realize as much as they are worth. It is time for you to do what is best for you and the family, and get out of so much pressure of the duties and work there, and first of all have the time needed to study for Th.D., which has been your aim all along these many years. This should be [your] first consideration, and it is too much for you or anyone to continue in the mission work and also study at the same time. There is a limit to what one can do, and doing both at the same time is far more than you should undertake. Just think how much better job you can do in teaching, and by so doing teach so many to take over the mission work and be able to do a much better job from having been taught and [being] better equipped to do the work.

I feel that by my good job and having a nice increase in income [His new job paid $5,400 per year.] I can help you over the next few years. I have always considered my greatest assets was the investments made in my children and their families, and I am rich in having such children and their families, and [I] want you and Ruth to know that I am behind each of you and consider it a duty and pleasure to see you through and will help with everything needed. I feel that I have been blessed beyond measure with having good health these many years, and having good jobs with good pay, and mother and I want by all means to help you reach the goal you most want, and that is the Ph.D., and with some of your savings and ours forget about income for the time required to study and get the Ph.D.

Now one other thought which I know you and Ruth have and will consider and that is Alan and Larry's education. Each of them need to be with you and Ruth. They need you and each of you need them with you to help them over the rough spots in school, and by all means when each of them enter their college days and work. Their future is at stake, and your greatest assets are in Alan and Larry, and you and Ruth will be much happier by them having received the best education possible, which neither of them can have if you remain in mission work, so make up your mind now to do that which is best for all of you. Get that Ph.D without delay.

Hugo, this is my personal feelings. I am not being dictatorial in the matter. The final decision has to be with you and Ruth, but I just had to let you know our personal feelings.[25]

The next month, Hugo wrote the following letter to Dale Moody at Southern Seminary analyzing the options before him.

Dear Dale:

We want to congratulate you on the recent study grant that will make possible a year of study in Germany. The committee showed good judgment, and I'm sure it will make a real contribution to your continued growth and development in the field.

About the time you return from Germany we shall be arriving in the States at the end of this five-year term of service (July, 1958). I am writing this letter to you as a personal friend, sharing with you confidentially some of my thoughts and problems, and seeking from you your reactions in the light of your experiences and observations. Certainly anything you might write in reply will be taken as coming from a friend and not in your capacity as a professor.

I am considering staying on in the States with a view to finishing up my graduate studies and with the hope of teaching there somewhere. This has been a fruitful period of service, and I cannot but feel that the Lord brought us here for this particular time. The Mission of about 45 missionaries is very young; most of them are in their first term. It has been a time of transition. My former terms of service and limited experience have given me the opportunity of sharing fully here. I'm finishing up three years as president of the Mission, and have had to pinch-hit as acting president of the seminary (of 61 students) for a year and a half. This in addition to teaching 12 hours a week in classes, preaching on the weekends, teaching special study series in the churches from time to time, and serving on numbers of Seminary, Mission, and Convention committees. Just now for two or three years I am chairman of the Continuation Committee of the Rio Conference on theological education for Spanish-speaking Latin America. We are trying to get some good texts translated into Spanish and published at El Paso. Such works as Seeberg, Latourette's one-volume church history, etc. I've taken your time to mention all this to help you understand why I feel this term has been worthwhile. At the same time, the feeling has come to me of late that perhaps our work is done here.

---

[25] Mr. J. H. Culpepper, letter to Hugo Culpepper, 12 May 1957.

My interest in missions has been related to teaching all along. I've put in three terms now, and in none of them have found it possible to major on teaching, which I feel to be my vocation primarily. The mission field is no place for very much specialized teaching. In this respect, it has been disappointing. Neither does one find time from so many diverse activities to grow very much in the field; in this respect it is not too different from what a pastorate in the States would be. While I feel that it is all very worthwhile here, I cannot but wonder if I should not finish up my studies. This may take two or three years to do. I like to do a thorough job of whatever I go after. Because of that I have felt a certain frustration. If we return after this next furlough, probably I should forget about any further studies or certainly any degree work, and give all my time to doing the best I can the things that come to hand in the work here.

I have often thought of your comment to me one day in your office shortly before the end of the year when we returned here; you mentioned one or two letters you had received inquiring as to where they could get well trained men in theology, and then you commented, "There is plenty of room at the top." This was probably just a casual comment in passing, with no point to it in relation to me. However, as has happened at other times in my past experiences, such passing comments have turned out to be suggestive to me. The aspect of "the top" doesn't interest me; I realize that I am very late in life in even thinking of getting around to serious study. But the challenge of serious study is still there in my personality, regardless of what it might lead to or what type opportunity might open up later on. It could be that the Lord could use me in some small college, and the combination of our rather unusual experiences and further studies would be helpful to some students.

This brings me to several questions that come to mind: I began my candidacy for the degree in theology in September 1952, and put in the full session till May 1953. If I should stay on till I finished up, what would my time limit be? How much time would I have left now, by returning in September 1958?

I have savings which could see us through three years of study if necessary (mostly back salary and government compensation from the concentration camp experience); I have planned to save this for the education of our two boys. This is one serious factor in the situation. Having the savings means I could study anywhere. Would I do well to stay on at Louisville till I got the degree there? Should I stay there till I get the preliminaries off, and then go somewhere else for the thesis research? Would I do well to consider starting from scratch for a degree somewhere else, since I "know" Louisville pretty well as a school (Forget that you are a professor in Louisville when you face this question). I raise it from the broad viewpoint of professional preparation, as I think you will understand. You once remarked to me that a certain prof. had never been "off the hill" to study, for example.

Of the five parts to the field of theology at Louisville, I find myself more attracted to either N.T. theology or systematic theology as a thesis area and any further specialization. Perhaps my comparative facility in the use of N.T. Greek on the basis of past studies is a factor here, as well as personal interest. Do most other schools have as broad a field as the five areas? I see the value of them as a foundation (especially for college teaching), but I doubt if one ever becomes very proficient in all that vast area. What do you consider the strongest center (& man) for N.T. Theology and for Systematic Theology respectively?

If I should go in for further studies, I have thought of the schools up east (especially Yale), of those in Great Britain (especially Manchester or Edinburgh), and of Germany (perhaps, Basle—I would like to acquire facility in reading German; my two years at Baylor have long since faded badly!)

Since you have been at some such similar point, your suggestions will be helpful. (I remember your telling me that you "figured you had burned your bridges behind you" when you drove out of Louisville heading for Union). In the nature of the case, since my future relationship with the Foreign Mission Board is involved, please keep this whole matter confidential. It could be that I shall give up further study and stay on here to do what I can, in which case I would prefer that these thoughts of mine not be spread around, as you can understand. If I do stay, however, I shall probably always feel a disappointment in not having "finished the job" as regards the fullest preparation.

I hope this letter reaches you before you leave for Germany, although I am afraid it may not, and that it will not be too much of a drain on your time to work in an answer—perhaps on your trip over, if [it is] not convenient before then.

Best wishes for a good year. Why don't you write an occasional "report to the people" for publication in the State papers, or some more congenial medium, in which you would share your observations of the current theological scene in Europe, etc.?

Cordially yours.

Hugo Culpepper[26]

Moody responded that the best combination of biblical and systematic theology to be found at the time was in Basel, with Karl Barth, Bo Reicke, Van Oyen, and Walther Eichrodt. In answer to Hugo's questions, Moody replied,

---

[26] Hugo Culpepper, letter to Dale Moody, 24 May 1957.

According to our regulations here at Southern, you have used only one year of your graduate time. You would have at least five years if you came here to Louisville. I do not doubt that our field of theology is becoming about as strong as any in the United States, but I would still recommend that if at all possible you earn a Doctor's degree in one of the German-speaking universities. I believe that the study at Princeton, Union, and Yale would be the only schools superior to what we have to offer, so my advice would be to take a good look at either Basel or Princeton.[27]

Hugo wrote back, suggesting that he might finish a year at Southern, completing the preliminary examinations, and then go on to Princeton to write his dissertation there. Moody thought that was a "splendid" plan. By August 1957 Hugo had decided definitely to pursue his Ph.D. The decision then was whether to finish at Southern, where he had already done a year's work on the degree and was known by the faculty, or go to Princeton, which was further from Little Rock, where they did not know anyone, and where it would take a year longer to complete the degree. By the end of August, Hugo had already purchased their tickets to return to the States by boat, leaving Buenos Aires on 21 June and arriving in New Orleans on 9 July 1958. Still, Hugo was wrestling with the uncertainties of the future. Physically and emotionally the strain was taking its toll on him. He was having trouble sleeping, and the fatigue merely compounded his problems. In response to a long letter describing his problems, his father wrote:

Hugo, your letter dated August 27th (three pages) received. We have read it over several times, and we appreciate more than words can express your frank and complete outline to us of your problems, and we wish we could give you the answers.... On page three you open with a clear statement which reads as follows: "I think I have come to recognize the factors in my problem quite clearly," and mother and I agree and have known for some time that you have taken over much more work than one person should have had. Burning the candle at both ends is bad for anyone, but in your case I think you have broken your candle in half, trimmed the wicks at each end of the two smaller candles and lit all four ends for the last two years. This has caused all the tallow to be used up; one half was burning for all the mission work,

---

[27] Dale Moody, letter to Hugo Culpepper, 31 May 1957.

and the other half was family obligations. You need and must have more light in order to see the way to go. You just cannot go two routes. Mother can in a way understand why and what the reason is for your waking up at nights (from needed sleep) and thinking, thinking, thinking your plans as to what to do and how things will work out. You make up your mind on part of the problems, then the next night you work on a different plan, and this goes on and on.... We are glad you explained your problems to your doctor, and by all means take the Placidon pills as directed. You must have sleep and be able to relax.[28]

In the remainder of the letter, Hugo's father urged him not to try to have two plans but to burn his bridges, start liquidating their possessions, and plan to come home to stay. He assured Hugo again that they would step in and help financially all they could while Hugo finished his degree. He then added that there were still guards around Central High School (following the integration of the school that fall) and that they did not know what the outcome would be.

Hugo took a prescribed tranquilizer for two or three weeks, and gradually his condition began to improve—more quickly than the conflict at Central High School in Little Rock, which dragged on, making news around the world. By the end of November, Hugo notified Frank Means at the Foreign Mission Board of his intent to stay in the States and pursue a Ph.D. Means supported Hugo in his decision and worked out a plan whereby his furlough (with pay) could be extended six months. The Culpeppers planned to spend the first two months (July–August) in Little Rock and then to go on to Louisville at the end of the summer. With the decision finally made, Hugo began to have more peace of mind and to look forward to the opportunity for further concentrated study. In December, the Culpeppers and the Glazes took a vacation together, hiking and fishing at Sierra de la Ventana, which is located in a low mountain range about 350 miles south of Buenos Aires. Behind the lodge was a "Cropogo" course—a combination of croquet, polo, and golf, which was played with wooden mallets and balls, tees, rough "fairways" through the woods, and holes with obstructions, as in miniature golf. Both families and both generations enjoyed the game, and the relaxing trip helped Hugo to get back on his feet.

Throughout the early months of 1958 the family made plans for their return to the United States. Hugo decided not to sell their belongings in

---

[28] Mr. J. H. Culpepper, letter to Hugo Culpepper, 8 September 1957.

Argentina, not to burn any bridges, so as to leave their options open. The final weeks were busy with packing and storing their belongings and telling fellow missionaries, students, and church members goodbye. Hugo's detailed records reveal that he preached 205 sermons during the five years in Argentina.

On 21 June they sailed from Buenos Aires on the *S.S. Del Mar* (Delta Lines), leaving most of their possessions behind but not knowing whether they would be back or not. Once again, Hugo was going to Louisville to continue his graduate studies, as he had in 1939 and again in 1951. Along the way, the Del Mar put in for brief periods at Sao Paulo, Rio de Janeiro, and Curacao.

International Baptist Theologial Seminary.
Buenos Aires, Argentina, 1953.

Chapter 8

Southern Seminary
1958–1964

"Any evangelistic and missionary activity which is not
consistent with a Biblical basis of mission is vulnerable to
superficiality and shortsightedness."[1]

The *S. S. Del Mar* arrived in New Orleans on schedule on 9 July 1958,
in spite of skirting a storm in the Caribbean, and the Culpeppers celebrated
a joyous reunion with both families there. After spending a couple nights
in a new Holiday Inn, they made the drive back to Little Rock, taking in all
the changes that had occurred in five years' time.

The Invitation to Join the Faculty at Southern

Events that would shape their future were already unfolding. Cornell
Goerner, who had been professor of missions at Southern Seminary since
1935, had resigned in 1957 to become the associate secretary for Europe,
the Middle East, and Africa at the Foreign Mission Board, but the
seminary had not yet found anyone to succeed him. The seminary itself
was in turmoil. On 14 June 1958, the Board of Trustees had accepted the
resignations of thirteen faculty members who refused to sign a statement
agreeing to work with administrators elected by the board. Among the
letters Hugo's father brought with him to New Orleans was one from Paul
Geren,[2] and along with that letter was a copy of a letter Geren had written

---

[1] Hugo H. Culpepper, "One Mission—Missions and Evangelism," *Review &
Expositor* 60, 4 (Fall 1963): 388.

[2] See above, p. 103, n. 2.

to Henlee Barnette, then acting dean of the School of Theology at Southern. It read:

> Dear Henlee:
> This is a brief note concerning my friend Hugo Culpepper, a Southern Baptist missionary who has been teaching Theology and Church History in the Baptist Theological Seminary in Buenos Aires, Argentina; and who, I understand, plans to spend the year beginning in September in study at S.B.T.S. My suggestion is that Hugo would make an excellent faculty member in Missions, or one of his fields—Theology and Church History. In the latter case he would bring the impact of his experiences on the mission field to his teaching.
> Hugo and I were classmates at Baylor. We traveled together to hear Kagawa at S.B.T.S. in 1936. He did his work in the Seminary and went out as a missionary to China. He and his wife were prisoners of the Japanese during World War II. After the war and repatriation to this country, he completed basic medical studies, but felt that his calling lay in the teaching field. Of all my classmates at Baylor, his consecration and devotion, which has been replete with struggle, impressed me above that of any other, and continues to impress me in the same fashion.
> If I had any real authority in this connection, I would see that he became a member of our faculty [at Baylor] in September. Since I don't have that authority, I am hoping that the Louisville Seminary can get him in some combination of professor and advanced graduate student.
> Sincerely,
> Paul Geren[3]

A letter from Geren to Hugo reported that Barnette had responded, saying, "We are definitely interested in him as a visiting professor and perhaps as a permanent member of our staff."[4]

After only ten days in Little Rock, the Culpeppers set off for Foreign Mission Week at Glorieta, New Mexico, in a new pink and white 1958 Chevrolet Bel Air sedan. By the end of August, the Culpeppers had settled once again into the missionary apartments at Southern Seminary. Geren wrote again, saying that he was trying to arrange an invitation for Hugo to speak at Baylor. He added, "Best of all is the fact that you are settled at the Seminary with a high purpose and a sense that you are doing the right

---

[3] Paul Geren, letter to Henlee Barnette, 24 June 1958.
[4] Paul Geren, letter to Hugo Culpepper, 8 July 1958.

thing. Thanks for sharing your talk with Dale Moody. I am sorry degrees are counted so important. You can have yours soon, and the opportunities of work wherever you choose will be abundant then."[5]

Dale Moody urged Hugo to get his Th.D., even if it took him the full three years. He also invited Hugo to be his teaching fellow that fall and grade the papers for his classes, which allowed Hugo to review the basic theology courses. Hugo gratefully accepted the position and the stipend of $50 per month. His father wrote: "Remember we are ready to help you, and you need have no fear of having to live on cornbread and buttermilk."[6]

By October, Southern Seminary began talking to Hugo about finishing his degree and joining the faculty there, teaching missions. His parents were thrilled:

> There is no doubt but that the Lord has been leading Hugo all along over the past 20 years, and as you mentioned two years ago even [while] you folk was half of the world away from Louisville, things began to take shape. No one but the Lord could have caused things to start in the direction of what is to develop in the near future. I wish it were possible to put in words our feelings about the subject matter, but this is something words cannot describe, so we will just say we are happy and thankful to the Good Lord for all the blessings and prayers answered.[7]

The fall of 1958 was turbulent. The faculty and president at Southern were working through the fallout from the faculty resignations in the spring. Hugo's future course was becoming clear; he was working on his doctoral studies, and he still carried on a vigorous speaking schedule with trips to Southeastern Seminary, St. Louis, and Atlanta. From Southeastern, his friend James Tull wrote:

> We are still living in the good cheer of Hugo's visit. It was just too short. I have had a bad conscience, Hugo, for working you so hard. You made a fine impression here.... The chapel talk was excellent, and I thought that the class talk was even better. The students ate up what you gave them.... Ruth, you need not let Hugo read this, but we were

---

[5] Paul Geren, letter to Hugo Culpepper, 10 September 1958.

[6] J. H. Culpepper, letter to Hugo Culpepper, 19 October 1958.

[7] Ibid.

greatly thrilled with your husband. I have always admired him, and this time more than ever he seemed to show the mature qualities for which he has shown promise since I first knew him—depth of mind and spirit, sanity, balance, understanding, breadth of comprehension, and geniality. That last quality you might sometimes doubt![8]

By December the decision to stay at Southern had been made, and a spate of letters followed. Hugo sent a letter to Dr. Frank Means at the Foreign Mission Board, advising him of his plans to accept the appointment at Southern.

Dear Dr. Means:

It is with mixed emotions, but with a clear sense of providential guidance, that I am brought to the point of writing this letter to you.

Last Monday, December 8, the faculty of the Southern Baptist Seminary voted to nominate me for an assistant professorship in the Missions department. Wednesday morning, the 10th, Dr. McCall had a long conference with me. Thursday afternoon I talked with a committee of the Trustees. This morning, Dr. McCall advised me officially that the appointment has been made, to become effective June 1, 1959.

You will recall that, in the course of our conversation while riding from your hotel to our home for breakfast, during your last visit to Buenos Aires, I indirectly expressed some misgivings as to my future work in Argentina. The "upsetting thought" that perhaps my work there was done, first came to me in January 1957. I did not know that some of the professors here had begun to think of me as a possible faculty member shortly after Dr. Goerner left. In fact, I did not know that I was being considered until after I arrived home on furlough. Shortly after arriving on the campus in September I learned that I would probably be facing such a decision sooner or later. It has not been easy to face up to. The "agonizing" that some of my friends know I went through during the last year I was in Argentina, together with these months this fall here, prepared me for a decision when it was presented to me. I accepted. (By "agonizing" I mean the spiritual wrestling with the definite impression that the Lord had something else for me, but not being able to see into the future as to what it would be.)

It is with a clear realization of the difficulty of the work in normal times, and of the unusual difficulties because of the "crisis" through which the seminary is passing, that I accept the challenge. It surely is something that one would not

---

[8] James Tull, letter to Hugo Culpepper, 10 December 1958.

be inclined to seek. Yet, I have the same conviction toward it that I have had about other aspects of my foreign mission vocation. In no sense do I feel that it is an altering of that vocation; it is only an institutional and geographical change. For me to decline, in the nature of the case, would be to shirk.

Sometime next May I shall be writing to you to present my resignation to the Foreign Mission Board as a missionary, to become effective May 31, 1959. However, I wanted to write today to share this information with you at the earliest possible moment. I hope to find a sympathetic understanding on your part and that of other friends in Richmond. For my part, I am looking forward to the same close cooperation in the years to come that I have enjoyed thus far....

Today I am writing the Argentine Mission, and also Bro. W. L. Cooper. Our ties there are strong. However, it is gratifying to know that Dr. Cecil Thompson (theology) and Dr. Justice Anderson (Church History) will be able to take over my work there without any considerable inconvenience.

Please remember us in your prayers. I hope to see you in Dallas in January.

Cordially yours,
Hugo H. Culpepper[9]

Then came the painful task of telling friends in Argentina—especially Jack and Jean Glaze and Bill and Kitty Cooper—that they would not be returning.

Dear Jack and Jean,
We have to share with you some news, but I hardly know how to go about it. I think it is more difficult to write you of it than anyone else, and that is why I have put it off a few days, although I have not mailed the other letters (waiting to get this one written). Friday, December 12, we accepted appointment to the faculty of Southern Seminary as Dr. Goerner's successor in the Missions Department—to become effective June 1, 1959.

You knew, better than anyone else, the struggle I went through for the last year or so we were in Argentina. We had thought we would be spending our lives in Argentina (as our house furnishings would indicate), but I had come to feel that our work there was done and that the Lord had something else ahead for us. Yet the way was dark and I was deeply torn. We sincerely had no idea what it would be....

---

[9] Hugo Culpepper, letter to Frank Means, 12 December 1958.

Two different friends on the faculty told me in September that we would be facing this decision before the year was out and that they (the faculty as a whole) wanted us for Missions. In October, Dale Moody told me he thought that I could take my choice of Missions, Theology, or New Testament—whichever one I could really put my heart in. Later, I told him that while my "sugar-stick" would be Theology, I did not feel I could say "No" to Missions since that was my vocation—and in the light of the consensus of opinion in the faculty here and our past experiences. They like my studies in Greek N.T. and Theology along with our various mission experiences—with a view to having our emphasis on the Biblical Basis of Missions and the Principles and Practice of Missions. Dr. Jackson had his work in the History of Missions with Latourette, and has as his specialty Comparative Religions, which doesn't particularly interest me....

On last Monday, the 8th of Dec., the Theology school faculty voted unanimously to suggest my nomination for Missions. On Wednesday morning, the president talked with me for an hour and twenty minutes making the offer. That afternoon the combined faculties (of all the schools) had it presented to them. On Thursday afternoon I was interviewed by a trustee committee on faculty placement, and Thursday night the Trustees officially approved the appointment. I was notified on Friday morning. Actually I had already done my "agonizing" over the change while still in Argentina, before I knew what it would be. The three months here on the campus, having known what was up, gave me time for this to come to the surface of my mind from the subconscious, and made possible an immediate acceptance this week. That is how it came about. To me it is in a small way something of a "Peter-Cornelius" experience, because it seems that the Lord was working at both ends of the line, without the other party knowing it.

I am continuing on furlough until the end of May, since we have a number of speaking engagements yet. Although the matter of my exams is not an immediate condition, they are naturally interested in my completing the work in Theology, and I still hope to take the preliminaries in May, the week before the Southern Baptist Convention. Then on June 1st, I take up the status of assistant professor in Missions. Next year I shall teach about 6 hours a week so as to have time to work on a thesis. (I am still interested in existentialism as the field and Miguel de Unamuno as the subject.) Once I complete the thesis and get the degree, I shall be eligible for associate professor.

It will probably be necessary for me to make a flying trip to B.A. in June, at my expense, to liquidate our situation there. We are interested in getting a few personal effects, the copperware and pictures, and my library. Everything else is for sale. If any of the missionaries are interested in buying at a very reasonable price anything we had, I shall be glad if they would drop me a line and I shall quote them a price. It would be quite O.K. for them to make monthly payments.

We are all sad over the separation from friends like you. Alan is the saddest member of the family! He was ready to return and fish and hunt with you. We feel terrible about Blackie [our cocker spaniel; Jack Glaze reported that the Cockburns asked for Blackie for their son Johnny, and they took Blackie to him on Christmas Day: "Johnny was the most thrilled boy I have seen in a long time, and Blackie 'wagged' all over with the love he received."]

Our food costs twice as much here—literally—$75 in Argentina and $150 per month here!

Now we are looking forward to welcoming you home on furlough here next year. We shall have to buy a home by September, I guess, if we find what we want.

With our love,
Hugo[10]

Hugo's letter to Bill Cooper was much the same but included a couple of interesting paragraphs of his reflections on this transition:

While Theology was my "sugar-stick," I could see that possibly God had been preparing me for Missions. For the first time the pattern of these years and their activity began to fall in place: that is, the various mission assignments in Chile and Argentina. In the light of this experience, and of my feeling that my work was done in Argentina, and that the faculty here was unanimous in thinking I should take Missions here I came to feel that I would be "shirking" God's leadership if I were to say "No," or were to insist on a personal temperamental preference for a field of study....

I am fully aware of the difficulties of the job I am taking even in normal times, and the crisis through which the school is passing makes it all the more difficult. However, I love the school here for its rich heritage and believe that it has a future of greater usefulness in the Lord's work. Just because a ship is passing through stormy seas is no adequate reason to abandon ship. However, it surely is not a job one would seek nor even accept without a strong sense of God's leadership.

Our ties are strong to our friends there in Argentina. Until one comes to the point of change, it is impossible to fully feel the rupture that it involves. The

---

[10] Hugo Culpepper, letter to Jack and Jean Glaze, 15 December 1958.

Mission was exceedingly good to us, and we shall always be grateful for the years of fellowship in the seminary with all of you.[11]

The letters Hugo received in response expressed friendship, support, and confirmation of the sense of God's leading that he was feeling. Cornell Goerner, whose place he was filling at Southern, and who was then area secretary for Africa, Europe, and the Near East at the Foreign Mission Board wrote:

Dear Hugo:

Perhaps it will not be entirely amiss for me to be the first to congratulate you and express my enthusiastic approval of the action taken by the Seminary and of your acceptance of the invitation, since actually in a very real sense it is I whom you are replacing.

As I first read your letter I shared the mixed emotions with which you had faced the decision. But before I had come completely to the end of the letter, as I quickly reviewed in my own mind your technical studies at the Seminary, some of them with me, your rich experience in the Orient, and then your valuable experience and service in Latin America, I had a growing conviction that all that has happened to you thus far has been fitting you in a most admirable way to interpret the missionary task to the students with whom you will come in touch there at the Seminary. I am well aware of your philosophical bent, your deep concern with practical problems of missionary admini-stration, and your own deep personal commitment to world missions, as well as your intimate knowledge of Southern Baptist missionary procedures, from the inside. All of this will place you in a very strong and understanding position, and it will enable you to complement Dr. Jackson within the department. He has his own special interests and points of great strength, and you and he together should make an excellent team.... I have a real sense of satisfaction as I contemplate the possibilities of your future in that position.... You will have a two-fold task. Perhaps most important is to help produce a generation of missionary-minded pastors and denominational leaders. Then you will give basic training to an increasing host of future missionaries, I trust.

You have my prayers, my whole-hearted support, and my best wishes as you take up this important task.

---

[11] Hugo Culpepper, letter to Bill Cooper, undated, probably 15 December 1958.

Cordially yours,
Cornell Goerner[12]

Friends in Argentina responded with expressions of a genuine sense of loss. Jean Glaze wrote:

> We know you have had a hard decision to make because everybody here loves you, and you mean so much to our mission—but I'm sure that God has directed you in your decision. Someone said, I would think Hugo the most contented person in Argentina because I never meet a student, pastor, or Baptist that doesn't sing his praises. You will never know how deeply we feel the loss of all of you to our family life as well as mission work. We have realized this year just how much we depend on you all for sound thinking in making decisions. We feel that Southern Seminary is being blessed by adding Hugo to its faculty and are sure that many lives will be influenced in class by a sound theological background expressed through missionary action. May God bless you and give you a fruitful ministry there. We will always love, appreciate, and miss you here.[13]

James Tull, their friend at Southeastern Seminary, provided a different perspective.

> Dear Hugo and Ruth,
> Of the great honor involved, there is no question, and to say that we are thrilled is putting it mildly. I feel that Hugo has the opportunity, not to succeed Cornell Goerner, but to succeed W. O. Carver. Hugo thinks like Carver, and has some of Carver's breadth and depth (and none of his classroom dullness!).... This will be an opportunity, as Ruth said, for which the last 18 and more years have well prepared you.
> I think I know two things about Hugo. The first is that he is not politically ambitious, and the second is that, though affable and cooperative, he doesn't allow anyone to run over him. Both of these qualities will come in good stead as you help the school to weather the crisis into which it has come....
> I am hoping that Dale [Moody] will stay because his great prestige in the denomination can be a constructive influence in rebuilding the

---

[12] Cornell Goerner, letter to Hugo Culpepper, 17 December 1958.
[13] Jean Glaze, letter to Hugo and Ruth Culpepper, 23 December 1958.

school. To the same end, I believe that Hugo will be a tower of strength....

I know you must have some heart-rending when you think of severing from your work in Buenos Aires, but you both doubtless are upon the threshold of your greatest work. Virginia wants me to add her heartiest congratulations to mine....

Love,
James[14]

At the end of December Hugo and Ruth attended an informal reunion of some of the internees from the concentration camp in Indianapolis. Early in January 1959 Jack Glaze offered to serve as Hugo's agent in sorting and selling their possessions and packing the rest for shipment back to Louisville.

Of all the letters Hugo received that month, Bill Cooper's letter must have been the most painful:

Dear Hugo,

It is with mixed emotions, but with a deep sense of loss, that I write this letter. I wish that I could feel as clearly that you were providentially guided in your decision as you do. I am surely glad that you have that assurance. My emotions are profoundly stirred personally, in their relation to the Seminary, the Mission and the Baptist work here in Argentina, in all of which you were having so large and so important a part.

Since I practically never had a brother (The other son of my parents was born after I was in college. I seldom saw him until we lost him in the war.), others came along to whom I felt a strong brotherly attachment. It was so with Gillis, Ramsour, Kilgore, but most especially with you. In losing each of them, I felt a real personal loss. But in losing you I find myself receiving one of the hardest blows I have ever suffered. It will go hard with me personally.

The Seminary will continue to function. The students will come and go. The faculty will meet and treat its problems. The staff will still work at the solution of its problems. At the same time each of these groups will go along feeling that an essential part of its being is missing. You must know that the seminary came to have prestige as a real teaching institution due in great part to your contribution. It will be a

---

[14] James Tull, letter to Hugo and Ruth Culpepper, 30 December 1958.

long time, if ever, before we find another that can make so worthy a contribution.

The Mission, in which you have had so large a part in guiding it into a wider and better plan of work and life, will miss you. Many times when the rough spots come and when the sailing is hard, we shall miss your steadying hand. The denomination, yet in its formative years when so much guidance by a wise head and a strong heart is needed, will miss you. They have already spoken to me, and many more will.

Your going makes a great difference in the entire picture. It is not a vacancy into which most any other can step in order that there be proper balance. That blank spot will be a long time closing in, it will not be filled in.

You know even without our saying it—which makes us no less desirous of saying it—that our love, prayers, and interest will follow you. May the Lord help to heal the wound made.

Sincerely yours,
Bill[15]

Letters followed from other friends in Argentina, expressing their sadness and making arrangements to purchase various items, and students wrote touching expressions of their appreciation for Hugo's teaching and their regret in not being able to study with him further.

Doctoral Studies (1959–1961)

The press of activities in Louisville kept Hugo from looking back. He spoke at a pastors' conference in Dallas in January, and that month Ruth began looking for a home for the family in Louisville. Hugo received a letter of appointment to the faculty from President Duke K. McCall, to be effective 1 June, "subject to passing preliminary examinations for Th.D. degree before effective date indicated."[16]

By the end of the month they had bought a three-bedroom, two-bath ranch house with a basement and carport in St. Matthews, about three and a half miles from the seminary. In the midst of moving and settling in,

---

[15] Bill Cooper, letter to Hugo Culpepper, 5 January 1959.
[16] Duke McCall, letter to Hugo Culpepper, 20 January 1959.

Hugo made a trip to Richmond, kept up the work for his seminars, and prepared for his preliminary examinations in May.

Finally, twenty years after he began his doctoral studies, the time came for his preliminary exams. On 12–16 May 1959, Hugo wrote for four hours each day on five questions.

On 27 May 1959, Hugo and Ruth submitted their formal resignations to Dr. Frank K. Means at the Foreign Mission Board. The next day he received a one-sentence letter from the administrative dean: "Dear Brother Culpepper: I am happy to advise you that you have passed your preliminary examinations in partial fulfillment of the requirements for the Th.D. degree."[17] On 1 June, Hugo became assistant professor of missions at Southern Seminary, at a salary of $6,000 per year. Later in the month, he moved the first of his library of about 1,000 books into his office at Southern. Jack Glaze brought the rest of his books from Argentina at the end of the year.

In a letter to Ruth, while she was away at a GA meeting in August, Hugo wrote:

"Last night we each took a Bible and are reading five verses each, going around till we read a chapter. We are going to read a book at a time this way. We are reading John now. I hope it will help them form the habit of reading their Bibles some. I am going to let them pick the time but leave half an hour free tonight between TV programs to read again tonight."[18]

In September Ruth accepted a position with the Kentucky Baptist Convention's WMU, directing work with junior and intermediate girls and planning and presiding at state meetings, camps, workshops, and conferences around Kentucky.

Hugo spent all available time during the latter part of 1959 and 1960 working on his courses and his dissertation. Two letters to Ruth in the winter of 1961 recall the way dissertations were written before the advent of the computer:

After getting them off to school this morning, I came back and proofread the typing.... By 10:30 I had both folders ready to deliver—one to Mrs. [Lillian] Arnett [who typed Hugo's dissertation] and one to Rust—Chs. 5 and 6 respectively.... Then I checked—by counting—on how many cards I

---

[17] Hugh Peterson, letter to Hugo Culpepper, 28 May 1959.
[18] Hugo Culpepper, letter to Ruth Culpepper, date? August 1959.

have left. I have used 716 [note] cards so far. I have 334 left.... I left after lunch in time to stop by Mrs. Arnett's and leave Ch. 5 with her. She gave me through Ch. 2 in a box in finished form—all three copies. Tonight she called and said she had finished Ch. 3, and that it went through page 152 on her numbering. That is through Part I. This was 119 pages of my long hand. That means she gets 1.2773 pages per my one page. I have written 200 pages long hand. Therefore, this will be 255 pages from her, and this is through Ch. 6. I expect to hold Ch. 7 to 25 pages.... Then Part III, Chs. 8–10 will be about 55 pages, or 65 pages from her. So it looks like it is going to turn out to be about 350 pages, plus the Bibliography!... But from here on my problem is more selecting, rejecting, and organizing the remaining cards, rather than actual time spent in writing. I must not write over 80 pages more, so that is only about 10 hard days, but what goes into that is important.

I spent all day yesterday organizing Chapter 7. I had 145 cards to go through. I selected 83 and eliminated 62, and then organized the 83 in sequence, outlined the chapter, and even typed it (. . .) so as to let Rust see it before Saturday. I hope to get the whole of Part III, which is three chapters—8, 9, 10—done this way too. There are only 195 cards for these three chapters.... (Actually, I want to see Rust day after tomorrow, on Friday; that means some hard thinking between now and tomorrow night to go through these 195 cards). Then starting Saturday, I can write about nine pages a day through Sunday or Monday week and be through....

By 5:30 I was groggy from sitting and thinking hard all day, so I took a workout and a shower.[19]

Hugo's engagement with Unamuno was so profound that one must understand something of his interpretation of Unamuno's thought in order to understand Hugo himself.

"The Christian Faith and Modern Man in the Thought of Miguel de Unamuno"[20]

In the preface of the dissertation, Hugo explains why he was attracted to Unamuno:

---

[19] Hugo Culpepper, letters to Ruth Culpepper, undated, January 1961.

[20] Hugo Culpepper, "The Christian Faith and Modern Man in the Thought of Miguel de Unamuno" (Th.D. diss., Southern Baptist Theological Seminary, 1961).

It is a satisfying experience to make an exhaustive study of any significant subject. This is true in a special way when the subject is related closely to one's sense of vocation. In the course of nineteen years as a foreign missionary, I became concerned to develop an effective apologetic for approaching students and intellectuals in the Spanish-speaking world. When I encountered the personality and thought of Miguel de Unamuno, I realized that he was a man of influence among people of his own culture. Further exploration of his works revealed him as a dynamic person of deep passion and genuine existential concern. His spirit is contagious. It has been something of a personal spiritual pilgrimage to live with him for a while on the edge of the abyss, as he struggles with an unknown future. At the same time, he leaves one with a deeper appreciation for an evangelical faith and a Biblical theology—both of which he lacked. He encourages one to live the paradox of tension between struggle and peace, and to share the meaning of life with others.[21]

Up until 1947, Hugo had only seen Unamuno referred to in relation to a seminar described in the catalogue of Union Theological Seminary in New York. That same year, however, he became aware of Unamuno's influence among Latin American intellectuals through his friend Honorio Espinoza, then president of the Baptist seminary in Santiago. The idea of writing a dissertation on Unamuno occurred to Hugo at this time, but he did not settle on the topic until he met John A. Mackay when Mackay gave the Carnahan Lectures in Buenos Aires in 1953. On 28 July 1953, Mackay suggested to Hugo that "a helpful subject for a doctoral dissertation would be something dealing with Unamuno's interpretation of Christianity or the Christian life."[22] Nearly all of the reference material Hugo consulted was in Spanish:

"Eighty percent of the material has been primary sources. Seven volumes of a projected ten-volume *Complete Works*, whose publication began in Madrid in 1951, have thus far become available.... The collection constitutes about eight thousand pages thus far, and all the principal works of Unamuno have been published. In addition, some two thousand pages of secondary sources have been studied, mostly in the nature of 'critical' evaluations by Spanish authors."[23]

---

[21] Ibid. vi.

[22] Ibid., 6.

[23] Ibid., 8

Part One: The Sources of Unamuno's Thought

The Life and Setting of Unamuno

Miguel de Unamuno.

Born 27 September 1864, in Bilbao, Unamuno was raised by his mother, a Catholic "of simple and heart-felt piety."[24] He began reading philosophy at the age of fourteen, then spent four years studying philosophy at the University of Madrid. From 1884–1891, he lived in Bilbao and tutored students while he tried to secure a university appointment. He was passed over four times before he was made professor of Greek at the University of Salamanca. This appointment enabled him to marry his sweetheart of twelve years, with whom he enjoyed more than forty years of marriage, and together they had nine children.

In 1901 he was made president of the University of Salamanca at the age of thirty-six. In 1914, at the beginning of the First World War, he was removed from office because he favored the Allies. Finally, after he attacked the Spanish king in his writings, he was sentenced to sixteen years in prison, then given a royal pardon. When he opposed the military dictatorship that came to power in 1923, he was exiled to the island of

---

[24] Ibid., 14

Fuerteventura (one of the Canary Islands). He was rescued by a secret expedition and took up residence in Paris until 1925, when he moved to Hendaya, France, on the Spanish border. When the Republic he had worked for was established in 1931, Unamuno took part in the National Assembly that composed the new Spanish Constitution, and then was returned to his position as president of the University of Salamanca. When the Spanish Civil War broke out in 1936, Unamuno opposed the communists. He died suddenly on 31 December 1936, while a colleague was reading a manuscript to him.

Unamuno's Spiritual Orientation

Three spiritual influences shaped Unamuno's thought: religious, philosophical, and theological.

Unamuno was Spanish, Basque, and the son of Catholic families. The religious influence was the personal religious crisis he experienced in his reaction to orthodox Spanish Catholicism: "he believed that the soul of his country was medieval, and that Spain has experienced the Renaissance, the Reformation, and the Revolution without allowing them to affect its soul." [25] Throughout his life he joined in the religious practices of his family, morning and evening prayers, and (like Hugo) read his Greek New Testament daily; the "heresies which were to come later seemed to be more of the head and the pen than of the heart and life." [26] As a university student in Madrid, seeking to rationalize his faith, he finally ceased to attend mass and communion. When he returned to Bilbao in 1884, he was reading Kant, Hegel, and Krause rather than the Spanish apologists, [27] but still he experienced a nostalgia for the old faith. After trying to return, however, he made a second break from the church, "realizing that he was definitely an unbeliever in the orthodox sense of the term." [28] He hoped his fellow Spaniards would embrace the spirit of the Counter-Reformation [29]: "Only personally held faith is real; to 'believe' something just because the Church

---

[25] Ibid., 36–37; Miguel de Unamuno, *Tragic Sense of Life*, trans. J. E. Crawford Flitch (New York: Dover Publications, Inc., 1954) 322.

[26] Culpepper, "The Christian Faith and Modern Man," 39; Hernan Benítez, *El drama religioso de Unamuno* (Buenos Aires: Universidad de Buenos Aires, Instituto de Publicaciones, 1949) 95–96.

[27] Culpepper, "The Christian Faith and Modern Man," 42.

[28] Ibid., 43.

[29] Ibid., 45.

'believes' it is to believe nothing."[30] For his views, Unamuno was severely criticized by Catholic scholars, and when the monarch fell in 1914 Unamuno was deposed from his position at the University of Salamanca and excommunicated by the church.[31] When he rebelled against both the church and intellectualism and developed a faith based on sentiment and voluntarism, "his thought on immortality became a conscious preoccupation."[32]

The second influence on Unamuno's thought was philosophical. Hugo summarized the broad sweep of Unamuno's reading as follows:

He had strong preferences which are quite revealing. Above all, he esteemed the Scriptures (his most cited sources), especially the New Testament, and within it, Paul's epistles. Next, he emphasized the works of authors who were religiously motivated, one way or another: Augustine, Pascal, Spinoza, Rousseau, Senancour, Leopardi, Kierkegaard, Butler, Saint Teresa, Saint John of the Cross, Ignatius. Then, such thinkers as Kant and James, who have dealt with religious issues, and especially Protestant theologians such as Schleiermacher, Harnack, Ritschl, and Luther himself. The more rigorously philosophical authors held less appeal, and the Catholic theologians appear less frequently and then usually without approval. He was not attracted by Aristotle, Thomas Aquinas, Duns Scotus, Suarez, and Leibniz. Finally, he appreciated the poets in whom he found a profoundly religious sense of existence, such as the Greek tragic poets, Leopardi, Quental, Dante, and above all the English: Shakespeare, Tennyson, Wordsworth, Thomson, Byron, Browning.[33]

When Unamuno was exiled to the Canary Islands in 1924, he carried with him three books: the Greek New Testament, Dante's *Divine Comedy*, and the poems of Leopardi.[34] Hugo was especially interested in Unamuno's attraction to Browning:

For anyone who really has discovered Robert Browning, it reveals much as to the nature of Unamuno to know that with no other poet did he have so much in common. It is true that Browning did not share Unamuno's religious

---

[30] Ibid., 50.
[31] Ibid., 59.
[32] Ibid., 60.
[33] Ibid., 61.
[34] Ibid., 62.

anxiety. But apart from this, there was much that appealed to Don Miguel: the abstract thought, the concept of life as a battle, the exaltation of the will and of personal energy, the love of the paradox, and the belief in continued individual consciousness beyond death.[35]

In the rest of this section, Hugo analyzed the influence of these writers on Unamuno, citing both Unamuno's writings and the works of others. He gave particular attention to Unamuno's critique of positivism.[36] In a letter to his friend Jimínez Ilundain, who urged Unamuno to declare himself an atheist, Unamuno wrote: "The greatest miracle is to come to trust in the possibility of the Gospel after having passed through agnostic rationalism."[37] Unamuno had studied science, but primarily to refute and combat it: "Furthermore, the worship of learning terrified him, and the idolatrous worship of science seemed to him to be the most shameful and miserable of all."[38] In the end, he rejected positivism, not theism, writing again to Ilundain: "Every day I feel myself to be more Christian, and more a believer in the other life and less positivist, or whatever you want to call it."[39] Unamuno was attracted to the thought of Karl Christian Friedrich Krause (1781–1832) and his emphasis on pantheism and the intuitive perception of God. For example, Unamuno wrote: "And this vast I, within which each individual I seeks to put the Universe—what is it but God? And because I aspire to God, I love Him; and this aspiration of mine towards God is my love for Him, and just as I suffer in being He, He suffers in being I, and being each of us."[40]

Prayer, then, is "a way of life in which one does everything with one's whole soul to such an extent that it brings him to live in God."[41] Nevertheless, Unamuno safeguarded the distinction of his own personality from the divine personality. Summarizing Unamuno, Hugo's statement echoes some of his own deepest sentiments: "The secret of human life is the desire to be all without ceasing to be oneself—it is the appetite for divinity, the hunger for God."[42]

---

[35] Ibid., 62–63.

[36] Ibid., 76–85.

[37] Ibid., 82; Benítez, *El drama religioso de Unamuno*, 255 and 262.

[38] Culpepper, "The Christian Faith and Modern Man," 84.

[39] Ibid., 85; Benítez, *El drama religioso de Unamuno*, 405.

[40] Culpepper, "The Christian Faith and Modern Man," 91–92; Unamuno, *Tragic Sense of Life*, 208.

[41] Culpepper, "The Christian Faith and Modern Man," 93.

[42] Ibid., 96.

The third influence on Unamuno was theological. Between the ages of twenty-five and forty, Unamuno read Protestant theology passionately, especially Harnack. Nevertheless, "Unamuno could not be content with any theology which did not take seriously the problem of immortality, as he saw it. Without doubt this was a significant factor in his ultimate failure to find a spiritual home in Protestantism."[43] Reading Harnack intensified his critique of Catholicism, but it also led him to conclude that Christianity itself had become corrupted through its history. He was left yearning for that primitive Christianity that could no longer be recovered. The result was that he turned "within himself for his ultimate formulation of a faith."[44] He rejected *cristianismo* (a rationalized system of dogmas) but not *cristiandad* (the quality of being Christian, i.e., of being Christlike).[45]

If Harnack freed Unamuno from historical Christianity, Søren Kierkegaard introduced him to existentialism. In fact, Unamuno learned Danish in order to be able to read Kierkegaard. One does not find the metaphysical speculation of Heidegger in Unamuno.[46] Instead, "Unamuno was an existentialist in the original sense of moving out from the little world of self concern to be gripped and caught up by a cause, which sweeps him on to suffering and the tragic."[47] "At last, he had found one [in Kierkegaard] who could teach him to die 'agonizingly,' and not 'hiccoughing' the syllogisms of a corrupt Church."[48] There is a deep kinship between Kierkegaard and Unamuno; both were passionately concerned with the question of how one can become a Christian, especially since Christendom has done away with true Christianity[49]: "*Cristiandad* is playing at *cristianismo*" in the same sense that the nation was "playing at" nationalism.[50]

Unamuno was not concerned with the question "From whence have I come?" His only concern was "Where am I going?"[51] He had to know the answer in order to live. Therefore, "as a consequence of these various, and

---

[43] Ibid., 105.

[44] Ibid., 111.

[45] Ibid.

[46] Ibid., 116.

[47] Ibid., 118.

[48] Ibid., 115.

[49] Ibid., 121.

[50] Ibid., 122; Unamuno, "Dos mercados," *Obras Completas*, ed. M. Sanmiguel (Madrid: Afrodisio Aguado, S. A., 1950) 1:940.

[51] Culpepper, "The Christian Faith and Modern Man," 122.

sometimes antithetical, aspects of his spiritual orientation, there arose a struggle in his soul as an existentialist in quest of a satisfying faith."[52]

The Consequent Struggle in Unamuno's Soul

Hugo claimed that one cannot characterize Unamuno's thought more aptly than Carl Michalson's definition of existentialism: "Existentialism is a way of life which involves one's total self in an attitude of complete seriousness about himself."[53] For Unamuno, confronting the mystery of life resulted in unrelieved struggle. His struggle centered around two main ideas: "the sense of mission in life and the desire to live forever."[54] This struggle often led him to be impatient with others who, instead of struggling for ideals, were "rodents of malicious stories."[55] This concern "led him to conceive of his mission (...) as being to shatter men's faith in whatever unworthy object holds them, whether it be Catholicism, rationalism, or agnosticism, that they may struggle even as he does."[56]

Unamuno was one of the great "agonizers." Roland Bainton placed him in an elite company of troubled souls: "If anyone would discover parallels to Luther as the wrestler with the Lord, then one must turn to Paul the Jew, Augustine the Latin, Pascal the Frenchman, Kierkegaard the Dane, Unamuno the Spaniard, Dostoievski the Russian, Bunyan the Englishman, and Edwards the American."[57]

The struggle for Unamuno was not merely intellectual. It was existential, and it often involved a conflict between heart and head—faith and reason—in his own soul. In some respects, "he was a man with a Protestant mind and a Catholic heart."[58] He read Protestant theology but did not find it satisfying, and when his sister died he arranged for Gregorian masses to be celebrated "for the eternal rest of her soul."[59] He was impatient "with anything smacking of dogmatic provincialism."[60] Even before

---

[52] Ibid., 126

[53] Ibid., 128; Carl Michalson, ed., *Christianity and the Existentialists* (New York: Charles Scribner's Sons, 1956) 3.

[54] Culpepper, "The Christian Faith and Modern Man," 131.

[55] Ibid., 132; Unamuno, "A lo que salga," *Obras completas*, 3:539.

[56] Ibid., 132.

[57] Ibid., 133; Roland H. Bainton, *Here I Stand: A Life of Martin Luther* (New York: Abingdon-Cokesbury Press, 1950) 385.

[58] Culpepper, "The Christian Faith and Modern Man," 138.

[59] Ibid., 139.

[60] Ibid., 143.

Jean Paul Sartre's birth, Unamuno began writing existential novels as an expression of his "tragic sense of life." These are not psychological novels but novels that sketch the essential mode of being of his characters: "Unamuno's novel is interested in a life because life is a condition for understanding death, which is the real question. Death transcends life and brings one to the person who is dying after having lived."[61] His characters struggle with temporality and death, and they develop before him revealing the reality he sought to encounter. Furthermore, he believed that all the characters created by an author were necessarily extensions of the author himself, "parts of his very being."[62] Through his novels, therefore, Unamuno traced the theme that he would eventually take up in his magnum opus, *Tragic Sense of Life*.

Part Two: Unamuno's Presentation of the Christian Faith

His Central Problem: Death

The purpose of Unamuno's major work, *Tragic Sense of Life*, was to draw the reader's attention to "the only real problem": death. So troubling is the human inability to resolve the question of death that people spend their lives distracting themselves from it. Near the end of the book, Unamuno writes: "I took up my pen proposing to distract you for a while from your distractions."[63] Immanuel Kant was concerned with the same problem: "I mean with the only vital problem, the problem that strikes at the very root of our being, the problem of our individual and personal destiny, of the immortality of the soul."[64] He held that the real point of departure for all philosophy is "the human question...the question of knowing what will become of my consciousness, of yours, of that of others and of all, after each one of us dies."[65]

Concern with this central problem can be found in the thought of other philosophers, though at times in secondary forms. Religion is based "on an intimate sense of one's own substantiality and the desire to perpetuate it."[66] For Unamuno, "apart from duration, there can be no value."[67]

---

[61] Ibid., 146.

[62] Ibid., 150.

[63] Ibid., 156; Unamuno, *Tragic Sense of Life*, 330.

[64] Culpepper, "The Christian Faith and Modern Man," 157; Unamuno, *Tragic Sense of Life*, 4.

[65] Culpepper, "The Christian Faith and Modern Man," 159; Unamuno, *Tragic Sense of Life*, 159.

[66] Culpepper, "The Christian Faith and Modern Man," 164.

Unamuno confronted his fear of dying. For him, it was essential to do so and to probe within himself to attempt to discover why he had such a fear of death. Just as he could not remember having been born, so he hoped that death would overtake him by surprise—as it did—and that he would have no premonition of its approach. Still, he regarded the loss of consciousness in sleep and the sensation of solitude as foretastes of death. Since death cannot be relived, it must be pre-lived. Through the characters in his novels (who are extensions of himself), Unamuno carried out his attempts "to penetrate to the secret of death."[68] To understand death, he thought he had to come to know the real person, the person that exists only for God.[69] In *La Tía Tula* Unamuno treats death as absolute loneliness and as the world dying to oneself. In an exception to the aloneness with which one confronts death, Unamuno describes the deaths of two lovers in his narrative poem "Teresa" as they share the slow process of dying from tuberculosis. In a description that he could not have foreseen characterizing his own and Ruth's slow decline at the end of their lives as they struggled with dementia and Alzheimer's, Hugo summarized the poem: "But in a deeper sense, because of the union of their lives in love, each was dying in a deeper sense through the progressive death of the other. Finally, when one passed on, the other felt that part of his self had also died.... This note of fellowship in death is so exceptional in Unamuno as to be noteworthy."[70] More typically, death is the supreme solitude: We live together, but die alone. Nevertheless, through the death of Manuela in *La Tía Tula*, Unamuno introduced the concept of a "latent reality" to which one passes through death: "In the radical solitude of death, there is revealed to man the ultimate ground of his being, God, for he comes to be with Him."[71]

The Tension between Mind and Heart, Which Results in the Tragic Sense of Life

Unamuno's life was a battleground for the struggle between the head, which said there could be no reason to think there is life beyond death, and the heart, which demands that there must be, and for Unamuno this was "the tragic sense of life." Because he did not grant the final verdict to

---

[67] Ibid., 168.
[68] Ibid., 175.
[69] Ibid., 176.
[70] Ibid., 177–78.
[71] Ibid., 180.

reason, however, he did not despair. He agreed with Tennyson that "nothing worthy proving can be proven, nor yet disproven."[72] In a larger context, the Spanish soul is found in an inward tragedy, a conflict "between what the world is as scientific reason shows it to be, and what we wish that it might be, as our religious faith affirms it to be."[73] Reason and life can never agree. Yet neither can one maintain itself without the other. It is futile to attempt to establish the immortality of the soul by rational argument. On the other hand, reason can argue that individual consciousness depends on the physical organism, emerging slowly as one gains impressions from the world outside oneself and ending with death.[74] But the heart is not appeased by reason. Unamuno agreed with William James on the limitations of reason: The will to believe is the only faith possible for one given to analytical reasoning. Both poetry and religion are contra-rational. Unamuno cited Kierkegaard in support of this point: "Poetry is illusion before knowledge; religion illusion after knowledge," but "every individual who does not live either poetically or religiously is a fool."[75] Persisting in faith's claims against reason, Unamuno adopted an epistemology based on intuition. Who can say that there are not things that one can feel without knowing?[76] Perhaps what differentiates man from animals is not man's ability to think but man's ability to feel. Unamuno's motto, therefore was: *in interiore hominis habitat veritas*. He therefore "concedes a decisive value to intuition as a way of knowing,"[77] and his intuition leads him to believe in the existence of God: "I believe in God as I believe in my friends, because I feel the breath of His affection, feel His invisible and intangible hand, drawing me, leading me, grasping me; because I possess an inner consciousness of a particular providence and of a universal mind that marks out for me the course of my destiny."[78]

Believing, therefore, is a form of knowing; it is an immediate apprehension from within "arising from the springs of one's being."[79] The will then drives on from intuition, "actively moving toward the object of its trust."[80] Faith is not believing in the unseen; for Unamuno "faith is

---

[72] Ibid., 184.
[73] Ibid., 186; Unamuno, *Tragic Sense of Life*, 321.
[74] Culpepper, "The Christian Faith and Modern Man," 192.
[75] Ibid., 196; Unamuno, *Tragic Sense of Life*, 196.
[76] Culpepper, "The Christian Faith and Modern Man," 200.
[77] Ibid., 201.
[78] Ibid., 202; Unamuno, *Tragic Sense of Life*, 194.
[79] Culpepper, "The Christian Faith and Modern Man," 204.
[80] Ibid.

creating what one does not see."[81] Still, "simple faith" is valuable to the simple-minded, as Unamuno explored in one of his novels: It is "better for them to believe everything, even contradictions mixed in with the rest, than to believe nothing."[82] As for the critical agnostic, Unamuno's character believes that "for some holy but inscrutable end, the Lord had made them believe that they were unbelievers."[83]

Faith and reason, thought irreconcilable, must work together in fulfilling man's two basic instincts: conservation and self-perpetuation. For Unamuno, there are only three possible solutions to the problem of death: "(a) I know that I shall die utterly, and then irremediable despair, or (b) I know that I shall not die utterly, and then resignation, or (c) I cannot know either one or the other, and then resignation in despair or despair in resignation...and hence conflict."[84]

Unamuno would not let either faith or reason triumph, perhaps because he feared that reason would prevail. He preferred for the war to continue. He found meaning in struggling with the mystery. Moreover, rather than rendering ethics pointless, the tragic sense of life served as the basis of an ethic for life.[85] His religion was struggle, whether he won or not. Indeed, the prize may be the struggle itself. Unamuno formulated his principle for action succinctly: "Act so that in your judgment, and in the judgment of others you may merit eternity, act so that you may become irreplaceable, act so that you may not merit death."[86] In other words, live in such a way that if there is nothing beyond death, it will be an injustice. He agreed with Kant: "We cannot know that there is a God; but we ought to live as though there were one."[87] This "transcendental pessimism" provided Unamuno with a positive, even optimistic, outlook on life. In a peculiar way, therefore, religion was Unamuno's supreme preoccupation, and his orientation was Christian. Responding to Jesus' cry of dereliction, "My God, My God, why have you abandoned me," Unamuno sought the

---

[81] Ibid., 206.

[82] Ibid., 212.

[83] Ibid., 213.

[84] Ibid., 220; Unamuno, *Tragic Sense of Life*, 33.

[85] Culpepper, "The Christian Faith and Modern Man," 223.

[86] Ibid., 225; Unamuno, *Tragic Sense of Life*, 263.

[87] Culpepper, "The Christian Faith and Modern Man," 226; Miguel Romero de Navarro, *Miguel de Unamuno, Novelista-Poeta-Ensayista* (Madrid: Sociedad General Español de Libreria, 1928) 224; citing Edgar A. Singer, *Modern Thinkers and Present Problems* (New York, 1923) 129.

faith of Jesus rather than faith in Jesus.[88] Christianity is struggle, life, and agony, and therefore adventure, not doctrine.

The Existence of God

The opening paragraph of this chapter contains Hugo's summary of Unamuno's views on the subject:

One of the most perplexing problems in the thought of Unamuno has to do with the existence of God. There is no question as to his belief in God's existence, but it is not altogether clear as to what this means for him. He affirmed in a letter to Ilundain, in 1906, that every day he believed more in a personal God, the consciousness of the universe, the ordainer of everything. But in the next breath he said that every day he believed less in the validity of the traditional and logical proofs of his existence."[89]

The basis for Unamuno's belief in God was not rational but grew out of his own desire for God to exist and a heartfelt response to the revelation of God through the gospel, Christ, and history. Logical proofs and ecclesiastical doctrines present the idea of God, while Unamuno believed that what really mattered was the heart's desire for God. True knowledge of God can come only from love, not from reason.

For Unamuno the usual relationship between God and the immortality of the soul is reversed: "God is...deduced from the immortality of the soul, and not the immortality of the soul from the existence of God."[90] But it is not merely a rational matter, of course. The believer participates in the reality of God. Therefore, Unamuno said, "I persist in creating by the energy of faith my immortalizing God."[91] It is as though God were the dreamer of all that is, and we exist in God's dream. The alternative is "either God or oblivion."[92] While professing to belief in the personal God of Christian theology, Unamuno inclined toward pantheism: God is the consciousness of the Universe, the personalization of the Universe. Nevertheless, God "has an intellect and will that differs from those of men

---

[88] Culpepper, "The Christian Faith and Modern Man," 230.

[89] Ibid., 232.

[90] Ibid., 238; Unamuno, *Tragic Sense of Life*, 4.

[91] Culpepper, "The Christian Faith and Modern Man," 241; Unamuno, *Tragic Sense of Life*, 241.

[92] Culpepper, "The Christian Faith and Modern Man," 243.

only in degree,"[93] and Unamuno insisted on maintaining the distinction between God and men, who have independent feelings and wills.

Christ also retained an important place in Unamuno's theology. He wore a cross every day and insisted that it be represented in the bronze statue that was cast of him late in his life. Hugo agreed with John Mackay that for Unamuno the cross was "the emblem of Unamuno's lifelong struggle, his *agonía* to pierce the mystery of human existence."[94] Unamuno wrote a poem on the painting, "The Christ of Velazquez," who never ceases to agonize, is always dying in order that he may give us life.[95] Christ's struggle is projected into the life of his disciples, who find meaning and life in this redemptive struggle.

Unamuno's Eschatology

In a letter to Ilundain in 1900, Unamuno expressed his belief that "uncertainty as to whether there is a life beyond the grave is man's salvation."[96] If one were certain there is life after death, one would be tempted to commit suicide in order to enter immediately into that immortal life. On the other hand, if one were certain there is nothing beyond death, one might be led to suicide in order to escape the agony and meaninglessness of life. Either way, it is the lack of certainty and the desire for life after death that make life possible. Moreover, if the end of life makes life possible, then the chief aim of life is to make a soul for oneself, to create and cultivate one's soul for eternity. At times Unamuno turned his thought of God as the dreamer of life, regarding death as an awakening to life.[97]

Although Unamuno recognized the comfort of substitutes for personal immortality, he ultimately rejected them, demanding the hope of personal immortality. In a sense, one lives on in his or her descendents, in a material as well as a spiritual sense. Again, Unamuno maintained that he would live on in his writings and the fame of life's work. Just as Pascal and Kierkegaard lived on in him as he thought their thoughts after them through their writings, so he would enjoy a form of immortality by living

---

[93] Ibid., 249.

[94] Ibid., 255.

[95] Ibid., 257–58.

[96] Ibid., 262.

[97] Ibid., 265–66.

on in his readers.[98] But these substitutes for personal immortality, for a resurrection of the body, are unacceptable: "All this talk of a man surviving in his children or in this works, or in the universal consciousness, is but vague verbiage which satisfies only those who suffer from affective stupidity."[99]

Salvation, for Unamuno, was salvation from death, from nothingness, rather than salvation from sin. But salvation is not contingent on progress; instead, Unamuno was attracted to the understanding that "eternity is constituted of the past," as the sum of all that has gone before, taking one beyond the limits of time.[100]

What one really wants to be, therefore, becomes within him a creative force: "Unamuno expects God to reward or punish one by permitting him to become throughout all eternity that which he had really wanted to be."[101] The human person is being produced in this life, up to the point of one's death, so life is the making of one's soul. The process occurs primarily as one responds to and internalizes either love or hate. One therefore "passes through death to a life beyond which is in keeping with what he has become, through love or hate."[102] Old age and death are temporary obstacles in one's personal development. Beyond death lies "the pilgrimage, ever onward, in the realization of his selfhood."[103] This view led Unamuno to reject traditional notions of heaven and hell: "It is not the divine reward or punishment, but the judgment which one formulates in his own consciousness, that constitutes his reward or punishment."[104] Unamuno found the prospect of nothingness far more terrifying than hell. He thought that religion had been converted into a kind of police system in order to maintain order in society, but he found the fear of hell to be an ineffective deterrent. Moreover, while he did not believe in purgatory, he preferred the importance of the communion of the faithful in Catholicism to the isolated individualism of Protestantism: "One prays for the other, and each has someone in heaven to pray for him."[105]

Eternal life depends on an agonizing desire for it. For this reason, Unamuno was attracted to the notion of conditional immortality. Whether

---

[98] Ibid., 269.

[99] Ibid., 270; Unamuno, *Tragic Sense of Life*, 16.

[100] Culpepper, "The Christian Faith and Modern Man," 274.

[101] Ibid., 275.

[102] Ibid., 279.

[103] Ibid., 280.

[104] Ibid., 281.

[105] Ibid., 285.

one actually believed in life after death or not, one must desire it: "He even began to doubt that those so devoid of the desire for life could be awakened after death."[106] One's duty to one's neighbor, therefore, is to awaken "his sleeping consciousness to the central issue of life and eternity."[107] Nevertheless, given the alternatives of reward and punishment or a future life in which all will be saved, Unamuno inclined toward the latter. Only a wicked man could say there is no other life than this one, and "even a 'human God' would not condemn such a man for his despair."[108] Late in his life Unamuno moved increasingly toward universalism, concluding that "death is in itself a repentance and an expiation, and consequently that death purifies the sinner. It would follow then that all men would be saved."[109] One may continue on in the next life as one was in this, but life requires the possibility of change: "The joy of seeing Him [God] face to face will not be that contemplation of the whole Truth all at once. This would be overwhelming. It will rather be 'a continual discovery of the Truth, a ceaseless act of learning involving an effort which kept the sense of personal consciousness continually active.'"[110]

Hugo found this understanding of life after death personally appealing. Later, when asked what he thought life after death would be like, Hugo said he thought it would be a long, upward climb, and he was looking forward to it with a great deal of anticipation.

Part Three: The Significance of Unamuno for the Christian Encounter with Modern Man—His Weakness and Strength

The Plight of Modern Man and the Point of Contact

A major reason for Hugo's interest in Unamuno was the latter's influence among Latin American intellectuals and the value of his thought as a bridge to the gospel. In this regard, Unamuno's concern with modern man's search for meaning, his concern with man (humanity) as the most important reality, and his search for meaning within himself all made him appealing to others in their quest for answers to life's ultimate questions.

---

[106] Ibid., 287.
[107] Ibid., 289.
[108] Ibid., 293.
[109] Ibid., 294.
[110] Ibid., 296; Unamuno, *Tragic Sense of Life*, 229.

Unamuno described man as "a sick animal." The sickness was a manifestation of hatred, arising from self-hatred and the inability to love: "The worst thing is not to be able to love."[111] The plight of modern man is rooted within himself: "His life is empty and meaningless, insecure and anxious. Without a proper self-love, he is the victim of false passions toward others."[112]

Such being the condition of modern man, Hugo considered that existentialism could serve as preliminary to, and keep the way open for, a positive Christian faith. In this judgment he concurred with Carl Michalson, author of *Christianity and the Existentialists*.[113] As the principal forms of philosophy influential in Latin America, Hugo discussed, in order, the neo-scholasticism of the Roman Catholic Church; logical positivism, which attracted students in secondary school and the university; dialectical materialism (Marxism), which attracted students as they became conscious of the economic struggle to live; and existentialism, which resonated with their quest for a more satisfying understanding of life. Hugo had experienced encounters where Paul Tillich's "method of correlation" had been validated: the gospel correlated with existentialism, providing answers for the questions existentialism raised.

Unamuno's influence functioned as a point of contact with Latin American intellectuals. Unamuno was a Spaniard, well known in Latin America, and his personal spiritual pilgrimage gave him unique credibility. Like them, he had been raised in a Roman Catholic environment, struggled with positivism and rejected it, and recognized the significance of dialectical materialism. He had run the gamut of the philosophies that defined the conversation in Latin America and found them all lacking. Unamuno was also prominent in Latin America, where his books were readily available, newspapers and magazines carried features on him, and he was the subject of extensive discussion among other writers. Hugo's personal friend, José Míguez Bonino, president of the Union Theological Seminary in Buenos Aires, wrote to him on 29 June 1959: "The subject of your thesis interested me very much. Unamuno is constantly quoted, but one has the impression that he is quoted disconnectedly and that as yet he has not been adequately appreciated in his religious philosophy. It will be of

---

[111] Culpepper, "The Christian Faith and Modern Man," 306; Unamuno, "Abel Sánchez," *Obras completas*, 2:895.

[112] Culpepper, "The Christian Faith and Modern Man," 308–309.

[113] Ibid., 310, where Culpepper quotes Carl Michalson, *Christianity and the Existentialists* (New York: Charles Scribner's Sons, 1956) 20-22.

much value that we may be able to have soon a Protestant study of him in Spanish."[114]

Eduardo Font, one of Hugo's students in whom he took a special interest, wrote on Unamuno before going to the University of Buenos Aires to work on a doctorate in philosophy. Hugo also related his experience of conversations with a priest who came to him at night seeking firsthand knowledge of the evangelical faith from a believer. The priest eventually left the Roman Catholic Church and became an evangelical himself. Hugo's interest in Unamuno, therefore, arose out of his commitment to Christian missions and his recognition of the importance of being able to engage the intellectual leadership of the culture.

Unamuno's Weakness

As much as Hugo appreciated Unamuno's struggle with the human situation, he recognized deficiencies in Unamuno's thought, and his critique of his subject reveals some of the primary themes of Hugo's own theology. He noted first Unamuno's lack of any "experiential sense that God had been seeking man in an active, objective, historical way through the centuries."[115] Had Unamuno lived fifty years later, Hugo thought he would have come more heavily under the positive influence of biblical theology, with its emphasis on God's redemptive purpose, biblical vocation, election, covenant, and the people of God. Consequently, "life was not a gift of God to be filled with meaning for his glory."[116] Because Unamuno rejected the sacraments, Hugo wondered whether his limitation of grace to the sacraments was an obstacle that kept Unamuno from ever experientially discovering "the reality of Biblical grace."[117] Neither did he have a doctrine of sin that took seriously the self-centeredness of man: "Whatever shortcomings Unamuno sees in humanity, he tends to attribute to ignorance or the lack of development."[118] He was also more concerned with immortalization than justification by faith. While he read Luther, his experience did not resonate with Luther's. In this regard, he remained more Catholic than Protestant. Unamuno lacked faith both in the Catholic sense of faith in the truth of the Christian religion and in the sense of faith

---

[114] Culpepper, "The Christian Faith and Modern Man," 322.

[115] Ibid., 329.

[116] Ibid., 331.

[117] Ibid., 332.

[118] Ibid., 334.

in the capacity of human reason. Neither did he know the peace that comes from a personal trust in Jesus as Savior.

Perhaps because of the Spanish emphasis on individualism and his rejection of Catholicism, Unamuno lacked any appreciation for the corporate nature of Christian experience—the church. Hugo's critique at this point is borne out by the clearest definition of Unamuno's understanding of Christianity. In "La agonía del cristianismo" he wrote: "Christianity is a value of the universal spirit, which has its roots in the most intimate part of the human individuality."[119] In response, Hugo lamented, "He leaves no place for dwelling together in the beauty of holiness as the family of God in the Church. Indeed, he leaves no place for the family in any sense."[120] As a result of this extreme individualism, Unamuno's thought is highly self-centered and lacking in historical orientation. Hugo reacted strongly against this egoism. He felt that Unamuno was guilty of an exploitation of God for his own immortality: "There is nothing here of the Biblical teaching that end of life is to live for the glory of God."[121]

Unamuno's Strength—His Positive Contribution

Unamuno was a disturber of minds and hearts, an awakener of sleeping souls. He considered his vocation to be to arouse others from their slumbers, whether they be the dogmas of Catholicism or of free-thinkers and positivists. He sought to provoke interest in what he considered the real issues of life and to goad others to transcend the trivialities of life.[122] He was concerned with the growing of souls, and no growth comes without agonizing: "What this noble struggler wanted was to make a struggler for an ideal out of every man. He was not so much concerned as to what the ideal might be as he was that everyone become an agonizer."[123]

Unamuno continues to be relevant because of his profound conviction that the supreme virtue ought to be sincerity, by which he meant integrity. He was repelled by those who twist the meaning of Scripture to get it to say what they want it to say. The search for truth requires honesty and

---

[119] Ibid., 342; Unamuno, "La agon(a del cristianismo," *Obras completas*, 4:827.

[120] Culpepper, "The Christian Faith and Modern Man," 343–44.

[121] Ibid., 348.

[122] Ibid., 355.

[123] Ibid., 356.

openness before it. He was also repelled by mediocrity or settling for anything less than reality. One who claims to believe must be willing to examine the foundations of his or her belief: "If anyone says his religion embraces certain dogmas of which he is really ignorant, Unamuno would deny their significance. Only that is religion which is one's own in such a way that it makes a difference in one's very life."[124] Faith for Unamuno, therefore, meant sincerity (a holy desire for speaking the truth), tolerance (a recognition of the relativity of all knowledge), and mercy (which is the result of seeing the inherent spiritual value of another).

Unamuno was also in touch with the needs of his time in contending that one's "proper vocation is possibly the gravest and most deep-seated of social problems."[125] One should therefore find meaning in life through service—if one were a cobbler, to service the community with comfortable footwear, to "shod them for the love of them and for the love of God in them,"[126] to shod them religiously.

As an existentialist, Unamuno provides the opportunity for a missionary apologetic for the Spanish-speaking world. He feared not the Europeanization of Spain but its Americanization—a terrible expiation for Spain's colonization of America. He wanted to call the Spanish-speaking world on both sides of the Atlantic to a deeper regard for life and a deeper level of life. He also sought to free his culture from the corruption of Catholicism. Neither did he regard philosophy as a substitute for religion. In spite of his opposition to Catholicism, however, he still believed that only Christianity gives purpose and comfort in living.[127] In these respects, Hugo saw that Unamuno could have an apologetic significance for disaffected Catholics in South America and in Argentina in particular. Unamuno looked forward to an indigenous reformation in Latin America, breaking out from within.[128] For this reason, Hugo insisted, missionaries should grant full acceptance to the indigenous churches. For Hugo, however, "Unamuno's ultimate significance is that he and his thought can serve as an apologetic point of contact for the witness to the grace of God through faith in Jesus Christ. He can inspire both non-Christians and Christians,

---

[124] Ibid., 361.
[125] Ibid., 364; Unamuno, *Tragic Sense of Life*, 271.
[126] Unamuno, *Tragic Sense of Life*, 274.
[127] Culpepper, "The Christian Faith and Modern Man," 370.
[128] Ibid., 372–73.

but in a different sense, with his final legacy: 'And may God deny you peace, but give you glory!' "[129]

The dissertation was signed by Eric Rust (chairman), Dale Moody, James Leo Garrett, and Wayne E. Ward. On Friday, 10 March 1961, Hugo had his oral exam. The same day, he received a one-sentence letter from the administrative dean: "Dear Brother Culpepper: I am happy to advise you that you have passed your oral examination on your thesis in fulfillment of the requirements for the Th.D. degree."[130] On 14 March, the Board of Trustees of The Southern Baptist Theological Seminary, by unanimous action, promoted Hugo to the rank of associate professor, effective 1 August 1961. Hugo's parents paid for his academic regalia and drove up from Little Rock for his graduation on 19 May. The next day, the *Courier-Journal* carried an account of President Duke McCall's charge to the graduates under the headline "McCall Says Theological Revolt May Destroy Baptist Convention." Prophetically, McCall warned the graduates that "the rebellion now expressing itself within Southern Baptist life is all part of a basic disillusionment with the effectiveness of traditional and familiar religious forms.... The rebellions against denominationalism and church institutionalism are being fed by the genuine discovery of real Christian fellowship beyond and outside denominational and churchly institutional lines." The situation was all the more dangerous, he said, because Baptists have "tried to pretend that nothing important is happening."[131]

---

[129] Ibid., 375; Unamuno, *Tragic Sense of Life*, 330.

[130] Hugh Peterson, letter to Hugo Culpepper, 10 March 1961.

[131] *The Courier-Journal*, section 1 (20 May 1961) 6.

Dale Moody hooding Hugo,
19 May 1961.

W. O. Carver Professor of Christian Missions
and World Religions

In the fall, Hugo's Missions 51 syllabus carried the following explanation of the reading report required at the end of the course:

The student is required to certify on the final examination that he has read *all* the textbooks (5 books, total of 1163 pages). *NO CREDIT* for the course will be given without this certificate. He is requested to hand in at the last class period a summary (author, title of book, number of pages in each book citing exact pages, and the grand total) of any parallel reading for the course which he has done on his own initiative. There is *no requirement* for parallel reading, but it will be taken into consideration when the final grade for the course is assigned. (The exceptional student, and even the good student, will go beyond "the call of duty" out of sheer interest and display some initiative at this point.)

For the Comparative Study of Religions course offered the same semester, he required a certificate and summary of John B. Noss's *Man's Religions* (768 pages) and an additional 750 pages that the student could select from the suggested parallel reading. Little wonder that his students at times referred to him as "Dr. Skull Popper"!

In September Hugo and Ruth celebrated the news that President Kennedy had appointed their friend Paul Geren as the first director of the Peace Corps. By the end of the year, the future directions of the Culpepper boys were also becoming clear. A letter from Hugo's father says:

> We are very happy that Alan has decided to be a preacher. We have thought for some time that he would do this.... All of us agree that Larry can do anything that he wants to do or be. He has plenty of time to decide on his vocation. We think he will decide on Medicine. MD seems to be his choice now, but he can and will be tops in any vocation he wants to be. We are proud of them—[that] goes without saying, as you well know. We have lots to be thankful for. Our greatest assets are investments we have made with our families.[132]

The following spring (1962) Hugo was given tenure by the seminary trustees, and his parents celebrated that milestone also.

Hugo's schedule filled quickly, as it always did, with speaking engagements, meetings, faculty activities, and the boys' sports and school activities. In the summer of 1962 Ruth had to be in Glorieta, New Mexico, in July and in Ridgecrest, North Carolina, in August. The family drove from Louisville to Little Rock and on to Glorieta. Leaving Ruth at Glorieta, Hugo and the boys set out on a memorable, three-week camping trip in the family's 1962 Plymouth station wagon. Larry became the cook, Alan set up the tent and gathered firewood, and Hugo did most of the clean-up. The three drove leisurely from Glorieta north into Colorado, seeing sites along the way. When they stopped for the night near Pueblo, New Mexico, they made a huge fruit salad for supper and finished it for breakfast the next morning. When they could not find a campground in Wyoming, they just pulled off the highway about a half a mile and camped on the prairie. In Yellowstone, Hugo read, Alan fished, and Larry explored. When a bear came up to the picnic table where Hugo was working, Hugo shooed it away with his writing pad.

---

[132] Mr. J. H. Culpepper, letter to Hugo Culpepper, 17 December 1961.

On the way south, they stopped at Roosevelt Park, south of Alpine, Utah, and then swung by Salt Lake City so that Hugo could see the Mormon Tabernacle and gather information on the Mormons for the course he was teaching that fall, Comparative Religions. At the end of the standard tour, the college student who was working as a tour guide that summer asked the assorted group of tourists if they had any questions. Hugo said, "Yes, I wonder if you could explain to me the epistemology of Mormon eschatology." The man standing beside the boys turned to another man and said, "You can bet he ain't no hack driver!" The tour guide arranged for Hugo to visit with a professor of Mormon eschatology at Brigham Young University that afternoon, and Hugo was able to talk with the Mormon theologian and gather some resources for his course.

From there it was on to Bryce, Zion, and the Grand Canyon before returning to Glorieta. Stopping for a night near Amarillo, Texas, at a motel with a swimming pool was a refreshing break from the rigors of camping. The next day, near Sweetwater, they had a flat tire. After the boys changed it, Hugo took the lug wrench to be sure they had gotten the lug nuts tight enough—and twisted one of the bolts in two! Ruth always said that with his strength he tightened everything too tight!

Hugo in front of portrait of
W. O. Carver.

During its spring meeting in March 1963, the trustees of Southern Seminary established a new endowed chair, the William O. Carver Chair of Christian Missions and World Religions and named Hugo as the first professor to hold that chair. Because of Carver's influence on Hugo and Hugo's great appreciation for Carver's understanding of and passion for the mission of the church, there was no one better to carry Carver's legacy, and Hugo always took great pride in this appointment.

In this position, Hugo shaped the teaching of missions at Southern for the next generation, as he himself described in "Missions, Evangelism, and World Religions at Southern":

In 1963, when Culpepper was the only faculty member in the department, at his initiative, the name of the department was changed to Christian Missions and World Religions, and the curriculum in the department was changed. The introductory course, which was required for the B.D. degree, was expanded to four areas: the Biblical Basis of Missions, the History of Missions, the Principles and Practice of Missions, and World Religions. A month of introductory study was devoted to each of these subdivisions in the course. Each of these four areas was also offered as a full semester elective course for in-depth study. In addition, an increased number of electives was listed in the 1963–1964 catalog to be offered in alternate years or when indicated. These courses included area studies in three continents, Cultural Anthropology, History of Baptist Foreign Missions, History of Baptist Home Missions, History of Religions (three courses which together covered all religions), Religious Cults of America, History of Ecumenics, and the Theology of Missions.[133]

A sermon that Hugo preached in the seminary chapel and then published in a collection of sermons by Southern Seminary professors at that time relates experiences from his years in Chile and Argentina, explains his understanding of "the righteousness of God," and casts light on how he taught missions during that era.[134]

"God's Power and the World's Response"

As I have lived through the years, seeking to let God work through my life as he did through Paul's, I have been able to understand better what Paul meant in Romans 1:16-17, than I could twenty-two years ago when I first went to China as a foreign missionary. In both his life and mine two things made and kept us missionaries.

---

[133] Hugo Culpepper, "Missions, Evangelism, and World Religions at Southern," *Review & Expositor*, 82, 1 (1985): 68.

[134] Hugo Culpepper, "God's Power and the World's Response," *Professor in the Pulpit*, ed. W. Morgan Patterson and Raymond Bryan Brown (Nashville: Broadman Press, 1963) 54–61.

First, there is the personal sense of vocation. Paul had his "Damascus road" experience; in my own way, I am just as sure that God called me. It is not enough to become a foreign missionary simply because you have no good reason for not doing so. Everyone should face honestly the very real possibility that "God wants you!" However, unless you come to believe that God wants you as a foreign missionary so strongly that you cannot be happy at home, you had better not go. The way is too demanding for half-hearted recruits. But if you do feel that you must go, then by all means go, and God will go with you and the way will be glorious.

Secondly, there is an understanding of God's "plan of the ages," of what God is doing as he is active in history.... As I lived and preached the gospel in the chaos of China, during three years in a Japanese concentration camp in the Philippine Islands, among the upward struggling masses of Chile, and through a dictatorship and revolution in Argentina, I was grateful for some measure of understanding of what a living God is doing as he realizes his intention in history. Missionaries of the twentieth century can say with Paul, "I am not disappointed in the gospel, because I have seen that it is God's power manifesting a redeeming activity that bears fruit of eternal significance in the lives of men today."...

How can we explain this condition of man in his natural state? Man is a creature with two aspects to his life: horizontal and vertical. Horizontally, he is an animal and has much in common with all other animals in his biological structure and functions. But man is more than an animal, since he is related to God and has the potential in his life of fellowship with God. As a result he is conscious of his insecurity as an animal, but sin distorts his vision and thwarts his will and keeps him from enjoying fellowship with God, which would give him security. He is lost and hopeless! Yet he strives by his own efforts to achieve security, often by trying to become wealthy. Few succeed, and most of those who do are spiritually proud and more "lost" than ever. What happens to the masses who fail? They seek to forget their insecurity through drink, immorality, gambling, and other vices. All of this explains the seething caldron of lost men who confront us in a pagan world.

> Most men eddy about
> Here and there—eat and drink,
> Chatter and love and hate,
> Gather and squander, are raised
> Aloft, are hurl'd in the dust,
> Striving blindly, achieving
> Nothing; and then they die—

Perish;—and no one asks
Who or what they have been,
More than he asks what waves,
In the moonlit solitudes mild
Of the midmost Ocean, have swell'd,
Foam'd for a moment, and gone.[135]

But this hopeless condition of lost men, for whom life has no meaning, becomes acute to the missionary when he meets a lost individual. Several years ago a man off the streets came into the seminary in South America where I was teaching, and asked for me. The moment I looked into his eyes I knew I was talking with a desperate man. Beads of cold sweat popped out on his forehead. His hand quivered as he talked. He came to the point immediately. "Does God forgive?" "Does God forgive? " He repeated this piercing question several times.

Through sympathetic listening I soon learned his story. He had a faithful wife and children whom he loved and cherished. Always he had been a good husband and father, until the whim of a moment led him to fall into immorality some months before. Now his body was diseased. His doctor had forbidden him to live at home, out of consideration for his family. His family did not understand his strange behavior. He was depressed, burdened with a guilty conscience, and suffering acutely before God and man. His supreme concern was to know if there was any hope for him. "Does God forgive?" I preached the gospel to this one man. Only the certainty that God is able to save such a man can help one to point him to hope and life in Christ. But we do not become disappointed, because we know the gospel is the power of God unto salvation!

In the gospel a redeeming activity of God is being revealed. It was being revealed in the time of Paul, and it is still being revealed today. Paul calls it the "righteousness of God" which is being revealed. Usually we read this to mean either a moral quality of God's own character, or a moral quality in the life of the Christian which is derived from God. Both of these meanings occur at times in the Bible, but they are secondary, resulting from the primary, soteriological sense, as we interpret it here [where it means God's redeeming activity in history]....

God came to the climax of his redeeming activity in Christ, establishing a new covenant with the church as the body of Christ, through whom he continues to realize his purpose of redeeming men even in our time. Christ in

---

[135] Matthew Arnold, "Rugby Chapel," *The Poetical Works of Matthew Arnold* (New York: Oxford University Press, 1957) 288.

us, you and me, is the hope of glory for God and men—for God, as his true character is manifested in and through the followers of Christ (this is God's glory); for men, as they are laid hold of by this revelation and, through faith, come to have the living hope of becoming Christlike.

I think all of this is what Paul meant when he said that the "righteousness of God" is being revealed in the gospel. He had seen and understood the redeeming activity of a living God through history, coming to a climax in Christ and his death, and still expressing itself in and through the New Testament Church in Paul's own time. We believe that this same living God is still active through his people today in the gospel, and that only this adequately explains the response of the world as missionary advance bears fruit in lives changed by the gospel.

If life is worthwhile as one fills it with things beautiful to remember, certainly the missionary becomes wealthy as he sees the lives of those who have responded to God's redeeming activity in Christ changed through the gospel. Many powers are at work in our world. In Latin America, communism is constantly making a bid especially for the young people. A few years ago, when I returned to my office near the end of the day, a young Bolivian had been waiting for four hours to see me. Juan Lopez had come in quest of more truth. His life was changed already because he had seen God's power through the Christian faith of an humble Baptist girl in Bolivia whom he had married. She was a successful nurse with a scholarship for study in the States when he met her. By deception he led her to believe that he had given up communism. After their marriage, she learned that Juan was unchanged. He became active again, organizing cells of young Communists. Then he tried to get the help of his young wife in doing this. She had given up much in life because she loved him. "One thing I refuse to give up," she told her husband, "and that is my faith in Christ!" To young Lopez, this was a new power with which he was unable to cope. He had never known anything quite like it in his life. In a few months' time, through trial and suffering, God used his wife's influence to win him to Christ. Now he wants to live even more zealously as an evangelical Baptist pastor than he did as a young Communist.

In the seminary in Argentina, we had students from Peru, Bolivia, Brazil, Paraguay, Uruguay, Chile, Argentina; many of these had come directly, or their parents had, from various European countries such as Germany, Russia, Italy, Poland, and Spain. Their lives had been uprooted by the convulsions of twentieth-century Europe. Face to face, they had seen the stark realities of hunger, disease, torture, depravity, and death. No veneer of blinding materialistic prosperity had dwarfed their spirits. They were robust, and spiritually hungry, as they lived in quest of the truth.

One of those young men had been an artillery officer in the Russian army. He escaped after the war and made his way to Italy. In Rome, he lived the life of a derelict. One thing he swore to himself: "If I ever find the truth, I'll follow it!" That was enough! God's grace took hold of that speck of hope and integrity. One night as he slept in a railroad station, covered by newspapers, a wadded up page of New Testament Scripture fell nearby. On awakening, he read it and became interested. Soon he found a tract with the address of a mission to which he made his way and heard the gospel. A young Russian refugee who had been converted in the mission a month earlier witnessed to him. Soon afterwards, he was saved. Later he came to Argentina, was called of God to the ministry, was graduated from the seminary, and then became the first Baptist missionary in Patagonia. Argentine Baptists support him. He followed the truth with all his heart!...

Maria Gonzalez was reared in Paraguay, where there is so much poverty and suffering that radical political ideas find fertile soil. Her body felt the pangs of hunger and her soul the sting of seeming insignificance in her loneliness and yearning for community in fellowship. Perhaps it was only natural that she should respond to the appeal of the radical political party with its communistic emphases and eventually become a daring leader of its young people. On one occasion she rode at the head of the masses through the streets of Asuncion, holding the party banner high. Later she was pursued and was forced to swim a river under fire as she escaped from the country. Then she came to know Christ. She began to live for the first time. Her soul was at peace, and her life produced the fruits of it. The tremendous energies formerly directed toward revolution were now to be used in the service of her Lord. She has completed three years in our seminary where her interest in personal work, especially with questing, reckless young people, has been notable. Because she is righteous through faith, she has begun to live fully now.

It has come to be a commonplace observation that second-generation Christians have a better standard of living, more culture, and a keener sense of moral values than their fathers. However, it is anything but commonplace when dramatically accented in the life of an individual. Some years ago I had the opportunity to spend a week in a small interior town of Chile. While preaching and teaching in the small Baptist church there, composed of only twelve families, I lived in the home of a deacon as his guest. He housed his family in several rooms to the rear of his little corner grocery store. The floors were of brick. The roof was of thatch. It was the dead of winter. At night after church, we sat around a small charcoal fire in the center of the room, sipping a native tea and talking, or singing hymns and praying. The deacon was converted too late in life for his faith to affect his outward living conditions very much. He still worked in a flourmill, and his wife ran the grocery store. But what a difference his life made in his home! His children were growing up secure in a love such as only Christian parents can give. Later, some of them moved to the capital city, which is so characteristic of second-generation Christians, to find larger opportunities in life. They were not lost in the vices of a large city, but soon found their place in a Baptist church and honored their parents and their Lord with their way of life.

One afternoon while in that town, I visited and had tea in the thatch-roofed, dirt-floored, adobe home of another deacon. He was the father of three boys, all of whom were graduates of the national university and Christian professional men—one a lawyer, one a doctor, and one an outstanding leader as an evangelical theologian and denominational statesman. Their father's "righteousness through faith" had not only brought him to life, but had been used of God to give a better life to his sons. What a response in a church of twelve families to the power of God in the gospel!

A few years ago I was returning home about eleven at night on an electric train, after having taught a class of young people in a church across the city. I was amazed to hear the testimony of the young man at my side. He was one of the more zealous members of the class studying biblical theology with me. His mother had been abandoned as a young orphan. Years ago evangelical missionaries had taken her into their home to rear. There she learned of the love of God in Christ. She in turn reared her family in a Christian home. This son had come from the provinces to Buenos Aires, worked his way through the university, and is now a practicing architect. But he works at his profession only to make a living, in order that he may have more free time to live and work for his Lord! He is a lay preacher. What radiance and joy his life manifests!

None of these fruits of missions would be enough, even though they are important and impressive, were it not for the Christian's hope, Paul's and ours, that "he who is righteous through faith shall live" eternally. We have come into a fellowship with God, by grace through faith in his redeeming activity in Christ, which we believe shall be unbroken. We have seen God's power bring a new quality of life into being—life such as can reach its end only through eternal fellowship with God and the redeemed of all ages. We believe that because he lives, we shall live also, together with all those who are responding in faith as missionary advance moves on.

In July of 1963 Hugo met with the Study Group on Missions and Missionary Education, which was charged with preparing a report and recommendation for the Education and Promotion Coordination Committee of the Inter-Agency Council of the Southern Baptist Convention. At this meeting, Hugo first articulated the definitions of "mission" and "missions" that would guide his thinking for the rest of his life. As he said at a conference some years later,

I first had my introduction to this area when, back in 1963, I was invited to attend a conference in Fort Worth sponsored by the Coordinating Committee of the Inter-Agency Council [of the SBC], at which time the denominational agencies were trying to come to terms with each other in their understanding of three words: the word "mission," the word "missions," and the word "missionary education." They had no real problem with "missionary education," but they had great difficulty with the other two words. Apparently, they had been having considerable discussion and decided to take off a couple of days and get together at Southwestern Seminary. They invited four or five professors of missions from different institutions in our convention at that time, and we went into it rather as babes in the woods, I think, as reflected by our participation there, not really knowing the dynamics and inter-workings of the confronting of issues by the differing agencies of our denomination. That was my initiation into the situation.

After the initial afternoon session, when there was wide divergence of opinion, the same as there had been before they had come—and really the reason for the conference—I remember Jim Sapp, who was at the Brotherhood Commission at that time, was presiding.... He had the inspiration on the spot about 4:30 in the afternoon to dismiss the committee that had brought in the initial recommendations as to definitions of "mission" and "missions" and to appoint an ad hoc committee on the spur of the moment, composed only of seminary personnel. And so he selected three of us and asked us to get together between 4:30 and, around the dinner table, and be back at 7:30 with proposed definitions.

During the course of that three hours of discussion that there came into focus quite spontaneously and extemporaneously in my own mind the definitions which I proposed to the sub-group of three of us talking, and which they went along with, and which we carried back to the group.... As I recall, it was something like nine years before the matter was resolved in the context of the inter-agency relations—I believe along in the fall of 1972.... I got word of the approval of a document that incorporated these definitions.[136]

---

[136] Hugo Culpepper, "The Dialectic of Confrontation," tape recording of CTE Conference on "The Mission of Your Church" at Southern Seminary, 17–20 October 1977.

Later in the meeting, Hugo presented a paper titled "Why Missions?" in which he summarized the biblical basis for missions.

When Alan entered Baylor in the fall of 1963, Hugo sought to pass along his own study habits:

Don't be afraid of the German. Put in all the extra time you can spare this semester by reviewing the grammar in general, and when you have to run down a form learn that complete declension or conjugation thoroughly so you will not have to continue referring to it. The effect will be cumulative. Likewise, the vocabulary. It is just a matter of time, effort, and drill on a language like this, and especially consistent daily effort.[137]

When Alan reported how demanding his schedule at Baylor was, Hugo responded with sage counsel and a revealing summary of his week's activities:

You will be increasingly busy, if that is possible, the rest of your life till you retire! But then your capacity to carry an increasingly heavier load will also continue to increase—as it has by now in comparison with your high school days. For example, I thought I was busy in Argentina, but that was nothing compared to my load now. However, I manage to carry it and turn the necessary work off now at a good clip, it seems.... I worked hard all day long in my study at home Saturday preparing lectures for both classes this next week in Cultural Anthropology. I have done this all day today for Ecumenics. These are two new courses, and I have to dig in on the weekends to be ready since I have prepared no material on these subjects before.... Yesterday I left home at 7:00 A.M. and drove 140 miles in three hours to preach at Lawrenceville, Illinois, at 10:30 at the First Baptist Church. It was a small church with about 100 in Sunday School. I spoke twice last night and drove home getting here at 11:30 P.M. I am not as tired as I expected to be. Last week I got in three barbell workouts for the first time in one week since last spring, and that has made me feel good.

We are having Dr. Cecil Thompson out for supper tonight. You remember [that] he and his wife moved into the house we left in Buenos Aires. He is on furlough now and is here this week interviewing prospective appointees. We will enjoy the evening of relaxation and visiting for a welcome change. All my work is up to date, and I can forget it a few hours.

---

[137] Hugo Culpepper, letter to Alan Culpepper, 15 September 1963.

In the morning I am speaking out at Broadway [Baptist] Church for 30 minutes just before lunch, besides my three lectures for the day at the seminary.[138]

In October Hugo flew to Atlanta and gave four lectures on "The Biblical Basis of Missions" to the fall group of appointees at the Home Mission Board.

When Alan found it difficult to manage the demands of college courses and a part-time job during his first year at Baylor, his father's counsel was predictable:

The income from your work is not necessary for you to stay in school. It will enable you to have more for spending, since there is naturally a limit to what we can provide. It may even make it somewhat less of a strain on us. However, this angle is not a major consideration. The major factor is the constructive use of your time in living and growing in all respects to take full advantage of your opportunities now. Above all, try to live a balanced fourfold life: spiritual, intellectual, physical, and social. Spend some time relaxing with friends and cultivating a disposition of getting out of the inside of yourself and being with others.[139]

Alan kept the job a while longer. A letter a few days later sketches Hugo's recent and coming activities:

Last Friday I drove to Indianapolis, taking along Dr. Thurman Bryant (Visiting Professor from Brazil) with me in the Rambler, and then we went on to Chicago with Dr. Joe Smith to the Missions professors' meeting. Bishop Stephen C. Neill was a most stimulating personality. It was a spiritual and intellectual feast to hear him two times....

I am leaving at 6:30 tonight on the plane for Richmond, Virginia, to attend the meeting of the Missionary Educational Council to help plan the Missions Study Series for the next several years. This year I am chairman of the Adult Foreign Missions Committee, which plans the book for adults on foreign missions. I should get back midnight Friday....

Sunday afternoon I accepted an invitation to preach in a revival effort the week of November 17–24 up near Cleveland, Ohio, on the lake there. It will be

---

[138] Hugo Culpepper, letter to Alan Culpepper, 30 September 1963.
[139] Hugo Culpepper, letter to Alan Culpepper, 23 October 1963.

a treat for me to get away and engage in visitation, preaching, and personal work for the week, and I am looking forward to it a great deal.[140]

As suggested reading for Alan he enclosed copies of Emil Brunner's *Our Faith* and William Temple's *Readings in St. John's Gospel.* The next week Ruth reported that she had stayed home on Friday to clean house: "We are having all the students who are mission volunteers to come out tonight and just talk to some of the furloughing missionaries. It is their idea, though we do not know how many to count on. Daddy brought home 28 chairs for us to have in the basement."[141]

Hugo's week in Ohio was taxing, as Ruth reported: "Daddy is having it rough in Cleveland this week. It is really a mission situation. He stays a different place each night, and eats at a different place each meal. It is in the pioneer mission area, and the people are working people without much of a church. He stayed Tuesday night in a trailer. The men take off one day to take Daddy visiting. Because they take off they lose that day's pay, so it is a real sacrifice for them. I do pray they will have a good meeting and reach many in that area."[142]

The remaining weeks until the Christmas holidays were filled with speaking for the Lottie Moon Christmas offering and end of the semester activities, as always. At the end of the year, Hugo accepted an invitation from Robert Bratcher to serve on the review committee for a new Bible translation, "Good News for Modern Man."

Dr. Arthur Rutledge, who would soon become the new head of the Baptist Home Mission Board, was a visiting professor in missions at Southern in the spring of 1964, and a close friendship and mutual respect developed that spring between Hugo and Arthur. That spring Hugo taught ten hours a week: Introduction to Christian Missions (4 hours), Principles and Practice of Missions (4 hours), and Religions of the Orient (2 hours). In addition, he wrote a 140-page study guide for a seminary extension course, "Survey of the History of Missions," and maintained a full schedule of travel and speaking. As he was finishing that assignment, he received another, to write a background study paper for the Home Mission Board to be used by the staff in planning their program for approval by the Southern Baptist Convention. This paper involved Hugo in the planning of

---

[140] Hugo Culpepper, letter to Alan Culpepper, 29 October 1963.
[141] Ruth Culpepper, letter to Alan Culpepper, undated, November 1963.
[142] Ruth Culpepper, letter to Alan Culpepper, 20 November 1963.

programs for the Men's Brotherhood, the WMU, Home Missions, the Sunday School Board, and the seminaries.

Still, he was in the best physical condition he had been in in years. He also took a ham radio course that spring. Larry passed the exam for a second-class commercial license, and Hugo wanted to build up his speed with Morse Code so that he could get a license also. Hugo bought a reconditioned short wave transmitter for them to use, and he and Larry set about building an antenna for it.

Late in the afternoon we had to stop and make a trip to town and get some wire and things. It runs from the TV antenna pole strapped to the chimney to the big tree at the end of the house. There is one insulator in the center. Then there are four separate wires running to the same center insulator. At the two ends the wires are tied on one above the other about two feet apart. There is a door spring on the end of each antenna, so when the tree sways with the wind the spring gives and the antenna does not break. There is one common lead in. This is called a dipole type antenna. They are different lengths and are for the 40, 20, 15, and 10-meter bands. Whatever frequency the transmitter is on, the outgoing current will seek the right antenna and radiate from that one. Then from the center insulator there is also a 60-foot wire running across the backyard to the other tree, and also a 60-foot wire from the antenna across the carport driveway to the white wooden post in the corner of the front yard where the names of the streets hang. This is for the 80 meter band.... The new rig is working swell and Larry has already talked with New York, and North Carolina. He also talked with Denver, Colorado, and yesterday afternoon with someone at Guantanamo Bay in Cuba! It took us until 11:30 Saturday night to get this system of antenna put up. After laying it all out in the backyard and doing the soldering at the connections, we had to roll each wire up and take it up on the roof and then unroll them one at a time to make the tie-ups so as not to get the wires all tangled. We ran an extension with two light globes up the side of the chimney, plugged in in the carport, and then I stood on top of the chimney at 11:30 P.M. and made the tie-ups. Larry was up in the top of the tree with the lantern up there with him. I guess it was not surprising that cars slowed up as they passed to see what was going on![143]

The next summer (1964), Hugo and Larry decided they needed a more powerful antenna, so Hugo ordered a telephone pole from the telephone company and had it put in the ground in their side yard. Together, Hugo

---

[143] Hugo Culpepper, letter to Alan Culpepper, 12 March 1964.

and the boys built an antenna for the radio that looked like the frame of a box kite, with long bamboo poles for the crosspieces and copper wire strung around them. The whole apparatus was mounted on metal pipes. A rotor motor allowed them to change the direction of the antenna. All the kids in the neighborhood gathered when they bolted it to the top of the telephone pole. Alan handled the antenna at the top of the pole, Larry handled the cables, and Hugo drove the station wagon. With a pulley mounted at the top of the pole, they used the car to pull the antenna to the top of the pole and hold it there until it could be bolted into place.

In April Hugo went to Duke University for a stimulating conference on "Christianity and Social Revolution in the Newly Developing Nations" with 120 other invited participants. The following week he was elected editor of the *Review & Expositor* for a five-year term (1965–1970—a position that events unforeseen at the time would keep him from filling). In the midst of the other demands on his time, Hugo maintained a heavy writing schedule during this period, as one can see from this letter:

Well, at last I feel liberated again. For the last two months I have been working constantly until 11:00 P.M. on these writing projects I have done. I had gotten in 150 pages to the Seminary Extension Department. Then I had to start immediately on the WMU "Study Program of Christian Missions." The headquarters in Birmingham asked me to write this to provide them with a guide in Biblical, theological, and historical background for replanning their whole program for the future in preparing materials for all the churches in the Convention. I mailed the last of a total of 90 pages on this at 5:00 P.M. yesterday. It went first class special delivery and got there in time this morning for the deadline. Now I'm going to take a break for a few days before starting on other projects in writing. I hope to get started and not be under pressure on them. I have two magazine articles, which are not too difficult. But then I have a major background study due in August for the Home Mission Board and this will take considerable time. All of this explains what I have been doing. Since I could not get this WMU paper typed fast enough at the seminary, Ruth has done the typing on it. Since it was WMU work she could do it at her office on work time. She has also worked some at nights on it. We are both relieved now.[144]

---

[144] Hugo Culpepper, letter to families in Little Rock and to Alan Culpepper, 30 April 1964.

The study paper for the Home Mission Board created an opportunity that would involve him at the center of mission efforts across the United States for the next five years. A letter from Arthur B. Rutledge contains the following words of appreciation: "You did a masterful piece of work at Ridgecrest. I heard you all but one morning and was blessed personally. Many, many commented to me about their appreciation for your warmth as well as your scholarship. I regret that my responsibilities were such that I had no time for a full visit with you."[145]

The Decision to Move to Atlanta

In a Missionary Day address at Southern Seminary in 1968, Hugo recalled the events that led to his decision to accept a position at the Home Mission Board:

I must be very candid to recognize that as recently as four years ago I personally would not have dreamed that I would ever have seen the things that I have seen and felt in the course of these last three or four years. It may be of some interest to you to know that during the five and half years that I was here teaching I personally did not...offer a course in home missions. I say this to my rebuke from where I stand now, but I recognize that it was partly because I did not know enough about it in the first place to dare to attempt to teach a course in it, and I must say quite candidly that in the second place I did not have enough respect for the work of the Home Mission Board at that time to be too much interested in teaching a course at that time in home missions.

And so there was no one more surprised than I was on that particular September day three years ago last September when the phone rang at home one day. It was the day after we had returned from the faculty retreat at Frankfort, and Dr. McCall and I had played golf together the afternoon before, when the phone rang and Dr. Rutledge's voice was on the other end asking if he could see me and talk with me about coming to the Home Mission Board. My first reaction was, "Well, Arthur, you have made a mistake. I can't quite understand your confusion at the present moment, but you're not talking to the person you think you're talking to or intend to be talking to. There is something badly wrong here, and so maybe the best thing to do is just to say that there is really no point in our getting together." And yet a corrective sense

---

[145] Arthur Rutledge, letter to Hugo Culpepper, 28 August 1964.

came in my mind, and I thought, "I cannot react this way lest the Lord might conceivably be in it beyond my remotest imagination," and so the conversations began.[146]

On 11 September 1964, Dr. Arthur B. Rutledge, who had served for six years as director of the Missions Division of the Home Mission Board, and who had been tapped to succeed Dr. Courts Redford as executive secretary of the Home Mission Board on 1 January 1965, flew to Louisville to invite Hugo to succeed him as director of the Missions Division and to help him in giving direction to the work of the Home Mission Board's 2,369 missionaries. Hugo related their conversation in a letter to Alan, who was beginning his sophomore year at Baylor.

Dear Alan,

Dr Rutledge had arrived about 1:30 and rested and worked some and was waiting for me. We talked constantly until I took him to the airport about 8:15 P.M. to catch his plane returning to Atlanta. At 6:00 P.M. we went into the dining room and had a good dinner continuing our talk all the while. This gave us time to cover most all the ground we were interested in talking about.

He described the work of the Director of the Missions Division in detail. In his judgment it is the most strategic position on the staff of the Home Mission Board. There are 6 Departments in it now and he plans to organize and place a seventh one in it. There will be 22 in the division as Department Secretaries and their Associates, beside about 12 secretaries. Once a year I would have to travel to all 28 states in which there are working agreements now and have a conference with the State Executive Secretary and the Missions Secretary and their associates (Dr. Sanders and Mr. A. B. Colvin in Kentucky, for example) the Department Head in my Division would also go. I would preside over the meeting. It would be a conference on mission work in that particular state and the Home Mission Board's part in helping with it, etc. In Atlanta, I would have conferences with the Department Heads. These would be the two main kinds of conferences, and they would take about 25 percent of the time, outside of Atlanta and 30 percent in Atlanta, so that 55 percent of my time would be spent in conferences in administrative capacity. Then I would spend 25 percent in the study and planning of programs of work, and the final 20 percent in correspondence and office details. I'll type you a copy of the job description he gave me.

---

[146] Hugo Culpepper, tape recording of Missionary Day address in Southern Seminary chapel, 9 March 1968.

He said that I would be the only name he will submit to the Personnel Committee, if I agree to permit him to do it. We are discussing it and praying about it and I'll try to reach a decision by the middle of this coming week. The Personnel Committee meets on September 24. If they agree to consider appointing me, they will set a date for a meeting in Atlanta to interview me in person and I would have to fly to Atlanta. This would be not later than October 8 or 9. Then very soon after that the committee would make their decision as to whom to nominate to the full Home Mission Board, Dec. 1 and 2 in their annual meeting. Other members of the committee may suggest someone else, and they may interview more than one person. However, I would be the only one with the support of the new Executive, and this would carry a lot of weight. If the committee decides to nominate me to the full Board, that is practically equal to a certain appointment. He said there would not be over one chance in a thousand that the Board would do other than approve the Personnel Committee's nomination. After the Committee decided to nominate me, the decision being made by about October 10 or 12, then Dr. Rutledge would call Dr. McCall and tell him that he wants to approach me about a position on the HMB. This would be the first official contact. Until then we must keep it confidential. There are 6 people on the committee. I know only one of them personally!

It would never have occurred to me to be interested in the place or to seek it; however now that the approach is being made, we know of no real reason not to be open to consider and even to accept it, if officially offered the place, except personal selfish reasons. There are a number of things that have happened in bringing this about and leading up to it that seem to be Providential. We do not feel that we can refuse to be open to it simply because we would be personally more comfortable to stay on here in Louisville, where we have friends and many things that are congenial. Such might be refusing to follow the Lord's leadership. The feeling has been gradually developing that I must be available to them, if they want me for the place. However, if the Lord wants me to stay here, I hope he will lead the way for someone else to be suggested in the committee and for the nomination to go to that one. Then it would be a big relief to us to have been open to it but to have been permitted to stay on here. From this viewpoint, my letter will probably give him my approval for presenting my name to the committee. However, this will not be definitely accepting the place because as I told him, one cannot really say "Yes" or "No" until he is officially offered it. At the same time if I let him present my name, this will have some moral obligation to accept the place if it is offered, but not absolutely so if a strong feeling developed otherwise by then.

I shall no doubt attend the Annual Board meeting in Atlanta December I and 2 anyway as the seminary representative. Then if I take this position, he wants me to attend a conference in Atlanta January 5-8 for annual staff planning and then assume the new position February 1 at the end of the first semester here. Mother and Larry would stay on here in the house till Larry graduates and then we would move to Atlanta. I would do lots of travel in the spring getting acquainted with the work and would stay in a small hotel while there in Atlanta. This is all I know on the matter now. What do you think? I was awake until after 4:00 A.M. this morning thinking about it!

The Ex. Sec. is Grade 12, the top position; the Assistant Ex. Sec. is grade 11. As a Division head I would be grade 10 and beginning salary would be about $11,000 a year. The annual increase is $420 per year up to a maximum of $14,340. Because of Mother's work, at the beginning [and] for several years this would be a pay decrease for us. Also, I would not have the $1,000 per year college money, and would have to repay the $1,500 we have borrowed for you thus far. Mother would probably try to get a teaching job as soon as she could qualify so as to make about $300 per month at least for college expenses for you and Larry for the next couple of years, etc. If the Lord is in it, we believe He will somehow help us to work all of these details out. We will manage some way. Of course, when we sell this house, we can put only part of the money in on another one as a down payment and use the rest to pay off the car loan money and the college loans, etc....

This gives you some idea of what it would be like. Dr. Rutledge said that he supposed the main factor in directing attention to me was the Resource Paper I wrote (about 45 pages) recently at their request. He said it was the most helpful of the nine papers they had gotten written to help them with their program-planning. So goes it.

We shall be looking forward to hearing from you real soon.

With our love[147]

In a follow-up letter to their meeting in Louisville, Arthur Rutledge wrote: "Since returning to Atlanta, and being in the office two days, the conviction had deepened with me, Hugo, that you are eminently prepared by experience and training to bring to our home mission task a freshness and a philosophy which can add much to the strength and vigor of our outreach in the years immediately ahead."[148]

The following day, before their telephone conversation, Hugo wrote:

---

[147] Hugo Culpepper, letter to Alan Culpepper, 12 September 1964.

[148] Arthur Rutledge, letter to Hugo Culpepper, 15 September 1964.

I have been giving serious, even wakeful, consideration as to where under the Lord I might be able to be most helpful during the remaining years of my life. Monday I was in Owensboro all day (having preached Sunday and waiting to address the Brotherhood Monday night) and spent the time literally "holed up" in my room considering the matter. Some time was spent on my knees seeking the Lord's guidance as best I could. I believe that I have come to the point that my major concern is to be where I might be most helpful—where God could best use me. However, I have not come to a clear "breakthrough." Last night Ruth and I talked until midnight. I awoke again at 3:00 A.M. and spent a two-hour night-watch considering all the factors.[149]

A letter from Ruth the next day reports that Hugo was still struggling with the decision:

Yesterday afternoon he called Dr. Rutledge and talked with him twenty-five minutes on the telephone about various points that were not clear.... Everything was fine in the conversation, and last night Daddy was leaning strongly [toward] letting him put his name before the committee—which meets next Thursday. However, this morning he says that he feels that he just has no clear leading to leave Louisville. One of the strange things is that while he has come into a great appreciation of what the job is, and feels that with God's help he can meet the demands of it, there is still a great lack of any enthusiasm for the job. So as yet he has not really made up his mind.[150]

On 18 September, Hugo drafted a letter asking Dr. Rutledge to withdraw his name from consideration. As he later recounted the events:

I could not contemplate anything within my makeup which would be conducive to the demands and type of work which this would lead into. And there came a point in my struggle at which I sat down in my office over here and wrote a letter expressing appreciation and declining this invitation, recognizing that my place was here, and I should continue on in that which seemed to be most congenial to my temperament and to my nature. I had that letter of declining in my pocket and got up from my desk and started to walk to the post office to drop that letter in the box, and then the thought occurred to me, "but

---

[149] Hugo Culpepper, letter to Arthur Rutledge, 16 September 1964.
[150] Ruth Culpepper, letter to R. Alan Culpepper, 17 September 1964.

you have not talked to anybody outside of your own family about this question. You have gotten no objective appraisal of the possibilities and demands of this work. Perhaps you would do well to do this." And so, on my way to the post office to mail that letter I stopped by Dr. McCall's office, and he happened to be in at that moment, thirty minutes before chapel time.

As was characteristic, I received a warm welcome and in the course of that thirty minutes shared with him that which was upon my heart. He did not know that at that moment there was in my pocket a letter declining. I asked him to be quite objective with me as a friend and to seek to analyze the situation that I was confronting, and to give me his judgment and the value of his insight since he had had experience in denominational life in former responsibilities. He recognized something of the difficulty of this, but very honestly and candidly gave me an appraisal which was positive in terms of its recognition of the need for a revitalized ministry of the Home Mission Board in the life of our denomination, and in terms of the horizons of possibilities for the future in the life of this agency. And then he was kind enough to go on in the second place to seek to encourage me to staying here even in the face of these other factors because this was where being who I was that I perhaps more rightly belonged. This caused me to continue to reconsider, and I did not go and mail the letter.

After further prayerful consideration came to the conclusion that I must respond affirmatively to this invitation because in the first place I would have to live with myself in future years if I did not do it and would always have the question in my own mind as to whether I had been willing and dared to face up to the nature of the demand and of the responsibilities that would be involved and the second question as to whether I had deliberately chosen that way which was most congenial to my own nature—the life of the academic community and the thrill of the classroom dialogue with students and the opportunity for reading and study and personal growth. It was upon those bases that I answered affirmatively.[151]

The following day Hugo mailed Dr. Rutledge a letter in which the crucial paragraph read:

I feel quite clearly now that I ought to make myself available— available to explore the matter thoroughly with the Committee, and with you more thoroughly. I cannot withdraw from the situation in which your approach placed me,

---

[151] Hugo Culpepper, tape recording of Missionary Day address in the Southern Seminary chapel, 9 March 1968.

by deciding alone that I am not available. If the Committee, as men of God seeking His will, feel that I am the man for the job, this would be very meaningful; if they come to feel otherwise, I would have the sense of having been released for continuing here, but for continuing here not just because I was indulging myself in the more comfortable and convenient choice.[152]

The die was cast. Hugo's letter to Alan the following day summarizes the struggle and his thought processes:

I mailed a letter yesterday morning to Dr. Rutledge permitting him to present my name as his recommendation to the Personnel Committee of the HMB for their consideration as Director of the Missions Division. It has been an agonizing struggle. If it were merely a matter of our personal taste and preferences, we would not consider it. However, unless one is open to such responsibility, it is difficult to teach others that they should live up to discipleship even to the point of sacrifice. The matter is still open on both sides for further consideration even if the Committee desires to interview me in Atlanta. They meet next Thursday the 24th of September, and if they are interested in naming me to the position they would want to interview me, probably about October 8.

While it is still open, the fact that I am permitting my name to be presented involves me in a certain, moral obligation to Dr. Rutledge to be more seriously open to acceptance to the call if it should be extended. I talked with Dr. McCall yesterday morning. Indirectly he was an influence leading me to permit my name to be considered. While he was very kind in expressions of appreciation of my work here and of them being pleased with it, he also was objective enough to say that next to Dr. Rutledge's position as Ex. Sec., the position of Director of the Divisions of Missions is probably the most strategic place in the Southern Baptist Convention leadership ranks today because he believes that Southern Baptists are going into all the USA on a big scale and that this should be gotten under way in force now. It is the challenge of the opportunity, the sense of obligation not to shirk responsibility if the Lord is leading me to it as His choice, and the belief that theological study should have a practical application–all of this leads me to be open for further exploration of the matter.

On the other hand, every personal consideration would keep me here. I am tried and proven in the work of teaching; my experience is here; it is congenial to me; I have more leisure and a more relaxed schedule here; with

---

[152] Hugo Culpepper, letter to Arthur Rutledge, 19 September 1964.

Mother's work, our income is higher than my income alone would be in Atlanta (although my income will be greater than I would ever receive here); we would be with you and Larry more if you come here to the seminary and Larry should study medicine here—and on and on, not least of which is that we are comfortably situated in a community of friends. But none of these considerations can be overriding and decisive factors, unless one is to feel that he has chosen the way of self-indulgence and security—then he would lose the thrust and heart out of his message. In our world, as General MacArthur said, "There is no security; there is only opportunity!"[153]

In a handwritten note the following day, Dr. Rutledge expressed his pleasure with Hugo's decision to proceed with their conversation: "I am pleased that you are willing for me to present your name to our committee Thursday night, in the spirit of continuing to seek divine guidance. I share your feelings that God works at 'both ends of the line.' I am very grateful, Hugo, for the earnest and prayerful way in which you have moved to this decision."[154]

Plans were made for Hugo to fly to Atlanta to meet with Dr. Rutledge and the committee. Hugo and Ruth were still undecided about the matter, but word began to get around:

Those that know of the decision are doing everything they can to persuade us to stay here. Actually this is not a decision at all but just what we feel the Lord wants us to do. I am still very much in the dark as to what that is. Somehow it is getting around. Dr. Francisco stuck his head in Daddy's office this morning and asked if he was still around. A student was there but left, and so Dr. Francisco came on in. Daddy said tears actually came to his eyes as he tried to show Daddy he was indispensable here and that the mission spirit was just beginning to come out and what a blow it would be if Daddy left. Everybody has been so kind that it just makes it harder.[155]

Following the interview in Atlanta, the Personnel Committee voted unanimously to recommend Hugo to the board on 1 December, if he agreed to allow them to do so.

---

[153] Hugo Culpepper, letter to Alan Culpepper, 20 September 1964.
[154] Arthur Rutledge, letter to Hugo Culpepper, 21 September 1964.
[155] Ruth Culpepper, letter to Alan Culpepper, 9 October 1964.

Dear Alan,

I had a good trip to Atlanta and a very helpful and constructive conference with the Personnel Committee of the Home Mission Board. They voted unanimously in my presence to recommend me to the Board on Dec. 1, if I come to indicate that I am available. I am increasingly coming to feel that this is something that has sought me out and laid hold on me, and therefore will probably accept it. I have told them that I want to wait until I get back from the trip to Waco to give them a definite answer, and they agreed. This is to give my increasing inclination toward going a chance to "jell" and feel sure about it.

I became convinced that they feel deeply that I am the man for the job. If I should refuse it, I am afraid I would always feel that I was unwilling to accept heavier responsibilities or that I was indulging myself to staying by a more leisurely and pleasant way of life. It would not be easy to live with that feeling or continue to be effective in my teaching. It just seems to be one of those times when the Lord has opened a door to heavier responsibilities and broader fields of service. It is with some sense of fear and trepidation that I look toward entering it, and yet I have a quiet sense of confidence that I shall have His presence and be able to get on top of the job.

It will be a bigger job than I had realized. The budget this next year will be 2/3 of a million dollar increase just for this one Division over what it has been this year. This will bring it to 4 and 2/3 millions dollars, and I shall have to direct the spending of it in 10 out of the total of 14 Programs the Board now has. Three-fourths of the Operating Budget of the Board is spent in this one Division. There are 5 departments and a staff of 20 (besides the office secretaries etc.) that are in the Division under my direction. We shall fill one whole floor of the office building and possibly run over onto another floor.... All of this is secondary and incidental to the deciding factor that it will be an opportunity to be more helpful on a larger scale to the Lord's work than my present position affords; the two kinds of work are so different as almost to defy comparing, however.

I would need to go on Feb. 1. We would wait at least till Larry graduates to move to Atlanta. They told me to put the room cost of staying in Atlanta [at the Americana Motor Hotel, across the street from the HMB building] on my unlimited expense account, since I should not have double cost of housing.

What do you think of it all? It seems to me that it is a most crucial decision. On the one hand it is the chance of a lifetime in regard to larger fields of service; I probably would never again have such a wide open door. It is in effect being Area Secretary for the U.S.A. the same as the Foreign Board secretaries are for Latin America, Africa, the Orient, etc. If I stay here, I shall probably stay on here the rest of my life....

Well I started to write a note only but it has grown into a letter! I must run on to the seminary. The great Methodist missionary to India, E. Stanley Jones (now retired), is speaking in chapel this morning.

Love[156]

While en route to Tokyo on, Duke McCall wrote the following note:

Dear Hugo—

Just a note scribbled against the back of my passport case on a bucking plane.

This trip is confirming my feeling that a major re-thinking of foreign missions is now needed. That means SBTS must keep you for you are the one man I know in a position to do the job. The point is not SBTS but the mission enterprise.

If I were at the HMB, I would want you there. But you cannot have the full mission enterprise in focus under your leadership if you belong to any one part of it, no matter how important.

What about adding John Claypool for Brooks Chair? This would require three of you in Missions Department. The more I think about the seminary program, the more convinced I am that SBTS must reassert its leadership in missions at home and abroad—for the sake of our Baptist witness. Let us get aggressively about this.

I continue to pray not only for you but also for Rutledge and HMB. It is God's plan we seek.

Cordially,
Duke[157]

On the way back from the Baylor Homecoming, on 26 October, Hugo called Dr. Rutledge from Little Rock to tell him that he would be available if the Home Mission Board wanted him. Within an hour, Dr. Rutledge dictated his response: "It is with a deep sense of joy and satisfaction that I have your response to our invitation. I have had the consciousness of divine leadership throughout this period, and am now gratified to see the way open." The same day, Dr. Rutledge wrote to Dr. McCall, reporting Hugo's decision that he was available to serve as the director of the Missions Division if elected by the board on 1 December and asking that

---

[156] Hugo Culpepper, letter to Alan Culpepper, 14 October 1964.
[157] Duke McCall, letter to Hugo Culpepper, 19 October 1964.

Hugo be released to assume his new role as early in 1965 as possible. Dr. McCall responded:

> We, of course, cannot look with any calm upon the prospect of losing Hugo Culpepper from the Seminary faculty, but we are content to leave this matter to the direction of the Holy Spirit. Should present plans follow through as anticipated, it is my understanding that you would want him to take up his responsibilities with you January 1, 1965, or February 1, 1965. Just for the record I should note an old Seminary regulation requiring four months notice of faculty resignations. But in the light of your situation this, of course, is of secondary concern.[158]

It was agreed that Hugo would take up his new responsibilities 1 January 1965, but would spend a few days back in Louisville for conferences at the seminary and to give the final exams for his fall semester courses. In December the board voted unanimously to elect Hugo as director of the Missions Division. In that capacity he would coordinate the work of the departments of language missions, metropolitan missions, urban-rural missions, pioneer missions, work with National Baptists, and special mission ministries. These departments supervised the work of most of the board's 2,369 missionaries.[159]

On 3 December, Hugo sent Dr. McCall his letter of resignation, effective at the end of the year, 31 December 1964. He said, "I am sure that I shall always look back on these years as bright lights in my life pilgrimage."

A flood of letters from colleagues at the seminary, friends in other places, and former students followed, expressing loss for the seminary, hope for the Home Mission Board, and support for Hugo in the new challenges he would face.

---

[158] Duke McCall, letter to Arthur Rutledge, 11 November 1964.

[159] "Moseley, Culpepper Join Mission Board," Baptist Press release, 1 December 1964.

Chapter 9

Home Mission Board
1965–1970

"Perhaps the greatest problem in mission strategy is how to use money effectively to help achieve spiritual ends."[1]

On Sunday, 3 January 1965, Ruth and Hugo drove from Louisville to Atlanta for Hugo to begin his work at the Home Mission Board and for Ruth to begin to get acquainted with Atlanta, look for a job, and begin making plans for the move. Ruth was impressed with how different Atlanta was from Louisville: the traffic, the heavily wooded yards, and the hills. Among other impressions, she wrote, "We went across the street to a Chinese restaurant for a Chinese supper, which was quite good. You could certainly tell you had gone back south because the waitress was telling us all about her grandmother who uses one tea bag a day, and how they gave her a tea bag holder for Christmas, etc., etc., and you can just imagine something like that happening here in Louisville.... Atlanta is a Baptist town, and I mean nearly everybody we met was Baptist or Methodist."[2] She also had strong feelings about the Home Mission Board and Georgia Baptist buildings:

> Daddy's office is not nice, though it is larger than the one at the seminary. In fact, the whole building is a disgrace to Southern Baptists. They know it, and can you guess what they have under study now— moving the Home Mission Board within the next five years to St.

---

[1] Forms of this observation appear in Hugo Culpepper, "New Patterns and Trends in Contemporary World Missions," (Background paper for Missions Consultation, 30 June—3 July 1965) 2; and "Acts 4:12," *Review and Expositor*, 89 (1992): 86.

[2] Ruth Culpepper, letter to Alan Culpepper, 6 January 1965.

Louis, Chicago, or Denver. Nashville is out because they do not want to locate any more work there. Dallas was considered but dropped because of being in Texas, and they do not want the Texas influence that the Foreign Mission Board has acquired. Oklahoma City and Kansas City were considered, but travel connections are poor. So they are narrowing it down to the three mentioned, and in that order.... [Note: Later, the decision was made to relocate the Home Mission Board from Spring Street to a new building adjacent to I-85 in Atlanta.] After the lunch, we went back to the Georgia Baptist Building (another disgrace to humanity) for me to see the WMU office and meet with the personnel committee.[3]

The WMU of Georgia invited Ruth to become the state GA director, but Ruth was reluctant initially because the job called for traveling at least half of the time, and she did not see how she could do that, support Hugo in his work, and be home during the summer when the boys would be home from college. Over the next few weeks, however, she decided to accept the position, beginning in September, for a trial period of twenty-one months.

On 27 January, Hugo and 1,500 others attended a dinner for Martin Luther King, Jr., which 100 leading Atlanta businesses sponsored to celebrate his being awarded the Nobel Peace Prize. After the gala event, Hugo walked down the block and crossed the street to a little café to have a cup of hot chocolate before returning to the hotel. The owner of the café, not knowing that Hugo had just come from the dinner, made disparaging and racist comments about King, saying, "I don't understand why they gave a peace prize to a man who is turning the world upside down." Hugo was struck by the cultural divide, commenting later that these were the "two worlds of our time, divided by a city street."[4]

From January through May Hugo traveled, getting back to Louisville whenever he could. Ruth and Larry stayed in Louisville for Larry to finish high school and to get the house ready to sell. The few weekends Hugo was alone in Atlanta were especially lonely, but the workload left him little idle time. During the evenings, Hugo worked on the Today's English Version of the New Testament, responding to the translation done by Robert G. Bratcher. On 4 February 1965, he sent the translator his notes on the

---

[3] Ibid.

[4] Karen Waggoner, "Baptist Missionary Sees No Conflict in Church Roles: Evangelistic Zeal and Christian Social Concern," *Eugene Register-Guard* (5 November 1966): 2A.

translation of the Gospel of John, the three Epistles of John, and the Epistle of Galatians: "I am seeking to make it a regular procedure of reading one or two chapters a day in the Greek New Testament (sight reading) and then turning to your translation and immediately reading that, noting my reactions on the manuscript." Hugo's notes on the Gospel of John reflect a perceptive concern for its theology and the preservation of the sense of terms such as "flesh," "glory" (as God's true nature), and "signs" (of a revealing nature).

Shortly after it was published in 1965, Hugo wrote a critical review of a collection of essays on the church growth movement in which he took issue with its basic premises:

In the literature of missiology, this is the latest expression of a school of thought that dates back to the books of Roland Allen. The emphasis is essentially negative as an attack is made on the "mission station" methods of an earlier era in foreign missions. One lays this book (as well as the earlier ones) aside with the feeling that something is wrong with the basic structure of this theology of mission. The perspective as to the nature of the Christian mission and the purpose of missions is too limited. The resulting view is a distortion. The reviewer was the only Baptist participant in the Consultation on Church Growth at Iberville, Quebec, in August, 1963. He took issue there with this view.

The ultimate purpose of the Christian mission is the *redemption* of men. Jesus was filled with compassion for the *whole* man. He preached and taught and healed that men might have life and have it more abundantly. Missions is the implementation of this mission to redeem men. It is not enough, in our kind of world, to be satisfied with organizing churches in areas which are responsive. With the exception of Nida, these authors seem to make it all too easy![5]

While Hugo was still getting oriented in his new position, the invitation came from the Foreign Mission Board to present one of six papers for the World Mission Conference that summer on the theme of "Whither Missions?" The invitations to speak continued to pour in also, leading Hugo to write in one of his letters, "The only problem I am having with my work is that I have far more opportunities for service than I can accept. I would like to do it all!" The following excerpt from Hugo's letter

---

[5] Hugo Culpepper, Review of *Church Growth and Christian Mission*, ed. Donald Anderson McGavran.

to the family, summarizing his travel plans, would be typical of the pace he would keep for the next five years:

Hugo at the Home Mission Board.

I was invited this week by Dr. Chester Quarles, Ex. Sec. of Mississippi, to be the morning speaker during the Bible Study week at Gulfshore the week in August which overlaps with HMB week at Ridgecrest.... I had to decline. This coming weekend, Alan, I spend Saturday night in Waco as well as Friday night. Then we are due at the Park Cities Baptist Church by 10:30 A.M. [In the course of his sermon, Hugo told the story of his experience following the banquet for Martin Luther King, Jr., and said, "These are the two worlds of our time, and we all have to choose in which one we will live." The man sitting in front of Alan told his wife he had heard all he could take and got up and walked out.] We shall have lunch with the Howards and Homer Reynolds. At night on Sunday and Monday I shall speak in Homer's church. Monday noon I am speaking for 20 minutes to the Dallas Association of Pastors board meeting at Cliff Temple Baptist Church. I leave about 7:10 A.M. Tuesday to fly back to Atlanta. Then, Thursday morning I fly to Nashville and will be in the Holiday Inn Motel there Thursday night. Thursday afternoon and Friday morning I will be at the Baptist headquarters building for a conference. Friday afternoon, February 19, I fly to Louisville, arriving at 4:15 P.M. Then I fly back to Nashville on Monday morning the 22nd. I shall be in Nashville all week till 9:15 P.M. Friday night. I am going...to take the L&N train out of Nashville just after 11:00 P.M. Friday night the 26th and get in Louisville at 4:40 A.M. Saturday morning. Then I leave there about 7:00 P.M. Sunday the 28th of February and fly to Denver, getting there by bedtime. On Monday March 1 in Denver and then on the 2nd in

Oklahoma City and then on to Tucson, Arizona, Tuesday arriving by 7:15 P.M.... Then to Alexandria, La., for March 29, to Dallas March 30, and then from Dallas on the 30th I fly to Miami and on to Puerto Rico for the rest of that week.[6]

Because all of the staff members had heavy travel schedules, they designated one week each month as "at-home week" so they could have conferences and coordinate work with each other.

Hugo and Ruth's responses to one of Alan's letters from college reveal their values and their struggles. In February of his sophomore year, struggling to meet the demands of the honors program at Baylor, Alan wrote:

> I don't know why, but it always seems to be the case that about this time of year I have to keep re-motivating myself. This is the time of my life in which I could be the freest, and yet I am subjecting myself to most rigorous demands. But, it would not be so bad if it were only now that I had to work under the pressure of a high level of expected performance. The fact is that in our system of education the more and the better the work you turn out, the more that is expected of you.... The higher you can reach, the higher the mark is raised. It would be all right if this were the case only in college, but I know that it probably is not. Seminary will be the same way, and then when I finish my education, I will have an education such that wherever I work, in a church, as a missionary, or as a teacher, great demands will be made on me. Therefore it seems that now I am only charting a similar course for the future, when really I would very much like to have time in my life to be able to enjoy some of the simpler, finer joys, pursuits, and pleasures, such as time to read whatever I please, engage in creative hobbies, worthwhile projects, outdoor life, and leisurely family living.[7]

Ruth responded:

> I was tremendously impressed with your letter yesterday. I know I can be of little help to you except to say that we feel very deeply the tensions you are under. I have had the same ones all my life. How I have longed to be like Mary and Wanda [her sister and Hugo's sister], and just live an easy-going life in one place with family and friends. I

---

[6] Hugo Culpepper, letter to family, 9 February 1965.

[7] Alan Culpepper, letter to Hugo and Ruth Culpepper, 21 February 1965.

use to cry long and hard over the tension I felt at not being able to do so—and still have sometimes the same reaction. I particularly felt it last fall. We thought we had it made here [in Louisville]. [We] were over the hump financially, had attained a place of service that was demanding and yet not too demanding; had friends and roots, and everything we wanted. Therefore when this job [at the Home Mission Board] came along my reaction was "Lord, why can't you leave us alone and let us enjoy that which we have worked so hard to build." So you can see there will always be this tension....

I think it is the inner dedication of Daddy's to be the best that God gave him the possibilities of being that has taken him where he is today. It was not that he wanted to be top man, or to be important. You know Daddy is not of that nature. But I think the thing that God has always been able to use the most is his complete willingness to sacrifice himself to whatever He asked him to do. So I think you can begin to see that sacrifice is not always doing without something that you would have. I mean by that it is not always going to a mission field and doing without the latest appliances. There is a self-sacrifice that is paid dearly in application and long hours of work and struggle to do the best that you are able to do....

I also believe very firmly that as we persist in developing all the capabilities (talents) that God gave us, we are able to continue growing all through life. With this growing never stopping, we are thus put in more responsible places because God had found one worthy of the stewardship, as He illustrates in the parable of the talents....

Now, having said all this, I do believe that all four of us are guilty of being too intense in life. I feel that all of us should take more time out to play and get out from under tension (of the moment—not the tension that keeps us ever pushing forward toward life's full development).[8]

When he got a moment to write, after summarizing his activities that week, Hugo reflected:

From all this you can understand how your last letter struck a responsive, understanding chord with me. Your problem has always been with me! However, I believe we can be good stewards of God's gift of life and learn to "relax in flight." I'm trying to! But I wouldn't want a life determined merely by

---

[8] Ruth Culpepper, letter to Alan Culpepper, 26 February 1965.

what "I wanted to do" in the popular sense of the phrase. Actually, as one's character develops he does what he *really* wants to do. In fact, we come to be "determined" by our characters.... the ultimate issue is not what "I'd rather do"; it is the stewardship of life. There is an "art of living" in the sense of achieving up to the limits of one's possibilities and at the same time recognizing one's limitations and being content to live with them. We are more likely to commit the "sin of low aim" though, I suppose. [The last sentence is an allusion to something Dr. Armstrong told his classes: "Better to aim at a million and miss it, than to aim at a hundred and gain it."][9]

By the middle of April, Hugo and Ruth had found a house they both liked. Since it was still not finished, Ruth could work with the builder and choose the wallpaper and carpet she wanted. They signed a contract, hoping that their home in Louisville would sell before the closing date.

In mid-April Hugo had an opportunity for the kind of serious dialogue he enjoyed so much and one that foreshadowed the turn of his interests a decade later:

Alan, I had a most interesting time last weekend.... I took a cab to the airport at noon and flew to St. Louis. There I was met and driven during the afternoon the 190 miles to the Lake of the Ozarks in central Missouri. It is a beautiful modern State Baptist Camp. I was in a motel as nice as a Holiday Inn. There were 175 foreign college students there for a BSU sponsored conference. I had three seminar discussion conferences and brought the major address Saturday evening; it was really a personal testimony on "My Life Pilgrimage with Christ." It was a thrill to have the conversations that followed and to witness and share in a quest for truth and meaning with Moslems, Hindus, and Buddhists from all over the world. Most of them were science and engineering majors, and it was exciting to discuss religion with them.[10]

About ten days later he flew with Dr. Loyd Corder in his private plane to Jackson, Mississippi, to confer with the National Baptist state secretary who was heading the Committee of Concern, which was rebuilding the African-American churches that had been burned in the Civil Rights violence.

---

[9] Hugo Culpepper, letter to Alan Culpepper, 2 March 1965.
[10] Hugo Culpepper, letter to Alan Culpepper and Mr. and Mrs. J. H. Culpepper, 21 April 1965.

Their house in Louisville sold early in May, to a couple who wanted to take possession of it on 17 June, the exact date they had already set with a mover to move them to Atlanta. Two weeks later, Hugo presented a paper, following the meeting of the Baptist World Alliance. In it he surveyed the current situation in regard to missions, articulated a theological basis for missions, and took sharp issue with the church growth and people groups philosophy of missions that continue to influence Baptist thinking about missions even today:

Another movement which is attracting considerable attention today emphasizes "peoples' movements and church growth." This is fostered by those sympathetic with a school of thought that may be traced from the writings of Roland Allen (. . .) and those of Donald McGavran (. . .). There are points of value in this school of thought. The authors know the problems on the mission field and point them out clearly, although their comments are more relevant to the older mission station era than to the emerging future. (I think much of Allen's concern would have been relieved had he been a Free Churchman, and especially if he had been a Baptist!) This school of thought recognizes, in its more recent expression, the value of cultural anthropology, but it seems to be limited too much to one mission front, as I shall mention later. Also, a contribution is made in directing attention to the need for expecting and securing church extension. (I fear that it leaves the impression with some of us, however, that it does not emphasize quality in Christian discipleship, concern with relevance to ethical issues, concern that missions be "the crossing of barriers"—social, economic political, etc., as well as geographic and statistical church extension.) Desirable attention to mission strategy has been provoked. This is good. Out of honest differences progress can come through constructive discussion.

The leading exponent of this school of thought is Dr. Donald McGavran. He has begun a school in Eugene, Oregon, which is called the Institute of Church Growth. In August of 1963, the writer had the privilege of attending a Consultation on Church Growth at Iberville, out from Montreal, Canada. Dr. McGavran was also a participant. Having read his books, I was glad to have the opportunity of hearing him personally give exposition to his views and of discussing with him the things in his thought that give me concern. His answers were not such as to remove my concern. At one point in the discussion of the whole group, I suggested that a strategy of missions needs an adequate biblical and theological basis and that we should give some attention to this before developing a strategy. Dr. McGavran replied, "We (at the Institute) have considered theology and have found it to be a dry well." I was shocked at this statement and considered it to be irresponsible. (In this connection, I am pleased to see that the latest book related to the Institute includes a chapter on "Theological Foundations.") The concept of "peoples' movements" has not been reconciled with the historic Baptist (and New Testament) emphasis on a regenerate church membership. I asked Dr. McGavran personally about this; he denied there is a problem, but gave no satisfactory explanation. His thought is directed to a diminishing frontier in missions, i.e. tribal, animistic, primitive peoples and cultures. I recognize that such phenomena as the Institute deals with may be relevant on this front, pragmatically speaking, but it is not the major front of today and tomorrow. I suggested to Dr. McGavran that he would make a better contribution if he could develop a strategy for the metropolitan centers of the world where by the end of this century 90 percent of the world's population will live (according to Barbara Ward). Here people are becoming isolated individuals holed-up in high-rise apartments and not influenced by the patterns of group cultures which are basic to peoples' movements.

This school's emphasis on harvesting where the fruit is abundant and immediately ripe, which involves a highly mobile missionary force that can be concentrated in responsive areas, leaves unanswered some valid questions and neglects a necessary dimension in a complete strategy (from the New Testament viewpoint). In combating acknowledged weaknesses in "our missionary methods," the total impact comes to be unduly negative.[11]

After the Baptist World Alliance and the mission conference came the missions weeks at Glorieta and Ridgecrest, then a conference in Washington with the American Baptists concerning work in Puerto Rico.

In August, Hugo also received a letter from Cecil Thompson in Argentina, relating the current discussion there concerning whether the seminary should continue to be an international seminary or serve Argentina only. Dr. Thompson also indicated that since Dr. Cooper was retiring from the presidency, he and others wanted Hugo's permission to put his name in nomination to succeed Dr. Cooper as president of the seminary. Hugo's response is typically revealing:

In regard to your suggesting my name to the trustee nominating committee for the position of president of the seminary, I am honored and most

---

[11] Hugo H. Culpepper, "New Patterns and Trends in Contemporary World Missions," background paper for missions consultation, Miami Beach, Florida, 30 June 30–3 July 1965.

appreciative of this expression of confidence on your part. I must recognize that this struck a note of nostalgia in my heart. After sharing this letter with Ruth and our two sons, I remarked that I wish I had three lives to be living simultaneously. It was a most difficult struggle as to our vocation last fall for two or three months when we wrestled with the question of leaving Southern Seminary and coming to the Home Mission Board. Last night as I read your letter it made me realize how wonderful it would be if I could be living one life in Buenos Aires and have all of the thrill of involvement there, if I could still be at Southern Seminary with the challenge there, and at the same time continue my ever deepening involvement in the strategic area of missions in the United States. I appreciate your concern that the academic level and standard of excellence among students be maintained in the future. It seems to me that this is imperative and that everything possible should be done to continue to mold that school into a truly great seminary, rather than permit it to become a national institute. This period of transition through which you are passing can and should be made a stepping stone in that direction. Some of the happiest years of our life were spent in ministry there. Had this situation arisen last fall or slightly earlier, it would have been a most difficult thing to deal with. Larry enters Baylor this fall, and we realize that from this point on both of the boys will be increasingly away from home. Life there was deeply satisfying in terms of well-balanced involvement in study, teaching, and creative administrative and executive involvement, as well as ample opportunities for fellowship and ministry to people in the churches. Our interest in world missions has not decreased in any way.

However, I do not think it would be wise for you to suggest our name to the committee because we have so recently come to this place of responsibility and because of the deepening involvement in which we find ourselves in the life of our denomination and of missions at the national level here in our own country. The demands are far greater than I can possibly live up to in terms of time and energy in my present opportunity for service. Sometimes it is a bit frustrating because of the absolute lack of time to continue my reading and study as I have been accustomed to do in the past and even to have reasonable fellowship with friends and family.[12]

In the fall of 1965 Hugo participated in a retreat at Callaway Gardens with four other agency people and nine seminary professors, working on convention goals for 1970–1980. Hugo and Ruth co-authored the mission study book for 1966, titled "Panama: The Land Between," and taught it

---

[12] Hugo Culpepper, letter to Dr. and Mrs. Cecil Thompson, 31 August 1965.

several times that winter. The demanding schedule of meetings and travel continued. From 21–27 May 1966, Hugo and Ruth were at the Southern Baptist Convention meeting in Detroit. While they were there, Hugo gave a brief presentation to the Men's Mission Conference:

In the eyes of men he was a railway postal clerk. His daily schedule was somewhat uncertain. Many men under similar conditions would have thought it impossible to become involved in missions. After all, a man must have some time for himself! But he had become possessed by One greater than himself. He had come to feel that his life was not his own. Not that he was a mystic or a man of special spiritual gifts. He was really quite ordinary.

It all began when his pastor shared a vision of what his church could do for the glory of God if the men would work with him. The pastor organized a missions committee in the church and asked the railway postal clerk to serve as chairman. He recruited others to serve with him. None of them knew very much about what they should do, because missions committees were still new. But he grew with his increasing responsibilities. During the next decade mission points were established, lay preachers were secured from among the men of the church, church sites were acquired, buildings were erected. He was never out front in it all. But he was always *there*. He was the means of relating *many* to the work of missions.

Thirty years have passed. At least ten of the missions took root and are strong churches today! The pastor went on to give leadership to the 30,000 movement. Numerous student preachers in those missions remember the chairman of the missions committee with gratitude.

He influenced their understanding and appreciation of missions more than he ever dreamed. One of them became a medical missionary. Another is director of the Division of Missions.…

Yes, men saw him as a railway postal clerk—but in God's sight he was mighty like the Father's own Son![13]

Responding to a longstanding invitation, Hugo gave a series of lectures at a pastors' conference in Buenos Aires, 29 May–5 June, and then in Santiago, 6–10 June. Hugo gave four lectures on "The Biblical Basis for Missions" and enjoyed renewing friendships in Buenos Aires. The main difference Hugo noticed was that there were twice as many cars in Buenos Aires as when they had left eight years earlier. Hugo was treated with the

---

[13] Hugo Culpepper, "Men Involved in Home Missions," tape recording of presentation at Men's Mission Conference, 23 May 1966.

kind of hospitality only dear friends can extend. The Carrolls took Hugo to La Cabaña for a "baby befe," and Jean Glaze sent him breakfast the next morning on a tray. One morning he was served hot biscuits and fried quail for breakfast. At the end of one letter, however, he commented: "We are remembered most here by the 'escapades' of the boys!"[14]

In the spring of 1966 Hugo had been invited to become a member of the Faith and Order Colloquium, organized by the National Council of Churches of Christ in America. Individuals from all the major denominations participated. The first meeting was in Chicago in June 1966, on the theme "The Nature and Meaning of Conversion." Hugo had to leave two days before the colloquium was over to fly to Fresno for a missions conference, then to Portland, and on to Alaska for two weeks. From Anchorage, Hugo wrote:

The Captain Cook Hotel is modern in every respect and yet it has a continental air to it such as a foreign hotel in Asia. My eighth floor window looks out to the west over Cook Inlet (from the Pacific). In the distance to the right is a snow-capped mountain.... To the east are mountains which are like the Andes in Santiago. I have the strange feeling of being in a western frontier town of 50,000 with the Chilean mountains overhanging on one side and the sea on the other!... It is light around the clock here now—all night.[15]

Hugo preached at Calvary Baptist Church in Anchorage, then began a tour of mission points in Seward. Next, he went to a small town with a church started by a soldier who hitchhiked 120 miles each way every Sunday to preach to nine people, Kenai, Fairbanks, Fort Yukon, where they took in fresh fruit and vegetables to Dan and Mary Ann Rollins and Hugo preached at a worship service that began at 10:45 P.M. At midnight they all went out to see the sun, still up on the horizon since they were eight miles north of the Arctic Circle on the longest day of the year. That night, they flew back to Fairbanks. He preached there the next night, and then they drove back to Anchorage (500 miles), visiting pastors and churches along the way. Then they flew to Kotzebue, on the Bering Strait, Kiana, Shungnak, and Kobuk. The next day they flew to Nome and Unalakleet. From there they traveled to Emmonak to visit the first Eskimo native missionary, then returned to spend the night at Unalakleet before returning to Anchorage and going on to Juneau. The return flight brought

---

[14] Hugo Culpepper, letter to Ruth and the boys, 1 June 1966.
[15] Hugo Culpepper, letter to Ruth and the boys, 18 June 1966.

him back to Atlanta by way of Seattle and Chicago. By the end of the
month, Hugo had traveled 27,000 miles, covering the western hemisphere
from one end to the other.

The First Annual Pastors' Conference at Baylor, 4-8 July
1966. On the front row (l-r): James Leo Garrett, Riley
Eubanks, Jack Flanders, Ray Summers, and Hugo Culpepper.

Hugo was one of the three speakers at the first annual pastors'
conference at Baylor, 4–8 July. The theme was "The Renewal of the
Church." Dr. Ray Summers interpreted Ephesians as a biblical basis for
church renewal; Dr. James Leo Garrett discussed the theological basis for
church renewal; Hugo spoke on the practical aspects of the theme. Dr. Jack
Flanders preached each evening.

On 6 August, Sherryl Bedell, Hugo's niece, was married in Little Rock.
Hugo and the boys drove over from Atlanta, while Ruth flew to Little Rock
from Glorieta, following WMU week. After the wedding, Hugo flew on to
Glorieta for Home Missions Week, while Ruth and the boys returned to
Atlanta. At the end of the month, the family drove to Corpus Christi for a

few days of fishing for king mackerel with Dr. Lewis Newman before the boys returned to Baylor for the fall semester.

Larry, Alan, and Hugo, fishing at Padre Island, August 1966.

In the fall of 1966 Hugo visited several college campuses as part of a listening team, listening to students sound off about the church, denominational life, problems, hopes, and materials. Hugo and Ruth also took part in the orientation and commissioning service for the new home missionary appointees. Ruth described the event in a letter to Larry and Alan: "We had a very nice weekend at Toccoa with the new appointees. There were seven or eight who had been Daddy's students at Louisville, so it was fun to renew acquaintances. Daddy did well in the Bible studies, and they were greatly appreciated. The women and I talked a great deal. So many wanted conferences that they set up a conference for just the women, and we just sat around and talked some things over. It was interesting to see the problems of these young, new missionaries."[16]

Christmas provided a much needed break and time with the family. It had been a hard year for the extended family. Hugo's mother had tuberculosis early in the year, his father was suffering from emphysema, and his mother fell and broke her pelvic bone just before Christmas. Ruth's brother had been burned over sixty-five percent of his body in an oil well explosion in New Mexico, and age was taking its toll on her parents, too. The younger generation, however, was thriving. Alan gave his college sweetheart, Jacquelyn McClain, an engagement ring in January of 1967, and Larry was compiling a strong college record in the pre-med program at Baylor.

---

[16] Ruth Culpepper, letter to Larry Culpepper and Alan Culpepper, 1 November 1966.

In a letter to Leroy Seat, a former student who had just gone to Japan as a missionary, Hugo gave advice and reflected on the year past:

Let me share with you once again, as I so often mentioned in the classrooms at Southern, concentrate on the language above all else during these early months and years. It will pay rich dividends of satisfaction in your service in the years to come....

We have been here at the Home Mission Board for nearly two years now. It continues to be an arduous task but full of challenge and satisfaction in many ways. It is an entirely different life than that which we lived at the Seminary. However, we are finding opportunities continuously to make use of experiences and studies in years gone by. One has the sense of being involved on the front lines of mission activity in this country.[17]

A visit to Southern Seminary in January to talk to students about vocational opportunities at the Home Mission Board gave Hugo a chance to visit with former colleagues there. In March of 1967 Hugo had an occasion to make his first trip to Europe. The Foreign Mission Board invited him to give a series of lectures on metropolitan missions at the seminary at Ruschlikon, Switzerland, for a conference considering strategies for reaching the cities of Europe.

The press of activities at home continued. In May, Hugo had cooperative missions conferences in Little Rock, Albuquerque, Phoenix, Salt Lake City, San Francisco, and Portland, before the Southern Baptist Convention meeting in Miami. When he could find the time, he was writing Sunday school lessons.

In May, Ruth resigned from her position as the GA director. She said there were a lot of factors in the decision, not the least being her desire to be at home that summer while the boys and Jacque were in town. In a delightful serendipity, 1 June 1967, Dr. Arthur Rutledge, executive secretary of the Home Mission Board, spoke at the baccalaureate service at Baylor, and the next day, when Alan and Jacque graduated, Baylor awarded him an honorary doctorate. Three weeks later, on Hugo and Ruth's twenty-eighth anniversary, 24 June, Alan and Jacque were married in Houston, Texas, and Hugo performed the ceremony. That same month Ruth accepted a position as a cataloger in the library at Emory University.

At Glorieta that summer, 3,027 attended Home Mission Week, and 2,000 other requests for room accommodations had to be denied. In a letter

---

[17] Hugo Culpepper, letter to Leroy Seat, 19 December 1966.

to Mr. Roberto Gonzalez, a student in Buenos Aires, Hugo explained the nature of his work at the Home Mission Board and his understanding of the relationship between the church and the kingdom of God:

You raised the question as to why so much emphasis has been given recently to the church rather than the kingdom. I do not believe that this is to de-emphasize the importance of the kingdom of God in any way. However, too little attention in the past has been given to developing a Biblical doctrine and understanding of the nature and work of the church as the instrument of God in achieving the growth of the kingdom of God. By kingdom of God, I mean where the will of God is done. Wherever the will of God is done, there is the kingdom, in a spiritual sense. The church is the body of Christ, the people of God, and the servant of God. It is the mission of the church to carry on the mission of Jesus Christ to the world and to achieve the realization of the purposes for which He gave Himself. I believe that we Southern Baptists have great need of giving attention to understanding the nature of the church and its mission. This will do more than anything else to help us win people to faith in Jesus Christ and to bring them into the kingdom of God.[18]

In the fall of 1967, Hugo's close friend Paul Geren left the state department to become president of Stetson University. In passing, he suggested that if Hugo ever left the Home Mission Board he might consider going to Stetson. The move to Stetson never materialized, however. Two years later Hugo and Ruth received the sad news that Geren had been killed in an automobile accident near London, Kentucky, on 22 June 1969.[19]

Another letter, this one from John R. Carter, who had been one of Hugo's students at Southern, foreshadowed events that would develop a few years later. Carter related how meaningful for him his study at Harvard had been, at the Center for the Study of World Religions, and with Professor Wilfred Cantwell Smith.

Life in Atlanta, continued to be fulfilling, and filled with a balance of activities:

Thursday night [2 November 1967] we go to the Atlanta Symphony concert and Friday night to the Atlanta Music Club (Mantovani will be on this program). Robert Shaw is conducting the Symphony now as the permanent conductor. Saturday we see Duke play Tech. Saturday night we are having the

---

[18] Hugo Culpepper, letter to Roberto Gonzalez, 11 August 1967.

[19] See p. 103, n. 2.

discussion group of six couples over to our home at 7:30 for a discussion of cybernetics. A professor of Electrical Engineering at Tech is leading this particular night. Sunday morning at 10:00 I leave for Hawaii. It will be non-stop to Los Angeles by Delta and then change to a Pan American plane on to Honolulu. It will take about 11 1/2 hours for the trip, but I will arrive there at 3:30 P.M. Sunday because of gaining six hours going that way. I attend the Hawaii Baptist Convention and speak and then visit all the mission work on all the islands. I'll return on Wednesday, November 15 and spend the night in Los Angeles. On Thursday, November 16, I take a non-stop flight to Atlanta and get here after lunch. That night is another Atlanta Symphony concert with Yehudi Menuhin, the violinist. That Saturday the 18th, Notre Dame plays Tech here. Then on the following Monday, the 20th I go to Nashville for the Coordinating Committee of the Inter-Agency Council meeting and will leave there Thanksgiving morning to come up to Louisville. I've got to present the outline for a proposed 60-page paper that will define and interpret Southern Baptist mission strategy at that meeting.... I've enjoyed reading a new book Mother checked out of Emory for me: Carl Michalson's *Worldly Theology*.... It is very contemporary as to theological trends, and he has a very readable style.

I completed reading the Old Testament in Spanish today, having read three chapters a day in it since last January 1. Now I am going to start through the RSV in the Old Testament. I read one chapter of Greek a day along with it in the New Testament.

I wish I could work in about two hours a day of serious theological reading into my routine also. I am coming to appreciate it more than ever as personal pilgrimage in living and thinking. Glad you are getting some exercise along the way. Hope you all are enjoying living these days of your lives!

With love,

Dad[20]

Hugo preached the Sunday evening he arrived in Hawaii, although it was nearly 1:00 A.M. Still, he found it invigorating: "Got a thrill out of the visit. Gave me a sense of nostalgia because of the spirit of heart-felt religion of new Christians."[21]

Hugo's travel schedule continued unabated in 1968, but he attended Paul Geren's inauguration at Stetson (25 January 1968) and visited with Alan and Jacque in Louisville, where Alan was a student at Southern

---

[20] Hugo Culpepper, letter to Alan and Jacque Culpepper, 31 October 1967.

[21] Hugo Culpepper, letter to Ruth Culpepper, 7 November 1967.

Seminary and Jacque was in her first year of teaching. Following the visit, Hugo wrote, philosophizing:

> I think you are both to be commended for the way you have settled into the responsibilities of life and for the manner in which you both are applying yourselves and getting on with the task. In a way I know it may seem to be rough at times—and it really is. But I have come to see that life is a continuing struggle and that the strength acquired in overcoming today prepares you for bigger tasks tomorrow. I suppose it will be a vigorous effort all the way until the end—and maybe into eternity!"[22]

Hugo was reflecting on his own experience. The pace he was keeping was exhausting, but Hugo was making a contribution that reached beyond the Home Mission Board by helping to define the mission strategy of the Southern Baptist Convention:

> I have been very busy lately, and by last weekend I was worn down to almost exhaustion. I was in Nashville for four days last week, and the committee went over a 40-page paper I had written to set forth Southern Baptist mission strategy. They took two days for this. It was an interesting experience. They made no changes of any significance. Dr. Frank K. Means is writing the Foreign Mission Board part. I wrote the introduction, Biblical and Theological basis part and the history and strategy of the Home Mission Board part. His will be about 25 pages long. When it is finished later on this year, after having been circulated among about 75 Southern Baptist Convention agency leaders, and finally adopted by the Coordinating Committee of the Inter-Agency Council, it will be the official Convention inter-agency source paper on the subject of Southern Baptist mission strategy. It has not been too much work getting it done because I am using what I have long since worked out in my own studies and thinking and teaching.[23]

In the same letter Hugo reported that plans were being made to move the Home Mission Board to a new building near I-85 in Atlanta later that summer.

Other building plans were underway that year also. Their church, Second Ponce de Leon Baptist, was supporting the effort to open the new Atlanta Baptist College (which would later merge with Mercer University)

---

[22] Hugo Culpepper, letter to Alan and Jacque Culpepper, 5 February 1968.
[23] Hugo Culpepper, letter to family, 20 February 1968.

that fall: "We went out there Wednesday night for a chicken box supper to see the four new buildings that have been erected."[24] In the spring of 1968 Hugo was writing Sunday School lessons on Romans, for which he worked through the Greek text and five substantial commentaries. He was also working on a resource paper for Dr. Rutledge to take to the Baptist World Alliance meeting in Liberia that summer.

When Alan was called to be pastor of a small American Baptist church near Madison, Indiana, Hugo had advice for the young pastor:

> While you will be taking their preferences into consideration as regards what they expect their pastor to do, at the same time you have a responsibility to the Lord as his 'under-shepherd' to pastor the flock in respect to what it seems to you that is needed. You do well to try to be creative in the way of fresh sermon approaches. Still, over the long pull, you will do well to lean heavily on Bible exposition as the basis and source of your sermons. Otherwise, sooner or later, you will run dry.[25]

The pace of life was unrelenting, with missions weeks at Ridgecrest and Glorieta, parents in failing health in Little Rock, and the Sunday school lessons on Romans. At Glorieta, Hugo gave the charge to the newly appointed missionaries, drawing from texts and perspectives that he had found meaningful across the years.

"Charge to Newly Appointed Missionaries"

As newly appointed missionaries of Jesus Christ, you stand tonight on the threshold of a boundless life. You have responded to the leadership of the spirit of God in your hearts and lives, you have turned your back upon a way of self-preservation and self-realization primarily to a way of self-sacrifice, willing to be led of the Spirit of God to know and to do His will....

You see, you are being sent to a world where life seems to be cheap and meaningless—where in some cases it is no more than just a bubble that bursts and vanishes away. And God has called you to go to lend meaning to life where tonight there is no meaning. You are being sent, but you are a missionary of Christ Jesus. You have responded to God's leadership to make his mission your mission. Your mission, henceforth, in life is to glorify God—to live in such a way that the very character and nature of God himself may come

---

[24] Hugo Culpepper, letter to family, 28 April 1968.
[25] Hugo Culpepper, letter to Alan and Jacque Culpepper, 30 June 1968.

to be known in your life—through what you do and through what you say....
For where you are will be the growing edge of the church as it confronts the
world today. And just as the flame is to the candle your life is to the people of
God—to the church of Jesus Christ—this day. For even as the candle is
consumed in bringing light round about it, even so you as the flame of the
church will be spent in bringing light into the lives of others. For you will be a
missionary of Christ Jesus, a missionary of Christ Jesus through the will of
God.

Though you stand on the threshold of a boundless life, may I assure you
from twenty-eight years of personal experience that there will be dark days
ahead. There will be days of struggle, there will be days of anguish and
uncertainty when you will seemingly have lost a sense of direction and only
then can you find strength if you are always assured that you are there
because of the will of God.... For there is no other form of security in our kind
of world today. Indeed in a sense humanly speaking there is no security.
There are only opportunities for the self-giving in the love of God for the redemption of others. And so as you go into this glorious walk with Christ Jesus
in a benighted world to bring love and faith and meaning and confidence and
hope, may you go with enthusiasm. May you go with a sense of assurance that
will make your step steadfast. May you go with that poise of character, with that
serenity of spirit, with that nobleness of character that your lives might truly be
Christlike. And may it be said of you by those who know you and have seen
you work through the years that as they saw you work they often wondered
whether it was life or death that held you most in bondage. But that by the end
of the way they will have come to know that for a missionary such as you there
really is no day or night, no end and no beginning, but that all is one great
dawn that sees in golden glory, eternity itself as a sunrise.[26]

In September Hugo spoke at Alan's ordination at Macedonia Baptist
Church. Ten days later, while returning from a visit with Larry in Waco,
Hugo and Ruth had a wreck near Meridian, Mississippi, when another car
pulled in front of them. While their injuries were minor, Ruth lost two of
her teeth as a result of the accident. In October, Hugo wrote, "We have
been in such a whirl this past two weeks that I have become almost oblivious to
time!"[27] Part of the whirl was lecturing seven times in four days at
Southern, and Hugo was leaving the next day to give five lectures in forty-

---

[26] Hugo Culpepper, "Charge to Newly Appointed Missionaries," tape recording
of presentation at Missions Week, Glorieta, New Mexico, 3 August 1968.

[27] Hugo Culpepper, letter to family 14 October 1968.

eight hours to the foreign mission appointees at their orientation at Ridgecrest. Later that month, Hugo made a visit out West. After summarizing his exhausting schedule for the week, he added:

Let me give you a tip though. This sort of life takes a lot out of one physically and [it] grows old soon. I am glad you are planning to get an early start on a scholarly life as your vocation.... At the same time, the practical pastoral experience you are now getting will be invaluable later on also. I wish I had gotten it as a student. It will stimulate you to assimilate truth into your life day by day as you live it now, and it will help you share the best you find with others along life's way.[28]

From January through 6 April 1969, Hugo was interim pastor at Redan Baptist Church, just south of Stone Mountain. In February, Hugo's mother went into Baptist Hospital in Little Rock for a month for treatment for TB. Meanwhile, Hugo's work continued to demand all he could put into it. When snow shut down the city of Atlanta in February, Hugo wrote:

This last week has been one of the hardest work-weeks I have put in. It was an 'at home' week, and we had lots of hard decisions to make and also extra meetings at night, etc. I am really glad to get a little break and a chance to relax a bit, catch up on work and things I need to do here [at home], even if the weather has forced it on us.[29]

When Alan became interested in a Ph.D. in New Testament studies, Hugo talked with Raymond B. Brown, dean of Southeastern Seminary, who recommended Duke, saying that Professor W. D. Davies was the most outstanding English-speaking New Testament scholar in the country and that Duke had a young professor who had recently finished his Ph.D. at Yale, D. Moody Smith, Jr. Hugo immediately purchased Smith's published dissertation and those of Davies' books that he did not have and began to read them. In response to a letter from Alan about his growing attraction to New Testament studies, Hugo wrote:

I can well understand your comment that you find your interest more on the academic side of religion than in its practical value. I am also probably

---

[28] Hugo Culpepper, letter to Alan and Jacque Culpepper, 3 November 1968.
[29] Hugo Culpepper, letter to family, 16 February 1969.

disposed in this way too. However, I think it is important to assimilate academic questing for religious understanding and truth in an existential way for the nourishment of an ever-deepening personal trust and sense of discipleship and pilgrimage. Also, increasingly I find that it is rewarding to open one's life to others in ministry, although others usually enrich my life through fellowship more than anything I can consciously give to them. To withhold ourselves from others, whether from timidity or self-centeredness, is to impoverish our lives since we were made for each other.[30]

The second week of May 1969, Hugo went to Wake Forest University for a Catholic-Baptist Dialogue sponsored by the new Ecumenical Institute there. Then, on 12 May, Hugo left for twelve days of travel in the West: Albuquerque, Phoenix, Las Vegas, Salt Lake City, Fresno, Portland, Anchorage, Fort Worth, and back to Atlanta. After visiting Las Vegas, Hugo wrote: "We had dinner about 8:00 P.M., and then the three of us (Emmanuel McCall and Quentin Lockwood) spent about two hours walking through the gambling casinos both downtown and on the strip. I found it depressing! There were so many older people! They were seeking distraction from empty lives it seemed."[31]

Larry graduated from Baylor in May 1969 and entered Baylor Medical School that summer, working on a project on "EEG and the Regulation of Electrocortical Activity and Behavior by the Nonspecific Thalmo-Orbitocortical Synchronizing System." In the fall of 1970 Alan entered the Ph.D. program at Duke University. Hugo took pride in the advanced work both boys were pursuing—each in an area to which he had been attracted: New Testament studies and medicine.

In July Hugo visited the language school in Guadalajara, Mexico, to evaluate whether the Home Mission Board should begin sending Spanish-speaking missionaries there for their language training. The following week he and Ruth left on a three-week trip to Europe. They flew Icelandic to Luxembourg, where they took delivery on a new Volkswagen squareback. From there they drove down the Rhine Valley, taking what Ruth called "a theologian's trip" through Europe. They visited Worms ("Luther country"), the universities at Heidelberg, Strassbourg (where they saw the small church where Albert Schweitzer preached, the medical school where he studied, and further south, his birthplace), and Basel, then across to Salzburg and on to Vienna, before arriving at Baden bei Wien, Austria,

---

[30] Hugo Culpepper, letter to Alan and Jacque Culpepper, 4 May 1969.
[31] Hugo Culpepper, letter to Ruth Culpepper, 14 May 1969.

for the Baptist World Alliance meeting. At Baden they visited with many old friends, including Dr. Frank Means; Dr. John Watts, then president of Ruschlikon Baptist Seminary; Dr. James Wood, professor at Baylor; Dr. James Leo Garrett, professor at Southern Seminary; and Dr. Duke K. McCall. The last was particularly significant, because Dr. McCall asked Hugo off-handedly, but seriously, whether he was ready to come back to Southern. The seed was planted. Hugo said the meeting of the Baptist World Alliance gave him "many back-stage, behind the scene" insights.

For the Home Missions Week at Glorieta in August 1969 they had to decline 2,000 requests for housing for the week because everything was booked. In September, while Atlanta was caught up in the National League pennant race, Hugo was involved in meetings with state directors of missions, exploring the language school preparation of missionaries to Spanish-speaking people. When Hugo's travels started again in the fall, he wrote Ruth: "I hated to leave home after being spoiled for the last two months by getting to be with you all the time!... I miss you and love you very much. I want us to cultivate more devotional life, relaxation, and play together and with friends when I'm there."[32]

After Clarence Jordan, founder of Koinonia Farm in Americus, Georgia, died in October, Hugo wrote:

When I entered [Southern] seminary in 1936, he was a graduate student and did some of the instructing in my class in baby Greek. He got into working with Negroes there in Louisville and then went back to his home setting to simply "be" a Christian.... I have no doubt he was a radically Christian spirit and one of the true Baptist prophets of our time. Of course, the local Baptist church there, culturally bound as it was, ex-communicated him ("withdrew fellowship" is the Baptist phrase). He was not eccentric, as one might think from the [newspaper] write-up—just radically and simply Christian in his scale of values, even to the simplicity of being buried unembalmed in a cow pasture without a gravestone. Apparently he wanted his family to take a Christian view of death and regard him as returning home to the Lord and just let his dead body fade away, returning to dust.[33]

In November 1969 Hugo visited three of the San Blas Islands, offshore on the Atlantic side of Panama.

---

[32] Hugo Culpepper, letter to Ruth Culpepper, 14 August 1969.
[33] Hugo Culpepper, letter to Alan and Jacque Culpepper, 1 November 1969.

On the first island we were met by the school band, all out in their uniforms, playing for our reception. There were about 3,000 people on each island. The Indian chief and his three spokesmen councilors met us, and we went to the nipa hut Congress Hall for a conference with them. Then we visited the church and the pastor. On the second island we had lunch. Our menu was: rice cooked in coconut milk, fresh lime juice punch, sliced tomatoes, roasted fresh lobsters (out of the shells), and fresh papaya!

It was delicious—all of it! We sat near the edge of the island looking out through the palms on the beautiful blue Atlantic as the gentle breeze blew by on the clear sunny day. On the third island we visited our medical clinic, where there were 45 bed patients. It is a primitive operation with one medical missionary and one RN—a US-2 [volunteer] who is just out of college and nurses training. They are doing a remarkable work. She lives in a nipa hut with a dirt floor and sleeps on an army cot under a mosquito net. Pays five dollars per month rent for the hut. They do practically every kind of case there and have good success, it seems. It was very inspiring.[34]

On the same trip Hugo read Eldridge Cleaver's *Soul on Ice*, which he found worthwhile as a commentary on the thought and life of a segment of the culture at that time. Still, "his value system is distorted, and he manifests a lack of positive orientation in life. He does provide an insight as to what the product of many of the injustices of society today is.... The book is an insight to the malady of today's unjust social order, but provides no clue to reality nor positive insight as to what can or should be done about it."[35] The next Sunday he heard a Sunday school lesson on the Israelites' return from the exile taught by a layman. The teacher took the theme "return," talked about the demonstrations in Washington, D.C., and other social movements of the time, and then talked of

returning to the social order of yesterdays, etc. It was an extreme right wing perspective, voicing nostalgia for the good ole' days, the vested interests of the status quo people, etc. It was a good insight to the mentality of the "solid, upper middle class" in today's culture.... I realized that he was just as mistaken as Cleaver, but at the other end of the spectrum. Then, I had the insight that both the Sunday School teacher and Cleaver lacked a truly Biblical, prophetic, theological understanding and perspective as to what truth and reality is from

---

[34] Hugo Culpepper, letter to family, 16 November 1969.
[35] Ibid.

God's perspective and what is the truly redemptive course of action in keeping with God's intention in history.... But only eyes of faith can see it![36]

At the end of the year, a letter from Dr. Arthur Rutledge, executive secretary of the Home Mission Board, expressed his appreciation for the contribution Hugo had made there over the past five years.

> Dear Hugo:
> Five years have passed quickly! As we approach January 1, 1970, I recall your beginning in the responsible and challenging post of director of the Division of Missions. As I have had occasion to say to you orally, your leadership year by year has been strong and extremely effective, and I rejoice in the way you have shouldered your heavy responsibilities.
> I know something of the challenge which you have felt and which I trust you feel increasingly. You are in one of the most sensitive spots and one of the potentially most influential spots in Southern Baptist life, and it is a joy to me to see you provide dynamic and prophetic leadership at this crucial time in the life of our nation and of our world.
> Vesta joins me in genuine appreciation for both you and Ruth as friends, as well as co-workers.
> May the years ahead be even more rewarding and satisfying as you carry your heavy responsibilities.
> Cordially yours,
> Arthur B. Rutledge[37]

The Decision to Return to Southern Seminary

In the spring of 1970, the seed planted by Dr. McCall the summer before at the Baptist World Alliance meeting bore fruit. On 12 March, William E. Hull, dean of the School of Theology, notified Arthur Rutledge that he was in conversation with Hugo about the possibility of his return to the faculty at Southern. Two weeks later Dean Hull extended a formal invitation to Hugo to return to Southern as a full professor with tenure and to occupy the W. O. Carver Chair of Christian Missions and World Religions. One

---

[36] Ibid.

[37] Arthur Rutledge, letter to Hugo Culpepper, 30 December 1969.

part of Dean Hull's letter projected the faculty's desires for the position to which Hugo was being invited:

In evaluating the prospect of your return, the faculty identified three areas of particular concern. First, there is the desire to achieve greater specialization in the area of World Religions. To achieve this goal, it is felt that you and Dr. Hicks would need carefully to differentiate your respective assignments. The faculty would like for a strong emphasis on the history and phenomenology of religions to be developed at the graduate level in addition to other emphases which have been associated with the teaching of Missions. Second, the faculty would like for you to attract, develop, and eventually train for future faculty service exciting young men who might bring new approaches and perspectives in a rapidly changing field. Finally, the faculty is open to curricular experiments both in content and technique so as to introduce greater stimulus into the classroom in order that the teaching of Christians Missions and World Religions might have a broad appeal and make a significant impact on the student body.[38]

President Duke McCall added his personal support for the faculty's action:

Dear Hugo:

On this Saturday I find on my desk the letter of March 26 from Dean Hull to you. I want you to know that I am enthusiastically behind this invitation to you to return to Southern Seminary. You will know that from my conversation with you in Baden last summer.

Perhaps it is important to say that I have deliberately stayed out of the discussion because it fell into the area of responsibilities of the new school dean and because the circumstances made the faculty's judgment even more important than normal. That is to say the faculty has such knowledge of you as to make its evaluative judgment more accurate than a conversation in an hour's coffee would have permitted.

I am delighted at the enthusiasm with which this invitation is extended to you. Marguerite and I would be pleased to have Ruth back in Louisville. In fact, the only way you can decline this invitation is to get a divorce and send Ruth back if you won't come with her. We want both of you, and we want you badly. We believe that there is an

---

[38] William Hull, letter to Hugo Culpepper, 26 March 1970.

unfinished ministry here. I further believe that you have laid the foundation in the Home Mission Board on which others can build in the future. Come back and train those others for the long future, for home and foreign missions.

Cordially,

Duke K. McCall, President[39]

In a telephone conversation, Hugo asked Dean Hull for clarification about the opportunity for an early sabbatical leave. Dean Hull responded that his previous teaching for over five years would be counted and that he would support an application for a sabbatical leave for Hugo in 1972–1973, which would still leave him five years of teaching before he reached retirement age at sixty-five.

Again, the invitation to change his role and place of service had come to Hugo unsolicited. A number of factors led Hugo to accept the invitation to return to Southern. First was a feeling that he had already made whatever contribution he was capable of making at the Home Mission Board in providing a biblical and theological basis for its work and helping to shape its mission strategy in that era. Second was his commitment to the vocation of teaching and scholarship, for which he had had little time in the past five years. Third was the wear and tear of constant travel that his position at the board required, his separation from Ruth for so much of the time, and her loneliness. Fourth, both of them loved Southern Seminary and their friends and colleagues there. Ruth especially longed to return to Louisville. Finally, Hugo was already picking up signs of theological change in various quarters of Southern Baptist life that he found disconcerting: a superficial understanding of evangelism, the demand that mission programs be measured by the number of baptisms, an emphasis on programs rather than incarnational ministry, and the move toward more centralized control of agencies and programs. For all these reasons, Hugo accepted the invitation to return to Southern and submitted his letter of resignation to Dr. Arthur Rutledge, to be effective September 15, saying, "I shall always be grateful to you, my colleagues here, and the Home Mission Board for these almost six years of ministry with this agency. It has been a privilege to be a part of your administration. My interest in Home Missions will continue, and I hope to be helpful to this Board as a Missions professor. May our fellowship continue in the years ahead in service to our Lord."[40]

---

[39] Duke McCall, letter to Hugo Culpepper, 28 March 1970.

[40] Hugo Culpepper, letter to Arthur Rutledge, 8 April 1970.

Accepting Hugo's resignation with regret, Dr. Rutledge responded:

I find it difficult to express to you my own feeling. Your departure in September will leave a big gap to be filled. However, I respect your integrity in the decision which you have made, and am grateful for the almost six years of outstanding service which you have given to home missions as director of the Division of Missions. You have served with distinction in this position which I count one of the most strategically important positions in the life of the Southern Baptist Convention. The directions which you have set and the leadership you have provided will continue to shape our missions ministries, as well as other activities of this Board, for a long time to come.

It has been a personal joy to me to be associated with you as a co-worker as well as a friend. You have acted with decision and forth-rightness as well as Christian compassion in every situation. I have felt relaxed and free with you, and have rejoiced in your comradeship.[41]

Thanking Dr. Rutledge for his personal letter, Hugo responded:

I believe that the work of this agency has made a distinctive contribution to the life of Southern Baptists in these years and that it will continue to do so. The opportunities for involvement have been almost limitless in the position of director of the Division of Missions. Within the limitations of time and energy, I have sought to give the best I have in effort. There has been a deep-seated sense of satisfaction in such involvement....

I think the one decisive factor which has brought me to accept the invitation to return to the seminary is a seep-seated sense of the stewardship of life, training, and experience. A large part of my life, in terms of time and effort, has been devoted to study and preparation and participation in teaching. These almost six years here of activity near the nerve center of the denomination have broadened the experience and enriched the potential resources for what has always been the major direction of my sense of vocation. While I had not anticipated nor sought such a change as has come upon us, when this door opened recently, it seemed to me to be right that we should respond.[42]

---

[41] Arthur Rutledge, letter to Hugo Culpepper, 16 April 1970.

[42] Hugo Culpepper, letter to Arthur Rutledge, 22 April 1970.

Letters from friends at Southern and at the Home Mission Board; fellow missionaries from years past; Porter Routh, executive secretary of the Executive Committee of the SBC; Herschel H. Hobbs; and others expressed their support for Hugo in the move he was making.

Ernest J. Kelly, assistant to the executive secretary of the Georgia Baptist Convention, offered a revealing comment on the changing context of Baptist missions at the time:

> Your spirit and attitude, your depth of understanding, and evaluation of mission work have served a real benefit in my ministry. I am going to miss you, and I am sure I speak for other men who serve as state mission directors in other states.
>
> In a very unique way the person who replaces you at the Home Mission Board will have a tremendous influence in the ministry of each of our states. It seems that there is a widening breach in the theological, philosophical, and practical understanding of mission involvement. I sincerely trust that they will seek out a man who shares your views and attitudes toward the work of missions. A radically different attitude could make my work much more difficult, if not impossible to interpret in Georgia.
>
> Please forgive the foreboding and awesome overtones of the preceding paragraph, but I think so very highly of you, and your life has greatly influenced my ministry.[43]

Hugo with Alan, at Alan's graduation. *The Tie* (1970)

PROFESSOR AND SON — Hugo H. Culpepper (left), who was re-appointed to the faculty of Southern Seminary in April in the W. O. Carver Chair of Christian Missions and World Religions, points to familiar landmarks on the Louisville campus as he chats with his son Richard Alan Culpepper, a May 1970 graduate of the seminary.

The closing months of Hugo's tenure at the Board moved quickly. In April Hugo and Ruth purchased a home across the street from the seminary

---

[43] Ernest Kelley, letter to Hugo Culpepper, 15 April 1970.

without even having seen it. Alan (who was graduating from Southern that spring) and Jacque handled the initial arrangements and inspection of the house. Hugo would be able to walk to his office. At the end of the month Hugo led a retreat of state directors of missions from across the country at Toccoa, Georgia, planning a national strategy for missions.

In July Hugo and Ruth joined with the Rutledges in a group of nineteen, touring the Orient and ending up in Tokyo for the meeting of the Baptist World Alliance. It was their first trip back to the Orient. The group made stops in Honolulu, Wake Island, Manila, Baguio, Singapore, Bangkok, Hong Kong, and Osaka before arriving in Tokyo. Ruth described their return to the Philippines:

> We were surprised at how dirty and poverty-stricken everything is.... Friday morning five of us left Manila and drove to Baguio. We left at 9:00, got there about 3:00, and started back about 6:00, arriving at 11:00. So it was a hard day, but we saw where we had been interned, the house we lived in, and had tea with the landlord of the house where we lived. It was a sentimental journey that left us awfully sad. It is hard to believe the filth and dirt of Baguio. It was nice, clean, attractive place, but now is squalor and shacks. We just could not believe the difference.
>
> Arriving here in Singapore just heightened the contrast. This place is clean, alive, the people smiling, and poverty is at a minimum. You can say what you please but colonialism is not all bad.[44]

In August Hugo and Ruth attended the Home Mission Weeks at Glorieta and Ridgecrest before moving to Louisville at the end of the month. Hugo's charge to the appointees at the missionary commissioning service at Ridgecrest was one of his last acts at the Home Mission Board, a handing on of the baton to a new generation of home missionaries.

"Charge to Missionary Appointees"

Tonight you are being commissioned as missionaries. You are standing on the threshold of a possibly boundless life. And yet your life will be lived in a time when the night cometh. While the shadows close about us, ushering in the darkness, men—especially young men and women—are questing desperately for meaning. But this does not mean that your message will be

---

[44] Ruth Culpepper, letter to Alan and Jacque Culpepper, 5 July 1970.

popular.... Mission in our world today demands a radically new understanding of ministry. Human society is becoming far more regimented than has ever been necessary before. Any mission effort whose activity is largely identified with that of representative people in ecclesiastical places is going to end up in total bureaucratic captivity, its bounds set and its functions limited by the planners. The mission can only be carried on insofar as the church becomes a divine infection of the whole body of mankind. The *diakonia* of the people of God, the servant-church, must no longer be a bit of Christian theory. It must be earthed; it must be embodied visibly. The times in which we live will permit nothing less! Verbalization of the gospel is not enough; it must become incarnate. Even God could not find a better way!

As missionaries, your ministry must be functional. No longer can you think of it in terms of structure and authority. Your training probably has not completely qualified you to meet what lies ahead. Some of you will need to be *pastors*, exercising the counselor's role concerned with the wholeness of persons. Remember to include the teaching of prayer and the life of holiness which is wholeness. Some of you will be *evangelists*, not in the traditional sense, but in the truer sense of entering into dialogue with unbelievers and of developing a Christian apologetic for the day in which we live. It must include the approach to the people of other faiths and ideologies, the approach to secular humanism (even to the shaking of the foundations of some of the "pillars of the church") and the approach to the thoughtless uncommitted. Some of you will be *prophets* devoted to the service of the secular city through social action and community care. Be ready and alert for the ministry of community-building, of community mobilization, of the fight on behalf of man's humanity amid the structures of technopolis, of the deliberate involvement of the congregation in movements for peace, for civil rights, for integration and in action to deal with neighborhood needs. Though we cannot agree with those who seem to assert that today this is the whole meaning of ministry, we must at least allow that this is a full-time ministry for those who are called to it.

Some of you will be *teachers*, providing leadership for those believers who would grow in grace and the knowledge of God and be able better to give a reason for the faith that is in them.

Some of you will be *apostles* "overseers" (the *episkopé*) for mission. Your oversight will be concerned essentially with the gospel, and only by derivation with the church. You will lead your fellow Christians in service and witness to be as effective as possible. You will be the helmsmen in your area, directing the course of the ship.

In *all* of these functional ministries, you are called to shine as stars in the night. My fear is that the church is changing too late and too slowly *from* what has virtually become one sacred ministry *to* many sacred ministries, *from* a monopoly which is like the sun *to* the multiformity of starlight. That is George Herbert's metaphor, a suitable one for a time when night cometh....

As missionaries, give of yourselves by the grace of God to warm our cold hearts with a redemptive fire—the fire of God's Spirit![45]

Several years later Arthur Rutledge reflected on the significance of Hugo's service to the Home Mission Board:

Rutledge: And another significant move in personnel was to invite Dr. Hugo Culpepper, former foreign missionary and then professor of missions at Louisville, to come to be our director of missions, filling the place that I was vacating. One of the things that attracted me to Dr. Culpepper was...in the area of some of the goals that I wanted to see accomplished, the feeling that though we are an activist oriented agency, and I think we need to be—we are an action oriented people—still I had the feeling that there was a great need for clarity of theological base, clarity of biblical base, for what we were doing. And whatever else he would be able to do, I felt he could help us at understanding our theological base better. He stayed with us five years and then felt that he should go back to the seminary. I think he helped us turn a corner there. But I must say that in addition to his helping us with his biblical insights, and theological insights, that he is a strong administrator. I really wasn't sure he would be as strong an administrator as he was. He was not afraid to face hard questions; he handled the conferences, the planning conferences with state conventions, well. But that was one of our objectives—let's identify our theological bases a little more clearly.

Knight: I remember that he worked hard at that and wrote a number of articles and many of these you still see in many of the planning papers of the denomination.

Rutledge: That's right. Some were written for the denomination as a whole, some for us in-house.

Knight: What was your first contact with him?

Rutledge: Well, my first was way back in college days. I met Hugo when we both were in Baylor, and I met his wife Ruth. They were single people then. We were, I think, in the same class though I think

---

[45] Hugo Culpepper, "Charge to Missionary Appointees," tape recording of presentation at Missions Week, Glorieta, New Mexico, 22 August 1970.

Hugo transferred. He went to a military academy, or naval academy, for at least a year and felt he was called to the ministry, and I think he went to some other school [Ouachita], and then came to Baylor the last two years. But we had no contact in the intervening years until I was on campus in 1964. Of course, I worked alongside him, really under his leadership, that year as a visiting professor, that semester, I mean. So I had a fresh contact in 1964.

Knight: You found out how compatible you were.

Rutledge: I had such great admiration for the man as a man and as a scholar. So when I needed someone to fill the missions place, it seemed to me here was a man with beautiful credentials. I really had mixed feelings. I hated to see him even consider leaving Southern, thought he was needed there, but I felt we needed him, so maybe for him to come and stay five years was a good compromise.

Knight: He found a lot of this kind of frustrating, too, didn't he—the amount of time he had to spend on the road and in these conferences. I remember the pressure of getting around to all those state agreements was pretty heavy on the Division of Missions Director, wasn't it?

Rutledge: Yes, it really was a heavy responsibility. It was when I was in that place. Then year by year it got larger, as our resources increased, it got larger.

Knight: And you were in agreements with more states each year, too, were you not?

Rutledge: Yes. So the job just got very heavy. And as you know, we did some dividing of it after he left, something I think we would have had to do had he stayed on because of the unmanageable nature of it.[46]

At the end of August 1970, grateful for the experiences of the past five and a half years but looking forward to returning to teaching and a more settled life, Hugo and Ruth moved back to Louisville.

---

[46] Arthur Rutledge, interview by Walker Knight, 1975 or 1976.

Chapter 10

Southern Seminary,
1970–1981

"My teaching has been an overflow of my seeking
the knowledge of God."[1]

The move to Louisville marked the beginning of a more settled period for Hugo and Ruth. Hugo could enjoy the life he loved, reading and teaching, and Ruth had her close circle of friends at Crescent Hill Baptist Church and the Crescent Hill Women's Club. As a result, the move from involvement in the day-to-day activities of the Home Mission Board to a more relaxed pace of life allowed Hugo more time for reflection and exploration, and his assignment to develop graduate studies in world religions brought him more directly into dialogue with persons of faith in other religious traditions.

Because of his administrative experience and the esteem in which his faculty colleagues held him, Dean Hull asked Hugo to become the director of professional studies at Southern.[2] The Professional Studies Committee was assigned the responsibility for overseeing all phases of the M.Div. program (the basic three-year degree) and for the design of a new degree program—the Doctor of Ministry, a professional doctorate for ministers. By December of 1971 preliminary information on the new degree program was made available to prospective students.[3]

Hugo was still writing Sunday school lessons for the Sunday School Board when the announcement was made that Dr. Leo Eddleman had been

---

[1] Audio Tape collection.

[2] "Professional Studies Committee Appointed, Will Investigate Doctorate as Basic Degree," *The Tie* (September 1970): 1.

[3] "Information on New D.Min. Degree Now Available to Interested Persons," *The Tie* (December 1971): 8.

appointed as "doctrinal reader" for the Sunday School Board—one of the early steps taken in response to pressure within the Southern Baptist Convention to secure greater control over the content of its literature. Hugo sent copies of the following letter to his editor, to Dr. James L. Sullivan, and to Dr. W. L. Howse.

Dear Mr. _____ :

Since the release of the news item concerning the appointment of a "doctrinal reader" at the Sunday School Board, I have felt uncomfortable with reference to my present writing assignment. You will recall that I am working on the exposition of the Scripture (Acts 13–28) for the Adult and Young People's quarterlies of the Life and Work Curriculum for the third quarter in 1972. Three of these units have been completed and sent to you and you have acknowledged receipt of them. I have ten units yet to write.

I am writing to request specific information as to what procedure you plan to follow. Will my integrity as a writer be respected in the sense that nothing will come out under my signature without my approval of it? I shall not agree to the publishing of anything under my name if changes are made in the manuscript after I have last seen it.

I recognize your right as an editor to determine what your agency will or will not publish. At the same time, as a writer, I expect to have the confidence of your agency as to what I write and also I expect your agency to respect my integrity as a writer in all areas, including doctrinal integrity. I shall have no problem in making suggested modifications in the text where I do not feel that a matter of intellectual integrity is involved. If no theological principle is at stake, or if the question is of uncertain determination, I am quite willing to co-operate in a matter in which any reference is made to a given problem or in the deletion of any such reference. However, I anticipate the possibility of some issue coming up, which in my judgment would be a matter of intellectual integrity and theological principle. I would not be able to conform in such a case. I have too much respect for Baptist heritage and for my freedom as a Baptist to express my convictions regarding the meaning of Scripture. Although I am a Baptist by heritage, by training, and by conviction, it could be that we will come to an impasse on such questions which would make it impossible for me to write for your agency. I do not anticipate this necessarily. It will depend upon the meaning and the manner in which your new policy is implemented.

Personally, I regret very much that this action was taken. I do not think that it is a tenable position for any man to successfully fulfill. I felt that an earlier position of the Sunday School Board was quite firm and defensible. This was the position which answered its critics by saying that this agency sought to serve the Southern Baptist Convention as a whole and that there were differing views within the constituency of the Southern Baptist Convention.

I would appreciate hearing from you at your early convenience regarding these questions which I have raised.

Sincerely yours,

Hugo H. Culpepper[4]

His editor wrote that his response to the appointment of a "doctrinal reader" for the Sunday School Board was similar to Hugo's. He assured Hugo that the doctrinal reader would work with the editor and that as editor he would work with Hugo to resolve any question that might arise. As editor, one of his responsibilities was to ensure the doctrinal integrity of material he approved for publication, so in that respect nothing was changed. He concluded by saying, "We have never selected writers because of supposed theological positions but because of ability in Bible study and competence as writers. However, if all of those who disagree with Dr. Sullivan's decision refuse to write, then our materials would have to be written by persons of only one point of view. This would not be healthy or helpful in the long run for Southern Baptists."[5]

The invitation to preach at Crescent Hill Baptist Church on 27 September 1970 allowed Hugo to return to another of his continuing interests, the promise of eternal life.

"Eternity as a Sunrise"

During my junior year at Baylor University, I was initiated into a national honorary English fraternity—Sigma Tau Delta—along with several other students. We were required to present an original literary composition as a part of the initiation. A fellow student, Louise Harper, read an original poem. While she did not reveal it in the poem, she was thinking of A. J. Armstrong when she wrote it. He was our professor of English, the sponsor of the fraternity and the founder of the Browning Collection. Because of my appreciation of Dr. Armstrong, the poem was meaningful to me in a special sense. But even more than this, the philosophy of life which it expressed "grabbed me" at the moment and has been a life-long influence. The poem began:

I often wondered as I saw you work,

---

[4] Hugo Culpepper, letter to his editor, James Sullivan, and W. L. Howse, 21 September 1970.

[5] Letter from Hugo's editor, 23 September 1970.

If it were life or death

That held you most in bondage.

How true it is that most people live all their lives in bondage—to life or to death! Not just in a superficial sense to the routine of a rat race, but in the sense of a deep, intense fear—a fear which is always there in the background, try as we may to forget it. To whatever extent such a fear controls us, it disqualifies us for the fullest, most creative living!

Job knew what it was to feel the weight of this fear of death. In the fourteenth chapter of the book of Job, he was speaking for all mankind. He depicted man's mortality. One of the tragic dimensions of life is its brevity. Even the longest life is all too brief. The religious rites and beliefs in the ancient Near East cultivated the hope of a resurrection after the grave. But Job spoke bluntly against these attractive illusions, as he saw them. "Man lies down and rises not again," he said. Emil Brunner listed, as one of the axioms of modern man, the statement, "If you are dead, then you *are* dead." Men today have an idea that they know what kind of world they are living in. Death seems to them on the face of it to be fairly conclusive.

But Job was speaking out of the context of the Hebrew religion. The popular Hebrew notion of the so-called "life" after death was that it goes on as being, but it amounts to no more than a dreary sort of not-being. It has been said that the pessimism of the author of Job is more profound than that of any other of the writers of Israel, profounder even than that of Ecclesiastes; for in Job life seems "incurably evil, unbearably sad, atrociously tragic."

The determination with which Job rejects the hope of life after death betrays the fascination that such beliefs exercise on his mind. He rejects them, but he cannot help dwelling upon them a little longer. He gropes toward some assurance of an afterlife, then he rises from the level of meditation to that of warm and intimate dialogue. "O that thou...wouldst...remember me!" This call from person to person enables him to restate his wildly imaginative hope in the form of a question, "If a man die, shall he live again?" This is the cry of anguish from the heart of man, "If a man die, shall he live again?" With all the stored-up yearning of his soul, he reaches out his hands for what his mind has forbidden him. Is the wish father to the thought, or is God father to the wish?

We are reminded of the life-long struggle of Miguel de Unamuno, president of the University of Salamanca at the early age of thirty-seven. The purpose of his major work, *Tragic Sense of Life*, was to draw his reader's attention to "*the* problem." At the very close of the book, he states this purpose in an indirect manner, which at the same time strikingly suggests that usually people try to evade it, when he says, "I took up my pen to distract you for a while from your distractions." In other words, most of what we do in life, he thought, was to distract us from remembering our mortality. One does not read long in *Tragic Sense of Life* before the centrality of the problem becomes emphatic. He says, "I mean the only real vital problem, the problem that strikes at the very root of our being, is the problem of our individual and personal destiny, of the immortality of the soul." As the only "real" problem, it caused Unamuno anguish in his deepest being. He wrote, "The problem of the duration of my soul, of my own soul, tortures me." Death and the uncertainty of any life beyond were ever present with him. Again he said, "This thought that I must die and the enigma of what will come after death is the very palpitation of my consciousness." It was a deep conviction with him that if his soul was not immortal, and the souls of all the rest of men and even everything, then nothing is worthwhile or worth the effort. Life's value is utterly dependent on immortality, he believed. Again he wrote, "If consciousness is, as some inhuman thinker has said, nothing more than a flash of light between two extremities of darkness, then there is nothing more execrable than existence."

Unamuno learned eighteen languages to read philosophy and the religious literature of the world in the original languages as he quested for some sure answer to his problem. The more he read, the more he became convinced that it is not reasonable to expect to live on beyond death. But the more his mind became convinced of this, the more his heart cried out that there must be life beyond death, because he so deeply longed for it to be so. There resulted a tension between mind and heart which he called the tragic sense of life. By this tension he came to live, as though it were his sustaining faith. At least it kept him from despair, he believed. His courage to face up fully to what he called the only real question in our existence was admirable. He challenged us to have the courage to look life and death squarely in the face! He believed in the value of the agony of soul struggle it caused him. His final legacy to us would be, "May God deny you peace, but give you glory!"

The tragedy of his life is that he seems never to have found the answer to his only real problem—and Job's: "If a man die, shall he live again?"

It was the privilege of a humble woman, who lived with her sister and brother in a village near Jerusalem, to hear the answer to this ultimate question from the lips of the Lord of life and death, Jesus said to Martha, "I am the resurrection and the life. The one believing in me, even if he should die, shall live; and everyone living and believing in me shall never die." Martha had been brought face to face with the reality of death. At the moment, her brother was dead and buried. A few days earlier she had hoped that the Master might come and save her brother. But he arrived too late, it seemed.

When the message of the illness of Lazarus reached Jesus, he was away—probably beyond the Jordan River—with his disciples. He deliberately stayed two days longer before going to Bethany. From the moment he heard, Jesus was confident of the outcome. What appeared to be evil, he would change to be good. The disciples feared for his safety, if he went back to the vicinity of Jerusalem. Bethany was only two miles from Jerusalem. Already his enemies were seeking to destroy him. When he determined to go, they were resigned to go with him, even if it meant to die with him.

He arrived and discovered that Lazarus had been buried for four days. Many Jews had come out from Jerusalem to console Mary and Martha. When Martha heard that Jesus was coming, she went out to meet him. Disappointed as she must have been at his late arrival, she still expressed her faith and a message of hope. "Lord, if you had been here, my brother would not have died. And even now I know that whatever you ask God, God will give you." Was it too much to hope still that her brother could be saved? Did she realize what she was saying? Apparently, not fully. When Jesus said to her, "Your brother shall rise again," she thought he meant in the last days at the end of time. She responded with words that she had been taught. "I know that he will arise again in the resurrection at the last day." This was the orthodox theological doctrine of the Pharisees as over against the Sadducees. But really it seemed to be so far in the future that it was of small comfort now. Meanwhile, where was her brother?

One Sunday when I was preaching at a country church in Indiana, the Sunday school lesson was on the life beyond. A lady was teaching the adult class. I soon learned that she had lost her husband a few months earlier. She shared with the class her emotions of the weeks immediately following his death. "I wanted to know where he was now—the man of flesh and bone—the man who sat across the breakfast table from me, and laughed, and lived, and loved!" Even so, it must have been with Martha. The hope of reunion at the last day was but poor consolation for Martha. It was conventional comfort such as she had already had from many of the Jerusalem friends.

The reply of Jesus was unexpected. "*I am the Resurrection and the Life.*" These were startling words! Resurrection was not only future; it was a present possibility. It was not just a doctrine; it was conditional upon a personal relationship. Because he was life in the absolute sense, he was the resurrection. To be in full fellowship with him was to have a quality of life which finds its fullest expression in triumph over death. Jesus substitutes for adherence to dogmatic truth confidence in his person. Anyone having this personal trust in Jesus Christ, even if he should die a physical death now, shall go on living life in the fullest sense of the word. The spirit of this truth was revealed by Edward the Confessor in his last words, "Weep not; I shall not die but live. And as I leave the land of the dying, I trust to see the blessings of the Lord in the land of the living."

But Jesus went on to an even stronger affirmation of the meaning and result of his being the Resurrection and the Life: "Everyone living and believing in me shall *never* die." William Temple saw the depth of meaning here. He said, "Life is a larger word than Resurrection; but Resurrection is, so to speak, the crucial quality of Life.... There is no denial of a general resurrection at the last day; but there is an insistence that for those who are in fellowship with Jesus the life to which that resurrection leads is already present fact. "If a man believes in Him, although his body dies his true self shall live; or, as it may be put in other words, no believer in Jesus shall ever die, so far as his spirit is concerned." Jesus would say to us as to Martha, "Your brother is alive now, for in me he touched the life of God which is eternal; in me, he had already risen before his body perished." This is the meaning of life in Christ.

In other words, whether the gift of eternal life is conceived as a present and continuing possession, or as a recovery of life after death of the body and the end of this world, the thing that matters is that life is the gift of Christ—and Christ's gift to men, we know, is Himself.

Jesus realized the need to explain the nature of eternal life to Martha as clearly and as fully as he could. He wanted to affirm the truth which she had already come to appreciate, "the resurrection at the last day." But even more, he wanted to lead her gently on into fuller understanding of the nature and significance of eternal life as a present possession. Only the experience and possession of this quality of life in the present world could liberate her from the bondage of death and life. Jesus was free on that occasion, even in the presence of death. His desire was for Martha and others to have that same freedom to live fully. But explaining and teaching alone would not bring it to pass. They too must believe and place their trust in him. As John later wrote, "This is eternal life, that they should know thee the only true God, and Jesus Christ whom thou hast sent." Because of this, he came to the point directly and asked her the question to which each of us must ultimately give an answer in our lives: "Do you believe this?" It was a deeply personal question. Only her experience of God in Christ could provide an adequate answer.

Stanley Jones has told of an early experience when he went to India as a missionary. He organized spiritual life retreats—called Ashrams—and took the students aside for several days at a time. He sought to share with them as fully as possible what he had been *taught* about God in Christ. One day a young intellectual looked him straight in the eyes and said, "Tell me what *you* know of God."

The Lord's question to Martha was crucial. On it hung the issue of life or death. So it is with us. Do you *believe* this? Do you *really* believe? Do *you* believe this? Sometimes we give our most honest answers to this question in attitudes expressed when we are caught off guard. On one occasion I was a guest in the home of an uncle. We were seated at the table. Someone mentioned having read of the death of a well-known pastor whom I had known as a truly spiritual minded man. I made the comment, "Death for him must have been a glorious experience. I imagine it was like walking through that door into the immediate presence of the Lord whom he knew so well and loved so much." My uncle was somewhat startled. "Do you really believe that?" he asked. His reaction was a surprise to me. All his life he had been an active church member, a Sunday school teacher, and a deacon. I thought to myself then, "How strange that what he professes to believe seems not to make a real difference." Since then I have lived longer and can empathize more fully with my uncle. But I still have a conviction that death was a glorious experience for my friend.

It was not the intention of Jesus that Martha should come to have a morbid preoccupation with death. Neither is this his desire for us. He came that we might have *life* and have it abundantly! The point of his conversation with Martha was *not* to emphasize death, but rather to emphasize eternal life and the consequent insignificance of death for those believing in him. As close as Martha and her brother and sister had been to Jesus in their friendship, only now did she seem to move *from* assent to the teaching of the Pharisees *to* a personal trust as the basis of an eternal quality of life in the present. And even yet, she relied upon the concepts of her Jewish religion to express this trust. Her answer to Jesus was, "Yes, Lord; I have believed and keep on believing that *you* are the Christ (the Messiah), the Son of God, the one coming into the world." But she was well on her way. She was growing in grace and the knowledge of God.

So it is with us. We do not begin the Christian pilgrimage as fully mature disciples. We are learners. We must go to school in God's school of life. We catch visions of inspired hope, but then at times we are lost in the darkness for a while. As Robert Browning wrote in "Bishop Blougram's Apology":

> Just when we are safest, there's a sunset touch,
> A fancy from a flower-bell, someone's death,
> A chorus-ending from Euripides,—
> And that's enough for fifty hopes and fears
> As old and new at once as nature's self,
> To rap and knock and enter in our soul.

And so we must turn our eyes once again to the Lord and look steadfastly enough to see life in the context of eternity. But we can grow in grace and knowledge of God to the point that we can have a steady assurance, a clarity of vision, an expectant hope. Life can become an exciting experience of living each day fully free, captive neither to the past nor the future. Then God can use us more fully in serving others and in bringing them to know him. We awake to welcome each day as a bright new challenge for creative living. We live on the tiptoes of expectancy!

I think this is what Louise Harper's poem went on to say:

> I often wondered as I saw you work,
> If it were life or death
> That held you most in bondage;
> But now I think I know:
> For such as you,
> Life has no day or night,
> No end and no beginning;
> But all is one great dawn
> That sees in golden glory
> Eternity as a sunrise![6]

Just a week later, on 5 October 1970, Hugo's father died. Hugo drove to Little Rock to accompany his mother, sister, and extended family on to Pine Bluff, where he conducted the funeral service. For Scripture readings he selected 1 John 3:1-2; 4:7-19; 1 Corinthians 13:1-13; John 14:1-7, 25-27. Then he spoke on the promise of life in Christ in John 11:25-27 and concluded with 1 Thessalonians 4:13-18. Afterward he said that speaking at his father's funeral was much more difficult than he had anticipated. The following March Hugo returned to Pine Bluff to conduct the funeral service for his aunt, who died from burns she received when her robe caught fire from a space heater in her home.

On 1 February 1972, Hugo gave his faculty address, titled "Missions in the Twentieth Century: A Perspective in the Theology of Missions," in which he articulated the understanding of missions he had come to over the years. While developing his long-term interest in the theology of missions, Hugo also found a new challenge in studying and teaching on the major world religion, as he related in a letter:

---

[6] Hugo Culpepper, "Eternity as a Sunrise," sermon preached at Crescent Hill Baptist Church, 27 September 1970.

Tomorrow morning I am speaking to the international students at the Tuesday 10:00 A.M. meeting of state groups here on campus on the assigned subject: 'Salvation in non-Christian Countries.' A South African student and Dickson Yagi will then serve on a panel with me on the subject. I am enjoying the World Religions class. We have 29 students. I'm using Ninian Smart, *The Religious Experience of Mankind,* and Robert Ballou's *Portable World Bible* (sacred writings of the religions) for the texts."[7]

Hugo continued speaking at conferences and preaching as he had opportunities to do so. Hugo and Ruth also enjoyed the friendship of other faculty couples and joined a discussion group composed of Findley and Louvenia Edge, Hugh and Ruth McElrath, Wayne and Mary Ann Ward, Eric and Helen Rust, and Frank and Evelyn Stagg. Work on the D.Min. continued to take a great deal of Hugo's time. In the spring of 1972, before the inauguration of the new degree program that fall, Ruth wrote, "There is still a great deal of faculty reservation and opposition to the D.Min. degree. How Daddy has been able to ride it out and work with it, I don't know."[8]

The Center for the Study of World Religions at Harvard

In the spring of 1972 Hugo and Ruth finalized plans for his sabbatical leave the following year. After a great deal of investigation, and with the encouragement of his former student John Ross Carter, Hugo decided to spend the year at the Center for the Study of World Religions at Harvard. Because housing there was so expensive, Hugo and Ruth bought a travel trailer, pulled it to Boston, vacationing along the way, and lived in it that year. Ruth worked in the admissions office of Harvard University Business School, and they enjoyed the fellowship of the Metropolitan Baptist Church.

The sabbatical experience proved to be both intellectually and spiritually stimulating as Hugo immersed himself in reading and dialogue with persons of faith from various religious traditions. During the fall he studied Sanskrit in order to learn some of the vocabulary one finds in the Buddhist and Hindu literature of India. At mid-year, he sent Dean Hull an interim report on his experience in Boston.

---

[7] Hugo Culpepper, letter to Alan and Jacque Culpepper, 15 February 1971.

[8] Ruth Culpepper, letter to Alan and Jacque Culpepper, n.d.

During the two weeks before the fall semester began, we took in as many of the Boston cultural and scenic opportunities as possible. Ruth was apprehensive of getting cabin fever once I got involved in my studies. She secured a job in the Admissions Office of the Harvard Business School. This has been a pleasant setting and an interesting experience for her. We are conveniently located in Peabody near the inner loop just forty-five minutes from Harvard via 128 and 93. The distance is twenty miles, which is about average for commuting in this area. We leave the trailer at 8:00 A.M. and return at 6:00 P.M. five days a week.

On September 21, I registered as a Visiting Scholar at Harvard Divinity School. This gives me access to all lectures, classes, and facilities at the Divinity School, and Harvard University, as well as the seven other institutions participating in the Boston Theological Institute. In addition to the B. T. I., this educational environment includes Boston College, M. I. T., Boston University, Brandeis University, Northeastern University, Tufts University and Wellesley College. The theological collections of the libraries total about 1,500,000 volumes. In all probability there is no academic and theological center in the world which offers more resources than those included within this complex.

An important part of the Divinity School is the Center for the Study of World Religions. The Center was established in 1958 to encourage the pursuit of a coordinated study and understanding of different religions and historical traditions. It is particularly concerned with the relationships between various religious communities in both practice and theory, past and present, and with the religiousness of men in its varieties. The small residence center has about twenty furnished apartments. Half of these are occupied by internationals and the other half by American Ph.D. students. This year we have in residence, among others, a Theravada Buddhist University professor from Ceylon, a Hindu University professor from India, a Jewish rabbi, a Chinese Christian girl from Taiwan working on a Ph.D. in Buddhism, a Muslim professor from the Near East, a Ph.D. student from Israel, a Hindu student from India majoring in Christianity, several Chinese, Japanese, and Korean students, and others making a total of about fifty in the community. Every Wednesday night we have a two-hour colloquium at the Center covering a wide range of subjects in the field.

In my academic pursuits I have an in-depth study of Buddhism with Professor Masatoshi Nagatomi, a Japanese Buddhist and Professor of Buddhist Studies at Harvard University. He is located in the Yenching Institute of Far Eastern Studies on the University campus. Professor Wilfred Cantwell Smith is Director of the Center, Professor of World Religions, and Chairman of the Committee on Higher Degrees in Religion at the University. He is a recognized international authority in Islam. I am studying with him in a general course on World Religions for purposes of bibliography and methodology. My study of Hinduism, in comparison with Buddhism, is directed by Professor John B. Carman, born and reared in India, and Professor of Comparative Religion. Last fall I studied Sanskrit with Professor Daniel H. H. Ingalls, the Wales Professor of Sanskrit at the University. This spring I have a seminar on Christianity and Traditional African Religions with Visiting Professor John S. Mbiti, from the Makerere University in Kampala, Uganda. For relaxation and to keep in touch with Christianity for a balance of perspective, I am doing the New Testament graduate seminar under the direction of Dean Krister Stendahl, assisted by the entire faculty of the New Testament department. We are doing an exegetical study of Romans with papers on related subjects.

I have a carrel in the stacks of Andover Library at the Divinity School where I study all my free hours. In my personal emphasis, the focus of my research is on World Religions and the Christian Faith. This helps to relate all my work to missions.

This is the most intellectually challenging year of my life. But the greatest single value of a sabbatical, as I am experiencing it, is the feel of being lifted to an objective perspective. What really matters is more clearly seen. The stimulus of new friends in different settings is exhilarating.

It was exciting to participate in a discussion at the Divinity School in the lounge on World Religions and the Christian Faith. Harvey Cox presented Alan Watts, who led the discussion with Leonard Bernstein seated on the floor at his feet: I have participated in weekend colloquia on missions at Harvard Divinity School, Gordon Conwell College, and the Greek Orthodox Seminary here. The theme was "Salvation Today." Among other resource personnel were George E. Wright and Avery Dulles. Ecumenical fellowship with the professors of missions at Boston University School of Theology and St. Johns Catholic Seminary has taken me to those two institutions....

We are grateful to the Trustees and the Administration for this sabbatical which has been so full of meaningful experiences. When we return in August, it will be with new energy and deepened devotion to our vocation.[9]

As he related to Alan and Jacque, the experience was driving him to raise probing questions about the relationship between Christianity and other religious faiths.

---

[9] Hugo Culpepper, letter to William Hull, 14 February 1973.

I am very pleased that we came here. I think I am going to get some value out of it. The first, most immediate thing is that I had my introduction to a much broader bibliography on a selective basis in the literature of world religions. I have bought a copy of a good many of these books and plan to read and underline as many of them as I can this year, and will work a lot of the material into the reworking of my courses in World Religions. That is the main objective I have for the year's work here....

Another whole area is the Center for the Study of World Religions, where they have about forty or so international students from all of the various religions, and we are finding the two-hour colloquia on Wednesday evenings very interesting there and the fellowship of the people, their viewpoints, and so forth. I go over some and talk with them in their rooms and visit there some also during the week....

I was talking about my studies here. In addition to surveying the field of World Religion, reading as widely and deeply in it as I can, with major emphasis on Hinduism and Buddhism, and to a lesser extent Islam, I am also very much interested in the question of the relation of world religions and the Christian faith, wrestling with the problem in what sense can you recognize a valid and possibly even salvific revelation in other religions, recognizing that there is one God of the universe, and if He has been at work in other religions in any meaningful salvific way for other men, how can you relate that and reconcile it to the uniqueness of the revelation of God in Jesus Christ without sacrificing something essential in the Christian faith on the one hand. The problem on the other hand is if you take an exclusivistic view and say there is revelation only in Jesus Christ and no revelatory truth in other religions, then you have a very difficult problem as to your idea of God in terms of the problem of theodicy—the justification of the ways of God with man in view of the long centuries and cultures and civilizations who have never known of or been related to the Christian faith. It is a very difficult problem on either side, and I am very much interested in the literature on this problem and wrestling with the problem afterwards in my own thinking.[10]

As usual, Hugo maintained his exercise regimen:

Preached last Sunday in the church here. Also celebrated my 60th [birthday] by taking a good barbell workout in the weight room of the Harvard gym. I did 12 exercises first for the full routine, including 20 rapid squats with

---

[10] Hugo Culpepper, tape recording sent to Alan and Jacque Culpepper, dictated 5 November 1972.

105 pounds in 52 seconds to work my pulse up to 145 per second just like jogging for three miles but only momentarily instead of sustained for 15 minutes or so. Then, just to see how a 60-year old compared with earlier years, I did three squats with 200 pounds and a press with 135 pounds. So, I guess I can manage to get around for a few more years![11]

Early in the spring, Hugo requested to be relieved of his duties as director of professional studies when he returned to Southern so that he could spend more time developing courses at the graduate level in world religions, and his request was granted. His suggestion that the Christian Missions and World Religions Department be moved to the Historical/Theological Division was received less positively because of the fear that it would be perceived as a move away from nourishing a missionary commitment on the seminary campus.

The Wednesday colloquia for the spring continued to be diverse and stimulating: Last night we stayed in for supper, and Mother went to a baby shower for the international new mothers at the Center for the Study of World Religions. This is the first night we have been home for some time. It feels strange—but good. Tomorrow we stay in for the usual Wednesday night Center program. It will be a film on "Chinese Ghost Festivals in Urban Hong Kong" with comments by Whalen Lai. On March 21, Professor Charlotte Vaudeville of Paris will lecture on "Popular Lyrical Poetry in Indian Literature." Monday, Tuesday, and Wednesday at 4:00 P.M. in the church in the Harvard Yard, Professor Raymond Panikkar of India will give three Noble Lectures on the general subject: "The Supername: The Idolatry of the Name and the Apostasy of the Silence." The title of the three lectures will be: (1) The Myth: Salvation, (2) The World: Christ, and (3) The Spirit: Life.... On March 29, a professor from Tehran will lecture. On April 11, a Theravada Buddhist from Ceylon who is living at the Center this spring, Professor Palihawadana, will lecture on "Is There a Theravada Notion Comparable with Grace?" On April 18, Huston Smith, of MIT, and soon going to University of Syracuse as Professor of Religion (changing from philosophy, which he thinks is sterile since linguistic analysis took over), will lead a discussion on "How and Why of Comparative Religion." On April 25, Prof. V. A. Devasenapathi of Madras, India, will lecture on "Of Human Bondage and Divine Grace," which is the title of a book he wrote. This gives you a rundown of what we have in store.[12]

---

[11] Hugo Culpepper, letter to Alan and Jacque Culpepper, 7 January 1973.
[12] Hugo Culpepper, letter to Alan and Jacque Culpepper, 13 March 1973.

When the possibility of a teaching job opened for Alan at Atlanta Baptist College, which had just recently merged with Mercer, Hugo wrote reflective advice:

It has been 72 hours since you phoned us about the possibility of something opening up in Atlanta. I have had time to reflect at bit on it and thought I would share my thoughts as you requested. It seems to me that by far the most important thing about the situation is the question of how this step would fit in with your vocational perspective. I do not mean that you should attempt to lay out a chess plan for your life and adhere strictly to that. I mean how much satisfaction would you find by doing the best job possible in that setting on an open-ended basis? Fifty majors in religion is no mean challenge in terms of life values. You would have a wide open opportunity to share the best you have found thus far along life's way with these who have not traveled quite so long and not so far as you have. Will that be rewarding enough to balance some other considerations?...

I think you are right in the possibility that taking this [position] would cast your lot toward denominational schools. There would be satisfactions and rewards in this. From observation here this year, I can see that university teaching is more impersonal (with colleagues and students) than [at] denominational schools. Inter-personal relations would be richer, and you would find more community in the long run in denominational schools, I think. At the same time, you will have more of a problem of "being all things to all people" in their expectations of you. You will sacrifice some measure of freedom of expression and initiative, but it can be handled and still maintain your integrity.

In any setting, the opportunity and achieving of excellence of work will be largely a matter of self-discipline.... You are *who* you are, wherever you are....

I would suggest you seek the counsel of the men there if the offer is made and see what their advice would be to you: Smith, Davies, Young, etc. They know you well, and they have a larger view of the academic scene from a different perspective than I do.[13]

While the situation was still developing at Atlanta Baptist, Alan received an invitation to explore an opening in the New Testament Department at Southern Seminary. By early in May he had accepted the position at Southern, to begin in February 1974. That same spring Larry graduated

---

[13] Hugo Culpepper, letter to Alan and Jacque Culpepper, 20 March 1973.

from Baylor Medical School and moved to do his internship at the Montefiore Hospital in New York. Alan wrote, "Behind every Watergate is a Millhouse." Hugo responded, "Impeach with honor!"[14]

From 17 June to 6 July 1973, Hugo participated in the summer workshop of the Case-Study Institute in Cambridge, Massachusetts, learning to use case studies effectively in teaching. The following week Hugo and Ruth left Boston, pulling their travel trailer across the country: Chicago, the Badlands, Cody, Yellowstone Park, the Grand Tetons, Salt Lake City, Bryce and Zion Canyons, the Grand Canyon, Flagstaff, Albuquerque, and on to Glorieta—getting almost seven miles to the gallon! At Glorieta, Hugo gave the keynote address, titled "Pass the Bread," on opening night of Foreign Mission Week, in one part of which he offered the following assessment of the challenge facing the church:

We live in a world of clashing ideologies, of conflicting value systems, of moral decay, of social disintegration, and contrasting lifestyles. In the long view of history, the world is struggling *to recover* the community of the Middle Ages *and*, at the same time, conserve the value of the individual, as recognized since the Renaissance, and *to synthesize* them into a unity. There will be further casualties in the fall of civilizations as the process continues. As America approaches her 200th anniversary, relatively young for a country, increasingly the question is being asked, "Do we have a future?" There is little real community in the basic sense of "having values in common." Provincialism is dominant. As a religious body, Southern Baptists run the risk of provincialism. There is a real danger that we will not become aware of the kind of world we are living in, of peoples of other cultures and religions and of how to relate to them. We may spend our little moment up on the stage of time, strutting with pride because of our size and resources and glorying in superficial achievements! To really be aware of the world is to recognize the deep hunger of people for meaning, purpose, values, direction, in the existence that for too many is empty struggle. In this kind of world, what is our task?

First of all, we are called to *be*—to be God's people. This involves a mission. It is God's mission. But he has entrusted it to the church as the people of God and the body of Christ. Indeed, the church becomes the mission. The *mission* of the church is to glorify God by leading people to know him through faith in Jesus Christ. Our mission is to reveal who God is, in his

---

[14] Alan Culpepper, letter to Hugo Culpepper, 10 May 1973; Hugo Culpepper, letter to Alan, 15 May 1973.

deepest character, and what he is like. In a sense, as W. O. Carver said, we are to become continuations of the incarnation of Jesus Christ. As people trust Jesus and commit themselves to him as Lord, they come to an experiential knowledge of God. God is made known—he is glorified. The meaning of life is to live for the glory of God.

If this is the nature of *God's People*, it involves them in God's purpose. This involvement leads to missions. *Missions* is what the church does to achieve its mission in areas of human need on the growing edge of its confrontation with the non-Christian world. The task of the church is to achieve its mission. Therefore, missions become its guiding principle and controlling activity.[15]

The Ad Hoc Advisory Committee

Hugo's return from sabbatical was anything but tranquil. In the fall of 1973, growing tension between the faculty and the administration of the seminary reached a point at which faculty morale was so low that some were beginning to talk about a recurrence of the kind of conflict that led to the resignations of thirteen faculty members in 1958. On 26 November 1973, the Faculty Affairs Committee submitted a report to the joint faculty and the president with the following addendum:

In a called meeting of the committee which lasted for more than two hours this morning, attention was given to the problem of faculty morale. An effort was made to analyze the nature and cause of the problem of low morale. It is the judgment of the committee that the basic problem is long standing and extends back over a period of fifteen or twenty years. This relates to administrative philosophy and style. As illustrative in the School of Theology, there has been a trend during this period for the locus of authority, and therefore responsibility, to move from departments to divisions and more recently to standing committees, which function somewhere in the area between divisions and the administration. In the spring of 1972 a trustee advised the Joint Faculty in a called meeting of a change in procedure for selecting faculty additions. This was vigorously resisted by members of the faculty, but without effect. To the faculty this was a climactic symbolizing of the shift of involvement from faculty to administration. It provoked a strong reaction

---

[15] Hugo Culpepper, "Pass the bread," tape recording of presentation at Missions Week, Glorieta, New Mexico, 1973.

among faculty members resulting in the feeling of non-involvement in the area of significant decisions which vitally affect the life of the institution and their personal lives and work. Faculty members, while still under the shock of this sudden shift in policy, seemed to react with an attitude of everyone withdrawing to "sit under his own vineyard" and do his work as an individual to find what satisfaction he could.

Simultaneously accompanying this trend during the last couple of years, the faculty has felt that increasing emphasis has been placed on administration, as evidenced by facilities, number of administrative personnel, etc., while the needs, requests, and concerns of the faculty have received little response. There have been numerous other problems, differing from one faculty member to another, but the Faculty Affairs Committee feels that the above analysis is basic to the present problem of low faculty morale.

We share this statement with the Joint Faculty requesting your reaction, both corporately and individually, as you may desire. The committee needs the positive expression of the faculty regarding the nature and cause of low faculty morale in order to represent you faithfully as a Faculty Affairs Committee.

Respectfully submitted,
Hugo Culpepper
Secretary of the Faculty Affairs Committee

In response, President McCall called for the formation of an Ad Hoc Advisory Committee and gave the faculty the following instructions regarding the selection of faculty for this committee: "You are therefore asked to return no later than Monday, December 10, the enclosed sheet nominating seven members for such an Advisory Committee. The first person you list will receive the equivalent of seven units, the second person will receive six, etc. The person receiving the highest number of units will be the chairman. Of the other six, at least one shall be from the School of Church Music and one from the School of Religious Education."[16]

By this process, his colleagues selected Hugo to chair the Ad Hoc Advisory Committee. E. Glenn Hinson was the secretary, and the other members were Findley Edge, Clyde Francisco, Hugh McElrath, J. J. Owens, and Frank Stagg. The next day, Hugo wrote the following account of the

---

[16] Duke McCall, memo to the Joint Faculty regarding "Called Faculty Meeting, Thursday, December 20, Gheens Hall, 9:00 A.M." The memo began: "This may be the most important faculty meeting in terms of the future of Southern Seminary you will be asked to attend."

events to Alan and Jacque (giving more confidential information than he otherwise would have because within a matter of weeks Alan would be assuming his position on the faculty):

Dear Alan and Jacque,

Last Monday morning the faculty affairs committee met for over 2 hours. Dr. Oates resigned from the committee as a "lame duck" [He had recently resigned from the seminary faculty.] In the discussion I suggested my analysis as to the nature and cause of "low faculty morale," as expressed in relation to Oates' resignation and Hinson's consideration of it. In a word it was a trend through the years of gradual loss of faculty involvement in decision-making that involved the life of the institution. The committee asked me to write it up during the noon hour and read it to the committee at 2 P.M. They made one deletion of a sentence that spoke of faculty members feeling like "second-class citizens." They introduced a phrase at the beginning of a sentence that made it apply to the three schools of the seminary and not just to the School of Theology. And, they inserted a very significant sentence to more sharply focus the cause as being "the philosophy and style of administration." This happened to be inserted near the point where I had spoken of the gradual trend as being over the "last 15 or 20 years." The committee asked me to read the statement at the Joint Faculty meeting at 2:30 P.M. that day. The purpose was to elicit the view of the faculty by inviting reaction to the statement so the committee could more accurately represent the faculty in working with the administration and trustees.

Dr. McCall was presiding when I read the paper. Dr. Edge moved its approval. The vote had only one negative and that was Dr. Allen Graves. I had to leave then to catch a plane to Atlanta. When I got back, I learned that later on the agenda under misc. items was an administration proposal to set up the proposed Boyce School as a fourth school in the seminary. It turns out that McCall had not wanted to bring this up, but Graves had insisted and persuaded him to do it at the last minute. It was a classic example of non-involvement of faculty and provoked much discussion, I am told, with such questions as "Does the faculty have a part in this decision?"

Yesterday morning as I was walking down the hall past the president's office he happened to be standing there talking with a student. Just as I passed he terminated the conversation with the student and asked me if I had a minute. We went into his office and talked for one and a quarter hours I "exegeted" the statement to him, so he would understand how it came to be, etc. He understands that I am not emotionally involved in the matter but am serving as a faculty member discharging my responsibilities on the faculty, and that I do not intend to be used by any other faculty members with different views to press, nor do I intend to be drawn into anything by administration or trustees, but rather will try to remain objective and "be my own man." At the same time, I can see his point that the faculty and committee will have to explain more fully what they mean by "philosophy and style of administration" and by the last "15 or 20 years." He points out that it will be applied by some in such as way as to be related to the '58 controversy: 15 years ago was 1958, and 20 years ago was the beginning of his administration. Also he points out that the mention of "trustee" by me in relation to the change of procedure for faculty additions will bring the trustees alongside the administration as over against the faculty. He is apprehensive that the first steps have been taken toward a renewal of something like the '58 controversy. I pointed out that there is no T. D. Price in the picture to pressure faculty conformance, etc. We parted understanding each other and with mutual goodwill.[17]

Over the next six months, Hugo and the other members of the Ad Hoc Advisory Committee met weekly and worked with the president and the faculty on a number of issues related particularly to the faculty's role in faculty appointments and the granting of tenure and promotions. As late as 20 May, the committee and the administration were still at an impasse. The president rejected the committee's proposal regarding rank-to-rank promotions and dissolved the committee because he felt that no useful purpose would be served by their continuing to meet. He then requested that the faculty reaffirm or rescind the addendum of 26 November 1973. Owens, Hinson, and Culpepper met with the president again on 28 May, with no progress. When the committee met again the next day, Owens presented the first draft of a proposal. The committee reworked it. Owens, Moody, and Culpepper presented it to the president later that day, and agreement was reached with limited revision. Harmony was reestablished. Owens and Culpepper reported to the committee late that afternoon, and the committee voted unanimously to approve the proposal as revised in conference with the president. The next day, 30 May 1974, the faculty adopted the report of the Faculty Affairs Committee that rescinded the statement of 26 November 1973, affirming that "some of the causes of faculty morale problems have subsequently been discussed fully and openly by the Ad Hoc Advisory Committee and the Joint Faculty" and that many of them had been resolved. Other items were referred to standing committees. The report concluded:

---

[17] Hugo Culpepper, letter to Alan and Jacque Culpepper, 1 December 1973.

We affirm the work of the President and the Ad Hoc Advisory Committee. Conversations between the President and the Ad Hoc Committee, though dealing with difficult and complex issues, were positive and profitable. We feel that both the President and the Ad Hoc Committee acted with openness and integrity in these meetings. Unfortunately, due to the difficulty of the issues, they were able to report out only a few issues for consideration and action by the Joint Faculty. We want, therefore, to affirm the spirit of cooperation and mutual trust that the issues assigned to the various committees will continue to be dealt with, by each Committee and others who may be involved, in the same spirit of cooperation and mutual trust.

A crisis had been averted, but just barely. The process had been difficult, but agreements were reached that allowed the faculty to have a greater role in faculty appointments and promotion and that fostered more consultation and cooperation between the faculty and the administration in the following years.

Alan and Jacque moved to Louisville at the end of January 1974, so except on rare occasions there was no need for written correspondence with Hugo and Ruth from that point on. On the other hand, the four enjoyed living near each other and sharing their work at Southern Seminary. In March Hugo and Ruth moved to a new home near where Alan and Jacque had located. On 3 April 1974, Louisville was hit by a devastating tornado, and the whole community spent the next several weeks cleaning up from the storm. On 24 May, Erin Lynn Culpepper was joyfully received into the family—Hugo and Ruth's first grandchild.

Hugo with Erin, 1975.

The importance of the implications of religious pluralism for Christians was becoming the cutting edge of Hugo's thinking, as he reflected on the significance of his sabbatical experience at the Center for the Study of World Religions, as the following statement illustrates:

As we think of bold new plans for missions, we should look beyond the immediate future to the end of the century and on. We must also broaden the spectrum of our thinking to include the experiences and wisdom of others beyond our own tradition. Rich as our heritage is, we need to tear down the walls that may separate us from an understanding appreciation of what God is doing through others in our time. In our kind of world, increasingly pluralistic as it is, we must dare to raise the windows and let the fresh breezes of God's spirit blow through our souls. God has not given up on persons anywhere. We must not "stiff-arm" others (and their views) in whom God is also at work in our world for its redemption. God is at work in other people, other traditions, and other structures. May he give us the vision to see where he is going and the spirit to work with him and his people to be used in his redemptive purpose for his glory!"[18]

Hugo found fulfillment in the balance of life during this period, the stimulation of students and colleagues, time for reading and exercise, and opportunities to preach and speak at conferences. Hugo especially enjoyed teaching a Sunday school class of questing young adults at Crescent Hill Baptist Church. In April of 1976, Hugo's mother died. The following month the family celebrated the birth of Rodney Alan Culpepper on 24 May 1976.

Hugo continued to develop his interest in world religions and the relationship between Christianity and other religious faiths. A tape of a lecture he gave on religious pluralism for the Continuing Theological Education Conference at Southern in October 1977, ends with the comments made extemporaneously during the dialogue after the lecture:

I just read, earlier in the morning, a letter written by a missionary in Bangladesh...in which he is raising the question as a missionary in the mission in Bangladesh as to whether what they are doing there all adds up to anything, or is accomplishing anything. He is simply saying that the lifestyle of the missionaries there in the institutional approach and the whole history of missions in that area among the Bengali, going clear back to William Carey—William Carey made a significant contribution, but he began thorough-

---

[18] Hugo Culpepper, *Missionary Intercom*, 10, 3 (March 1975): 1.

goingly institutional mission work. It has come down to what they are doing—activities giving expression to the subsidizing of what is going on through funds from another country. They are hiring people when they become Christians, and getting them a job, and involving themselves in a lot of institutional work and activity, but the spontaneity of the proclamation and receiving of the gospel as a revolutionary spiritual power in an indigenous lay movement simply has not caught on. Max Warren had this in mind, I think, when he said, "We have walked around Jericho, and the walls have not collapsed."

And I must confess that I think there is just basis for a lot of this criticism. I can't help but feel that if the Lord's will is ever going to be done in our world it is going to have to come with a revolutionary understanding of the nature and mission of the church, within our own selves, within our own communities, our own churches, and our own denominations, and unto the ends of the earth. I have said this most any place I have been in recent years. I said it to the study committee on the Bold Mission Task. When I first heard the concept of Bold Missions, I was excited because always there is hope for some progress, but when I stopped to realize it, I was not too excited. I had mixed feelings because, knowing us as I do, having sat where we sit in the planning councils of our denomination, I realized that probably it will result in the sifting of papers, a reshuffling of everything that is out there, and really we are having to come up with a new angle and emphasis and so forth, but it would be doing the same old thing.

Quite frankly, it seemed to me that if we as a denomination which is unique in the sense that we have for the first time in world history—it is the first time that any people who call themselves the people of God have ever had the tremendous material and personnel resources that Southern Baptists have at their disposition today. I think that what will have to be done before we will have any revolutionary impact upon our world will be to re-educate our whole constituency as to what the Christian faith is all about. Now, it is just that thorough-going and that deep. And you cannot be too optimistic at the feasibility of doing it....

Let me go on and comment in the context of this that while what I have said may add up to...negativism, I do not intend it to be that. I intend it to be the effort to be realistic in an analytical posture. I think within myself the fact that I keep on keeping on is not attributed to any disposition on my part but what ultimately for all of us is the fact that something beyond ourselves has laid hold of us, and ultimately we don't have a option here. We are simply crying out in the dark, but we are not on our own. We have been apprehended by God, and this is where the anchorage of my own life is. I have no option here. I think this what Paul meant when he spoke of being a slave to the Lord, and so while we are crying in the dark in the interest of realism, we are laid hold of by something beyond ourselves, and we keep on keeping on....

I suppose the thing I am most grateful for in my own personal, spiritual pilgrimage, in coming back to the Seminary in September of 1970...I was requested as one of the aspects of my returning here, that somebody in the Department of Missions would specialize in World Religions. I had the opportunity to give a year in doing this in '72–'73, and since then I have been rather constantly reading the scriptures and literature of other religions. Along with it I have tried to continue to read a chapter in the Greek New Testament each day, realizing that I need to counterbalance experientially the impact of the exposure of myself to these other traditions by the anchorage of my soul here. I have tried to open up and dare to look, and I think as a result of that [I have changed my understanding of] what before has been almost an exclusive emphasis in my teaching on the Heilsgeshichte, or salvation history from the viewpoint of Oscar Cullmann, of the particularistic and almost exclusive way in which God was working in our world. I have come to appreciate greatly the universal dimension, not in the sense of theological universalism—I am not a theological universalist because I take seriously the freedom of man, and I think man can say no to God. I think God limited himself when he made man free so that God is conditioned, and therefore I think there are men who are making evil their good and who are losing the power of discrimination, and who are drifting in the direction of ultimate, eternal alienation and separation from God. But I think God is the God of all the universe in a way that I did not appreciate a few years back. I think that he is the creator and sustainer of the life of all men. I think he continues to have this loving concern to try to get through to all mankind, and I think he is trying to do it in the world in a larger sense than just our structured, church approach, though he is still working with all of his resources in that direction....

I have come to take more seriously the potential of general revelation. I have come to think in terms of what we mean by Christian salvation, from the Johannine viewpoint largely. I am no longer particularly helped by the Pauline metaphors, which seem to me to be a status sort of thing, where through transaction you are moved from one status to another status in the sight of God. I have come to think more in terms of what happens to one when he comes and returns from the prodigal-son relation to God back into the family of God. What is it that happens? There must be some response, some assimilation, some change in one, if salvation is to mean anything. And I have come to see that through all the approaches of general revelation that the God of all the universe who is concerned for all mankind might be able to make there is conceivably the possibility of man encountering God through some other channels, so that I have left open the possibility of the knowledge of God coming through to all mankind in a way that formerly I would not have recognized perhaps and certainly not emphasized.

I find the locus of my emphasis in John 17:3, "This is eternal life (as a quality of life) that they (that is man, men) should know thee (that's *ginosko*, experiential knowledge), the only true God, and him whom thou dost send, even Jesus Christ." And so I think of salvation in terms of knowledge, in terms of the capacity to appreciate, to esteem, to be comfortable in the presence of God. I am much less concerned that I be rigid in trying to say how God can get through to men and how he cannot get through. I am wanting to be open enough to affirm what I see as evidence, and I am chagrined and embarrassed when I have to recognize that I have met people of other traditions...who have a quality of faith from their traditions, whereas there are many among us who profess a lot of things but who live like the devil, to be bluntly candid about it, and in whom I do not see evidences of the fruits of the spirit.

This is a very shaking perspective of realism, and so I am much less rigid, but you know the thing that is the anchorage of my soul—I still have a very high Christology. I really believe God was in Christ. If ever I lose that conviction, you can say he has cut the anchorage, he is adrift as a derelict upon the high seas of relativism, but as long as I have in the depth of my soul the conviction that God really was in Christ, then I conceive of myself as thorough-goingly Christian.... I keep on trying to look into the face of Christ through my Greek New Testament, all the while I am reading the Koran, Analects of Confucious, and these other literatures, and it is a great, exciting pilgrimage.

So really I guess all I am suggesting here is that it is time for us as pastors, in whatever opportunity we can, to begin to lead our people to some preparedness for this sort of pluralistic setting because I think here is where the mission of the church is going to have to be carried out in the years to come.[19]

Among the many students Hugo worked with, two with whom he cultivated a particularly close relationship at this time were Charles Kimball (who did his Ph.D. in world religions at Harvard) and Wayne Nicholson (who did his doctoral work at Southern under Hugo's direction). In a letter to Kimball, who was studying at Harvard at the time, he gave the following report of his work at Southern.

---

[19] From the dialogue following Hugo Culpepper's lecture on "Religious Pluralism: Christian Faith and World Religions," for "CTEC—The Mission of Your Church," Southern Baptist Theological Seminary, 17–20 October 1977.

We are making progress so far as student interest goes in the area of World Religions here. I have a good class in WR 141B this fall. At the present time three or four graduate students begin their study at mid-year with World Religions being one of their areas of study. They are all majors in Christian Missions with World Religions being one of the areas within the division. There are also two or three other students who are looking toward majoring in the area of World Religions within the next year or so. One or two of them begin next September. Wayne Nicholson continues to do exceedingly well in his program of study. I am very pleased with his progress. At the present time he is giving consideration to the following subject for his dissertation: "Religion and Faith: A Comparative Study of the Thought of Mircea Eliade, Karl Barth, and Wilfred Cantwell Smith." Dr. Smith might be interested in knowing that one of our students here is giving consideration to such a topic![20]

A letter from Wayne Nicholson expresses appreciation for the way Hugo had invested himself in him.

> Dear Dr. Culpepper:
> I want to express my deep appreciation to you for all the help and encouragement that you have given to me over these recent years. I shall never forget the countless hours we spent in your office exploring the lofty and sublime, as well as intricate and sometimes abstruse, thoughts of men about God and the universe. As I look back over the time that I spent in study under your careful supervision, I can see a change in my life for the better. I have matured, I think, both academically and spiritually. I still remember the conversation we had before I took the entrance examination in which you cautioned me about the difficulty and risk of such a study. Now at the end of my course of study I can appreciate the timeliness of your counsel and would wish only to assure you that while there were periods of perplexity my faith in God and appreciation of my religious tradition have been immeasurably strengthened and deepened.
> Thank you, Dr. Culpepper, for a stimulating and exciting pilgrimage....
> Cordially,
> Wayne I. Nicholson[21]

---

[20] Hugo Culpepper, letter to Charles Kimball, 20 October 1976.
[21] Wayne Nicholson, letter to Hugo Culpepper, 1 January 1979.

Nicholson's topic evolved further, and on 15 December 1978, Hugo proudly signed the approval sheet of Nicholson's dissertation, "Toward a Theology of Comparative Religion: A Study in the Thought of Hendrik Kraemer and Wilfred Cantwell Smith." Two years later Robert Don Hughes completed his work under Hugo's direction, and these were the only two students who completed their graduate programs with him.

The M.Div. students found Hugo challenging, but appreciated his spirit, the life stories he shared in class, and his famous "one-liners." Logan Smith, pastor at First Baptist Church, Cornelia, Georgia, recalls that he had Hugo for his very first class at the seminary, and he remembers how his head spun when Hugo said, "You could put all of Jesus into God, but you could not put all of God into Jesus."

Jeff Sharp, who became a missionary in Hong Kong, recalled Hugo's teaching and commitment to theological teaching, "but what impressed me most, and I am sure it was true for many, many others, was his life and testimony. His words, 'If God is the ultimate reality, our vocation is to be such as is in harmony with him,' were exemplified in his life."[22]

Hugo was also respected by his colleagues as a conversation partner, sage, and elder statesman. Walter Shurden penned the following note in August of 1977: "Just wanted to say in writing what an unusually good worship session you led at the faculty workshop. You made me stop and evaluate my first year at SBTS. You also made me reflect again on the tremendous heritage hanging over our heads on this campus. After your address I went to the office and looked up this quote by Henri Nouwen: 'Many places that are created to bring people closer together and help them form a peaceful community have degenerated into mental battlefields.' Thanks. Buddy Shurden"[23]

Faculty colleagues looked forward to gathering in the faculty lounge over a brown-bag lunch when Hugo was there because they could count on him to raise a provocative topic and lead in a stimulating and substantive conversation.

In April of 1978, Hugo received the following letter from Orman Stegall, an associational missionary for the Graves County Baptist Association in Kentucky, which reflect one of the many ways in which Hugo had multiplied his ministry and influence over the years.

---

[22] Jeff Sharp, email to Alan Culpepper, December 2000.
[23] Walter Shurden, letter to Hugo Culpepper, 15 August 1977.

Dear Dr. Culpepper:

Last night I preached on union with Christ using Romans 6:1-11. I read again your comments as published by the Sunday School Board in 1969. You remember me getting permission to reprint for distribution portions from Romans chapters 5–8.

In all the years of being an associational missionary I think of this being one of my best projects. I just want to thank you for this great work you did. I wish I had another thousand copies for distribution.

I find many Christians hungry to know the truth about victory in Christ. This accounts partly for the modern charismatic movement. If only they knew your understanding of these rich truths. I am active since retirement in sharing these truths in many churches.

Yours very truly,
Orman Stegall[24]

Because Hugo turned sixty-five in 1978, he had to retire, following the mandatory retirement policy then in effect. Nevertheless, the seminary made him a "senior professor" so that he could teach for the next three years. At the end of the fall term in 1978 the faculty honored the professors who were retiring that year: Hugo Culpepper, Earl Guinn, Eric Rust, and Frank Stagg. Still, Hugo remained active. That fall he walked twenty-two miles for the "Summer Missions Walkathon"—the longest distance turned in that year—and the next summer he supervised the work of fifteen students who were serving as summer missionaries in the Church Extension Field Seminar sponsored in conjunction with the Home Mission Board.[25]

In June of 1979, Hugo spoke at the National Conference on Bold Christian Education and Bold Missions, sponsored by the Education Commission of the Southern Baptist Convention in Galveston, Texas. His address there is perhaps the best summary of his mature understanding of the biblical and theological basis of missions.[26]

---

[24] Orman Stegall, letter to Hugo Culpepper, 3 April 1978.

[25] Teresa Sanders, "Summer Fields Provided by Extension Program," *Towers*, 6, 6 (23 September 1979): 1.

[26] Hugo Culpepper, "The Rationale for Missions," tape recording of presentation at National Conference of Bold Christian Education and Bold Missions, June 1979.

"The Rationale for Missions"

It was Tuesday afternoon, March 10, 1942, about 7:00 P.M. The place was Camp Holmes, a civilian concentration camp in the Philippines, located about five miles north of Baguio on Luzon Island. The scene was a beautiful sunset over the China Sea. The situation was existential: it was a matter of life or death, both physically and spiritually. Physically I had lost twenty pounds of muscle in ten weeks time and had been suffering from bacillary dysentery for ten days. For four days I had been isolated from the community, living outside the barbed-wire fence in a cottage with six other patients fasting on rice-water. Spiritually I was sinking in a state of lethargy, not caring much, whether I lived or died. As I was leafing through this copy of the Greek New Testament, looking for some word of *hope* from God, I came upon I John 3:23: "And this is his commandment"—a word from God for me in that hour of crisis. I looked more closely; it said two things: (1) "that we should *believe* in the name of his Son Jesus Christ"; and (2) that "we should *love* one another." My heart leapt up! I had found a reason for being—a rationale, an underlying reason, for life: first, the basis of *trust* in life is the *character* of God revealed in the nature of Jesus Christ; second, what one does in life is to spring from "*loving* one another," from respecting the inherent worth of one's fellow human being.

As we "face the realities of the contemporary world," the predicament of humanity is not too different from what I experienced in that crucial hour. We need to find a reason for living, both individually and corporately. Inherent in the Christian's reason for being is a sense of mission. Once we have trusted in God as he has come to be *known* in Jesus, the focal point of our life should be to share the *knowledge* of God by helping others come to *know* him through faith in Jesus Christ. This mission is implemented in the activity of missions. To be effective in missions, we need to understand the basic principles involved—to see clearly the rational foundation—to have a rationale.

The origin of missions is to be found ultimately in the heart of God. His are the redemptive purpose and plan. No thought of God is true to his revelation of himself that does not rest on the fact that he "so loved the world that he gave his only son" that by believing in him" the world should be saved through him.".... This attitude of God is eternal and is determinative in all his dealings with people.[27] It makes a difference to God what happens in the world. As the Creator and Sustainer of the universe and of all life within it, he has been involved throughout time with the condition of persons in history.

---

[27] W. O. Carver, *Missions in the Plan of the Ages* (New York: Fleming H. Revell Co., 1909) 125.

Although persons were created in the image of God (Gen. 1:27), because of sin they have failed to reveal the true character of God; that is, they have failed to glorify God and are missing the meaning of life. They are alienated from fellowship with God and each other and have no hope in themselves for this life or for eternity. This is the predicament of all persons when left to themselves.

After God had demonstrated his concern for people of all nations (cf. Gen. 1–11), he began working toward their redemption through a *particular* people. He called Abraham to become the father of that people. God promised to bless him, but at the same time charged him with the responsibility of being a blessing to all peoples (cf. Gen. 12:1-3).

God took his second great step in redeeming activity when he heard the cry of his people in Egypt. He sent Moses to lead them out (Ex. 3:7-10). After crossing the sea and going south to the wilderness of Sinai, Moses went up into the mountain. There, God gave him a message for the people. They needed to understand, first of all, that it was *God* who had brought them to himself. While all the earth was his, they were to be his own possession from among all people, if they kept his covenant. They were to be a priest-nation. It was here, in this time and place, that the nation of Israel was formed.

The covenant was an agreement between God and the people which involved both sides in responsibilities and privileges. He was to guide and care for them, but he had the right to expect them to obey him and to fulfill his purpose. They were to do his will and therefore had the privilege of expecting him to provide for their needs. Because they would come to know him experientially as their God, they were to live among the peoples of the world, serving as a priest to introduce others to God. The covenant (Ex. 20:22–23:33) was read to the people by Moses, and they committed themselves to it (Ex. 24:7).

The people failed to keep the covenant during the period of the judges and later during the kingdom. Sin led to the division of the kingdom and finally to the Babylonian captivity (587 B.C.) of the southern tribes. During this captivity, a man of God pointed to the promised Redeemer in the four Suffering Servant passages (Isa. 42:1-4; 49:1-6; 50:4-9; 52:13–53:12). His prophetic vision is consistent with the messianic prophecies, e.g. Gen. 3:15, down through the centuries. The references to the servant probably begin with the nation in mind in Isaiah 42 and later refer to the remnant. However, the servant is clearly personal in the last song, Isaiah 53. The characteristics of the Redeemer are set forth: vocation, Isa. 52:13; witness, Isa. 53:1; suffering, Isa. 53:3; and blessing (of the many), Isa. 53:5, 11. It is inspiring to note that these should also characterize the life of the missionary today.

When the fullness of time came, God sent forth his son (Gal. 4:4) into the world. He was the cosmic missionary coming from the Father into the world; the Word became flesh and dwelt among us (John 1:14). He lived at the center of history.

On the one hand, he was the climax of God's redeeming activity under the old covenant. He went to John for baptism in order to link on to the redemptive movement at its growing edge. When John was reluctant to baptize him, he said, "Permit it now: it is proper for us to fulfill all redeeming activity (righteousness)" (Matt. 3:15).[28] He intended to carry on to completion what God had begun with Abraham.

On the other hand, Jesus was also the transition from the old covenant to the new, and therefore he became the initiator of the new covenant. As the God-man, he did what was necessary to overcome sin by his death on the cross and by his resurrection.

The life and teaching of Jesus are inseparably related. His life was no play-acting. He was tempted just as we are, yet he was able not to sin (Heb. 4:15). Because of this quality of life, he was able to teach with authority, that is, out of his being (Matt. 7:29). His teaching was existential: just as he was on a mission and lived in the light of it, he taught his disciples that they too must live on mission for the glory of God.

When the Greeks requested to see him, he seems to have pondered the meaning of their coming in relation to his mission. This led him to express the basic principle of his life which must also come to be that of his disciples: "a grain of wheat falling into the ground abides alone if it does not die; if it dies, it bring forth much fruit." He came then to the existential choice that could make the difference between life and death..."what should I say?" He thought of the way of self-preservation: should he say, "Father, save me from this hour?" But that way out would mean renouncing his mission.

He chose the way of self-sacrifice, which was also the way to realize his missionary vocation: "Father, glorify your name" (John 12:23-28). To live for the glory of God, that is, to live so as to make *known* the very character of God, was the purpose of his life; he taught his disciples that this was also to be the purpose of their lives (Matt. 5:14-16). In his teaching, to be his disciple is to share his mission.

The life and teaching of Jesus were such as to make clear that the love of God in him was always leading on beyond himself. Its outreach involved him in the lives of others. From the beginning of their ministry, the disciples of Jesus

---

[28] The primary meaning of the word "righteousness" is redeeming activity, as illustrated in Paul's use of the same word in Romans 1:17.

followed his example in going beyond themselves and reaching out to those in need.

It was the Apostle Paul who expressed for us the fullest understanding of God's *eternal purpose*. He gave the best exposition of this insight in Ephesians 3:1-13. Having written of God's purpose in chapters 1 and 2, he turns in 3:1 to offer an introductory prayer for his readers. Then it occurs to him that they may not have understood. In a parenthetical statement (3:2-13), he summarizes his insight as to God's eternal purpose. A stewardship (rather than dispensation) of the grace of God had been given to him on its way to them. By a process of revealing, an open secret (mystery...that which had been hidden but was now revealed) had been made known to him (3:3): the nations were joint heirs, of the same body, and partners (fellow-partakers) of the promise in Christ Jesus...along with the Jews.

Paul was a servant of this good news which was to become known "through the church according to the purpose of the ages which God centered (literally, 'made') in Christ Jesus our Lord" (3:11).

Jesus knew that no one had ever seen God (John 1:18a), but he also knew that inasmuch as the disciples had seen him they had also seen the Father (John 14:9); he had interpreted (literally, exegeted) the Father (John 1:18b). Therefore, he could say, no one comes to the Father except through me (John 14:6).

Accordingly, he said to the disciples who constituted the Church, "You are witnesses of these things" (Luke 24:48), and again, "Just as the Father has sent me, even so send I you" (John 20:21). This perspective of Jesus indicated the nature and set the course of the early Church in keeping with its being his body.

After the resurrection, Jesus met the eleven disciples on a mountain in Galilee. With quiet confidence he affirmed, "All authority in heaven and on earth has been given unto me" (Matt. 28:18). On the basis of this fact, he was able to point them to the mission of the Church: "Going therefore, disciple all the nations, baptizing them in the name of the Father and of the Son and of the Holy Spirit, teaching them to observe everything I have commanded you" (Matt. 28:19-20).

There is only one imperative here; it is "disciple." The going, baptizing, and teaching are secondary in emphasis to that. The heart of the mission of the Church is to disciple all the nations. *Insofar as*—and *only* insofar as—it does this, the Church can expect to receive the promise of the Lord, "I am with you all the days until the consummation of the age" (Matt. 28: 20).

The Apostle Paul permitted the mission of the Church to come to a focus in his life. He stated it, while in jail because of his proclamation and witness, in this way:

> Now I rejoice in my sufferings in behalf of you and I am filling up that which is lacking of the tribulations of Christ in my flesh in behalf of his Body which is the Church, of which I became a servant according to the stewardship of God being given to me on its way to you to fulfill the word of God, the open-secret having been hidden away from the ages and generations—but *now* is manifested to his saints, to whom God willed to make known what is the wealth of the glory of this open-secret among the nations, which is *Christ in you,* the hope of glory (i.e., of God's glory—or God's being made *known*): whom we proclaim admonishing every man and teaching every man in all wisdom, in order that we might stand every man alongside (Christ) having reached the goal of maturity in Christ (at the consummation of the age). Unto this end I labor, struggling according to the operative power of the One energizing me with potential power (Col. 1:24-29).

The Christian's purpose and goal in life, as here set forth by Paul, is to bring all men to *know* God through Jesus and someday to see them stand alongside Christ fully mature in his likeness.

We have been giving an exposition of the biblical basis of missions because that is foundational to a rationale of missions. Now we move on to the definition and interpretation of selected theological concepts whose understanding is crucial to a theology of mission.

Because God is love, he has taken the initiative in revealing himself to men in the context of history. Biblical *revelation* is the coincidence of divinely guided events with minds (of the prophets as men of God) divinely illumined (by the Holy Spirit, and therefore inspired) to interpret those events in the light of the conditions of their time for their contemporaries and for us of later generations. God is sovereign and providential. He is active in history, achieving his purpose through his mighty deeds.

Men of God lived in close enough fellowship with him to understand, under the inspiration of the Spirit, what he was doing and to be his spokesmen. The *Bible* is the record and interpretation of God's mighty deeds in history and of the experience of his people in relation to them. The study of biblical revelation brings one to understand *God's purpose of the ages* which he made in Christ Jesus (Eph. 3:11). Such an understanding provides the basis for Christian missions. The more profound one's knowledge of biblical revelation becomes, the clearer is his vocation for mission.

The *mission* of the Church is to glorify God by leading persons to know him through faith in Jesus Christ. For clarification, it should be helpful to paraphrase this definition. According to the New Testament, the reason for being is to live for the glory of God. (This is true for the individual Christian and for the Church.) To glorify God is to reveal or to manifest his true character, to make him *known* as he is. The Church's mission is the same as that of her Lord; it is the carrying out of the mission of Christ himself.[29] "As the Father has sent me, even so send I you" (John 20:21). The mission of the Church is to make Jesus Christ known to the world and to accomplish the mission that Jesus himself came to achieve.[30] Ultimately, it is God's mission,[31] entrusted to his Son, and passed on through his Church to us in this day.

God's redemptive activity in history has been expressed through persons who came to be a particular people and as such are *the Church*, the people of God and the body of Christ. *A Church* is the church in a given place and time.

Missions is the implementation of the mission of the church. Missions is defined as what the church *does* to achieve her mission in areas of human need which are on the growing edge of the Church's confrontation with the non-Christian world.

When we become involved in what "the Church *does* to achieve her mission," we are at the point of transition from the theological basis of mission to *the practice of missions*. To be complete, a rationale must include a critique of the practice of missions, otherwise we are dealing only with ideal principles that never find realization in action.

There are three major areas of concern in which the missionary movement seems most likely to go awry in our time: (1) making mission less than our reason for being, both as individual disciples of Christ and as the Church; (2) doing missions with unworthy motives and mistaken goals and objectives; (3) falling into a spirit of triumphalism, or even arrogant pride, in a world that is religiously plural.

Most people in our churches do not take missions seriously. This is true even though there probably has never been so large a part of the people of

---

[29] Lesslie Newbigin, *One Body, One Gospel, One World: The Christian Mission Today* (London: International Missionary Council, 1958) 17–18.

[30] J. Allan Ranck, *Education for Missions* (New York: Friendship Press, 1961) 3.

[31] See Georg F. Vicedom, *The Mission of God* (Saint Louis: Concordia Publishing House, 1965).

God entrusted with so many and so much to be used for making *God known*. There is a reason for this indifference.

During the Middle Ages the church became diverted and corrupted and increasingly lost the sense of mission to a large extent. Even during the Reformation the reformers did not recover a sense of mission. Only Martin Bucer thought that missions was a continuing responsibility of the church. After the Reformation, church members who recovered a sense of mission formed missionary societies of like-minded persons, having failed in their efforts to lead the church to become aware once again that mission is its reason for being. This resulted in mission being thought of as only one department of a church's activity, and in some cases as an optional appendage. Most churches are still living under the influence of this basic misunderstanding of the nature of the Church!

The conception of the Church, which is still operative in (one may guess) the majority of congregations, is that a church is the receptacle into which the results of missionary activity are deposited. A church is not regarded as itself being, the missionary agency involving all of its members in the work of missions. (As I heard one deacon say in a church business meeting, "We *pay* missionaries to do that for us.") Mission is not understood as the reason for being of the whole body of Christ. If it were accepted as such, there would be a profound transformation in the pattern of congregational life, of ministry, and of Christian action in the world.

The second area of concern is doing missions with unworthy motives and mistaken goals and objectives. Painful as it is, let us dare look at ourselves through the eyes of a spiritual-minded Theravada Buddhist friend of mine:

> I must confess that I am no admirer of the tremendous power and efficiency ascribed to the organized church in Christendom.... It seems to me that far less damage would have been done to the Christian image had the movement been less institutionalized and more divorced from power. Less institutionalization would, for example, have led to less "denativization" of christianized Asians and Africans. This loss of cultural identity is one of the least pleasant effects of the spread of the Christian movement in the world. Does it also not lie among the possibilities within Christianity to replace its pre-dilection for institutional power with a preference for real spiritual power, which one must suppose was the source of its original strength? It is, however, a given fact of the present historical situation that Christianity and Christian societies in general have at their disposal a vast reservoir of temporal power. The strain between

Christians and non-Christians is due in considerable measure to their power relationship. While the Christian part of humankind is, by and large, affluent, the non-Christian, with a few exceptions, is poverty-stricken. While the one wields power, the other lacks and, of course, aspires to power. In this context, power is connotative of accumulated wealth, on the one hand, and potential violence, on the other.... There are great potentialities in Christian thought for correcting misconceptions on the power imbalance. Exploring these potentialities is imperative in a world where 80 per-cent of humanity lives in dire poverty, and the affluent have almost all the instruments to perpetuate that disproportionate distribution or, worse, to make the distribution even more disproportionate.... A passage that genuinely speaks to my heart...is one worth repeating a thousand times, Mark 10:17-26, especially verse 25 "it is easier for a camel to go through the eye of a needle than for a rich man to enter the kingdom of God." The comment of H. G. Wells on this passage is well taken. ". . . In the white blaze of this kingdom of his there was to be no property, no privilege, no pride and precedence; no motive indeed and no reward but *love*."[32]

Another critical issue today, in this area of concern regarding objective and goals, is "the relation of numerical growth to the message of the kingdom."[33] Lesslie Newbigin, in an important new work on missiology, gives us a telling critique at this point:

> Mission is not just church extension. It is something more costly and more revolutionary. It is the action of' the Holy Spirit who in his sovereign freedom both convicts the world (John 16:8-11) and leads the church toward the fullness of the truth which it has not yet grasped (John 16:12-15). Mission is not essentially an action by which the church puts forth its own power and wisdom to conquer the world around it; it is, rather, an action of God, putting forth the

---

[32] Mahinda Palihawadana, "A Buddhist Response: Religion Beyond Ideology and Power," *Christian Faith in a Religiously Plural World*, ed. Donald G. Dawe and John B. Carman, (Maryknoll, NY: Orbis Books, 1978) 39–42. See H. G. Wells, *A Short History of the World* (Harmondsworth: Penguin Books, 1960) 157.

[33] Lesslie Newbigin, *The Open Secret: Sketches for a Missionary Theology* (Grand Rapids: William B. Eerdmans Publishing Company, 1978) 138.

power of his Spirit to bring the universal work of Christ for the salvation of the world nearer to its completion.[34]

It is true that

in the Acts of the Apostles, we find a lively interest in numerical growth.... But when one has given due weight to this obvious delight in the numerical growth of the church, one must also observe that the rest of the New Testament furnishes little evidence of interest in numerical growth. In the Synoptic Gospels Jesus does not give the impression of being interested in large numbers.... Luke, who shows such evident delight in recording the multiplication of believers after Pentecost, also records several sayings of Jesus which suggest that the coming of God's kingdom does not at all depend on the number of those who expect it and pray for it (cf. Luke 12:32 and 18:8). The emphasis falls upon the faithfulness of the disciples rather than upon their numbers. Nor does a study of the Epistles seem to disclose any interest in numerical growth. Paul's...primary concern is with (the churches') faithfulness, with the integrity of their witness.... Peter (shows) a deep concern for the integrity of the Christian witness, but there is no evidence of anxiety about or enthusiasm for rapid numerical growth. In no sense does the triumph of God's reign seem to depend upon the growth of the church. In the Johannine Gospel and letters...there is nowhere any suggestion that the salvation of the world depends upon the growth of the church. Reviewing, then, the teaching of the New Testament,...there is no evidence that the numerical growth of the church is a matter of primary concern,...nor is there anything comparable to the strident cries of some contemporary evangelists that the salvation of the world depends upon the multiplication of believers.[35]

The third area of concern, triumphalism, a spirit of arrogant pride, stems easily out of the churches' concern for their own self-aggrandizement.

The church is least recognizable as the body of Christ when it is growing rapidly through the influence of military, political, and economic power.... When numerical growth is taken as the criterion of

---

[34] Ibid., 66.
[35] Ibid., 139–41

judgment on the church, we are transported with alarming ease into the world of the military campaign or the commercial sales drive. Sentences such as the following may be acceptable in the board room of a powerful mission agency with plenty of resources, but they sound quite different to those who are at the receiving end of the operation: "Unresponsive areas should be *occupied lightly*. A *Blitzkrieg* of missionaries in a resistant area usually serves to alarm the religious leaders and to harden the people in their unbelief. Better to keep the witness there light, ready to move in heavy reinforcements when the culture turns responsive."[36]

When the gracious love of God is present in the human heart, the only appropriate response is radical humility. With a spirit of profound gratitude to God, our deepest desire is that he may come to be known experientially, as he is by nature, in his own character. He is truth; he is ultimate reality. To know him is to glorify him. That is the rationale—the underlying reason—for missions.

The earth *will be* filled
With the *knowledge* of the *glory* of the Lord,
As the waters cover the sea.[37]

On 22 October 1980, Hugo preached in the seminary chapel. For over a year the Southern Baptist Convention and the seminary had been in turmoil. A fundamentalist resurgence in the convention was using "the inerrancy of Scripture" as a slogan and attacking alleged liberalism in the seminaries as a way of building support for their takeover. In this context, Hugo addressed central theological issues that were of utmost concern in the moment when he chose to speak on the nature of religious authority as he had come to understand it.

---

[36] Ibid., 141f. See M. R. Bradshaw, *Church Growth through Evangelism in Depth* (S. Pasadena: William Carey Library, 1969) 30.

[37] Habakkuk 2:14, New American Standard Bible.

"The Bible and Religious Authority"

Perhaps some of you noticed on the bulletin board that my subject is announced as "The Bible and Religious Authority." Let me hasten to assure you that my message is not at all like what you probably expect. About ten days ago, I was invited to speak on the theme "Where the Bible Speaks Most Personally to Me." By its very nature, this theme makes my message auto-biographical. Just last Friday I was asked what my subject would be, and I responded that I have no subject other than the theme which had been suggested, and I was told that I needed to have a subject so that they would have something to put on the bulletin board. So, immediately I responded, "Well, what I am really going to talk about is 'The Bible and Religious Authority.'"

Where does the Bible speak most personally to you? Suppose you were asked that question. How would you respond? Immediately my thoughts turned to what I consider to be the most profound of all writing: the Gospel of John. But the longer I thought about the question the larger the context of my thinking became. It mushroomed eventually from the Bible alone to the larger question of religious authority. While my parents were never very active as church members, and perhaps this left me more freedom and responsibility to develop my own personal living tradition, earlier than I can remember they began taking me to church; the church, as I would now express it as being the people of God and the body of Christ, became the first step in my experience of religious authority.

One Sunday night during the summer when I was eight years of age, as I saw it then and as I have seen it through the years and still see it, God took the initiative through a rather ordinary sermon (which has always been an encouragement to me personally) and came into my life in a new way. No one else happened to have responded that night to the invitation. I am sure the preacher was somewhat disappointed that only an eight-year-old boy came forth. But I felt that I must respond to the strong sense of God's leadership that I experienced in those moments. I accepted Jesus Christ as my Lord and Savior at that time. I did not understand much about the theology of that experience, but I have never for one moment doubted its authenticity or its validity. The Spirit blew where it would that night, and I heard its voice and was born from above. The personal experience of conversion then came to be the second step in my experience of religious authority, and I moved on into a period of some five years in which I was living in the afterglow, as it were, of this personal experience.

Then when I was thirteen years of age, I remember very well walking for two miles to church every night for a week with my grandmother to attend one of those old-time Arkansas doctrinal revival meetings. A preacher most of you probably never heard of, Dr. Allen Hill Autrey of considerable reputation in Arkansas circles, was the preacher for that occasion. It was a notable week of experience for me. For several years God as Holy Spirit had been very real to me. I remember so well as I was at the point of entering into the teenage years there began to weigh heavily upon my heart and mind the whole question of life, its nature, its responsibilities, the whole question of vocation. Who am I? What am I intended to be? And very frankly, I was overwhelmed by it. I turned the only place I knew to turn. Frequently at night after the house had become hushed and the family had dropped off to sleep, I would slip out of bed on my knees by the side of my bed in the darkness of my room and pray pretty much the same prayer time after time. It went something like this: "Lord, life is too much for me. I'm not sure that I'll be able to handle it. But you know who I am and you know what you intend for me to be. And Lord, I want to turn my life over to you and trust you to lead me into becoming and into being and doing that which you have for me."

During that week of revival the Spirit gave me eyes to see, and I discovered for myself the Bible. I would say that the Spirit was the third step in my experience of religious authority. The fourth step, under the guidance of the Spirit, came to be the Bible for the next decade or slightly more. Religious authority seemed to level out pretty much onto a plateau. I lived under the authority of the Bible per se. So much so, the Bible alone, I could almost say, was my authority. This carried me on through college and into the seminary here. And then my horizons began to lift under the leadership of the faculty of that time, and increasingly I was enabled to find under the leadership of the Spirit the living Word of God behind the printed words. I learned that the same Spirit who led me to discover the Bible for myself, to discover the living Word through the printed word, that this same Spirit had worked in the personalities and had illumined the minds of the writers of scripture when it was originally composed.

For me it was a great day when I discovered an adequate definition of what revelation is all about. I read it in William Temple's *Nature, Man and God*. With some modifications for clarity of understanding on my part, and in communicating it through the years to students, *revelation* became for me "the coincidence of divinely guided events with minds (of the men of God, of the prophets) divinely illumined (by the Holy Spirit and therefore inspired) to interpret those events" for their contemporaries and for us of later generations. I came to form my own definition of what *the Bible* is to me. I came to understand the Bible as being the record and the interpretation of the mighty deeds of God (of his historical redeeming activities) and of the experiences of his people in relation to those mighty deeds. A simple definition and yet a very functional definition which has been adequate for me through the years of my life. But then I moved on to what I considered to be a higher level. The Bible had come to be a distinct step in my experience of religious authority but I moved from it as the fourth step on to the fifth step to the higher level of authority of the Lord Jesus Christ himself as being until that time at least in my experience, the highest step in religious authority.

My response to the leadership of Jesus as Lord had led me to become a foreign missionary for nineteen years. As I look back now, I realize that I was almost heretical at times during this period in my understanding of the nature of religious authority. I almost held what Richard Niebuhr has called a Unitarianism of the second person of the triune God. And then I discovered that Jesus had not understood his own person in that way. I discovered that while the logos was God; God was not the logos. As John 1:1 is to be properly understood, in the nature of its grammar and syntax, where it says, "In the beginning was the Word and the Word was with God and the Word was God." The subject there which has the article is the Word. The predicate is God. As I understand Greek grammar, when there is no definite article in the predicate, subject and predicate are not interchangeable. And so we cannot say that God was the Word but we can profess with fullest enthusiasm that the Word was God.

My discovery happened one October afternoon some forty years ago now as I was preparing a chapel talk for the College of Chinese Studies in Peking, China. I was leafing through this very copy of the Greek New Testament, which has been by my side now for some forty-four years, for some message from God for that occasion. I came there to the passage in the twelfth chapter of the Gospel of John. You remember the occasion: Jesus was with his disciples on the road to go up to Jerusalem. And you remember the Greeks came and spoke first of all to Philip and then Philip went and spoke to Andrew and the two of them together went to Jesus with the request. And the request was interestingly expressed. It went this way, "Sir, we would see Jesus." Literally, it says, "Sir, we will," in the present tense or "We wish Jesus to see. " The abruptness of the present tense there is such as to suggest a strong volition and so it is well interpreted, "We would see Jesus." I came to see that this threw Jesus into a meditative mood in which he seemed to realize the depth of the nature of his vocation, standing as he was in the shadow of the cross almost. And he began something of a soliloquy in which he was thinking out loud of its nature and meaning for himself, but also of its meaning for his disciples who were within earshot. I think what he said was with reference to himself but also with reference to them as to their lifestyle.

You remember first of all he laid down the basic principle of his existence when he said, "Truly, truly I say to you, the grain of wheat falling into the ground, if it does not die, it abides alone, but if it dies, it bears much fruit." Now what I discovered on that particular occasion was the construction of that sentence which I had always read as it is usually put, "If a grain of wheat does not fall into the ground and die, it abides alone." But what I saw here for the first time is that "falling" is a circumstantial participle and that it is relatively secondary and incidental. And so I have since then translated it "the grain of wheat falling into the ground" to play that aspect down, and then to bring the full emphasis on the uncertainty (the third class conditional sentence), "if it should not die." I think it was quite significant that it was expressed with this class of conditional sentence. Because it uses the subjunctive, the hesitating mode of affirmaton, it is neither assumed as fulfilled or realized, or as unfulfilled and not realized, as the first two classes would be. It is not so highly unlikely to happen as the fourth class with the optative mood would be. It is exactly on target with the third class. It is an open possibility but not a forgone conclusion. Now, as I always do, I tried to relate the message of Scripture to where I was in my own pilgrimage in life; there I was recently having crossed the Pacific Ocean, gone to the other side of the world, with the purpose of sharing the gospel with people there. I came to realize that this was purely circumstantial. It was no more than a grain of wheat falling into the plowed furrows. The crux of the question was whether or not the seed germinates because that determines whether or not it brings forth fruit. And I came to see that this was a general principle, that status or title or position has no consequence in Christian discipleship, that ultimately the crux of the matter is whether or not we die to self to live for God.

Then I read on to what seemed to me to be a commentary upon this basic principle, for the Lord went on to say the one loving his life is in the process of destroying it. I once had a friend, Harold Rutledge (who was professor of pastoral care at New Orleans Seminary and who heard me give this exposition and immediately followed me on a program of orientation for missionaries), correct me in saying—because I had just said that most of us are loving ourselves to death, "the one who is loving himself is in the process of destroying it"—and he said, "No, Hugo, the problem is not loving oneself; the problem is low esteem, lack of self-acceptance." I realized the truth, from his perspective as a psychologist, of what he was saying. Only just recently, when I raised these two contrasting viewpoints with my colleague, Dr. Thornton, he made a helpful contribution when he differentiated, as psychologists do, between an egocentric personality, an egocentric self and a centered self, pointing out in the second place that the centered self has the larger context than just one's ego. And so affirmation and self-acceptance and self-esteem come with the unselfish person who has his being in something larger than himself, the centered self; and this removes the contradiction. Then Jesus went on to say, "the one hating his life in this world shall guard it unto life eternal." "If anyone would serve me, let him keep on following me and where I am there also my servant shall be. If anyone would serve me, the Father will honor him." I must admit that those words "where I am there my servant shall be" have been some of the most disturbing words in all the New Testament. For with all of the hurt and suffering and need of mankind, there is always a sense of responsibility to identify in some way with the needs of people and to be there simply because the Lord would be there. Then Jesus came to that existential moment in which the issue was life or death for him personally. I think that is the time of discovery of truth and reality. He said, "My soul has been perplexed or troubled and what should I say. Should I say, 'Father, save me from this hour?'" I think at that moment he was standing at the forks of the road and he looked down the way of self-preservation. The answer came back quite clearly. "But for this purpose came I into the world." Then he looked down the way of self-sacrifice. Someone has well said that sacrifice is that which we would not do except for love in our hearts. And the answer came quite clearly, "Father, glorify your name." What I discovered there was that Jesus clearly understood his own nature and vocation as being living for the glory of God: living in such a way as to manifest the true nature of God, to make God known to others. Jesus lived and died, then, for the glory of God and he called us to follow him.

I came to see...that ultimately the authority in my own religious pilgrimage was the character of God himself.... In John 17:3 I had read, "This is eternal life, that they should know thee, the only true God." An experiential knowledge of God is life, absolutely and eternally. Now this brought me to the sixth step and to the highest level in my experience of religious authority: the character of God himself.

Let me briefly review these earlier steps by working backward. I have a high Christology. I really believe that Jesus Christ was the incarnate Son of God. I believe that this living Word speaks to us through the written word, the Bible, as the same Spirit who inspired the writers gives us eyes of faith to interiorize the Truth, the living Truth which corresponds to reality, God himself. Then, we experience this knowledge of God for ourselves. We are converted, and all of this takes place in the context of the church. There is a particular salvation history, a particular Heilsgeschichte. And yet, and yet, in some sense, I am coming to see *all* of history is Heilsgeschichte. Paradoxical as it is, the New Testament teaches that the true light, the logos, illumines every person in some sense. In John 1:9, we are told this. During the last decade, this perspective has grown in meaning for me. Perhaps I am being lifted to a larger view in my knowledge of God. I believe that eternity is a long, long climb upward. And, frankly, I am looking forward to it with the greatest of anticipation.

Now in closing, I have two further observations in a word. The first is that when the Bible has spoken most personally to me, I was first of all deliberately seeking God. Jeremiah was right when he said to the children of Israel in Babylonian captivity, "You shall seek me, and you shall find me, when you seek me with all of your heart." Yet I hasten to say in the second place that it is by grace—this is in the instrumental case here, the means by which God has saved me—by grace through faith, through trust (the secondary, lesser means), that I am having been saved. And that, all that went before, not of myself, not of my own works, of God the gift. So I have these two things in relation: the necessity of deliberate, authentic seeking of God, the base line of our existence, nothing else mattering so much to us; and second, God giving us that which we seek. Now the knowledge of God is not an end in itself, something to be grasped. It only qualifies us to be used by him in making himself known. And so my prayer should come to be as was the prayer of our Lord, "Father, glorify your name or make yourself known." The highest of all religious authority is the character of God himself. May we pray.

Our Father, as we have thought of the mystery of our existence and of the providence of God, and as we have expressed gratitude for the manifestation of Thy very self to us, help us to realize our opportunity and our responsibility to become Thy agents unto the ends of the earth and the lives of all mankind, and may our sincere prayer and our characteristic lifestyle be, "may the earth be filled with the knowledge of the Glory of the Lord as the waters cover the sea." Amen.[38]

In his last year of teaching, Hugo's attention turned toward retirement. He said, "I am enjoying relaxation from a heavy teaching load. I think I'll be able to handle retirement with no problems, but with great joy!"[39] In the spring of 1981 Larry Culpepper accepted a position as associate professor at the Brown University Medical School and moved to Barrington, Rhode Island. On 26 May, Wayne Ward shared "Reflections about Hugo Culpepper" at the faculty dinner in honor of Hugo, Clyde Francisco, and Forrest Herren. Two days later, Hugo and Ruth flew to

---

[38] Hugo Culpepper, "The Bible and Religious Authority," tape recording of sermon preached in Southern Seminary chapel, 22 October 1980.

[39] Hugo Culpepper, letter to Alan and Jacque Culpepper, 10 December 1980.

England to spend several weeks traveling and visiting with Alan and Jacque and the children. Together, they enjoyed tracing the family's origins back to the Culpeppers of East Sussex and Kent, and visited Salehurst, Goudhurst, and the Great Wigsell Manor House, which was once owned by Culpeppers. When Hugo and Ruth returned to Louisville, they were pleased to learn that the trustees of the seminary had accorded Hugo the honor of naming him Professor Emeritus of Christian Missions and World Religions, effective 1 August 1981.

Hugo with Rodney, 1980.

Chapter 11

Retirement
1981–2000

"Grow old along with me!
The best is yet to be,
The last of life, for which the first was made!
Our times are in his hand
Who saith, 'A whole I planned,…
Perfect the cup as planned!
Let age approve of youth, and death complete the same!"[1]

Hugo's retirement years began in Louisville, where he was surrounded by friends, seminary colleagues, and his grandchildren. During the early years of his retirement, life changed very little. He continued to read vigorously, announcing at one point that he hoped to read all of Barth's *Church Dogmatics*. He taught Sunday school classes in various churches on a regular basis and preached when he had opportunities to do so. His thought moved increasingly toward the issues involved in religious pluralism and the relationship between Christianity and other religious traditions. In the fall of 1981 he delivered a paper on the thought of Wilfred Cantwell Smith, with which he resonated so deeply, for the College Theology Society meeting in Cincinnati. Indeed, Hugo was so influenced by Smith that in his interpretation of Smith's thought one can see many of the themes and emphases of his own thought at this time.

---

[1] Robert Browning, "Rabbi Ben Ezra," *The Complete Poetic and Dramatic Works of Robert Browning* (Boston: Houghton Mifflin Company, 1895) 383, 385.

"The Thought of Wilfred Cantwell Smith"

His inaugural lecture at McGill University on December 8, 1949, disclosed the seedbed of much of his later thought. In the course of his lecture he said,

> And it is only in so far as each religious community is consciously seeking Truth that they all can come together. So long as Christians are searching for the real Christianity, and Muslims for the real Islam, they cannot even talk to each other. But immediately both are looking for truth—for God, as they might well put it—then they can talk very warmly; and of course can learn from each other.[2]

On September 30, 1964, Smith delivered his inaugural address at the convocation of Harvard Divinity School. It was entitled, "Mankind's Religiously Divided History Approaches Self-Consciousness." Smith offered, in concluding his address, a means of understanding man's hitherto divided religious history. He proposed, first of all, that the Christian (or Muslim, Hindu, etc.) view all history as Heilsgeschichte. Given the situation of today's world one must approach the study of man's religious consciousness in terms of the historical rather than formally philosophic.[3]... And, secondly, one must bear in mind that the study of religions is primarily a study of persons not traditions.[4]

Smith's characterization of his own religious interests may best sum up this survey of his life and work:

> I am a Presbyterian, and will never shake off my delightful Calvinistic Puritanism until the day I die; yet the community in which I participate is not Presbyterian but the Christian. I participate as a deliberate though modified Puritan in the Christian community, and the Christian process. In much the same way, I choose to participate as a Christian in the world pro-cess of religious convergence.[5]

---

[2] Wilfred Cantwell Smith, "The Comparative Study of Religion: Reflections on the Possibility and Purpose of a Religious Science," *McGill University, Faculty of Divinity, Inaugural Lectures* (Montreal: McGill University, 1950) 58.

[3] Wilfred Cantwell Smith, "Mankind's Religiously Divided History Approaches Self-Consciousness," *Harvard Divinity Bulletin*, 29:8 (1964): 15.

[4] Ibid.

[5] Wilfred Cantwell Smith, "Participation: The Changing Christian Role in Other Cultures," *Religious Diversity: Essays by Wilred Cantwell Smith*, ed. Willard G. Oxtoby (New York: Harper & Row, 1976) 136f.

We turn now to a synopsis of Smith's thought....

Faith as a quality of human beings is (a) difficult to articulate, certainly to an outsider, and (b) is diverse among men. Faith is the personal involvement of a person who is the locus of an interaction between the transcendent, which is presumably the same for every person, and the cumulative tradition, which is different for every person.[6] Because of this historical and dynamic view of faith Smith declares that there can be no such entity as "*the* Christian faith."[7]

A major consequence of Smith's understanding of religious life is the contribution it makes toward inter-religious understanding. To the question "Can one know the faith of another?" Smith would respond, "Yes." In the first place, personal faith is expressed through various ways. Through familiarity with the religious tradition and observation of the character of the individual or community one can gain a valid insight into the nature of that faith. Secondly, the preliminary knowledge and observation can be confirmed and enhanced through the cultivation of a friendship with an adherent of a tradition and subsequent dialogue.[8] Finally, one can recheck the personal disclosure through the religious materials available pertaining to the tradition concerned.

Smith has found the Western notion of religion to be a problem. He proposes that usage of the term be discontinued as well as such terms as Buddhism, Taoism, Christianity, et al. In the place of religion he would substitute cumulative tradition and personal faith as more meaningful, and certainly more personal, since, after all, these concepts interlock in the life of the person himself....

Wilfred Cantwell Smith assumes as a working hypothesis that man is *homo religiosus*, by which he means that man has a capacity for faith. This position is based on his studies both as a historian and comparativist of men of diverse cultures. Smith proposes to explore this dimension of man's being and to try to understand it, for to know more of man's faith is to know more of man. Heretofore, philosophers and theologians have devoted themselves to a study of man's beliefs. Smith queries whether faith is not more fundamental and endeavors to elucidate this intensely personal quality of human life....

Faith, then, is a universal quality of human existence to Smith, who is reluctant to define it because it has hardly been studied. The following is the

---

[6] Wilfred Cantwell Smith, *The Meaning and End of Religion: A New Approach to the Religious Traditions of Mankind* (New York: The New American Library, 1964) 168.

[7] Ibid., 112.

[8] Wilfred Cantwell Smith, "Comparative Religion: "Whither and Why?", *The History of Religions: Essays in Methodology*, ed. Mircea Eliade and Joseph M. Kitagawa (Chicago: The University of Chicago Press, 1973) 39f. n. 18.

closest he comes to giving it a definition: "Faith is observably a universal hu-man characteristic, which has in empirical fact characterized the whole of hu-man existence from the beginning, as man's capacity to perceive, to sym-bolize, and to live in terms of, a transcendent dimension in his life."[9]

As a "universal quality" faith is primary, belief secondary. Smith has a choice aphorism to express this connection pungently. He avows one could almost say that "men's faith is given by God; men's belief, by their century."[10] Consequently, while there is Christian faith, it is unlikely that one should speak of "Christian beliefs";[11] rather, of beliefs that articulate faith from age to age. As a universal human quality, moreover, faith is holistic. There are several "strands" of faith; faith may assume varying degrees of form (e.g., a Christian, Buddhist, or Muslim form). But underlying these multiple forms of faith is a universal faithfulness itself. Therefore, Smith never uses the word faith in the plural, since his study has indicated that faith is a unitary phenomenon. The Muslim man of faith and the Buddhist man of faith, while participating in diverse traditions, may nonetheless be grouped together under the singular quality of human life designated by "faith."

The position to which Smith is drawn is that for far too long Western (and Christian) thought has emphasized belief over faith. The consequences have been disastrous. Beliefs divide; faith unites. Belief itself has had a dramatic shift from an act of commitment, out of what was recognized to be true, to a proposition that possibly (or likely) may be false. Faith is a quality by which man responds to what is meaningful and recognized as such and which is symbolized through beliefs. As such, faith is a more pristine and helpful category than (modern) belief.

Because Smith has argued for the personal quality of faith it is not surprising that he argues for the personal quality of truth as well. Smith's work in comparative religion has contributed to his elucidation of the notion of truth. In the western world there has been a divorce between what is real and what is true (truth is that which conforms to reality and therefore the two are in-separable), between knowledge and morality....

Religious truth involves personal faith and not some reified entity by the name of Christianity or Hinduism; moreover, it is historical, so that one's faith at

---

[9] Wilfred Cantwell Smith, "Faith: As a Universal Human Quality" (paper presented at Bea Lecture, Woodstock College, New York City, 18 March 1971) 28.

[10] Wilfred Cantwell Smith, "Faith and Belief: As Seen by a Comparative Religionist" (unpublished paper presented as the Centennial Lecture, University of Toronto, 9 January 1968) 37.

[11] Ibid.

the moment may be more true than it was the preceding day; or, one Christian may have a truer faith than that of another Christian at a given point in history. Religious traditions, like everything else in history, are in a flux, so that "Even those who like to think that religions have been false in the past should hope that they will become true in the future."[12] However, religious traditions are not theories; they are the contexts in which people have nurtured personal faith. Neither traditions nor propositions but persons are true or false....

Smith is quite cognizant of the problems of religious pluralism. Nevertheless, his intent as a historian and comparativist is to understand as clearly as possible the history, metaphors, and dynamic of the various religious traditions and summon men of faith to a collaborative enterprise in the pursuit of truth. He is ultimately concerned, not with the strident discord that erupts in polemical debate over truth claims that "conflict," but with the mutual sharing by men of faith of their experience of, and response to, God. It is upon this basis that he feels the responsibility rests for the development of a theology of comparative religion....

This means that because man is religious, man himself—in his involvement with his tradition, and through that with the transcendent—is the focus of study. One is not so much concerned with a reified entity called Hinduism, but with people who are called Hindus.[13] Not man as an object, but man as a (religious) person is the subject of investigation. For Smith humane knowledge is ultimately self-consciousness, which must be placed in a global context (viz., corporate) and made rational (viz., critical). Humane knowledge (or, corporate critical self-consciousness) is therefore an encounter of persons, a "we all" talking with each other about "us."...

Missionaries consciously and purposefully participate in countries foreign to their own. Moreover, given the emerging interdependence of nations, multinational corporations as well as government agencies may and do participate in several streams of man's religious consciousness. With regard to the missionary, Smith opines that the effective missionary "must be welcomed by the religious leaders" of the host country.[14] The prototype of the contemporary missionary should be Martin Buber, who although a Jew was made welcome by the Christian tradition in various cultures, not for his

---

[12] Wilfred Cantwell Smith, *Questions of Religious Truth* (London: Victor Gollanez Ltd., 1961) 76.

[13] See, for example, Wilfred Cantwell Smith, *The Faith of Other Men* (New York: Harper & Row, Publishers, 1962) 24ff.

[14] Wilfred Cantwell Smith, "Participation: The Changing Christian Role in Other Cultures," *Religious Diversity*, 131.

proselytism (which was not his intention) but because he enriched its understanding of God and man. Finally, there is participation in interreligious communion, a possibility that has emerged only recently. Following the lead of the missionary, men and women of faith may now contribute to, and learn from, one another, to consciously "participate in each other's processes of moving toward God."[15]

It might be objected here that Smith has ignored the matter of Christian revelation. That is not the case, for he maintains that, like truth, the locus of revelation is personal. God does not reveal religions, nor doctrines, nor propositions, but himself. In fact, Smith wonders whether one may declare that God has disclosed himself unless he has done so to a person. Such a view of revelation places it in human history, so that the most anyone can say is that God has revealed himself in such-and-such a manner to me. It becomes questionable to merely declare that Jesus Christ is God's full revelation of himself, because such an assertion is ahistorical; it is far better to add the words "to me."[16] Consequently, Smith is able to affirm that God was revealed to al-Ghazzali of the eleventh century A.D. through the Qur'an for both historical and theological reasons. Historically, it is evident through the study of his books and life that al-Ghazzali is disclosed to be a man of faith. Theologically, such a conclusion is congruous with "what I know of God, as revealed to me in Christ, and as instructed to me in Christian theology...that presumably God is...trying to speak to men in love and justice and mercy wherever they may be, in and through whatever context in which they find themselves."[17]

It is not surprising then that in his Cadbury Lectures Smith calls for a theocentric, instead of a Christocentric, orientation of *theologia religionis*.[18]

Such a view of revelation renders the question of religious authority irrelevant. It becomes dubious to aver that truth is in Buddhism, or Christianity, or a book merely on the basis of some presumed external authority; rather, truth is in persons, people of faith, who have encountered God. "God is both transcendent and immanent; and no form can contain Him. God is greater than any of the religions; and man is potentially great because man is the much-

---

[15] Ibid., 137.

[16] Smith, *Questions of Religious Truth*, 91.

[17] Ibid., 92ff.

[18] Wilfred Cantwell Smith, "Towards a Theology of Comparative Religion" (Cadbury Lectures delivered at the University of Birmingham, January–February 1972) VII-31f.

loved child of God. God transcends Islam, but is immanent in Muslims. God transcends Christianity, and yet is immanent in us."[19]

Just as the church has done theology in the context of Greek philosophy and subsequently science, so today theology must be worked out in a religiously plural world. This recognition poses three problems. First, there is the intellectual problem: how to understand the faith of other men? Something like a Copernican revolution has occurred in the Christian church as it has come to realize that it is but one type of faith in a world of multiple variants of faith. The problem is enhanced because there has not been a Newtonian revolution: "Newton's mind was able to conceive an interpretation... that without altering the fact that on earth things *do* fall to the ground and in the heavens things *do* go round in circles, yet saw both these facts as instances of a single kind of behaviour."[20]

The implication for Christian theology is significantly important: that no longer is one able to regard his Christian tradition as faith and other traditions as superstitions, but, rather, one must avoid such dichotomy by viewing the faith of all men as a "single kind of behaviour."

Second, there is a moral problem, for religious pluralism has hindered community.[21] Whereas in the past men of diverse traditions have fought or ignored one another, today the need is for collaboration. Unless men co-operate with one another across religious and cultural boundaries the future of the earth is bleak. Here Smith raises the question of the moral aspect of truth. If God is revealed in Christ then the Christian is morally obligated (a) to pursue and promote brotherhood among all men and (b) to construct theology accordingly. Christian theology is arrogant if it antagonizes others by asserting that without a knowledge of Jesus Christ men do not know God. The logic of such a position is that if Christianity is true and salvific then other traditions are false and damnable. "If one's chances of getting to Heaven—or to use a nowadays more acceptable metaphor, of coming unto God's presence—are dependent upon other people's not getting there, then one becomes walled up within the quite intolerable position that the Christian has a vested interest in other men's damnation."[22]

Finally, there is a theological problem of the extent to which men of other faith know God. Traditionally, theologians have argued that if Christians know God, then, because other religions are different, they do not. But, as Smith

---

[19] Smith, "The Comparative Study of Religion," 57.

[20] Smith, *The Faith of Other Men*, 124.

[21] Ibid., 126.

[22] Ibid., 131.

argues, it seems questionable to condemn the majority of the world's people by logic alone. Empirically, Smith has found evidence that others have known God. To entertain this question theologically, one must begin with trinitarian theology, not Christology. "Is God not Creator? If so, then is He not to be known—however impartially, distortedly, inadequately—in creation? Is He not active in history? If so, is His spirit totally absent from any history, including even the history of other men's faith?"[23]

The question must then be turned around so as to become: "Does God let Himself" be known only to those to whom He has let Himself be known through Christ?"[24] His conclusion is that man is not saved by knowledge or membership in any tradition, but only by "the anguish and love of God."[25]

When Hugo's review of Wilfred Cantwell Smith's *Towards a World Theology* appeared in the *International Bulletin of Missionary Research* in January 1983, Smith wrote Hugo, saying, "What a joy to have one's works reviewed by someone who so clearly has understood deeply what one is trying to say!"[26]

In May 1982 Hugo received the disturbing news that his sister had cancer of the pancreas and that little could be done for her. After battling the illness for a year, she finally succumbed to it.

The Baptist Program published a complimentary letter from Wayne Nicholson in October 1983 in which he said that Hugo personified for him "the aura of greatness" of the "tradition of scholarship coupled with piety" at Southern, with "a great cloud of witnesses (including the likes of Boyce, Broadus, Robertson, and Sampey), seemingly encouraging each succeeding generation of young preachers."[27]

Ruth retired from her position at the University of Louisville library in February 1983, when she turned sixty-five. The following fall Hugo and Ruth spent at Mississippi College in Clinton, Mississippi, where he taught as a visiting professor and they enjoyed the hospitality of the college and of Jack and Jean Glaze, with whom they had remained close friends since their days together in Argentina nearly thirty years earlier. The following fall, Hugo was teaching again, World Religions 3360, at Southern. On the

---

[23] Ibid., 137.

[24] Ibid., 139.

[25] Ibid., 140.

[26] Wilfred Cantwell Smith, letter to Hugo Culpepper, 25 January 1983.

[27] Wayne I. Nicholson, "Prof's Influence Lives On," *The Baptist Program* (October 1983): 5.

course evaluations, one student wrote, "The strength of this course lies not only in the relevance of the material but also in the professor. He radiates a life given to the pursuit of truth, one that has grown to maturity in the grace and knowledge of Jesus the Christ." Parenthetically, Hugo continued to lift weights regularly and water ski with the boys until his doctor advised him to stop weightlifting at the age of seventy-two because of his arthritis.

The qualities of a life of faith had long interested Hugo, and a sermon he preached at Crescent Hill Baptist Church in Louisville allowed him to gather up his understanding of faith.

Hugo, 1989.

"A Living Faith"

About ten days ago some of us here this morning attended a Valentine party sponsored by the faculty wives of the Baptist seminary. A distinctive feature of the program was the projection of slides made from the wedding pictures of those present. Beginning with the Ellis Fullers, married in 1925, they covered a span of almost sixty years down to those most recently married. As you can imagine, it was a hilarious experience—seeing how some of us looked way back then! My most immediate reaction was the youthful appearance of most of the men or should I say "boys." It seemed to me that in many cases the ladies had "robbed the cradle." But a more sober and enduring reaction was the brevity of life!

Perhaps I was conditioned for this more serious reaction by a traumatic experience Ruth and I had on January 15. It had caused me to begin reviewing my spiritual and religious pilgrimage across the years to determine where I am now. In this context, I invite you to think with me for a while about "a living faith."

The faith of most of us has been determined largely by the religious tradition in which we were born and reared. During the early years of life a form of *pedagogical authority* shaped our experiences. What we learned from our parents and teachers guided us as we developed. As we became older and were more influenced by our peers, *sociological authority* took over! We were likely to want to do and be what our social group dictated. Remember the ultimate argument, "But mother, everybody is doing it!" It seems that most people, even as older adults, never go very far beyond sociological authority. We like the cozy comfort of being accepted by "the group"—as we say. In a general context, we find it all too easy to be content to "keep up with the Joneses." The easy way in life is to escape responsibility by allowing others to have authority over us. There is a third level of authority to which it is difficult to rise—the authority of truth or reality, which is called *ontological authority*!

Early in life, I owed much to the teaching I received from Sunday school teachers in a small-town Baptist church. During my formal education, I was influenced by three great teachers: my English teacher during the last two years of high school taught, who me to love to read; Dr. A. J. Armstrong of Baylor University, who gave me a vision of the possibilities of life; and Dr. W. O. Carver, who shaped my theological perspective....

Tradition is the outer or objective aspect of religion. It is a bridge over which religion passes from one generation to the next. It is a necessary, but dangerous, aspect if one's religion stops there. We tend to "reify"—to make a thing of it. We try to keep it as "the faith of our fathers" by capturing it as a confession of faith or a creed. We use these statements or propositions as tests of orthodoxy. This has led across the centuries to thinking of revelation as being prepositional in nature. It has resulted in what is called the "plenary verbal view of inspiration," that is, that every word in the Bible is fully inspired. I have come to think that people who insist on this view would be more comfortable as Muslims. Islam teaches that the Qur'an pre-exists in heaven and that it was dictated to Muhammed, who recited it word for word as he received it. His disciples wrote it down word for word. Very early in the history of Islam all existing copies of the Qur'an were collected and edited so as to make one official version that has remained unchanged as their "Bible." It is about eighty percent as long as the New Testament. A student must memorize it in Arabic before being permitted to enter one of their seminaries.

This is not the nature of revelation or of the Bible. Revelation is the coincidence of divinely guided events with minds divinely illumined to interpret those events for their contemporaries and for us of later generations. God came into our historical world to make himself known through what he did. The Bible is the record of God's redeeming activity and of the experiences of his people in relation to them. The personalities of men were enlightened to see and record God's redeeming activity. The style of each writer is reflected in the book he wrote. Therefore, the Bible is a divine-human book. For me, the Bible is not the highest authority in my faith. God is the highest authority. "This is eternal life that they should know thee experientially." Ultimately, the character of God himself is the highest authority. To know him is personal and relational. The second aspect of religious authority, for the Christian, is Jesus Christ, the Son of God. He mediates to us the knowledge of God. The third aspect of religious authority is the Bible, the indispensable source of our knowledge of Jesus Christ. The Holy Spirit, in the fourth place, illumines our understanding as we read the Bible to sense the presence of God understood through Christ. The awareness of God's presence in our life through the Holy Spirit brings us to a personal conversion, in the fifth place, in which we turn from self-centeredness to God. And, finally in the sixth place, the church as the people of God is the context in which all of this comes to pass. For me, the six factors in religious authority are God, Christ, the Bible, the Holy Spirit, conversion, and the church.

Turning now from tradition as the objective side of religion, we must explore faith as the subjective or inner side. Instead of "reifying" tradition, i.e. making religion a thing, we should interiorize tradition to produce faith as a quality of our lives. Faith is insight toward transcendent reality (i.e., God). It is a sensitive awareness of Truth and a responding commitment that produces involvement and personal relationship with God. We see, we respond, we become involved, and we walk with God in a personal experiential relationship. This is the purpose of life: to live for the glory of God, to make him known as he is in character, to esteem and appreciate his very self.

Perhaps you remember with me as we were growing up that we were taught salvation is by "believing in Jesus"—that this meant trusting personally in Jesus, not "believing" this, that or the other about Jesus. It seems that now the emphasis has come to be on "belief" (related to propositional revelation). The idea that believing is religiously important turns out to be a modern idea. A great modern heresy of the church is the heresy of believing—the view that to believe is of central significance—this is an aberration. Faith, rather than belief, is the fundamental religious category. The noun "belief" occurs only once in the King James Version of the Bible (2 Thess. 2:13), i.e., "belief of the truth." Even here it is better translated "faith in the truth"; see Charles B. Williams's translation.

Faith is a quality of life—a quality of human living. At its best it has taken the forms of serenity and courage and loyalty and service: a quiet confidence and joy which enables one to feel at home in the universe, and to find meaning in the world and in one's life, a meaning that is profound and ultimate, and is stable no matter what happens to oneself at the level of immediate event. Men and women of this kind of faith face catastrophe and confusion, affluence and sorrow, unperturbed; face opportunity with conviction and drive; and face others with cheerful charity.

At the beginning I mentioned a traumatic experience Ruth and I had on January 15.... A phone call came from a Louisville friend who is the sister of Jesse. Jesse and her husband Bill [Junkin], lifelong missionaries in China and Taiwan, were dear friends from concentration camp days during the war.

They were in our home overnight in November. The sister said Jesse and Bill had five Chinese students in their home a week or so earlier. They lived on the side of the mountain in the Smokies in a small house which was originally a mountain shack. Bill, who was the son of missionaries to China, had worked every furlough to repair and enlarge the house. Before the students could leave, it was necessary to shovel snow. In time, Bill said, "Well, it is finished." As he turned, he struck his foot on a block of ice, fell, and fractured a leg in five places. They took him to the nearest city hospital, about twenty miles away, and an orthopedic surgeon set the leg. Things went well for two or three days. Then Bill became confused and a discouraging medical condition developed. After three days he broke out in a heavy sweat, slumped over in the presence of his wife and two nurses, and was dead.

Immediately after receiving the news Friday morning, we phoned Jesse. She said Bill's body had been cremated, and the urn was there near her at home. The next day she and their three grown children were going up the mountainside to the edge of their property and bury it in an accessible place under a big oak tree. Then a memorial service would be held at their church about 3:00 P.M. Jessie was composed and determined to carry on there in retirement, living alone, although she has a deteriorating spinal condition.

She and Bill had worked in the mountains of Taiwan since the war, traveling a week at a time among the native tribal people. They had not acquired much of this world's goods. But Jesse assured us all was well with them. God was real to them, and they knew that God is good. As the Psalmist said, describing his own experience, which also described Bill's and Jessie's,

"Even though they walked through the valley of the shadow of death, they feared no evil for God was with them." You see, they had a living faith![28]

Hugo mailed a copy of the tape of his sermon to his friend, Admiral James Kelly, former Navy Chief of Chaplains, whom they had visited recently. He responded,

> I listened to your sermon twice. In all the years we have known each other, that taped sermon is the first time I have ever heard you preach. Absolutely outstanding!—permeated with loads and loads of integrity—substance in every word and sentence—creatively fresh from your introduction to the conclusion—and so relevant and appropriate for the present time in our Southern Baptist Convention. Your positive affirmations all the way through the message—and too, you didn't put anyone down or belittle anyone.
>
> The first time I listened to the sermon I was lying on the bed face down. My back and legs were in pain, and Frances was giving me a rub down. I hung on to every sentence, and when you came to that belief-faith part, my ears really perked up—something I have always known but had never had it spelled out for me—you did it—and then when you mentioned visiting here and the active living faith, my eyes flooded and humbly flowed with tears. I couldn't keep them back. I am so grateful for what you said.[29]

On Thanksgiving night, 1988, Hugo suffered a heart attack. He and Ruth had driven to Tampa, Florida, to pick up a new Avion travel trailer. On the way back, they stopped at a camp ground near Adairsville, Georgia, for the night. After Hugo had gone to bed, about 11:00 P.M., he felt severe pressure and pain in his chest. Ruth ran to call for help. Fortunately, there was an EMS station less than a half a mile away, and help came quickly. Hugo was transported to the hospital in Cartersville, where he remained for the next six days while his condition stabilized. Members of Heritage Baptist Church in Cartersville responded with gracious hospitality for Ruth. Several weeks later Hugo had heart by-pass surgery. On the afternoon before his surgery, Alan was sitting with him in his hospital room. Hugo said that he was not afraid of the surgery the next day, though

---

[28] Hugo Culpepper, "A Living Faith," tape recording of sermon preached at Crescent Hill Baptist Church, 21 February 1988.

[29] James Kelly, letter to Hugo Culpepper, 23 March 1988.

no one could know what the outcome of it would be. The question of life after death had fascinated him for years, and he had read all the great thinkers on the subject. He said that in the final analysis, all the theories of eschatology really did not matter. It all came down to a conviction that "God is." And if God is, then one can face the unknown with every confidence.

As he later said in an interview with Brian Burton, "Because I have a confidence and trust in one ultimate conviction, 'God is,' I can say that at no time in my life have I experienced fear. If 'God is,' then that's enough. At times I've had a consciousness that I might be entering into the mystery of transcendence. But I viewed that as more of an interest in death as a next step instead of fear."[30]

Hugo, 24 June 1989.

On 24 June 1989, Hugo and Ruth celebrated their fiftieth wedding anniversary, with all their family and friends from the seminary and the church. The family arranged for a reception for them on the lower level of the Carver School building on the seminary campus, and Hugo and Ruth basked in the warmth of that day. Among the many letters they received was one from Roy Honeycutt, president of the seminary, in which he wrote:

---

[30] Brian W. Burton, "Hugo H. Culpepper: Seeker of God," *The Philippine Baptist*, 30 (June 1989): 9.

At a personal level, June and I continue to appreciate your friendship and recognize that you are among those friends who have created such a warm and caring community here in Louisville.

From the perspective of the seminary, I want, as President, to express appreciation to both of you for the splendid contribution which you have made to this institution. Through your teaching, Hugo, we have been greatly enriched. Although I was not here during your first tenure on the faculty, I remember with appreciation our association which began in 1975. Unless I am mistaken, you were on the search committee when I came as Dean of the School of Theology, and I have continued to appreciate your friendship since that date. You have always manifested the highest qualities of scholarship and integrity coupled with a creative openness to truth which I appreciate.[31]

In 1991 Alan and Jacque moved their family to Waco, Texas, where they both joined the faculty at Baylor University. Hugo and Ruth did not want to leave their community of friends in Louisville, but the following year they decided they needed to be near family and moved to Waco. They bought a house two doors from the Dan Carrolls, missionaries who had been their next-door neighbors in Buenos Aires.

In the winter of 1992, Hugo published his last article, a short expository article on Acts 4:12, a verse that interested Hugo because of its insistence on salvation exclusively in the name of Jesus. Brief as it is, it shows that his understanding of missions was still developing and that his experience at the Center for the Study of World Religions had led him to a deep appreciation for religious pluralism. Hugo was never a universalist, however, because he was convinced that God allowed human beings the freedom to seek or reject God's fellowship. Primary in his understanding of salvation was the reality of one's having a living faith that brought one into fellowship with God.[32]

"Acts 4:12"

The next morning Peter and John were brought before the Sanhedrin and asked, "By what power, or in what name have you done this?" Then Peter was filled with the Holy Spirit and replied, "In the name of Jesus Christ...does this man stand here before you whole." Peter soon commented, "and there is

---

[31] Roy L. Honeycutt, letter to Hugo and Ruth Culpepper, 11 July 1989.
[32] "Acts 4:12," *Review & Expositor*, 89, 1 (1992): 85–87.

not in any other one salvation. For neither is there another (kind) of name under heaven given among men in whom it is necessary for us to be saved."

The understanding of this last word, "saved," is crucial to the exposition of this verse. If we follow the popular understanding of salvation as being something objective which we can "have" or "not have," i.e. as being an objective status, we miss the mark. It becomes legalistic, juridical, judicial. It has nothing of the personal, of what we are in ourselves, or of the relational, of how we relate to God and other human beings. If God is the ultimate reality our vocation is to be such as is in harmony with him. As Paul put it in his mysticism, "Christ in you is God's hope of glory," of his being made known as he is. To be saved is used in three tenses in the New Testament. We have been saved, we are being saved, and we shall be saved. We have entered into relationship with God, we continue to grow in grace and the knowledge of God, and ultimately we shall come to be like God. "In the name of" is a New Testament idiom that means "all the name stands for" and all that stands behind the name.

From the literal text of Acts 4:12, we move to ten different commentaries.[33] They all agree that this verse is Luke's way of stating that Christianity is absolute. To stop here is to see missions as the answer. But we cannot stop here. We are concerned to understand the mission of the church *in the context* of religious pluralism. By religious pluralism we mean the existence of many different religious traditions at the same time throughout the world. Contemporary communication facilities and rapid transportation make religious pluralism of far more significance than ever before.

It raises the question of the nature of the church's mission today. Should the church seek to transplant itself as it is here at home? Should missionaries dominate national leaders? How can money be used to achieve spiritual results? Should missionaries simply go to other countries and ask what they can do to be helpful? What attitude should missionaries take toward existing religions in other countries? Should they seek to displace them, to cooperate with them, to fulfill them? Will these questions have the same answers for all other religions or will the answers vary from one religion to another? The writer would suggest a series of four books that will help answer these and other more profound questions; all four are written by Wilfred Cantwell Smith.[34]

---

[33] The ten authors are Haenchen, Munck, T. C. Smith, F. F. Bruce, Carver, Foakes-Jackson, Stagg, Rackham, Winn, and Packer.

[34] Wilfred Cantwell Smith, *The Meaning and End of Religion* (San Francisco: Harper & Row, 1962); *Belief and History* (Charlottesville: University of Virginia Press, 1977); *Faith and Belief* (Princeton: Princeton University Press, 1979); *Towards a World Theology*, Faith and the Comparative History of Religion (Philadelphia: Westminster Press, 1981).

The writer spent 1972–73 on sabbatical at Harvard University. At the Center for the Study of World Religions, located across the street from the Divinity School, W. C. Smith directed every Wednesday night a three-hour dialogue session of about fifty graduate students and visiting scholars. Most all of the religions in the world were represented. Each religion was considered a tradition which served as a bridge across which the person of that persuasion had crossed to become a person of faith. The bridge was not of greatest importance; where it led is what matters. If it led the person crossing it to become a person of faith, that is what is of supreme importance. There were numerous "persons of faith," saved people, who had crossed differing bridges. Professor Palihawadana from Sri Lanka was a quiet, soft-spoken man who had crossed the bridge of Theravada Buddhism to become a person of faith. He had crossed the bridge of a non-theistic religion to become "saved" as a person of faith.

A brilliant German graduate student, who was a Roman Catholic, was working on two Ph.D. degrees simultaneously: one in science and one in comparative religion. He was preparing to go to Lebanon as a missionary and serve as a professor in a university. A young American Jewish rabbi read a paper and led the discussion on another evening. In the Harvard Ph.D. degree program, the student had to master his own tradition and one other tradition. There were many traditions which served as bridges to lead to the production of persons of faith.

In the light of all that has been said, it is easy to see that the church today has a great challenge in seeking to achieve its mission in the context of religious pluralism. Because different churches have differing understandings of their mission, even different ideas of what they mean by "being saved," they differ in their work of mission.

If there is a God beyond all gods, surely He uses every culture, all the differing religious traditions, even all history in seeking to get through to as many people as possible and bring them voluntarily into relationship with Himself!

Gradually, age began to take its toll on Hugo and Ruth. In 1993 Ruth fell and broke her hip. Shortly thereafter she began to show symptoms of Alzheimer's disease; she could not find her way around Waco or remember the names of new friends at church. Hugo, too, slowly lost his mental acuity. By 1995, when Alan and Jacque moved to Atlanta, where Alan became the dean of what would become the McAfee School of Theology at Mercer University, it was clear that Hugo and Ruth needed to move to an assisted-living facility. They chose the Renaissance on Peachtree in

Atlanta, where they joined Weiuca Road Baptist Church and attended whenever they could. Shortly thereafter, Larry accepted an appointment as chair of the Department of Family Medicine at the medical school at Boston University.

Chapter 12

Sunrise

"Perhaps I am being lifted to a larger view in my knowledge of God. I believe that eternity is a long, long climb upward. And, frankly, I am looking forward to it with the greatest of anticipation."[1]

By March 2000, both Hugo and Ruth needed a higher level of care, so they moved to the Rosemont Nursing Home in Stone Mountain, near Alan and Jacque. Both at the Renaissance and at the Rosemont, Hugo's devotion to Ruth made a great impression on the staff, and they commented on it often to Alan and Jacque. When Ruth could no longer walk and Hugo could barely walk, he would lean on Ruth's wheelchair and push her down the hall to and from the dining room. His last and perhaps his purest testimony to others of the love of God in his life was his love for Ruth and their love for each other. In November Hugo came down with pneumonia and died the day after Thanksgiving, 25 November 2000. His last words were to ask Alan, "Where's Ruth?" When Alan said she was in the other room, he persisted, "Why can't I see her?" The next day, after his death, the nurses at the Rosemont reported that Ruth had asked for Hugo, and those were among her last words, though she lived until 26 March 2001.

The funeral service for Hugo was held at Smoke Rise Baptist Church on 29 November 2000. The "Farewell—Foreword" at the beginning of the book contains the tribute to Hugo that Alan delivered at that service. It ends with the following paragraph:

Now we are left to carry on. We will miss his gentle spirit. Looking back, there is no question but that we experienced God's love for us through his love. We will miss his questing spirit, living life "on the

---

[1] Hugo Culpepper, "The Bible and Religious Authority, sermon preached at Southern Seminary, 22 October 1980. See above, p. 334.

tiptoes of expectancy" (as he was fond of saying), open to new experiences, new opportunities, and new depths of understanding. But he leaves a great legacy in spirit, and were he here today he would challenge us all to cultivate an appreciation for the character of God, to live more fully in response to God's redeeming love, and to be thankful that we were made for God and that we are restless until, like Dad, we find our peace in him—now and forever!

Hugo and Ruth are buried in the "Old Rugged Cross" section of the Floral Hills Memory Gardens on Lawrenceville Highway in Atlanta. On the grave marker, between their names, is a reproduction of the clasped hands of Robert and Elizabeth Browning. It recalls their love of Browning and their love for one another. The hands, clasped in a handshake, also symbolize their meeting God in the continuing adventure of eternal life, and beneath their names are inscribed the words, "meeting eternity as a sunrise."

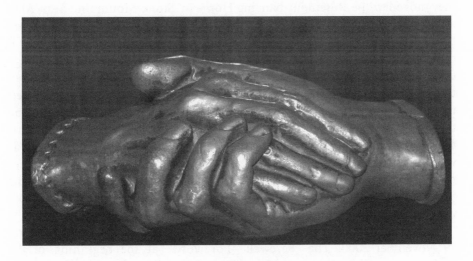

Clasped hands of Robert and Elizabeth Barrett Browning.
(Armstrong-Browning Libray, Baylor University)

Bibliography of the Writings of Hugo H. Culpepper

1945

"I Perish with Hunger." *The Commission*, 8/9 (October 1945).

1954

"I Am a Missionary." *The Commission* (June 1954): 8.

1958

"Argentina, Mission in." *Encyclopedia of Southern Baptists.* Nashville:
    Broadman Press, 1:59.

1959

"Advance in Argentina." Pamphlet for Foreign Mission Board.

1960

"Why Send Missionaries to Latin America?" Pamphlet for Foreign Mission
    Board.

1961

"The Christian Faith and Modern Man in the Thought of Miguel de
        Unamuno." Th.D. diss., Southern Baptist Theological Seminary.
"Immortality and Modern Thought: A Study of Miguel de Unamuno." *Review
        & Expositor*, 58 (July 1961): 279-95.
"World Challenges to Mission Advance." *Royal Service* (December 1961): 7-9.

1962

"Lengthen Thy Cords." *Home Missions* (February 1962): 10-11.
"Bibliography: Christian Missions." *Review & Expositor* (July 1962).
"Pluralism." *Home Missions* (October 1962):12ff.

1963

"Why Missions?" *The Commission*, 26,3 (March 1963):12ff.
"A World to Win." *Royal Service* (April 1963).
"Brass Tacks." *Royal Service* (August 1963).

"One Mission: Missions and Evangelism." *Review & Expositor*, 60 (Fall 1963): 388-98.

"World Missions Confronts World Religions." *Life Lines* (October 1963).

"God's Power and the World's Response." *Professor in the Pulpit*, compiled and edited by W. Morgan Patterson and Raymond Bryan Brown. Nashville: Broadman Press, 1963, 54-61.

"January Bible Study—Ephesians." *Home Missions* (November 1963).

1964

"Missions 144: A Survey of Christian Missions." Study Guide and Teacher's Edition for Seminary Extension Course. Nashville: Seminary Extension Department of the Southern Baptist Convention.

A Resource Paper for the WMU.

"A Resource Paper on the Background and History of Southern Baptist Home Mission Work." Prepared for the Southern Baptist Home Mission Board.

1965

"Inadequate as a Theology." *Home Missions*, 36 (April 1965):4.

"Whither Southern Baptist Missions?" *Review & Expositor*, 62 (Winter 1965): 4-10.

"Missions and the Seminaries." *World Vision Magazine* (January 1965): 6-7.

"New Patterns and Trends in Contemporary World Missions." Background Paper for Mission Consultation, Miami Beach, Florida, 30 June–3 July 1965. Richmond: Foreign Mission Board.

1966

"The Changing Challenge of Missions." *Home* Missions, 37 (April 1966): 26- ; (May 1966): 25-; (June 1966): 24-.

1967

"What is the Church to Do?" *Home Missions*, 38 (December 1967): 19.

"World Missions: Potential Breakthroughs." *Quarterly Review*, 27/1 (January 1967): 23-30.

"Look Ahead, and Act!" *Royal Service*, 62 (September 1967):9-.

1968

"The Bible Explained" (Second Quarter). *Life and Work Lesson Annual 1968–69*. Nashville: Convention Press, 1968, 102-202

1969

"How Will the Home Mission Board Use $6,500,000?" *Tell*, 16 (March 1969): 5-.

"War and the Christian Conscience—One Man's Struggle." *The Southern Baptist Chaplain*, 1/3 (July–September 1969): 1, 4, 5, 8.

1970

"Great Truths from Romans." *Adult Bible Teaching Guide* and *Young People's Bible Teaching Guide*. Life and Work Sunday School Lessons (January–March 1970).

"Reflections on Missionary Strategy." *Southwestern Journal of Theology*, 12 (Spring 1970): 29-41.

"Southern Baptist Mission Strategy: An Inter-Agency Council Position Paper." Coordinator: Albert McClellan; Writers: Frank K. Means and Hugo H. Culpepper. Distributed, 1973.

1971

"Home Mission Board of the Southern Baptist Convention." *Encyclopedia of Southern Baptists*. Volume 3. Nashville: Broadman Press, 1971, 1759-62.

"Is Everyone a Missionary?" *Concepts in Vocations in Home Missions*. Atlanta: Home Mission Board, 25-29.

1972

"Acts—What God Expects of His People." *Adult Bible Teacher*. Life and Work Sunday School Lessons (July–September 1972).

"A Basic Understanding of Southern Baptist Missions." With Albert McClellan, Frank K. Means, Winston Crawley, and M. Wendell Belew (January 1972).

1973

"Faith, Mission, and Salvation." *Royal Service*, 67 (February 1973): 31-.

"Genuine Religion and Mission." *Royal Service*, 67 (March 1973): 47-.

"God's Inclusive Circle of Concern: Preaching on the Imperative of Missions." *Proclaim*, 3 (January 1973): 37-.

"Mission Includes Faith and Action." *Royal Service*, 67 (January 1973): 31-.

"Missions in the Twentieth Century: A Perspective in the Theology of Mission," *Review & Expositor*, 70 (1973): 87-98. [Hugo's Faculty Address]

"Rationale of the Current Curriculum: A Symposium by Hugo Culpepper, Ernest J. Loessner, Forrest H. Heeren, and Wesley M. Patillo." *Review & Expositor*, 70 (Winter 1973): 39-48.

1974

"The Incarnation in the Dialogue of the Religions." *Review & Expositor*, 71/1 (Winter 1974): 75-84.

1976

"Every Knee Shall Bow." *Sunday School Lesson Illustrator*, 2 (April 1976): 60-.
"New Worlds for Christ." *Sunday School Lesson Illustrator*, 2 (July 1976): 18-.

1977

"The Christian Message Amid the Religions." *Review & Expositor*, 74/2
    (Spring 1977): 199-208.

1979

"Bold Missions Personified: Missionaries Who Have Led the Way." *Baptist
    History and Heritage*, 14 (January 1979): 50-.
"Ephesians—A Manifesto for the Mission of the Church," *Review & Expositor*,
    76 (1979): 553-58.

1981

"The Legacy of William Owen Carver." *International Bulletin of Missionary
    Research*, 5/3 (July 1981): 119-22.
"The Rationale for Missions." *Educating for Christian Missions: Supporting
    Christian Missions through Education*. Edited by Arthur L. Walker.
    Nashville: Broadman Press, 1981, 37-47.
"The Thought of Wilfred Cantwell Smith: A Historian of Faith." College
    Theology Society (25 September 1981).

1982

"What Every Woman Needs to Know about Women in Home Missions."
    With Deena Williams Newman. *Contempo*, 12 (June 1982):20-.

1984

"God and His Love for Us All." *Probe*, 14 (January 1984): 7-.

1985

"Missions, Evangelism, and World Religions at Southern." *Review &
    Expositor*, 82/1 (1985): 65-75.
"The Scholar and Missiologist." *God's Glory in Missions: In Appreciation of
    W. O. Carver*. Edited by John N. Jonsson. Louisville, 1985, 1-13.
    [Reprint of "The Legacy of William Owen Carver"]

1987

"The Early Church's Struggle." *Biblical Illustrator*, 13 (1987): 17-18.

1991

"Evangelism and Missions." *Handbook of Themes for Preaching.* Edited by
James W. Cox. Louisville: John Knox/Westminster Press, 1991, 99-
102.

1992

"Acts 4:12." *Review & Expositor,* 89/1 (1992): 85-87.

1994

"William Owen Carver, 1868–1954: Mentor of Southern Baptist
Missionaries." *Mission Legacies: Biographical Studies of Leaders of
the Modern Missionary Movement.* Edited by Gerald H. Anderson et
al. American Society of Missiology Series, n. 19. Maryknoll, NY:
Orbis Books, 1994, 85-92 [Reprint of "The Legacy of William Owen
Carver"]

Unpublished Papers

"Basic Missions Concepts" (14 September 1965).
"Biblical and Theological Bases of Missionary Education and Their
Implications" (1977 or later).
"The Biblical Basis for Understanding Man."
"Care Finds a Way—through Mission Ministry" (9 October 1968).
"Church Growth through Ministry" (after 1972).
"God and His Love for Us All."
"Man and the Gospel in Religion-oriented States" (1968?).
"Mission and Missions" (1965–1970). Two parts.
"Missions" (1965–1970).
"Missions and the Seminaries" (1964 or later).
"Missions U.S.A.: 1965–75." Speech for WMU Convention, Dallas, 31 May
1965.
"On Mission in the 70s."
"Potential Breakthroughs in World Missions" (1966).
"Some Major Doctrines of Major World Religions"

Person Index

Scripture Index